Slave trading in the early Middle Ages

Manchester University Press

MANCHESTER MEDIEVAL STUDIES

Series editor

Professor S. H. Rigby

The study of medieval Europe is being transformed as old orthodoxies are challenged, new methods embraced and fresh fields of enquiry opened up. The adoption of interdisciplinary perspectives and the challenge of economic, social and cultural theory are forcing medievalists to ask new questions and to see familiar topics in a fresh light.

The aim of this series is to combine the scholarship traditionally associated with medieval studies with an awareness of more recent issues and approaches in a form accessible to the non-specialist reader.

To buy or to find out more about the books currently available in this series, please go to: https://manchesteruniversitypress.co.uk/series/manchester-medieval-studies/

Slave trading in the early Middle Ages

Long-distance connections in northern and east central Europe

Janel M. Fontaine

Manchester University Press

Published by Manchester University Press
Oxford Road, Manchester, M13 9PL

www.manchesteruniversitypress.co.uk

British Library Cataloguing-in-Publication Data
A catalogue record for this book is available from the British Library

ISBN 978 1 5261 6009 6 hardback

First published 2025

Typeset by Newgen Publishing UK

Contents

Acknowledgements vi
List of abbreviations vii
Maps ix

Introduction 1

Part I: The economics of slave trading

1 Slavery within the slaving zones 19
2 External demand 46
3 Making slaves 75

Part II: Logistics and strategies of slaving

4 Warfare and enslavement 105
5 Small-scale slave trading 143
6 High-demand systems 165
7 Slaving and power 201
Epilogue 230

Bibliography 243
Index 273

Acknowledgements

The origins of this book lie in an undergraduate thesis submitted in 2011. It would be impossible to thank every person and institution involved in shaping my ideas about medieval slavery since then, but I am deeply grateful to each and every one. This particular project was developed as part of a Past and Present Fellowship at the Institute of Historical Research, University of London, from 2018 to 2020 and owes its completion to the support of the Department of History at the University of Glasgow. It has benefited immensely from the comments and critiques of Alice Rio, Andrew Roach, Jonathan Shepard, and David Kalhous, and any remaining errors are my own. The maps included would not have been possible without the enthusiasm of Daniel Dougherty, who patiently helped visualise my ideas.

Since leaving academia in 2021 I have been overwhelmed by the kindness and encouragement of my former and present colleagues at Edinburgh Napier University and National Museums Scotland, especially the Treasure Trove team. I am most of all indebted to the continuous support of my friends and family, especially my husband, Dan, and my feline writing companion, Delphi.

Abbreviations

AF	*Annales Fuldenses*, ed. G. Pertz and F. Kurze, MGH, SS rer. Germ. 7 (Hanover, 1891).
AFM	*Annala Rioghachta Eireann: Annals of the kingdom of Ireland by the Four Masters*, ed. and trans. J. O'Donovan (Dublin: Hodges and Smith, 1848).
AI	*The Annals of Inisfallen (MS. Rawlinson B. 503)*, ed. and trans. Seán Mac Airt (Dublin: Dublin Institute for Advanced Studies, 1944).
AL	*The Ancient Laws and Institutes of Ireland,* ed. and trans. W. N. Hancock et al., 6 vols (Dublin: Stationery Office, 1865–1901).
ARF	*Annales Regni Francorum,* ed. F. Kurze, MGH, SS rer. Germ. 6 (Hanover, 1895).
ASC A	*The Anglo-Saxon Chronicle: A Collaborative Edition*, vol. 3 *MS A*, ed. Janet Bately (Cambridge: Brewer, 1986).
ASC C	*The Anglo-Saxon Chronicle: A Collaborative Edition*, vol. 5 *MS C*, ed. Katherine O'Brian O'Keeffe (Woodbridge: Brewer, 2001).
ASC D	*The Anglo-Saxon Chronicle: A Collaborative Edition*, vol. 6 *MS D*, ed. G. P. Cubbin (Woodbridge: Brewer, 1996).
ASC E	*The Anglo-Saxon Chronicle: A Collaborative Edition*, vol. 7 *MS E*, ed. S. Irvine (Cambridge: Brewer, 2004).
AT	Stokes, Whitely (ed. and trans.), *The Annals of Tigernach*, 2 vols (Felinfach: Llanerch, 1993). Reprinted from *Review Celtique* 16–17 (1895–6).

AU	[To s. a. 1131] *The Annals of Ulster*, ed. and trans. S. Mac Airt and G. Mac Niocaill (Dublin: Dublin Institute of Advanced Studies, 1983). [S. a. 1132–1201] *Annals of Ulster*, ed. and trans. W. M. Hennessy and B. MacCarthy (Dublin: Stationery Office, 1887).
BT	*Brut y Tywysogion: Peniarth MS. 20 Version*, ed. and trans. Thomas Jones (Cardiff: University of Wales Press, 1952).
Capit.	*Capitularia regum Francorum*
CDB	*Codex Diplomaticus et Epistolaris Regni Bohemiae*, ed. G. Friedrich, 3 vols (Prague: Czech Academy of Sciences, 1904).
CS	*Chronicum Scotorum*, ed. and trans. William M. Hennessy (London: Longmans, 1866).
FA	*Fragmentary Annals of Ireland*, ed. and trans. Joan Newlon Radner (Dublin: Dublin Institute for Advanced Studies, 1978).
LL Nat. Germ.	*Leges nationum Germanicarum*
MGH	*Monumenta Germaniae Historica*
MMFH	Bartoňková, Dagmar (ed. and trans.), *Magnae Moraviae Fontes Historici*, 5 vols (Brno: Masaryk University Press, 1967).
SS	*Scriptores*
SS rer. Germ.	*Scriptores rerum Germanicarum*
SS rer. Germ. N. S.	*Scriptores rerum Germanicarum* (*Nova Series*)
SS rer. Merov.	*Scriptores rerum Merovingicarum*

Maps

Map 1. The British Isles: some locations discussed in the text

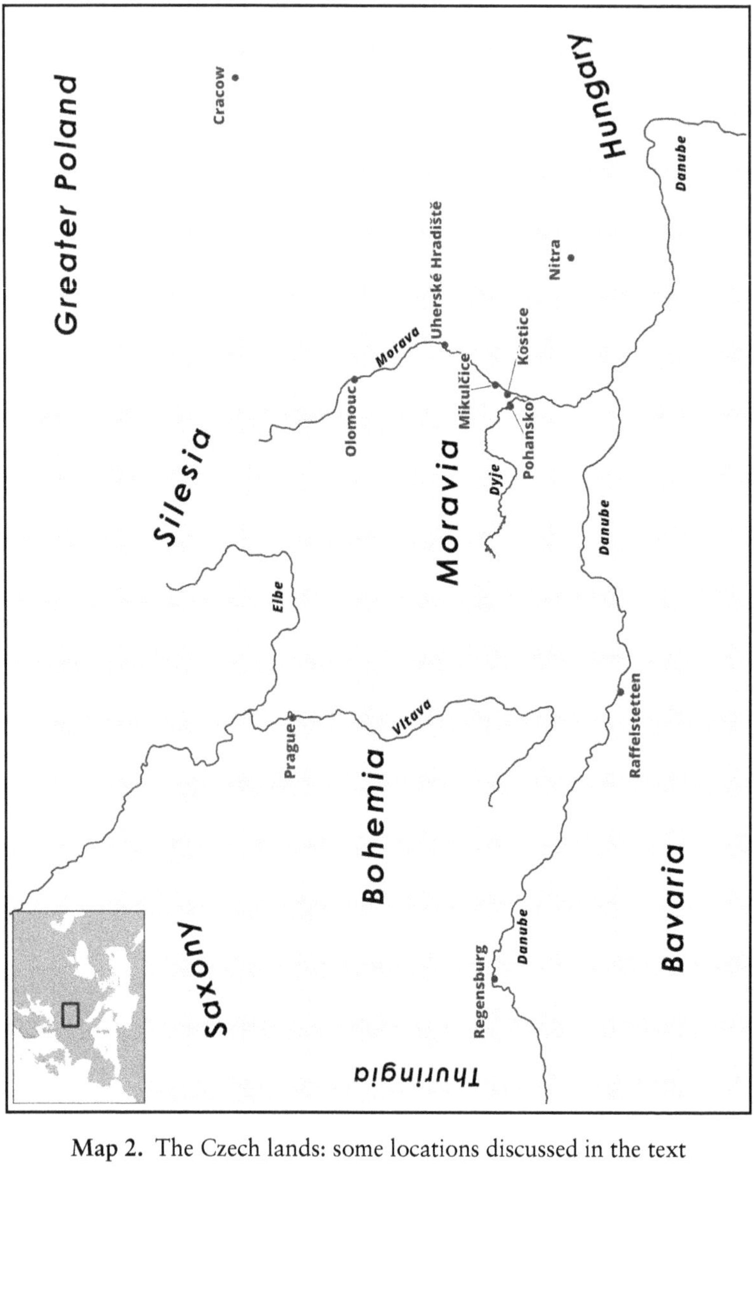

Map 2. The Czech lands: some locations discussed in the text

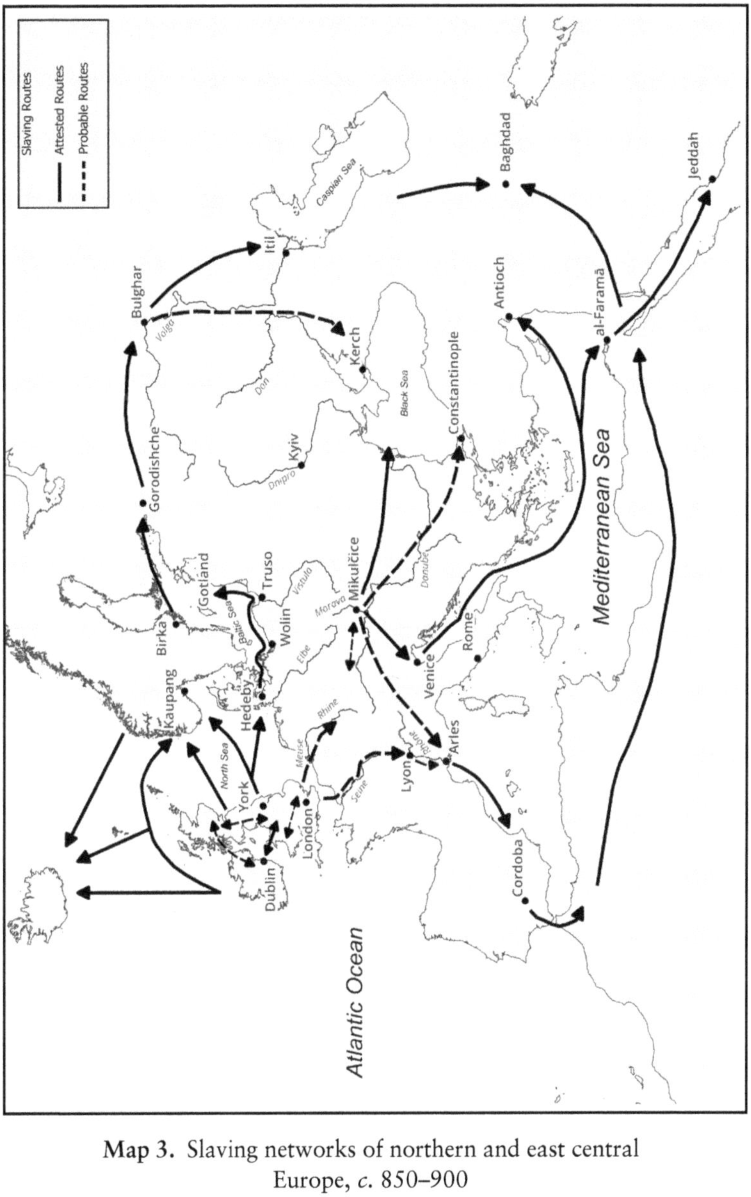

Map 3. Slaving networks of northern and east central Europe, *c.* 850–900

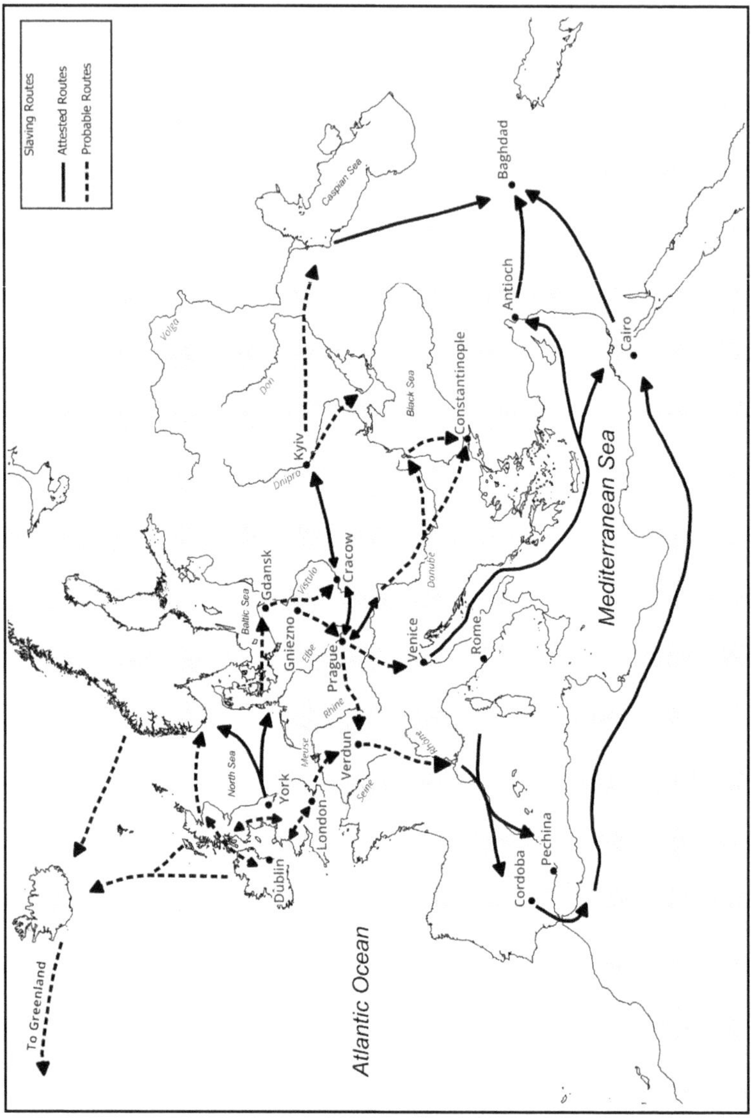

Map 4. Slaving networks of northern and east central Europe, *c.* 950–1000

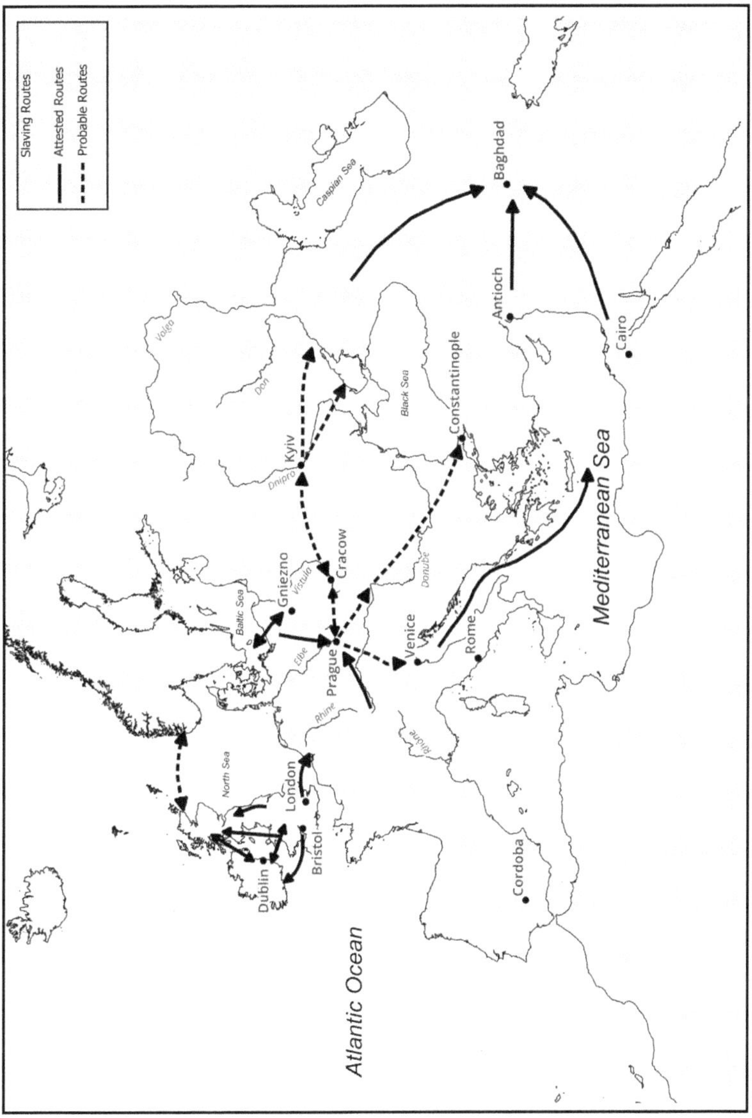

Map 5. Slaving networks of the British Isles and the Czech lands, *c.* 1050–1100

Introduction

Slavery and the sale of people as chattel have been part of most global cultures from the earliest records of human history to the nineteenth century. Europe in the early Middle Ages was no exception, and evidence of these practices, both institutional and customary, is scattered throughout a wide range of texts and hinted at in archaeological material. To understand the pervasiveness of medieval slave trading, however, we need look no further than the etymology of the word 'slave' in modern western European languages. Derived from the Latin *sclavus/-a*, similar forms such as the Spanish *esclavo/-a* and German *sklave/-in* can trace their origins back to the original, early medieval meaning of *sclavus*: 'Slav'. The elision of this ethnicity and unfree status may have taken place in East Francia as early as the tenth century, where the enslavement and sale of Slavs was a major feature of this frontier region, becoming widespread in usage by the thirteenth century.[1] Although the trade in Slavs left the most noticeable impact, it was only one of a number of slave-trading systems that operated throughout Europe between the fall of the western Roman Empire and the widespread enslavement of Africans by Europeans a thousand years later. Some societies, such as those in the Mediterranean and eastern Europe, enslaved and sold people for the entirety of this period, while others, in western, central, and northern Europe, moved on to other forms of unfreedom well before interest developed in enslaving Africans. This book tells the story of the nearly ubiquitous slave trading in early medieval Europe – its victims, its perpetrators, its enablers, and how these people shaped their own societies.

Enslavement was perceived by early medieval people as a legitimate expression of political and social dominance that served to meet both the judicial and labour needs of their societies, while the sale of these people as chattel allowed for their humiliation, the removal of difficult or problematic individuals, and financial gain. While localised, often small-scale trade supplied slaves from within a particular society, long-distance trade, especially when it occurred on a large scale, meant that enslavement undertaken in one region could be targeted to support the distinct aspects of slavery in another. Major developments such as the expansion of slave trading or its demise in one society therefore did not necessarily correlate with the scale of slave labour or even the end of slavery in that society; even when slave ownership remained limited and static, slaving could still respond dynamically to external demand. The interdependence of slaveholding peoples thus makes a wide geographical scope crucial to our understanding of slaving practice and significance.

Because of this separability, enslavement and slave trading could exert social and economic influence in fundamentally different ways from slave labour, status, and ownership. Slave trading attracted middlemen, introducing a third group of people directly involved in slavery, separate from yet dependent upon enslaved people and slave owners. Slaving also posed questions to its practitioners that slavery itself did not: who could be enslaved and why? To whom could they be sold? How could those with power protect certain people from becoming chattel? The involvement of Christians, Muslims, Jews, and pagans in slave-trading networks imposed a religious dynamic on these questions by forcing Christian ecclesiastics and rulers to consider what defined good behaviour and the extent to which secular authority could oversee moral, religious responses to slave trading. The study of enslavement and slave trading, then, illuminates social and political processes very different from the legal definitions of unfreedom, landholding systems, and judicial strategies highlighted by the study of slavery as an institution.

This book focuses on two major slaving regions, the British Isles and the Czech lands, in order to understand functions and strategies of enslavement and slave trading, to determine the extent to which practices were regionally distinct, and to observe the ways in which societies hundreds or thousands of miles away could directly influence slaving practices elsewhere. These two geographic areas have been selected for comparison because they account for slave-trading networks both within and outside the Viking trade and illustrate the pull of Mediterranean demand on lands not directly adjacent, all of which demonstrates that slave trading in these two disparate regions was not self-contained; it both attracted and responded to raiders, merchants, and buyers from across Europe and even beyond the Mediterranean. The extended chronology of the seventh through eleventh centuries provides the opportunity to perceive broad changes over time and the prevalence of different actors. The result is a model of early medieval slave trading in which contemporary, parallel shifts in scale drove fundamental changes in the social, legal, and economic spheres of distinct regions, specifically the conduct of warfare, the expansion of trade, and the centralisation of administration.

Although both these regions functioned as interconnected areas of concentrated slaving activity, the British Isles and the Czech lands were not cohesive units in the early Middle Ages. The Czech lands, constituting Bohemia, Moravia, and Czech Silesia, loosely corresponds to the modern Czech national state. Over the course of the period in question, these areas became increasingly linked by language, material culture, and religious identity, and by the middle of the eleventh century they were governed by continuous Přemyslid rule. Geographically and politically, they also comprised the core territories of Great Moravia and the Duchy of Bohemia, both of which at times extended into parts of modern Slovakia, Austria, Hungary, and Poland. The peoples of Britain and Ireland before the Viking Age did not share overarching political, linguistic, or material aspects beyond subsidiary groups such as Picts, Scots, Anglo-Saxons, the Irish, and the Welsh. Christianisation established a new type of network through which people and ideas could move, though there was notorious disunity in religious practice. Raiding, trade, and piracy had linked slavery in these islands well before the seventh century, and these connections only strengthened with Viking settlement and accompanying trade networks. Throughout the early Middle Ages the peoples in the British Isles and the Czech lands were closely linked by slave-trading systems in response to both internal and external demand.

Like most of Europe at the time, the British Isles and the Czech lands both experienced a demand for slave labour and participated in slaving, but they remained largely disconnected from each other despite their individual importance in slave-trading networks. Merchants do not appear to have travelled between them, neither served as an outlet of slaves for the other, and even political links were mostly indirect when they existed at all. This means that, when similar and contemporaneous developments occur in these regions, they are potentially indicative of much more widespread phenomena. Despite their points of separation, however, the peoples of these regions possessed similar social, political and religious contexts that influenced slaveholding and that serve as important points for the comparative study of slaving. They practised slavery for nearly the entirety of this study's chronology, or at least for whatever portion information survives, and likewise relied upon captive taking through warfare. Northern and east central Europe were also Christianised relatively late, making this era one of religious contention and negotiation. Particularly from the ninth century onwards, England, Bohemia, and – to a more limited extent – Moravia and Scotland experienced programmes of centralisation and territorial expansion by rulers in places that had been politically fragmented. Comparing these areas directly highlights regional distinctions in enslavement and slave-trading practices and helps us to evaluate the ways in which external demand could shape this slaving. We can observe similarities such as the methods of enslavement deployed and the types of people targeted, as well as in the roles of merchants, markets, and central authorities. Differences nevertheless resulted from distinct cultural and legal traditions, access to markets, and proximity to people who could be enslaved. On a macro level, similar, contemporary changes to slaving practices appeared in these unconnected areas, such as their rapid ninth- and tenth-century expansion and late eleventh-century decline and the changes in warfare, trade, and administration that resulted from these shifts.

The study of slave trading

Historians and anthropologists have long argued for the central importance of slaving in effecting political and economic change. It was a strategy by which individuals could consolidate personal power and wealth, and thereby advance their own position,[2] and it was a tool by which rulers and their administrations could develop their hegemonies and suppress rival polities politically, socially, and economically.[3] Acceptance of both enslavement and slave trading forced rulers to respond to questions of the legitimacy of these practices and necessitated official perspectives on when, where, and against whom slaving should be tolerated.[4] These arguments have proved to be invaluable methods for interrogating a variety of historical iterations of slavery, but, despite their influence on the study of slavery globally, they have only rarely been investigated in a medieval context. Attempts to understand early medieval slave trading in broader historical settings have instead tended to centre on the role of Christian thought in restricting enslavement and sale or the ways in which Marxist theory can illuminate the disappearance of agricultural slavery. Medieval clergy and rulers continuously grappled with theological perspectives on slavery and the acceptable limitations of slaving practices, and some scholars have attributed an important role to Christian thought in the decline and eventual end of slave trading, as the expansion of Christendom and the prohibition on the enslavement of Christians eventually eliminated the European slave supply.[5] Past studies also leaned heavily into the idea that the equality before God preached by the Church led to slave owners' increasing appreciation for their slaves' humanity, which in turn ended slavery and, by extension, slave trading.[6] Subsequent studies, however, have highlighted the lack of ecclesiastical objection to slavery as a social institution and to the enslavement of Christians by other Christians.[7]

Marxist analysis has interrogated land tenure through frameworks of class struggle and modes of production, often seeking to understand for how long and why 'ancient slavery' persisted into the Middle Ages. The constant fight by slaves against their own position and the oppressive state has been credited as a social impetus for the end of slavery,[8] while other work focuses on the economic relationships between medieval 'states', land-owning elites, and the free and unfree labourers who worked the land.[9] Western Marxist studies tend to marginalise or omit discussion of slave trading and its impact, instead prioritising rural agricultural unfreedom over the domestic and urban slavery that continued to exist in parts of Europe long after the demise of agricultural slavery.[10]

Marxist theory has had a tremendous influence on Czech studies of slave trading, stemming in part from Czechoslovakia's twentieth-century political contexts and from a long-standing interest in the charter record surviving from the late tenth century onwards. In the late nineteenth and early twentieth centuries, the study of estate development and state formation in early medieval Bohemia credited slave trading with supplying revenue and a rural labour force.[11] Substantial studies of peasant labour produced decades later under Communist and Soviet regimes could not disregard the prevalence of slave trading in source material.[12] Domestic and craft-working slaves, if they did exist, were dismissed as having an insignificant role in economic production, and ideas of agricultural slavery in the Czech lands were rejected entirely. Slave trading, then, was almost exclusively an export business, and captive taking served either to supply this trade or to enable the forced resettlement of free people.[13] As a result, the potential for internal demand within Bohemia and Moravia is only beginning to receive attention, and the different forms of unfreedom that existed there are not as well understood as in other areas of Europe.[14]

Outside these theoretical frameworks, our understanding of early medieval slave trading has been greatly expanded by numerous case studies that illuminate the practicalities and targets of slaving. Some concentrate on the victims and perpetrators,[15] while others attempt to emphasise or redefine the role of a particular region within trade routes or a source of unfree labour for other societies.[16] Still more investigate the mechanics and strategies of slaving in order to better understand the provisioning of and impact upon the institution of slavery at the core of their study.[17] Case studies have also, crucially, emphasised the contribution of captive taking, slave trading, and the oversight of these practices to some key shifts of the early Middle Ages. Combatants' interest in captive taking as a means of enslavement has been identified as a factor in the escalating scale of raiding in Viking-Age Ireland and the conduct of warfare throughout Europe.[18] Studies of Mediterranean, Black, and Caspian Sea connections have pointed to slave trading as being a driving force of these long-distance trade networks, especially for eastern Europe and Scandinavia.[19] Revenue acquired through the oversight of slave trading may also have played a pivotal role in the consolidation of power in Carolingian Francia, Přemyslid Bohemia, and Piast Poland.[20]

Case studies have portrayed slaving as an economic strategy of profound importance that was characterised by the diversity of participants and trade connections. This is also reflected in studies of network connections, which emphasise the geographical scope that slave trading could achieve. Charles Verlinden has highlighted not only the links that slaving fostered between distant places but also the prevalence of slave trading in the early Middle Ages and, in Mediterranean contexts, well into the fifteenth century.[21] Michael McCormick has specifically focused on slave trading as one of the many links between Christianised areas of Europe and the Islamic world, thereby dispelling any remaining ideas of economic separation.[22] Most recently, Christopher Paolella has assessed the *longue durée* of human trafficking in medieval Europe, arguing for its adaptability to circumstances of time and place and the importance of political fragmentation in sustaining this activity.[23]

This book seeks to integrate case study and network perspectives in order to take this research further, not only through the comparison of a better-known 'slaving zone' (the British Isles) with a lesser-known one (the Czech lands) but by assessing the extent to which major shifts are attributable to slave trading in areas beyond those in which they were initially identified. Slave-trading systems in the British Isles and the Czech lands connected these areas of enslavement with most of Europe, and rising demand in the tenth century resulted in widespread and fundamental changes in these two zones. Warfare became driven by the need to make slaves. Trade networks expanded to bring slaves to buyers and move the wealth accumulated by these sales.[24] Rulers and ecclesiastical leaders stretched their jurisdiction to extend and maintain their control over the lucrative slave trade. Together, these changes driven by the mechanics and strategies of slave trading comprise an early medieval model of slave trading.

Identifying slaves and slave trading

This book focuses on chattel slaves, those people who could be bought and sold as property, making identification of our subjects easier than in broader studies of slavery and unfreedom. Problematic Latin terms such as *servus/ancilla* and *mancipium*, which can refer to a range of unfree statuses depending on date and location, appear only infrequently in the context of sale or transactions in the British Isles or the Czech lands. Instead, authors often chose to emphasise the characteristics most important to their narratives, deploying Latin and vernacular words for 'Christian', 'innocent', and 'captive' more frequently than actual status terminology to describe those being sold. Especially in western European hagiography, in which the saint's enslavement serves as part of a narrative, people are simply sold without further commentary, though their subordinate status amongst the captors or purchasers is often clear. Sale over long distances also tends to be more visible than local trading. Selling people to foreign lands indicated the failure or denial of ransoming and created a greater risk that Christians might be sold to non-Christians – a substantial concern for early medieval authors, and one that recurs throughout this study. Slaves and other unfree people could change hands through a variety of transactions – gifting, bequest, manumission, and marriage – but none of these contributed to slaving practices. Differentiating chattel slaves and people of other unfree statuses, such as unfree tenants, is often extremely difficult to do other than in sale contexts thanks to the Latin terminology noted above and a lack of clarity in much of our surviving source material. Discussion in this book is limited to people who can arguably be considered to have been enslaved and saleable, but their legal status is referred to only in terms as precise as the primary sources allow.

The period of this study has been selected because it is framed by the appearance of a substantial documentary record in the seventh century and the disappearance of slave trading from texts in the twelfth. The seventh century saw the advent of royal and ecclesiastical documents in lowland Britain and of a substantial body of texts in Ireland, including the development and maturation of genres that serve as our main evidentiary sources for slaving: law, penitentials, hagiography, and chronicles. Material for the Czech lands is extremely limited before the ninth century, with almost no reference to events that can be associated with slave raiding or trading. By necessity, discussion here principally addresses the period from the eighth century onwards, and in many instances it must be approached from the perspective of Frankish texts. Nevertheless, in all areas, slavery and associated enslavement and slave trading were established social and legal practices from the outset.

Throughout the eleventh and twelfth centuries, references to enslavement and slave trading diminished and disappeared from genres in which they had been common, suggesting an end to these practices. In England, raiding appeared only as perpetrated by the Scots and Welsh after 1066, and by the second half of the twelfth-century descriptions of such attacks rarely included enslavement.[25] In Ireland, raiding appears regularly in the annals up until the Norman conquest, but examples of captive taking decrease after 1115, though cattle rustling does not.[26] Narrative sources of the twelfth century often describe slave trading as an abhorrent and otherwise defunct practice, and hagiographers no longer counted concern for the welfare of slaves amongst their subjects' virtues. In the Czech lands, records of enslavement and slave trading likewise disappear by the end of the twelfth century. The disappearance of slaving from the sources of both regions seems to indicate that fundamental changes were taking place in the creation and sale of slaves, and it is this disappearance that serves as the end point of discussion.

Although enslavement and slave trading appear within a variety of texts, no one genre provides sweeping or impartial pictures of them. Documentary sources that illuminate slave trading in other historical contexts, such as inventories, tax records, deeds, and substantial legal case records, do not survive for our period in either of the regions studied here and may never have existed with regard to slaves. Instead, our sources are overwhelmingly normative, with law codes and penitentials demonstrating the ways in which elites attempted to control or restrict practices that could cause problems for free Christians. Narrative texts such as hagiography and chronicles occasionally address slavery, albeit, likewise, within the context of problems such as the sale of Christians to non-Christians, the enslavement of 'undeserving' people, and the particularly brutal treatment of slaves. Hagiography generally focuses on slaves and captives as the recipients of saintly charity, while chronicles in many cases lament the capture and enslavement of the author's own people by foreign or pagan attackers as part of the historical political record.

As a result, there are some gaping holes in the historical record, which will become clear throughout this study.[27] They include the limited visibility of Christian enslavers and slave traders due to the fixation of Christian authors on non-Christian raiders and buyers who threatened the souls of the enslaved. There is also a lack of detail regarding how captives became slaves, when and where slave trading occurred, and the extent of the oversight of these practices. Where there is information, this is often linked to the exceptionality of the circumstances, making it difficult to extrapolate common procedures. Despite the appearance of slaving in sources across a number of genres, it is worth noting that – as is often the case for studies of the early Middle Ages in Europe – there is a limited number of texts with which to work. Sufficient evidence survives to allow us to make a series of educated guesses in addition to concrete assertions, but in many cases the particularity of the source material makes further argument difficult to sustain. This is necessarily a theme of this work, and discussion returns to these blind spots throughout. Even so, the texts suggest that slave trading was a fact of life, a system to be regulated, and a tool for expositing social – and especially Christian – mores. Some of these intentions have skewed perceptions more than others, particularly when religious motives are at play, but even this outlook provides valuable insight into how medieval authors dealt with or reacted to slave trading. The ubiquity of enslavement and slave trading is evidenced by the quantity of anecdotal evidence in charters, wills, letters, and the accounts of travellers from the Arab world.

The potential contribution of archaeological sources to our subject is less clear. Shackles and deviant burial have been proposed as indicators of slave trading in either region, but connections here are tenuous.[28] Shackles appear in contexts often associated with administrative centres, and texts indicate a range of uses, such as penance, criminal restraint, and leashing dogs.[29] Slavery often emerges as an explanation for inhumations demonstrating a lack of respect for the deceased, but we must also bear in mind the influence of Christianisation on the treatment of death, as well as judicial and state-building contexts.[30] Even specialised slave markets may never have existed; comparative analysis of various medieval and early modern contexts indicates that slave trading occurred within a general environment of exchange.[31] Likewise, the movement of silver and other traceable luxury goods, especially from the Middle East northwards to Scandinavia, is indicative of slave trading only to the extent that slaves comprised one form of merchandise.[32] As such, archaeological evidence for slave trading, for the time being, best serves at the intersection of written testimony and the material record.

This book is divided into two parts, which address different facets of the early medieval model of slave trading. Part I examines the economic basis for slave trading, establishing such fundamentals as when and where the demand for slaves originated and how enslavement fluctuated to create a supply. Chapters 1 and 2 examine the uses of and demand for slaves within the slaving zones and outside them, respectively. Internal demand does not appear to have changed substantially at any point, though this may be symptomatic of limited source material given the development of towns and certain industries in both England and Bohemia, which probably expanded the roles available for domestic and craft-working slaves. External demand, on the other hand, increased sharply in the ninth and tenth centuries, notably in the form of enslaved eunuchs and soldiers in the Islamic world (Iberia, north Africa, the Middle East, and central Asia) and in agricultural labourers in the North Atlantic (particularly Iceland). Chapter 3 seeks to understand how societies in the British Isles and the Czech lands were capable of responding to this changing demand through different methods of enslavement, including penal enslavement, direct sale into slavery, and captive taking.

Part 2 addresses the strategies of enslavement and slave trading, as well as their impact on societies within the slaving zones. Chapter 4 argues that the sharp increase in the demand for slaves in the ninth and tenth centuries led to a fundamental shift in the conduct of war; captive taking was no longer an opportunistic side effect of conflict but became the impetus for it. The following two chapters work in tandem to outline changing logistics largely from a chronological perspective, focusing on markets and points of sale, the merchants involved in moving slaves, and the trade routes they followed. Chapter 5 examines opportunistic slave trading, which occurred predominantly in the seventh through the ninth centuries but which could encompass ad hoc sales through the eleventh century. Chapter 6 turns to the slave-trading networks established to meet the high demand from areas of Scandinavian settlement, Byzantium, and the Arab world from the middle of the ninth century onwards. Whereas slave trading had previously relied upon pre-existing markets and trade routes, high-volume slave trading contributed to the expansion of routes and relied upon new and emerging markets. The final chapter assesses how the strategies of enslavement and slave trading outlined were problematised and exploited by secular administrators and the clergy as more and more people were captured and sold to foreign lands.

What emerges from this study is a model of early medieval slave trading, in which demand for slaves in the European periphery led to substantial changes in our two particular regions. Political fragmentation in the British Isles and the Czech lands was exploited by insiders and outsiders alike to enslave people through war; trade routes were expanded to move slaves and the luxury goods their sale purchased; and rulers accumulated taxes from slave trading and harnessed their own ideological status as protectors to expand their authority. Their role in restricting and ending slave trading was reactive – both to the surge in demand and its later collapse. These changes attest the fundamental importance of slave trading in shaping early medieval societies.

Notes

1 Charles Verlinden, 'L'origine de *sclavus* = esclave', *Bulletin du Cange: Archivum Latinitatis Medii Aevi*, 17 (1943), 122–4. Michael McCormick, *Origins of the European Economy* (Cambridge: Cambridge University Press, 2001), p. 737. Timothy Reuter, 'Plunder and tribute in the Carolingian Empire', *Transactions of the Royal Historical Society*, 35 (1985), 93. Cf. Alice Rio, *Slavery after Rome 500–1100* (Oxford: Oxford University Press, 2017), pp. 166–7. For thirteenth-century usage, Verlinden, 'L'origine de *sclavus*', 111–12.

2 Joseph C. Miller, *The Problem of Slavery as History* (New Haven, CT: Yale University Press, 2012), pp. 36–72.

3 Claude Meillassoux, *The Anthropology of Slavery: The Womb of Iron and Gold*, trans. A. Dasnois (Chicago, IL: Chicago University Press, 1991).

4 David Brion Davis, *The Problem of Slavery in Western Culture* (Oxford: Oxford University Press, 1966).

5 Jeffrey Fynn-Paul, 'Empire, monotheism and slavery in the greater Mediterranean region from antiquity to the early modern era', *Past*

and Present, 205 (2009), 3–40; and, to a lesser extent, Marc Bloch, 'Comment et pourquoi finit l'esclavage antique', *Annales. Économies, Sociétés, Civilisations*, 2:2 (1947), 39.

6 Pierre Bonnassie, *From Slavery to Feudalism in South-Western Europe*, trans. Jean Birrell (Cambridge: Cambridge University Press, 1991), pp. 32, 37. David Pelteret, *Slavery in Early Mediaeval England: From Alfred the Great until the Twelfth Century* (Woodbridge: Boydell, 1995), pp. 89–101.

7 Rio, *Slavery after Rome*, pp. 227–8. Similarly, David Wyatt, 'The significance of slavery: alternative approaches to Anglo-Saxon slavery', *Anglo-Norman Studies*, XXIII (2001), 337. John Gillingham, 'Christian warriors and the enslavement of fellow Christians', in Martin Aurell and Catalina Girbea (eds), *Chevalerie et Christianisme aux XIIe et XIIIe siècles* (Rennes: Presses de universitaires de Rennes, 2011), pp. 237–56. Stefan Jurasinski, *The Old English Penitentials and Anglo-Saxon Law* (Cambridge: Cambridge University Press, 2015), p. 112.

8 Bonnassie, *From Slavery to Feudalism*, pp. 47–51. Ross Samson, 'The end of early medieval slavery', in Allen Frantzen and Douglas Moffat (eds), *The Work of Work: Servitude, Slavery, and Labour in Medieval England* (Glasgow: Cruithne, 1994), pp. 95–124.

9 For example, Jarius Banaji, 'Late antiquity to the early Middle Ages: what kind of transition?', *Historical Materialism*, 19:1 (2011), 109–44. Chris Wickham, *Framing the Early Middle Ages* (Oxford: Oxford University Press, 2005), pp. 259–302. Guy Bois, *The Transformation of the Year One Thousand: The Village of Lounard from Antiquity to Feudalism*, trans. Jean Birrell (Manchester: Manchester University Press, 1992). Pierre Dockès, *Medieval Slavery and Liberation*, trans. A. Goldhammer (Chicago, IL: Chicago University Press, 1982).

10 Susan Mosher Stuard, 'Ancillary evidence for the decline of medieval slavery', *Past and Present*, 149 (1995), 3–28.

11 Josef Šusta, 'Otroctví a velkostatek v Čechách', *Český časopis historický*, 5:1 (1899), 69–92. Kamil Krofta, *Dějiny selského stavu* (Prague: Rolnická tiskárna, 1949), pp. 22–37.

12 František Graus, *Dějiny venkovského lidu v Čechách v době Předhusitské*, 2 vols (Prague: Státní nakladatelství politické literatury, 1953). Matúš Kučera, *Slovensko po páde Velkej Moravy: Štúdie o hospodárskom a sociálnom vývine v 9.-13. storočí* (Bratislava: Veda, 1974).

13 Graus, *Dějiny venkovského lidu*, i, pp. 158–87. Kučera, *Slovensko po páde Velkej Moravy*, 259–73. Jiří Sláma, 'K některým ekonomickým a politickým projevům raně středověkého přemyslovského státu', *Archeologické rozhledy*, 37 (1985), 334–42.

14 Martin Ježek, 'A Mass for the slaves: from early medieval Prague', in Jiří Macháček and Šimon Ungerman (eds), *Frühgeschichtliche*

Zentralorte in Mitteleuropa (Bonn: Habelt, 2011), pp. 623–42. Tomáš Petráček, *Power and Exploitation in the Czech Lands in the 10th–12th Centuries* (Leiden: Brill, 2017), though note Petráček's sometimes interchangeable use of 'slave' and 'serf'. Even so, see Dušán Třeštík for the economic significance of slave trading, but only as an export system: '"Veliké město Slovanů jménem Praha": státy a otroci ve střední Evropě v 10. století', in Lumír Polanský, Jiří Sláma, and Dušán Třeštík (eds), *Přemyslovský stát kolem roku 1000: Na pamět knížete Boleslava II* (Prague: Nakladatelství Lidové noviny, 2000), pp. 49–70. Available in German as '"Eine grosse Stadt der Slawen namens Prag": Staaten und Sklaven in Mitteleuropa im 10. Jahrhundert', in Petr Sommer (ed.), *Boleslav II. – der tschechische Staat um das Jahr 1000: internationales Symposium Praha 9.–10. Februar 1999* (Prague: Filosofia, 2001), pp. 93–138.

15 David Pelteret, 'Slave raiding and slave trading in early England', *Anglo-Saxon England*, 9 (1981), 99–114. Lindy Brady, 'The "dark Welsh" as slaves and slave traders in Exeter Book riddles 52 and 72', *English Studies*, 95:3 (2014), 235–55. Erik I. Bromberg, 'Wales and the mediaeval slave trade', *Speculum*, 17:2 (1942), 263–9. Caitlin Ellis, 'Perceptions of the slave trade in Britain and Ireland: "Viking" and "Celtic" stereotypes', *Quaestio Insularis*, 19 (2018), 126–56.

16 Mary Valante, 'Castrating monks: Vikings, slave trade, and the value of eunuchs', in Larissa Tracey (ed.), *Castration and Culture in the Middle Ages* (Woodbridge: Boydell, 2013), pp. 174–87. Youval Rotman, *Byzantine Slavery and the Mediterranean World* (Cambridge, MA: Harvard University Press, 2009), pp. 25–81. Jukka Korpela, *Slaves from the North: Finns and Karelians in the Eastern European Slave Trade, 900–1600* (Leiden: Brill, 2019). Alfred P. Smyth, *Scandinavian Kings in the British Isles 850–880* (Oxford: Oxford University Press, 1977), pp. 154–68.

17 Carl I. Hammer, *A Large-Scale Slave Society of the Early Middle Ages: Slaves and Their Families in Early Medieval Bavaria* (Burlington, VT: Ashgate, 2002), pp. 53–5. Rio, *Slavery after Rome*, pp. 19–41. William D. Phillips, Jr., *Slavery in Medieval and Early Modern Iberia* (Philadelphia, PA: University of Pennsylvania Press, 2014), pp. 54–78. Ruth Mazo Karras, *Slavery and Society in Medieval Scandinavia* (New Haven, CT: Yale University Press, 1988), pp. 46–50. Stefan Brink, *Thraldom: A History of Slavery in the Viking Age* (Oxford: Oxford University Press, 2021), pp. 77–84.

18 Poul Holm, 'The slave trade of Dublin, ninth to twelfth centuries', *Peritia*, 5 (1986), 317–45. Matthew Strickland, 'Slaughter, slavery or ransom: the impact of the Conquest on conduct in warfare', in Carole Hicks (ed.), *England in the Eleventh Century: Proceedings of*

the 1990 Harlaxton Symposium (Stamford: Paul Watkins, 1992), pp. 41–59. John Gillingham, 'Women, children, and the profits of war', in Janet L. Nelson et al. (eds), *Gender and Historiography: Studies in the Earlier Middle Ages in Honour of Pauline Stafford* (London: Institute of Historical Research, 2012), pp. 61–74. Gillingham, 'Christian warriors', pp. 237–56.

19 Marek Jankowiak, 'Two systems of trade in the Western Slavic lands in the 10th century', in Mateusz Bogucki and Marian Rębkowski (eds), *Economies, Monetisation and Society in the West Slavic Lands, 800–1200 AD* (Szczecin: Polish Academy of Sciences, 2013), pp. 137–48. Adam Gaiser, 'Slaves and silver across the Strait of Gibraltar: politics and trade between Umayyad Iberia and Khājirite north Africa', *Medieval Encounters*, 19 (2013), 41–70. Oldřich Tůma, 'Great Moravia's trade contacts and the mediating role of Venice', *Byzantinoslavica*, 46 (1985), 67–77. Eduardo Manzano Moreno, 'Circulation de biens et richesses entre al-Andalus et l'Occident européen aux viiie–xe siècles', in Laurent Feller and Ana Rodríguez (eds), *Objets sous contrainte: Circulation des richesses et valeur des choses au Moyen Âge* (Paris: Éditions de la Sorbonne, 2013), http://books.openedition.org/psorbonne/26817 (accessed 31 May 2023).

20 Michael McCormick, 'New light on the "Dark Ages": how the slave trade fueled the Carolingian economy', *Past and Present*, 177 (2002), 17–54; Třeštík, '"Veliké město Slovanů jménem Praha"', pp. 49–70. Matthias Hardt, 'The importance of the slave trade for the Slavic princes of the Early and High Middle Ages', in G. Bührer-Thierry, R. Le Jan, and V. Loré (eds), *Acquérir, prélever, contrôler les ressources en compétition (400–1100)* (Turnhout: Brepols, 2017), pp. 81–93. Andrew P. Roach, 'The people-trafficking princes: slaves, silver and state formation in Poland', *Slavonica*, 25:2 (2020), 132–56.

21 Charles Verlinden, *L'Esclavage dans l'Europe médiévale*, 2 vols (Bruges: De Tempel, 1955, 1977).

22 McCormick, *Origins of the European Economy*, pp. 244–53, 733–7.

23 Christopher Paolella, *Human Trafficking in Medieval Europe* (Amsterdam: Amsterdam University Press, 2020); the broader arguments in this work are sound despite numerous errors in the early medieval material.

24 There is considerable overlap here with the ideas present in network theory, but, although some terminology is borrowed sporadically in this work (e.g. nodes), this study of slaving seeks to approach the subject without reliance on theoretical frameworks.

25 Matthew Strickland, *War and Chivalry: The Conduct and Perception of War in England and Normandy, 1066–1217* (Cambridge: Cambridge University Press, 1996), pp. 294–304.

26 For an overview of twelfth-century raids, see Holm, 'The slave trade of Dublin', 337. Large numbers of captives are mentioned in AU, s. a. 1130, p. 579 and AFM, s. a. 1149, p. 1081. Compare to large numbers of cattle taken in the twelfth century, A. T. Lucas, *Cattle in Ancient Ireland* (Kilkenny: Boethius, 1989), p. 151.

27 These are succinctly outlined in Rio, *Slavery after Rome*, pp. 19–21.

28 Joachim Henning, 'Strong rulers, weak economy? Rome, the Carolingians, and the archaeology of slavery in the first millennium AD', in Jennifer R. Davis and Michael McCormick (eds), *The Long Morning of Medieval Europe* (Burlington, VT: Ashgate, 2008), pp. 33–53. Joachim Henning, 'Gefangenenfesseln im slawischen Siedlungsraum und der europäische Sklavenhandel im 6.–12. Jahrhundert', *Germania*, 70 (1992), 403–26. Luděk Galuška, 'O otrocích na Velké Moravě a okovech ze Starého Města', in Jan Klápště, Eva Plešková, and Josef Žemlička (eds), *Dějiny ve věku nejistot: Sborník k příležitosti 70. narozenin Dušana Třeštíka* (Prague: Nakladatelství Lidové noviny, 2003), pp. 75–86.

29 Janel M. Fontaine, 'Early medieval slave-trading in the archaeological record: comparative methodologies', *Early Medieval Europe*, 25:4 (2017), 469–73.

30 Milan Hanuliak, 'Ungewöhnliche Bestattungen in Siedlungsgruben des 9. bis 12. Jh.', *Ethnographische-Archäologische Zeitschrift*, 36:1 (1995), 130–3. Leszek Gardeła, *Bad Death in the Early Middle Ages: Atypical Burials from Poland in a Comparative Perspective* (Rzeszów: Wydowca, 2017), p. 231. Andrew Reynolds, *Anglo-Saxon Deviant Burial Customs* (Oxford: Oxford University Press, 2009), pp. 236–7.

31 Ben Raffield, 'The slave markets of the Viking world: comparative perspectives on an "invisible archaeology"', *Slavery & Abolition*, 40:4 (2019), 692–7. Fontaine, 'Early medieval slave-trading', 473–8.

32 Mary Valante, 'Dublin's economic relations with the hinterland and periphery in the Viking age', in Séan Duffy (ed.), *Medieval Dublin I* (Dublin: Four Courts Press, 1999), pp. 69–83. Felix Biermann and Marek Jankowiak (eds), *The Archaeology of Slavery in Early Medieval Northern Europe: The Invisible Commodity* (Cham: Springer, 2021).

Part I

The economics of slave trading

1

Slavery within the slaving zones

The institution of slavery fulfilled numerous functions within any given society of early medieval Europe, be it domestic, agricultural, or pastoral. Honour-based cultures also perceived the enslavement of one's enemies as a visible reminder of subjugation and of the enslaver's warrior prowess; it was not necessarily labour that held the most value for slaveholders but, rather, the power and prestige conveyed by possessing slaves.[1] This was especially true regarding the ownership of expensive and exoticised foreign slaves. The relationship between this varied demand and slave trading can be complicated, as no one type of demand required or precluded the purchase of people. Foreign slaves could be sourced via commercial networks but also gifted, and enemies could be enslaved in warfare but also sold onwards by their captors. Although he had in mind the truly large-scale slavery of the ancient world, Moses Finley has identified three factors necessary for creating the demand that stimulated slave trading: first, landowners holding more land than could be worked by their own families, and thus in need of permanent additional labour; second, markets and commodity production that could support regular and large-scale transactions; and, third, a lack of labour supply internally, for which the forced labour of outsiders had to serve to compensate.[2] When high demand meant that slave labour dominated both rural and urban production, slave labour served as the basis of the economy, and archetypical 'slave societies' emerged.[3] The first two chapters of this book, however, explore how the varying roles of enslaved labour across early medieval Europe and the Islamic world created demand that was, in turn, fulfilled by slaving. The purpose of looking beyond roles linked to economic production is to emphasise the multitude of ways in which slavery was embedded in cultural and legal practices.

Questions about who wanted slaves, why, and whether that demand was sufficient to dictate the trajectory of commercial slave trading are complicated by the constellation of unfree statuses recognised in Europe from the seventh through the eleventh centuries. Could unfree people be bought and sold as property, or were they tied to a lord and estate via labour obligations? For most examples from the British Isles and the Czech lands, this question is unanswerable. On the one hand, this makes the true scale of chattel slave labour impossible to identify, even when we have documents that hint at unfree population sizes, as in the case of *Domesday Book* for late eleventh-century England. On the other, this quandary strengthens our perception of a flexible and pervasive slavery in which legal or juridical status did not necessarily dictate the types of labour performed. By focusing on the demand for slave labour within areas of intensive slaving, this chapter reinforces the accepted understanding that hard physical labour and time-consuming tasks fell to those of unfree status when they were available and that there was no customary division between enslaved and free labour. This chapter and the next work in tandem to assess where we find demand for slave labour and why, as well as how these societies sit in relation to each other. Beginning with the demand for enslaved people in a study of slaving tells us which enslaved people were considered desirable and by whom, and therefore why the British Isles and the Czech lands served as appropriate sources for them. In short, scrutinising demand allows us to understand the motivating factors of slave trading's growth and decline, as well as its geographical extent.

The British Isles

England

Both narrative and documentary texts survive from the early English kingdoms that elucidate the demand for unfree labour in lowland Britain. Most of these sources are only from the late tenth and eleventh centuries and are complicated by the number of Latin and vernacular terms for unfree status used that are rarely defined to the historian's satisfaction. The Latin words *servus* and *ancilla* are ubiquitous, as everywhere in Europe, but Old English terms such as *þeow*, *weahl*, *esne*, *æhtemann*, and *þræl* denote enslaved or slave-like status. David Pelteret has attempted to unpick these various labels through his exhaustive study of vernacular and Latin texts, though our interpretation of status must ultimately be contextual, and is discussed here as the terminology is encountered.[4]

Early sources indicate that enslaved people were deployed in a variety of contexts by the beginning of the seventh century. The earliest surviving law code, issued *c.* 600 by Æthelberht, king of Kent, mentions the work of female 'grinding slaves' who belonged to the king, who must have been dedicated to the exhausting and time-consuming task of processing grain into flour with hand-operated querns.[5] Slaves may also have performed agricultural labour on kings' estates; Bede attests in his *Ecclesiastical History of the English People*, completed in 731, that the exiled bishop Wilfrid was granted an estate at Selsey by the king of the South Saxons in the second half of the seventh century, on which he manumitted all the slaves – as many as 250 people.[6] From the tenth century onwards sources attest to the variety of tasks assigned to unfree people on wealthy secular and ecclesiastical estates. Men were normally associated with tending fields and herding livestock, while women typically worked at the household production of food and textiles. The will of a noblewoman named Æthelgifu lists a huntsman, swineherds, shepherds, and an unfree dairymaid among those manumitted or bequeathed as property from her estates in Hertfordshire around 990.[7] The exceptional administrative documents from the monastery at Ely known as the Ely Memoranda, dated *c.* 1016 to 1035, likewise note the reallocation and purchase of dairymaids, swineherds, and a madder-keeper for the monastery's estates.[8] A guide to estate management produced in the second half of the tenth century or early eleventh known as *Rectitudines Singularum Personarum* notes unfree swineherds alongside other enslaved men and women along with the provisions they were owed by their lord, possibly in the area of Bath abbey.[9] Whether or not the terms in this document were implemented in practice, its composition suggests that these workers were common enough for generic terms to be beneficial.[10]

Two wills of tenth-century noblewomen also attest unfree women and men in craft-working roles. Wynflæd, whose will dates to the middle of the tenth century, bequeathed a weaver named Eadgifu and a seamstress named Æthelgifu, and also manumitted an unnamed wright.[11] In her will, Æthelgifu manumitted a fuller and bequeathed a miller, a goldsmith, and – exceptionally – a priest.[12] These individuals would have regularly been entrusted with expensive cloth, precious metals, and liturgical vessels, indicating that enslaved people could hold trusted positions within their communities. The size and number of estates held by Wynflæd and Æthelgifu were not unique amongst the tenth-century English elite, and the women's unusually long and detailed wills probably serve to make visible the skilled unfree labour in place on many contemporary landholdings.

Later texts also imply that ploughing was the domain of unfree men, though it is unclear whether they were considered chattel slaves. Ælfric's *Colloquy*, a Latin teaching text from the late tenth century, introduces a ploughman responsible for driving and yoking the oxen, working the plough, and generally feeding and caring for the animals, who laments that he is not free.[13] Roughly a century later the extensive royal survey of land ownership known as *Domesday Book* listed *servi* alongside ploughs and other tools of the estate, where they are included both for records of 1086 during William I's rule and, in the case of Little Domesday, as having been in place at the time of Edward the Confessor's death in 1066.[14] This association between unfree men and ploughing may represent a later trend in estate organisation or chance glimpses at a long-standing practice, but, given the physically demanding nature of ploughing, it seems plausible that slaves and other unfree men would have been given this duty whenever possible.

The difficulty arises, however, when the numbers of *servi* and the rarer *ancillae* in Domesday are used to estimate the enslaved population of England in the second half of the eleventh century. The inclusion of these people among an estate's assets appears to have been at the discretion of the commissioner.[15] F. W. Maitland and Paul Vinogradoff both agreed that these people were part of a dying institution, evident from the fewer numbers recorded for 1086 than for 1066.[16] Maitland believed the *servi* and *ancillae* to have been chattel slaves, the *þeowes* of the vernacular English law codes, and this idea has consistently led to an estimated slave population of 10 to 12% at the time of the Norman Conquest.[17] Alice Rio has argued, however, that these *servi* were unfree labourers or tenants placed by the lord in the households of his free tenants to assist with their work. The ambiguity of status caused by such a situation could explain why some commissioners felt that *servi* could be omitted.[18] Other significant problems ought to prevent our use of Domesday data to estimate an eleventh-century demand for chattel slaves. *Ancillae* appear only rarely, and their presence is probably the result of having occupations that contributed directly to the production of the estate, such as dairying.[19] Domestic servants remain invisible, as do any potential wives or partners and children of the listed *servi*, though domestic chattel slavery carried on well beyond the demise of agricultural slavery in other parts of Europe.[20] By leaving out these people, Domesday probably omits the *servi* and *ancillae* most likely to have been purchased in response to immediate demand, as well as the women and children typically targeted by raiding (see Chapter 3). Overall, it probably fails to record most chattel slaves in late eleventh-century England, and therefore cannot be used to paint an accurate picture of the demand that drove slaving activity.

These limitations provide the most likely explanation as to why Domesday's geographical distribution of *servi* does not match anticipated zones of raiding and slave trading where chattel slaves would be more readily available. Documented *servi* are not more numerous immediately along the Welsh border than further inland; in fact, they are less so.[21] The majority of *ancillae* listed in Domesday did occur in counties along the Welsh border, but this may only be a particularity of the commissioner who recorded the counties of Circuit V, given the extreme paucity or complete lack of *ancillae* in all other circuits but Circuit IV.[22] The lower numbers of *servi* in Middlesex can be attributed to a higher availability of wage labour so near to London and the cash to pay for it, but this is precisely where we would anticipate larger numbers of domestic slaves purchased to staff urban estates.[23] Thus, while *Domesday Book* remains enormously important for our understanding of unfree labour in the second half of the eleventh century in England, it does not help us understand demand for chattel slaves.

Enslaved people fulfilled a variety of roles on secular and ecclesiastical elite estates in England, but no labour was exclusive to them, and their tasks tended to be common ones associated with farming and the maintenance of large households. The unfree agricultural labourers noted here were likely to have been a core part of the intensively exploited 'inland' on estates, where their work could be better controlled than on the outer 'warland'.[24] Although the visibility of slave labour drastically increased in the tenth century, this may only be a symptom of greater numbers of surviving sources related to estates, such as wills, rather than a direct indication of increasing demand. David Pelteret has argued that the increased appearance of manumission in the tenth and eleventh centuries actually reflects a rapidly declining slave population, even being the cause for it, but we have to remember other factors at work.[25] The act of freeing slaves served both to express piety and memorialise the manumittor and to create new dependent relationships.[26] Increased records of manumission are due in part to the growing popularity of written testaments in these later centuries, as well as greater local interest in recording this pre-existing custom, especially in southwest England. Secular lords more frequently manumitted slaves on lands donated to ecclesiastical institutions than on lands passed down to family members, which challenges the idea of a general fervour of manumission that accelerated slavery's demise.[27] Given the complications of interpreting *servi* in Domesday and the likelihood that most chattel slaves were omitted by commissioners, slave labour on estates may not have experienced a substantial decline until the Norman Conquest, when new lords may have chosen to overlook the legal status of their dependents in favour of their submission and continued productivity.[28]

There are some factors that are worth considering in relation to the demand for slaves, however. The Ely Memoranda placed the reorganisation of slave labour in the context of an especially wealthy monastery's agricultural investment in the decades following its re-foundation. Agricultural improvement may also have been known at un-reformed houses or even secular estates, but Ely's size and wealth may have rendered the creation of records more important in managing the improvement programme.[29] Monastic reform impacted houses only in Wessex and the Midlands, but this still may have affected almost 40 houses.[30] Apart from this trend, the ninth, tenth, and eleventh centuries saw an increasing number of non-royal secular land transactions, with sales between members of the lower social strata reaching normalcy by the middle of the tenth century.[31] As individuals ranging from well-off peasants to the nobility were able to make small land transactions, they too may have engaged in 'improvement' efforts, including the purchase of slave labour to facilitate production.

Towns also experienced rapid growth in the tenth and eleventh centuries, and the attestation of slavery in tenth-century Winchester hints at an urban population with enough purchasing power to encourage slave trading.[32] Lantfred of Fleury's *Translatio et Miracula Sancti Swithuni*, composed in the 970s, concerns itself greatly with the titular saint's protection of slaves as the most powerless members of society. In doing so, it reveals a wealth of details regarding urban domestic slavery, with enslaved people put to work as household servants in the burh by owners including a bell founder and a merchant with the Frankish name Flodoald.[33] The growth of an affluent, urban population would have certainly opened new demand gradually over a long period. Winchester is a probable case study for the otherwise undocumented enslaved labour in English towns, including London and York.

It is clear from numerous normative and narrative texts that enslaved women were seen as sexually accessible to their owners, but there is very little evidence to say that they were kept exclusively as concubines in England, even though sexual availability was an important component of enforcing submission and displaying masculinity.[34] The ecclesiastical authors of English penitentials, handbooks of penance for various sins, remained concerned about the extramarital sex that slavery enabled and seem to have been generally unsuccessful in enforcing a prohibition.[35] There is no direct evidence that the children of enslaved women and their owners could inherit, though there are hints of this in Old English legal and linguistic tradition.[36] Young and attractive women probably remained in high demand since they could perform a wide range of tasks, and sexual accessibility did not drive demand in and of itself.

Despite the proliferation of sources in the tenth and eleventh centuries, there is very little information overall about the origins of enslaved people beyond those who had been penally enslaved or who had sold themselves and who we can assume were English, if not local to the estate where they are documented.[37] There are indications that many chattel slaves in Wessex were Welsh, though this probably resulted from the impact of political geography on supply rather than from any specific demand for Welsh slaves. Already, by the late seventh century, Ine's West Saxon law code indicates that Welsh inhabitants of Wessex held lesser status than the English and that either Welsh or foreign slaves were a sub-category of unfree people.[38] This would have facilitated subsequent linguistic change; initially Old English *wealh* denoted a foreigner or outsider, but at some point it came to simultaneously mean 'Welshman' and 'slave', probably a change linked to cross-border raiding.[39] Other origins for enslaved people in England are hinted at by naming conventions, such as the Irish 'Muelpatrec' in a Bodmin manumission, but these cannot be relied upon; enslaved people could be renamed by their owners, and Scandinavian names had become popular in England by the eleventh century.[40]

Ireland

Slavery is clearly visible in Ireland from the earliest sources in the fifth century through to the Norman conquest in the twelfth, but the extent of demand for slave labour is less clear. Its prevalence in law tracts gives the impression that slave status was but one of many juridical categories, more important as the lowest status in a highly stratified society than for its economic contributions. Some scholars have even argued that demand for slave labour amongst the native Irish was so negligible as to create little need for slave trading.[41] Slavery's basic function within a lord's household may have been to clarify the various roles and positions of free and unfree members in relation to each other.[42] It appears to have been primarily related to household production and service, with little or no exploitation of unfree labour on the scale of estates – a situation that probably resulted from a less complex economy relative to other areas of Europe.[43] Slave labour may not have been fundamental to the Irish agrarian economy, but slaves were nevertheless highly valued and had been for a long time before the advent of texts in the fifth century. By the early Middle Ages the Old Irish term *cumal* had come to mean not only a female slave but also a transactional value.[44] Depictions of slave ownership often coincide with wealth and high status, and slaves typically appear as the property of kings, religious institutions, and even poets and druids. This could be symptomatic of sources that focus on the lives and deeds of elites, but owning and maintaining chattel slaves required resources, so their association with the wealthiest and most prestigious members of society is not surprising.

From their earliest appearances in the source material, tasks performed by enslaved people appear along gendered lines, as we have seen in England. Men are referenced in pastoral or agricultural contexts, while women were often deployed in domestic service and production. Ecclesiastical and secular legal texts from the fifth through the seventh centuries indicate that enslaved men herded and tended livestock and undertook piecemeal tasks such as chopping wood.[45] The author of the propagandistic twelfth-century chronicle *The War of the Gaedhil and the Gaill* attributes winnowing to Norse men enslaved by the Irish in the tenth and eleventh centuries.[46] This text's depictions of Irish slave ownership are intended to aggrandise Irish military victories, but we need not discount the author's understanding of slave labour; slavery is attested in Ireland as late as 1169, meaning the author may well have been personally aware of the sort of work assigned to enslaved people.

Enslaved women were also involved in the care of livestock through dairying, which included tending the cattle, milking them, and churning butter, but the importance and ubiquity of dairying in Irish society meant that this was also the domain of free women.[47] Both legal and hagiographic sources from before the tenth century otherwise depict enslaved women performing tasks linked to the home, such as baking and acting as personal attendants.[48] The early ninth-century hagiographical work about Brigit known as the *Vita Prima* also includes a story about an enslaved woman valued for her skill in weaving, though she probably performed other domestic duties, which enabled her to steal her mistress's silver jewellery.[49] The *War of the Gaedhil with the Gaill* similarly describes enslaved Norse women washing clothes, kneading bread, and operating querns.[50]

Whether as a stereotype or a reflection of reality, there was an enduring cultural association between enslaved women and grain processing, including baking bread, but most importantly grinding grain. Legends included stories about the first *cumal* to work at a quern in Ireland and asserted that watermills were introduced when a king took pity on his pregnant slave, who had to grind grain daily.[51] The tenth-century lexicographer Cormac mac Cuilennáin believed that the word *cumal* itself derived from the Latin *cum mola*, 'with the millstone', and linked *trulla*, Old Irish for 'kneading-trough', to *tráill*, itself a borrowing of Old Norse *þræl*, 'slave'.[52] Nevertheless, poorer free women were also expected to process grain, and one ninth-century saint's life indicates that grinding could also occasionally be assigned to men.[53] Based on Cormac's commentary, however, Fergus Kelly has suggested that the introduction of the watermill in Ireland may have reduced the need for female enslaved labour from the seventh century onwards.[54] This technology may have rendered manual grinding obsolete in places where watermills were regularly accessible, such as on monastic sites, but this may only have diversified the work of female slaves amongst the tasks already noted. Certainly, in England enslaved women were still present and deployed in diverse ways well beyond the appearance of watermills in the late seventh century, with an enslaved miller on one of Æthelgifu's estates, despite women's first appearance as 'grinding slaves' in Æthelberht's law code.[55] We must also consider that hand-operated rotary querns remained in use in remote parts of Ireland even into the twentieth century, and so the appearance of watermills probably did not have much impact on demand for female slaves.[56]

The prevalence of enslaved women is also suggested by the greater interest of Irish authors in them than in their male counterparts. As in England, sexual availability probably played an important role in the demand for women over men, and Irish canon law of the seventh and eighth centuries regarding this type of fornication served as the basis for what appears in later English texts.[57] Irish sources also depict these enslaved women working while heavily pregnant, such as the aforementioned legend about the introduction of watermills and the *Vita Prima*'s portrayal of Brigit's mother continuing her dairying up until the point of giving birth.[58] Regardless of gender, however, contemporaries undoubtedly perceived slavery as contributing to economic prosperity in agrarian Irish society throughout the early Middle Ages. The seventh- or eighth-century law tract *Di Astud Chirt 7 Dligid* claimed that freeing slaves would result in the destruction of milk and produce, an assertion illuminated by slaves' roles in dairying and grain processing.[59] The compendium of canon law known as *Collectio Canonum Hibernensis*, which dates from around the same time, drew from the late antique works of Jerome in stating that a slave, alongside a dog and an ox, was one of three essential possessions.[60] Although slave labour was not the crux of economic production in any sphere, there was undeniably a demand for enslaved men and women in a range of contexts.

Demand for foreign slave labour in Ireland is most visible in the twelfth century, though it may have persisted throughout the early medieval period. The early law tract *Uraicecht Becc* notes that foreign slaves were more valuable than Irish slaves because they had fewer chances of becoming free.[61] The twelfth-century document *Lebor na Cert* includes both male and female slaves amongst the fictitious stipends and dues owed to and paid by client kings in quantities and frequencies (sometimes numbers as high as 50), thus illustrating the importance of slave ownership as a demonstration of wealth and power, even if the numbers cited are wholly unreliable.[62] Several client kings were to receive five to ten enslaved men or women from overseas or 'who know not Irish', indicating that foreign slaves were prestige symbols by the time of the document's creation.[63] This attitude is also reflected in the *War of the Gaedhil with the Gaill*, whose author felt that describing numbers and production capabilities of Norse captives was an appropriate means of emphasising the military successes of the Irish nobility in the early eleventh century.[64] Although we do not have relevant source material regarding enslaved labour in the Hiberno-Norse towns that arose in the tenth and eleventh centuries, we should consider that Irish slaves may have fulfilled a similar prestige factor in places such as Dublin and Waterford, and that, as in England, urbanisation brought an increased demand for enslaved domestic labour.

Apart from stereotypes associating enslaved women with grain processing, there was little separation between the kinds of work performed by free and unfree people.[65] The deciding factor in what was considered free or enslaved labour was probably whether there were slaves present to take over the most menial or arduous tasks. The goal of having slaves, in addition to creating visible displays of wealth and power, was to shore up the multitude of gradations in free, unfree, and half-free legal status, which were of great importance to early medieval Irish law in a society where clear labour divisions scarcely existed.[66] The essential role of slavery as a 'bottom tier' in social and legal hierarchies explains both the endurance and perceived significance of slaveholding in early medieval Ireland, while its somewhat superfluous role in overall production capability may explain the lack of perceptible changes in demand for slaves before the eleventh century. By the end of our period of study, however, 'foreign' slaves, probably from Britain and Norse-speaking areas of Ireland, were considered essential to demonstrations of wealth and prestige. This demand may not have filtered below the uppermost echelons of the Irish nobility, but the source material does suggest a change in attitudes towards slave ownership between the eighth and eleventh centuries.

Wales and Scotland

Surviving Welsh and Scottish sources offer little information about specific uses of enslaved labour and the extent of demand for it. There is no doubt that the Welsh were slave owners in the early Middle Ages, and even law codes written down in the thirteenth century include several comparisons of enslaved people to livestock.[67] The origin and transmission of these laws are complex, but the inclusion of chattel slavery indicates that it was a component of Welsh legal tradition possibly as early as the tenth century.[68] One text of the *Llyfr Colan* sets an enslaved woman's *sarhaed*, or honour price, at 24 pence if she did not work with a spade or a quern.[69] This law suggests a similar situation to that in Ireland regarding menial tasks, but it also, conversely, implies the existence of labour not related to farming or food production. The *sarhaed* of an enslaved man was set in some texts at only 12 pence, of which one penny was for a rope and one for a sickle or an axe if he worked in a wood, likewise mirroring Irish law.[70] We also know that enslaved foreign women could serve as in-kind payments; a charter dated to *c.* 740 lists a Saxon woman alongside a sword, a horse, and other items as payment for land.[71] This woman's origin was probably an important part of justifying her exchange value, and provides corroboration for two Old English riddles from the Exeter Book that portray the Welsh as enslavers as well as captives.[72] Welsh law also attests a demand for foreign slaves from overseas as prestige goods since these people held a higher compensation value (*galanas*) than Welsh slaves.[73]

The limited evidence makes it difficult to identify events or trends that may have changed the demand for enslaved labour over time. Charters from the eighth through the tenth centuries indicate that slave or unfree labour was valued highly enough to comprise donations to ecclesiastical institutions by presumably wealthy families.[74] Slaves were deployed on estates and farmland, perhaps most commonly at the operational centre, where they could be exploited most heavily.[75] Land was nevertheless worked by a combination of slaves and hereditary tenants, and the more frequent occurrence of the latter in the Llandaff charters from southeast Wales suggests that slaves were a smaller proportion of agricultural labourers on donated lands.[76] Although nuances remain invisible, it is clear that demand for slaves persisted in Wales throughout the early Middle Ages.

The dearth of texts from Scotland before the twelfth century means that there is precious little information regarding enslaved labour there, though, as Part II of this book demonstrates, inhabitants certainly participated in slaving activities. There may have been an overlap with practices in Ireland in the seventh and eighth centuries when the kingdom of Dál Riada encompassed what is now the west coast mainland of Scotland and the Western Isles as well as a portion of northeast Ireland. Early sources associated with the Irish monastery at Iona give some indication that slavery existed in the area in the seventh century. Adomnán's *Life of St Columba*, a seventh-century work about a sixth-century abbot of Iona, depicts slaveholding in Scotland for an Irish ecclesiastical audience, including a parable about the ownership of a Christian girl by a pagan magician.[77] We can also presume that, from the ninth century onwards, Scandinavian settlers practised slavery similar to that described in Scandinavia itself in the following chapter. There is very little information regarding slavery amongst the Picts and later Scots. Margaret (d. 1093), the wife of the Scots king Malcolm III, was able to redeem English slaves throughout Scotland in the late eleventh century, indicating that raiding in Northumbria served to supply some demand for slaves.[78] At the very least, we can say that there are hints that slaving by the various societies in Scotland throughout the early medieval period was not exclusively undertaken to supply external demand.

The Czech lands

Sources for slavery in the Czech lands are generally associated with two political epochs. The polity of Great Moravia lasted from the ninth to early tenth centuries and encompassed modern Moravia and parts of western Slovakia, and it may have had hegemonic control over Bohemia in the late ninth century. This was relatively short-lived, as internal power struggles and Magyar raiding from what would become Hungary led to Great Moravia's collapse in the first decade of the tenth century. Bohemia, by contrast, began to emerge in the early ninth century as a confederation with numerous dukes (*duces* in Frankish sources) and gradually came under the rule of the Přemyslid family, a dynasty that endured until the fifteenth century. By the late eleventh century their control extended over Moravia and Silesia, having included Cracow and parts of Greater Poland at intervals.[79]

The paucity of information on enslaved labour in either polity is due to the late emergence of a written record and to rulers' seeming lack of interest in written law. There was no substantial legal corpus before the twelfth century, and even these later sources do not include the law codes and wills that might have offered more information about enslaved people. This silence has doubtless contributed to Czech historians' emphasis on external markets for captives, which began with twentieth-century Marxist analysis by František Graus and Matúš Kučera and has persisted to the present day. Despite the rarity of the evidence, however, enough survives to demonstrate slave ownership within the Czech lands from the earliest sources of the ninth century through the early twelfth.

Great Moravia

Great Moravian texts that mention slavery all relate to the Byzantine ecclesiastical mission of the brothers Cyril (born Constantine) and Methodius, which arrived in response to a request by the duke Rastislav in 862. The Old Church Slavonic *Life of Constantine* provides a narrative for the mission's early years, written by a close companion not long after the saint's death in 869.[80] Both Rastislav and Kocel, the ruler of Pannonia, allegedly rewarded Cyril's preaching and introduction of the Glagolitic alphabet with gifts of 900 captives each in lieu of gold and silver at Cyril's request.[81] Even though this figure is probably inaccurate, we have no reason to doubt the presence of slaves in either polity as told by someone familiar with the details. The *Zakon Suydnji Ljudem*, a Slavonic law code with a problematic history of transmission but probably promulgated in Great Moravia in the second half of the ninth century, also indicates the presence of an enslaved population.[82] Selective in its content (it makes no mention of homicide, for example), the code was adapted from the Byzantine *Ecloga* (736 × 741) and may have been drafted as part of the Cyrillo-Methodian mission.[83] The deployment of penal enslavement as an alternative for the *Ecloga*'s harsh corporal punishments hints at Moravian customary influence on *Zakon*, as this had been outlawed in the Byzantine Empire since 536. Nearly half of *Zakon*'s clauses involve slavery, including ones suggestive of a resident enslaved population, such as punishments for men who had sex with their or another person's female slaves.[84] Slaves could not serve as witnesses for or against their owners, a slave owner was held responsible for theft committed by his slave, and anyone who stole another person's slave was to be punished.[85]

Despite confidence that Great Moravia was a slaveholding society, there is very little indication of how and to what extent such labour was deployed. *Zakon*'s interest in sexual access to enslaved women suggests concubinage, but, as in the British Isles, there is nothing to indicate that this was an exclusive role. Jiří Macháček has tentatively suggested that slave labour in craft workshops at the urban settlement of Pohansko may explain the inhumation burials found within individual workshop plots, with their low status indicated by a lack of grave goods and possibly a pagan style of burial at a time when wealthy members of society were being buried with personal possessions in churchyards.[86] Nevertheless, there is at present no means of determining if these people were unfree, but it remains a worthwhile consideration that some enslaved people may have been highly skilled labourers similar to those attested in the wills of Wynflæd and Æthelgifu.

In domestic contexts, enslaved people did not perform enough of the workload to offset labour undertaken by women of higher status. Osteological comparisons of remains from the Mikulčice acropolis, from the suburbs, and from hinterland sites indicate that elite urban women performed as much strenuous physical labour as their poorer and rural counterparts.[87] Entheseal changes to the skeletons of these women, particularly at the wrists and shoulders, were consistent with intensive, everyday activities such as grinding grain, weaving, and hauling.[88] Wealthy women were therefore not afforded a more leisurely lifestyle by having substantial numbers of enslaved servants in their households. Although there was almost certainly demand for slaves in the stratified Great Moravian society, as attested by *Zakon* and the *Life of Constantine*, the archaeological evidence suggests that this was more likely to have been smaller-scale, household slavery, perhaps as in Ireland.

Přemyslid Bohemia

Despite the greater number and variety of textual sources for Přemyslid Bohemia, there is still very little information about an enslaved population there. The lack of explicit evidence has meant that historians have focused on the export market, with the feudalisation of agricultural production precluding any internal outlets.[89] The idea that slaves and unfree tenants may have coexisted should not be a radical one, and yet these two categories have often been seen as mutually exclusive. The result is an oversimplification of early medieval society, with sources stretched beyond the limits of interpretation. For Josef Šusta and Kamil Krofta, this meant that the *servi* settled on eleventh-century estates who paid taxes were chattel slaves, while, for Tomáš Petráček, the *servi* ransomed from Jewish owners in 1124 by the duke Vladislav I were serfs, or at least people of indeterminate unfree status.[90] We cannot fully address the impact of the slave trade, however, without examining potential internal demand.

A steady supply of slaves may have been absorbed in Prague itself and the surrounding area. Martin Ježek notes that slave trading and iron production appear to have flourished simultaneously in the Prague Basin in the tenth and eleventh centuries, and that linguistic evidence hints at the operation of iron workshops by slaves.[91] Although it is true that mentions of slavery disappear from Czech sources as iron production declined, this industry is unlikely to have been the sole consumer of enslaved labour. Vladislav I's redemption of Christians from Jewish owners in 1124 and prohibition on future ownership of Christians by Jews is attested by Cosmas of

Prague in his *Chronicle of the Bohemians*, whose narrative ended with the author's death in 1125.[92] Domestic servants in many urban households, Christian or Jewish, in Prague or elsewhere, were probably of slave status for as long as people were sold. The 1124 act was not one of manumission or abolition; the Christian slaves may not have been freed, only removed from Jewish ownership.[93]

Previous historiography has also emphasised the enserfment of war captives as part of the land clearance and settlement encouraged by Přemyslid dukes, an approach largely based on Cosmas's story of a Polish settlement that was relocated to Bohemia during Břetislav I's 1039 campaign. During the Bohemian siege of Giecz, both the *castellani* and *villani* surrendered on the condition that they relocate to land in Bohemia along with their cattle and belongings.[94] Jiří Sláma has seen this as a rare record of widespread colonisation undertaken with war captives in the eleventh and twelfth centuries, and Tomáš Petráček has argued that war captives played a significant role in Bohemian slavery only through the tenth century, after which those who were not sold abroad were resettled as serfs.[95] The Giecz event, however, occurred during the same campaign in which Břetislav was chastised by the Pope for selling captives 'like brute animals' on his return.[96] Given its singularity in the historical record, it is difficult to see the Giecz incident as anything more than a surrender specifically negotiated to preserve the residents' free status and moveable property.

Estates and farms within the Czech lands may have relied on enslaved labour into the eleventh century. Two charters attest to the presence of unfree people in specialised agrarian roles on monastic estates, as we saw in tenth- and eleventh-century England. In 1078 the Moravian duke Otto and his wife made provisions for the monastery of St Stephen near Olomouc to purchase seven ploughmen with ploughs and four fishermen, among others. Should they wish to leave servitude, these individuals were required to return their purchase price so that another could be bought in their stead.[97] Petráček argues that they must have been serfs with enough economic independence to save up the money to buy their own freedom, but this need not be proof of serfdom; enslaved people in ninth-century Wessex and fourteenth- and fifteenth-century Tuscany were also allowed to keep money that they themselves had saved.[98]

The alleged foundation charter of Kladruby monastery provides more tenuous evidence of enslaved labour via the donation of seven *servi* and a *gynaeceum*, a textile production workshop, consisting of 12 *ancillae*.[99] The text may be spurious, though the nature of the donation could date this content to the monastery's foundation in 1115 or to a compilation in the middle of the twelfth century.[100] Later copies supposedly written in 1186 leave out the *gynaeceum*, suggesting that this system was by then defunct and no longer worth recording. The copyists did retain the donation of the *servi*, indicating that the vaguer agrarian male service was still deemed relevant.[101] Although the text demonstrates that unfree women could specialise in textile production, the *gynaecea* attested in earlier Frankish charters were already made up of the daughters of unfree tenants, not slaves as they had been during the Roman period.[102] This Kladruby workshop may have been modelled on Frankish examples, but chattel slavery did continue to exist at the time of these donations. While unfree people in western European charters were certainly tenants by the middle of the twelfth century, the presence of slaves in 1124, albeit probably as urban domestic servants, means we cannot rule out their appearance in Bohemian charters. After all, even though Vladislav I prohibited Jewish ownership of Christians, there is no recorded prohibition of Christians owning slaves.

The purchase or donation of unfree workers in these charters raises the question of monastic foundations' role in creating internal demand for slaves. Beginning with the Benedictine nunnery of St George at Prague Castle in the last decades of the tenth century, during the later stages of the Přemyslid family's power consolidation, these dukes and the bishop of Prague oversaw the foundation of as many as nine monasteries in Bohemia and Moravia by 1131.[103] While monasteries were often founded in association with pre-existing settlements, the construction and provisioning of the new religious houses could take as long as 30 or 40 years and involve the establishment of new settlements designed to support the functioning of the monastery and to 'colonise' unpopulated areas.[104] If these monasteries required the purchase and provisioning of enslaved people, as the charters of Olomouc and Kladruby suggest, the spate of late tenth- and eleventh-century foundations and their establishment over decades could have contributed to a demand for slaves. This was certainly not on the plantation-type scale proposed by Šusta, but we can be equally certain that monasteries in the Czech lands operated with a substantial amount of unfree labour that may have included slavery.[105]

Internal demand

All the cultures and societies in the British Isles and the Czech lands that are the focus of this book practised slavery, as is evident from their earliest records through to the late eleventh century or even later. Enslaved people were deployed alongside free labourers, and no tasks, agricultural or domestic, were stigmatised to the point of being exclusively the domain of enslaved people. In such a context, there was probably a constant demand for slave labour, but there are no detectable surges that would have driven a long-term escalation of enslavement practices. Factors related to monastic land management in Přemyslid Bohemia and England may have increased demand but only in isolated, short-term circumstances. Nevertheless, the provisioning of enslaved labour for these projects alongside other sources such as the *Lebor na Cert* from Ireland suggest that slaves were readily available for purchase by the eleventh century, perhaps to the point that it was easier to buy enslaved workers than to obtain other unfree or free tenants and servants. Urbanisation from the tenth century in England, Ireland, and the Czech lands would also have exploited a ready availability of slaves, as well as created a longer-term demand for enslaved servants.

Within the British Isles there was a visible interest in acquiring foreign slaves, and in England this seems to have been related to availability more so than in Wales and Ireland, where the principal concern was prestige. Contrary to expectations, there are also no clear mentions of Scandinavian slaves in England in later centuries as we see in Ireland, but this may be due to political factors such as the Danish conquest of 1014, which ultimately suppressed the types of antagonistic relationships that continued in Ireland alongside the growth of an export market, as we will see in Chapter 6. Perhaps most surprising, however, is the paucity of clear references to slavery in the Czech lands in the tenth and eleventh centuries. Although this has led to the traditional view that slavery there was limited, if not rare, it seems extremely unlikely that an area so involved in exporting slaves would not practise slavery itself, especially given extant hints that enslaved labour was deployed in contexts very similar to that of the British Isles. Much of the interpretation here is admittedly speculative, but fewer texts survive from the Czech lands before the twelfth century than from England and Ireland, and these are not the legal and hagiographical corpuses that so enrich our understanding of slavery elsewhere. For both the British Isles and the Czech lands, however, we must look to other, external locations to identify significant surges in demand.

Notes

1 This is fully discussed in Chapter 3.
2 Moses Finley, *Ancient Slavery and Modern Ideology*, expanded edn, ed. Brent D. Shaw (Princeton, NJ: Marcus Wiener, 1998), p. 154.
3 Finley, *Ancient Slavery*, p. 150. This label is typically reserved for the heyday of the Roman Empire and the early modern Americas. For critiques of this model, see Noel Lenski and Catherine M. Cameron (eds), *What Is a Slave Society? The Practice of Slavery in Global Perspective* (Cambridge: Cambridge University Press, 2018).
4 For detailed discussion, see Pelteret, *Slavery in Early Mediaeval England*, pp. 261–334. Paul Hyams, 'Servitude in Anglo-Saxon England: searching for the serfs', in Stefan Jurasinski and Andrew Rabin (eds), *Languages of the Law in Early Medieval England: Essays in Memory of Lisi Oliver* (Leuven: Peeters, 2019), pp. 141–2.
5 'grindende þeowa', Æthelberht §11, in Felix Liebermann (ed.), *Die Gesetze der Angelsachsen*, 3 vols (Halle: Max Niemeyer, 1903–1916), i, p. 3.
6 *Bede's Ecclesiastical History of the English People*, ed. Bertram Colgrave and R. A. B. Mynors (Oxford: Oxford University Press, 1969), pp. 374–7. Wilfrid's purpose may well have been his own memorialisation. Rio, *Slavery after Rome*, pp. 115–26.
7 *The Will of Æthelgifu: A Tenth Century Anglo-Saxon Manuscript*, ed. Dorothy Whitelock (Oxford: Roxburghe Club, 1968), pp. 6, 8, 12, 14.
8 Rory Naismith, 'The Ely Memoranda and the economy of the late Anglo-Saxon fenland', *Anglo-Saxon England*, 45 (2016), 343. For discussion of whether these individuals were enslaved or otherwise unfree, see 359–60. A madder-keeper seems to have been someone who tended madder, a red dye plant.

9 *Rectitudines Singularum Personarum* §§8–10, in Liebermann (ed.), *Die Gesetze*, i, pp. 449–50. P. D. A. Harvey, '*Rectitudines Singularum Personarum* and *Gerefa*', *The English Historical Review*, CVIII:426 (1993), 18–21.

10 Pelteret believes the *æhteman* and *æteswan* in this text are probably enslaved. Pelteret, *Slavery in Early Mediaeval England,* p. 262. Cf. S. Jay Lemanski, 'Slave or free: the *æhtemann* in Anglo-Saxon rural society', *Haskins Society Journal*, 29 (2017), 53–80.

11 'The will of Wynflæd', in *Anglo-Saxon Wills*, ed. and trans. Dorothy Whitelock (Cambridge: Cambridge University Press, 1930), pp. 10–13.

12 *The Will of Æthelgifu*, ed. Whitelock, pp. 6, 8, 12.

13 *Ælfric's Colloquy*, ed. G. N. Garmonsway, 2nd edn (London: Methuen, 1947), pp. 20–1.

14 See Pelteret's detailed tabulations, *Slavery in Early Mediaeval England*, pp. 185–240.

15 *Servi* appear regularly everywhere except the counties of Circuit VI (Nottinghamshire, Derbyshire, Yorkshire, Rutland, Lincolnshire, and Huntingdonshire). The *Inquisitio Eliensis* attests *servi* on the Huntingdonshire estates of Ely abbey, suggesting their omission in Domesday. H. C. Darby, *The Domesday Geography of Eastern England* (Cambridge: Cambridge University Press, 1952), pp. 329–31.

16 F. W. Maitland, *Domesday Book and Beyond: Three Essays in the Early History of England* (Cambridge: Cambridge University Press, 1987), pp. 27–8. Paul Vinogradoff, *The Growth of the Manor*, 3rd edn (London: G. Allen & Unwin, 1920), pp. 332–5.

17 Maitland, *Domesday Book and Beyond*, pp. 27–8. J. S. Moore, 'Domesday slavery', *Anglo-Norman Studies*, XI (1988), 191–220. Pelteret, *Slavery in Early Mediaeval England*, pp. 185–240. See also F. M. Stenton, *Anglo-Saxon England*, 3rd edn (Oxford: Oxford University Press, 1971), p. 477. H. B. Clarke, 'Domesday slavery (adjusted for slaves)', *Midland History*, 1:4 (1972), 40–2. H. C. Darby, *Domesday England* (Cambridge: Cambridge University Press, 1977), p. 74.

18 Rio, *Slavery after Rome*, p. 171.

19 This would mean that recorded *ancillae* were unmarried or widowed. Pelteret, *Slavery in Early Mediaeval England*, p. 202.

20 Stuard, 'Ancillary evidence', 3–28.

21 Darby, *Domesday England*, pp. 76–7. Pelteret, *Slavery in Early Mediaeval England*, pp. 219–20.

22 Pelteret, *Slavery in Early Mediaeval England*, pp. 192–3. Circuit V consisted of Cheshire, Gloucestershire, Herefordshire, Shropshire,

and Worcestershire, Circuit IV of Leicestershire, Northamptonshire, Oxfordshire, Staffordshire, and Warwickshire.

23 Moore, 'Domesday slavery', 205.

24 Rosamund Faith, *The English Peasantry and the Growth of Lordship* (London: Leicester University Press, 1997), pp. 59–70.

25 Pelteret, *Slavery in Early Mediaeval England*, p. 253.

26 For strategies of memorialisation, Rio, *Slavery after Rome*, pp. 115–26. For examples of new dependencies, see Roy Flechner and Janel M. Fontaine, 'The admission of former slaves into churches and monasteries: reaching behind the sources', *Early Medieval Europe* 29:4 (2021), 586–611.

27 Rio, *Slavery after Rome*, pp. 115–17.

28 Rio, *Slavery after Rome*, pp. 208–9.

29 Naismith, 'The Ely Memoranda', 367–8.

30 John Blair, *The Church in Anglo-Saxon Society* (Oxford: Oxford University Press, 2005), p. 351.

31 Rory Naismith, 'The land market and Anglo-Saxon society', *Historical Research*, 89:243 (2015), 35–7.

32 For an archaeological overview of this process, John Blair, *Building Anglo-Saxon England* (Princeton, NJ: Princeton University Press, 2018), pp. 339–50.

33 Lantfred, *Translatio et Miracula Sancti Swithuni*, in Michael Lapidge (ed. and trans.), *The Cult of St Swithun* (Oxford: Oxford University Press, 2003), pp. 288–91, 302–3, 308–11, 330–3.

34 The possible exception is Wulfstan of York's claim that women were purchased, gang-raped, and then sold. Wulfstan of York, *Sermo Lupi ad Anglos*, ed. Dorothy Whitelock (Exeter: Exeter University Press, 1976), pp. 57–8. Ruth Mazo Karras, 'Desire, descendants, and dominance: slavery, the exchange of women, and masculine power', in Frantzen and Moffat (eds), *The Work of Work*, pp. 16–29. David Wyatt, *Slaves and Warriors in Medieval Britain and Ireland, 800–1200* (Leiden: Brill, 2009), pp. 173–242.

35 Penitential canons requiring penance from a man who fornicates with his female slave: *Poenitentiale Theodori*, in Arthur West Haddan and William Stubbs (eds), *Councils and Ecclesiastical Documents Relating to Great Britain and Ireland*, 3 vols (Oxford, 1869–1878), iii, p. 188 (I.xiv.12). *Das altenglische Bussbuch*, ed. Robert Spindler (Leipzig: Bernhard Tauchnitz, 1934), II.5, p. 175. *The Old English Canons of Theodore*, ed. R. D. Fulk and Stefan Jurasinski (Oxford: Oxford University Press, 2012), §110, p. 12. This is based on early Irish penitentials. See p. 144.

36 Margaret Clunies Ross, 'Concubinage in Anglo-Saxon England', *Past and Present*, 108 (1985), 16–18.

37 See pp. 77–8, 81.
38 Martin Grimmer, 'Britons in early Wessex: the evidence of the law code of Ine', in Nicholas Higham (ed.), *Britons in Anglo-Saxon England* (Woodbridge: Boydell & Brewer, 2007), pp. 102–14.
39 Pelteret, *Slavery in Early Mediaeval England*, pp. 319–22.
40 Benjamin Thorpe (ed.), *Diplomatarium Anglicum Ævi Saxonici* (London: Macmillan, 1865), p. 630. Oliver Padel, *Slavery in Saxon Cornwall: The Bodmin Manumissions* (Cambridge: Cambridge University Press, 2009), pp. 14–15. The Durham *Liber Vitae* attests the manumission of the Scandinavian-named son (Gamal) of one English-sounding Ælsie. David Pelteret, 'The manumissions in the Durham *Liber Vitae*', in D. Rollason and L. Rollason (eds), *The Durham* Liber Vitae, 3 vols (London: British Library, 2007), i, p. 72.
41 Colmán Etchingham, 'Slavery or ransom? Why vikings took captives in Ireland and beyond', in Matthias Toplak, Hanne Østhus, and Rudolf Simek (eds), *Viking-Age Slavery* (Vienna: Fassbaender, 2021), pp. 140–3. Dáibhí Ó Cróinín, *Early Medieval Ireland, 400–1200*, 2nd edn (Abingdon: Routledge, 2017), pp. 281–2.
42 Rio, *Slavery after Rome*, p. 145.
43 Rio, *Slavery after Rome*, pp. 178–81.
44 *Canones Hibernenses*, in Ludwig Bieler (ed. and trans.), *The Irish Penitentials* (Dublin: Dublin Institute of Advanced Studies, 1963), §4, p. 171. Fergus Kelly, *A Guide to Early Irish Law* (Dublin: Dublin Institute for Advanced Studies, 1988), p. 113. Fergus Kelly, *Early Irish Farming* (Dublin: Dublin Institute of Advanced Studies, 1998), p. 592.
45 Patrick, *Confessio*, in Ludwig Bieler (ed.), *Libri Epistolarum Sancti Patricii Episcopi* (Dublin: Royal Irish Academy, 1952; repr. 1993), §16, p. 65. *Bretha Éitgid*, in AL, iii, 179–81.
46 *The War of the Gaedhil with the Gaill*, ed. and trans. James Henthorn Todd (London: Longman, 1867), p. 115.
47 *Vita Prima Sanctae Brigitae*, ed. Ioannus Bollandus and Godefridus Henschenius, *Acta Sanctorum* (repr. Paris: Éditions Culture et Civilisation, 1863), Februarii I, pp. 119–20.
48 *Bretha Éitgid*, in AL, iii, 275. D. A. Binchy, 'The saga of Fergus Mac Léti', *Ériu*, 16 (1952), 43.
49 Enslaved professional craftspeople do not appear in Irish sources, probably because skilled craftspeople such as metalworkers held high legal status. Kelly, *Guide to Early Irish Law*, pp. 61–3.
50 *War of the Gaedhil with the Gaill*, ed. Todd, p. 115.
51 *Bretha im Fuillema Gell*, in AL, v, 395. *The Metrical Dindsenchas*, ed. and trans. Edward Gwynn, 5 vols (Dublin: Hodges, Figgis & Co., 1903–1935), i, pp. 20–3.

52 Cormac Úa Cuilennáin, *Sanas Cormaic*, ed. Kuno Meyer, *Anecdota from Irish Manuscripts*, vol. 4 (Dublin: Hodges, Figgis & Co., 1912), §324, p. 28; §1249, p. 109.
53 AL, ii, 153. *Vita Sancti Ciarani Abbatis de Cluain mic Nois*, in *Vitae Sanctorum Hiberniae*, ed. Charles Plummer, 2 vols (Oxford: Oxford University Press, 1910), i, p. 203.
54 Kelly, *Early Irish Farming*, p. 439.
55 Helena Hamerow, *Rural Settlements and Society in Anglo-Saxon England* (Oxford: Oxford University Press, 2012), pp. 152–3.
56 Nancy Edwards, *The Archaeology of Early Medieval Ireland* (London: Routledge, 1990), p. 63.
57 *Penitentialis Vinniani*, in Bieler, *Irish Penitentials*, §40, p. 88. *Poenitentiale Cummeani*, in Bieler, *Irish Penitentials*, §26–7, p. 116. *The Hibernensis*, ed. and trans. Roy Flechner (Washington, DC: Catholic University of America Press, 2019), §45.31, pp. 374, 754.
58 *Vita Prima Sanctae Brigitae*, p. 119.
59 AL, v, 451.
60 *Hibernensis*, §52.4, pp. 413, 783.
61 AL, v, 111.
62 *Lebor na Cert*, ed. and trans. M. Dillon (Dublin: Irish Texts Society, 1962). For a discussion of dating, see Kevin Murray, '*Lebor na Cert*: language and date', in Kevin Murray (ed.), *Lebor na Cert: Reassessments* (London: Irish Texts Society, 2013), pp. 77–102.
63 Catherine Swift, 'Taxes, trade and trespass in *Lebor na Cert*', in Murray (ed.), *Lebor na Cert*, pp. 47–50.
64 *War of the Gaedhil with the Gaill*, ed. and trans. Todd, p. 115.
65 Kelly, *Early Irish Farming*, pp. 438–55.
66 Rio, *Slavery after Rome*, pp. 144–5.
67 'Dimetian Code', in *Ancient Laws and Institutes of Wales*, ed. and trans. A. Owen (London: Public Records Commissioners, 1841), 2.18.53, p. 260; 3.3.8, p. 294. 'Welsh laws', in *Ancient Laws and Institutes of Wales*, 14.6.3, p. 691. 'Gwentian Code', in *Ancient Laws and Institutes of Wales*, 2.40.23, p. 387. Owen's Gwentian Code is now known as Cyfnerth and his Dimetian Code as Blegwryd.
68 T. M. Charles-Edwards, *Wales and the Britons, 350–1064* (Oxford: Oxford University Press, 2014), pp. 271–2.
69 *The Law of Hywel Dda: Law Texts from Medieval Wales*, ed. and trans. Dafydd Jenkins (Llandysul: Gomer Press, 1986), p. 156.
70 The rest of the money was allocated for clothing and shoes. *Tair Colofn Cyfraith: Three Columns of Law in Medieval Wales*, ed. and

trans. T. M. Charles-Edwards and P. Russell (Bangor: Welsh Legal History Society, 2005), §110.11, p. 275.

71 J. G. Evans (ed.), *The Text of the Book of Llan Dâv* (Oxford: Oxford University Press, 1893), p. 185. Wendy Davies (ed.), *The Llandaff Charters* (Aberystwyth: National Library of Wales, 1979), p. 111.

72 Brady, 'The "dark Welsh" ', pp. 235–55.

73 Certain versions of the tract *Three Columns of Law* place the value of a slave from overseas at one pound and 120 pence, whereas Welsh slaves were valued at only one pound. 'The Three Columns of Law from Iorwerth manuscripts *E* and *B*', in Charles-Edwards and Russell (eds), *Tair Colofn Cyfraith*, §110.10, pp. 274–5.

74 Evans, *Text of the Book of Llan Dâv*, pp. 207, 236, 243.

75 Charles-Edwards, *Wales and the Britons*, pp. 289–90.

76 Wendy Davies, *An Early Welsh Microcosm: Studies in the Llandaff Charters* (London: Royal Historical Society, 1978), pp. 43–7.

77 *Adomnán's* Life of Columba, ed. and trans. Alan Orr Anderson and Marjorie Ogilvie Anderson (Oxford: Oxford University Press, 1991), pp. 140–2.

78 Turgot, *Life of St Margaret Queen of Scotland*, trans. W. Forbes-Leith (Edinburgh: W. Paterson, 1884), p. 57.

79 Cracow was under Přemyslid rule at least during the reign of Boleslav I, in the middle of the tenth century, with Greater Poland briefly conquered by Břetislav I in 1038–9.

80 Mirela Ivanova argues that the text is a product of a Greek-speaking scholarly community in Rome, produced for a Byzantine audience and originally in Greek. Mirela Ivanova, 'Rethinking the *Life of Constantine-Cyril the Philosopher*', *Slavonic and East European Review*, 98:3 (2020), 439–40.

81 Cyril immediately freed the captives. 'The *Life* of Constantine', in *Medieval Slavic Lives of Saints and Princes*, ed. and trans. M. Kantor (Ann Arbor, MI: Michigan Slavic Publications, 1983), p. 71.

82 *Zakon* survives only in a fourteenth-century Russian manuscript. Its origin amongst the western or southern Slavs is contested and the debate strongly influenced by nationalistic historiography. For a summary and the strengths of the Great Moravian argument, see *Zakon Sudnyj Ljudem*, ed. and trans. H. W. Dewey and A. M. Kleimola (Ann Arbor, MI: Michigan Slavic Publications, 1977), pp. v–xii.

83 '*Life* of Constantine', p. 65.

84 *Zakon Sudnyj Ljudem*, §5–6, p. 11.

85 *Zakon Sudnyj Ljudem*, §20, p. 19; §27, p. 21; §32, p. 23.

86 Jiří Macháček, *The Rise of Medieval Towns and States in Central Europe* (Leiden: Brill, 2010), p. 306.
87 P. Havelková et al., 'Enthesopathies and activity patterns in the early medieval Great Moravian population: evidence of division of labour', *International Journal of Osteoarchaeology*, 21:4 (2011), 498–9.
88 P. Havelková, M. Hladík, and P. Velemínský, 'Entheseal changes: do they reflect socioeconomic status in the early medieval central European population? (Mikulčice – Klášteřisko, Great Moravian Empire, 9th–10th century)', *International Journal of Osteoarchaeology*, 23:2 (2013), 249.
89 See p. 13–14, nn. 11–14.
90 Šusta, 'Otroctví a velkostatek v Čechách', 82. Krofta, *Dějiny selského stavu*, pp. 25–6. Petráček, *Power and Exploitation*, pp. 222, 327–8.
91 Unlike other locations with even less evidence of iron processing, sources for Prague record no *ferrarii*, *fabri*, or *rudnici*. Instead, there are plenty of references to slaves and slave trading. Ježek, 'A mass for the slaves', pp. 637–8.
92 Cosmas of Prague, *The Chronicle of the Czechs*, ed. János M. Bak and Pavlína Rychterová, trans. Pavla Mutlová and Martyn Rady (Budapest: Central European University Press, 2020) p. 412.
93 In Spanish colonial New Mexico, Native Americans purchased by colonists from other non-Christian Native Americans were described as 'ransomed' or 'redeemed', though they continued to live in servile status akin to slavery. David M. Brugge, 'The Spanish borderlands', in Jacob Ernest Cooke (ed.), *Encyclopedia of the North American Colonies*, 3 vols (New York, NY: Maxwell Macmillan, 1993), ii, p. 97.
94 Cosmas of Prague, *Chronicle of the Czechs*, p. 156.
95 Sláma, 'K některým ekonomickým a politickým projevům', 334–42. Petráček, *Power and Exploitation*, pp. 104–6.
96 'Captivatos ceu bruta animalia vendere', Cosmas of Prague, *Chronicle of the Czechs*, p. 174.
97 CDB I, no. 79, p. 84.
98 Petráček, *Power and Exploitation*, p. 262. Alfred §43, in Stefan Jurasinski and Lisi Oliver (eds and trans.), *The Laws of Alfred: The* Domboc *and the Making of Anglo-Saxon Law* (Cambridge: Cambridge University Press, 2021), pp. 348–9. Iris Origo, 'The domestic enemy: the eastern slaves in Tuscany in the fourteenth and fifteenth centuries', *Speculum*, 30:3 (1955), 351.
99 CDB I, no. 390, p. 399.
100 David Kalhous, 'Creating bonds, creating memories: monasteries Kladruby and Opatovice in twelfth century and their forgeries', *Studia Historica Brunensia*, 65:1 (2018), 41–2.

101 Petráček, *Power and Exploitation*, p. 288.
102 Rio, *Slavery after Rome*, pp. 161–2.
103 Petr Sommer, 'České kláštery 10.–13. století ve světle archeologických vyzkumů', *Archeologia Historica*, 3:1 (1978), 338.
104 Sommer, 'České kláštery', 338–9. Rostislav Nový, *Přemyslovský stát 11. a 12. století* (Prague: Charles University, 1972), p. 131.
105 For a catalogue and discussion of Bohemian charters donating unfree people, see Petráček, *Power and Exploitation*, pp. 236–320.

2

External demand

Whereas slaveholding within the slaving zones appears broadly static in the textual record, with room for small fluctuations in demand due to political and economic changes, external regions experienced dramatic escalation in the demand for slaves in the ninth and tenth centuries. Although the Islamic world was the primary driver, urban Byzantium also took in far greater numbers of foreign slaves than those polities within the slaving zones, and Scandinavian settlement of Iceland in particular created a discrete period of labour shortages filled by enslaved people. The first half of this chapter examines these three contexts, while the second looks at other regions essential to connecting areas of supply with core areas of demand, namely Francia, Rus, and Hungary. Slavery was practised in all these areas, with sufficient evidence to indicate the presence of foreign slaves, but there is no indication of demand comparable to areas under Islamic, Byzantine, and Scandinavian control, suggesting that these were chiefly transit zones for slave trafficking.

Centres of demand

The Islamic world

The Islamic world of the early Middle Ages was not monolithic in its practice of slavery, but it was linked by a shared legal tradition and broad cultural similarities in areas conquered by the Arabs in the sixth, seventh, and eighth centuries. Enslavement had been a feature of Islamic society since its inception, but from the ninth century onwards slavery began to emerge as an institution linked not only to household production but to the governance and military security of the various polities, from central Asia to Iberia. The deployment of slave labour and rules surrounding enslavement differed substantially from the societies we have examined thus far, with circumstances that created a higher demand for foreign slaves than anywhere else, making the Islamic world the primary source of demand for long-distance slave-trading networks operating out of Europe.

It was a fundamental premise of Islam that Muslims could not enslave co-religionists, a prohibition that, following the early centuries of conquest in the Middle East, north Africa, and Iberia, necessitated extensive networks to supply enslaved people from Europe, east and south Asia, and sub-Saharan Africa. There were also specific factors that kept enslaved populations far less reproductive than in non-Muslim Europe. Enslaved women who became pregnant by their owner gained special legal privileges as *umm walad* if the owner acknowledged paternity, including manumission upon their owner's death and free status for the child.[1] Amongst enslaved men, military slaves were – in theory – manumitted in recognition of their service, and castrated men had no chance of producing children who could be enslaved. All these factors necessitated the continual sourcing of enslaved people from foreign lands.

Enslaved men and women in the Islamic world also fulfilled roles that were not economically productive, creating a demand beyond the number of servants a household could sustain. Concubinage appears to have been a primary role of enslaved women rather than the secondary function of household servitude as we have seen elsewhere. This applied to wealthy homes and royal harems rather than more modest households, at least in the Abbasid Caliphate.[2] Nevertheless, the care and keeping of caliphal and elite women required even more female servants; Hilāl al-Sābī claimed that as many as 4,000 free and enslaved women served the harem of the Abbasid caliph al-Muqtadir (r. 908–932), part of a labour force totalling 11,000 servants.[3] Courtesans, known as *qiyan*, were also highly prized, foreign-born women who were expected to be a drain on their owner's finances. These women were trained from a young age, at special schools, the arts of music and poetry in Arabic, with the best-known schools in Medina on the Arabian Peninsula. From there, *qiyan* were sold all over the Islamic world, including to al-Andalus, the Muslim-controlled area of the Iberian Peninsula, through the late eighth and early ninth centuries, though such women began to be trained in al-Andalus from early on in the reign of the emir ʿAbd al-Raḥmān II (822–852).[4] The owner's financial burden of the purchase of a *qayna*, her maintenance in high style, and her display at performance parties brought social, not economic, prestige.[5]

Enslaved men were also deployed in specialised, non-productive roles. Enslaved soldiers, most often referred to in modern literature as mamluks, were favoured for their total dependence and lack of conflicting loyalties.[6] Armies of enslaved foreign soldiers appeared in the first decades of the ninth century in Iberia and north Africa and were later adopted in the heartland of the Abbasid Caliphate in the Middle East.[7] Turkic slaves were especially prized in Abbasid armies for their skill in horsemanship and archery, but these men could come from other areas on the Islamic periphery, such as Europe and sub-Saharan Africa.[8] In al-Andalus under the emir al-Ḥakam b. Hishām (796–822), as many as 5,000 enslaved men were introduced to the Umayyad army.[9] These numbers needed constant replenishment by enslaved foreigners, as rulers quickly learned that the children of these soldiers held additional loyalties to their families and were too ingrained in the local cultural fabric to be the deracinated fighters they desired.[10] Foreign boys and men were also prized as eunuchs, who served in palaces and well-to-do residences as servants and guards with the unique ability to move anywhere in the house, including amongst women.[11] Like enslaved soldiers, their social isolation was believed to intensify the bonds of loyalty between the slave and his owner, and eunuchs could not start families that would divide this loyalty.[12] Eunuchs also served in the administrations and militaries of Islamic rulers, sometimes rising to very high positions of power despite their enslaved status. At the Abbasid court of al-Muqtadir in Baghdad there were as many as 11,000 eunuchs (of whom 7,000 were black Africans and 4,000 were Slavs), guarding and caring for 4,000 free and enslaved women.[13]

Enslaved men and boys were concentrated in high numbers at caliphal courts, but it is important to note that numbers of enslaved women here were also high, and that women were more likely to appear in urban homes of less wealth. Although it has not been the subject of as much research as these more 'elite' roles for enslaved people, domestic servitude continued throughout the Islamic world of the early Middle Ages. Sources suggest that even modest households were able to possess slaves, and that these people contributed extensively to urban household productivity.[14] Slaves could also be purchased and utilised for building projects.[15] Agricultural slavery, on the other hand, was very rare; most agricultural labour was performed by free peasants, and the land reclamation required of Zanj (east African) slaves in Iraq that led to their revolt in the 860s may have been the only large-scale agricultural deployment of slaves in the Islamic world.[16] Nevertheless, agricultural slavery, or even just economically productive slavery, was not essential for immense demand for enslaved labour.

Of critical importance to the institution of slavery in the Islamic world were the *saqāliba*, who served in bureaucratic, domestic, and military positions.[17] This term principally referred to people of Slavic origin, though foreigners such as Franks and Galicians could also be included.[18] Slavic slaves were so prevalent in the Islamic world that, as with *sclavus*, their ethnic name (sing. *saqlabī*) became synonymous with unfree status in the tenth century or later.[19] In his eleventh-century slave-purchasing guide, Ibn Butlān informed prospective buyers that enslaved male *saqāliba* had good digestion and were long-lived and that women were barren, implying that both were available for sale regularly.[20] Slavic women were prized as *qiyan* in the early Abbasid period in the second half of the eighth century, but *saqāliba* are most visible in male roles as eunuchs and soldiers.[21] Ibn Butlān believed *saqāliba*, along with Turks, to have been ideal purchases for warfare, and al-Jahiz, writing in Basra in the middle of the ninth century, believed that castration improved the intellect and skill of naturally stupid and clumsy Slavic men, making them ideal eunuchs.[22]

Demand for *saqāliba* throughout the Islamic world in the ninth and tenth centuries was staggeringly high. The last Aghlabid governor of Ifrīqiya was said to have fled his palace with 1,000 *saqāliba* and still more enslaved women in 909, leaving others behind to become the property of the Fatimid conquerors.[23] The Aghlabids had relied on *saqāliba* since the first decades of the ninth century, and the Fatimids continued to deploy enslaved *saqāliba* in high-profile military, administrative, and diplomatic positions throughout the tenth century.[24] In al-Andalus at the Cordoban court of ʿAbd al-Rahmān III (r. 912–961), there may have been as many as 3,350 *saqāliba* men and boys, while the court of al-Muqtadir in Baghdad was home to 4,000 *saqāliba* eunuchs alone.[25] There are no mentions of British or Irish slaves in the Islamic world, but there is no reason to think that individuals could not have been grouped together with Franks or Slavs, especially if traded via these regions, though their presence must not have been substantial enough to have drawn the attention of commentators.

Certain historical trends would have focused the peak of demand for foreign slaves in Islamic polities in the ninth and tenth centuries, particularly for Slavs from east central Europe. The institutionalisation of enslaved armies in the first half of the ninth century created a sudden, sharp increase in demand that became recurrent throughout the Islamic world. Eunuchs were constantly in high demand in royal and other households due to the exclusivity of access to women in Islamic society, and the opening of trade routes introduced large numbers of *saqāliba* to markets in the Middle East via eastern Europe in the ninth century and to al-Andalus in the middle of the tenth.[26] The conscious restructuring of political institutions such as through coinage reform and market intervention by the state in the eighth and ninth centuries and first half of the tenth fostered the sort of urban economic development that would have enabled the mass importation of foreign slaves.[27] Conversely, periods of political instability probably caused a decline in demand for – or, at least, the availability of – enslaved Europeans. We will see in Chapter 6 that dynastic crisis in the Abbasid Caliphate in the second half of the tenth century may have been directly responsible for a change in eastern and central European trade routes away from Abbasid connections around the Black and Caspian Seas. Likewise, the eleventh-century decline and disappearance of *saqāliba* in sources from al-Andalus coincided with the decline and collapse of the centralised Umayyad caliphate in 1031 and its replacement by unstable, fragmented Taifa states.[28] This shift and its impact on trade routes also changed the demographics of slavery in north Africa; *saqāliba* disappeared from this region at about the same time, replaced by black Africans.[29]

Byzantium

Slavery in Byzantium had its roots in Roman legal tradition, transmitted in late antiquity via Justinian's legal corpus and modified over the course of the medieval period by further imperial legislation. As a result, legal attitudes focused on the dichotomy between free and enslaved more so than in the British Isles or the Czech lands.[30] Unlike its Roman predecessor, however, the Byzantine Empire was not a 'slave society' by Moses Finley's definition.[31] The scale of slavery had already declined through late antiquity and appears to have predominantly existed in 'productive' contexts, though 'non-productive' slavery still existed.[32] Nonetheless, the study of early medieval Byzantine slavery is complicated by ambiguous terminology; there was no Greek word in use that exclusively meant 'slave', meaning that the vocabulary of slavery overlapped considerably with that of free labour.[33]

Scholars have nevertheless identified a slavery reminiscent of slaveries practised in the other Christianised areas of Europe. Enslaved people primarily appeared in urban domestic and craft-working settings and, to a lesser degree, in agricultural roles. The main difference, and the reason the Byzantine Empire was probably a significant pull for slave trading, was in scale. The best case for this is in the craft-working sector, for which the *Book of the Eparch*, a legal tract promulgated in the early tenth century, attests the commonality of enslaved workers at all levels of skill and business management. This document sought to regulate guilds in Constantinople, and references enslaved silk merchants, dyers, and candlemakers.[34] A number of other professions appear without reference to slaves, such as perfumers, grocers, saddlers, butchers, and construction workers, but slaves were only explicitly prohibited from banking and silk finishing.[35] One law even addresses the placement of an enslaved person in a workshop as foreman, a strategy that would in effect enable the business owner (and slave owner) to become his own guarantor, thereby encouraging the purchase and deployment of enslaved people.[36] In such a situation, foreign deracinated slaves may have been seen as more trustworthy than people from the city, due to a lack of social ties and conflicts of interest.[37]

Domestic slavery likewise seems to have been far more widespread in Byzantium than elsewhere in Christian Europe, and foreign slaves were common. Two works of hagiography authored most likely in the mid- to late tenth century, the *Life of St Andrew the Fool* and the *Life of St Basil the Younger*, take slavery in the well-to-do households of Constantinople for granted. Enslaved men and women appear as key characters or bystanders. Andrew himself is depicted as a 'Scythian', probably a Slav, purchased as a boy by a man who already owned many slaves. Favoured for his intelligence, Andrew was educated and trained to be his owner's secretary.[38] In his role as a holy fool, he encountered enslaved servants and eunuchs, and those in the home of his friend Ephiphanios are depicted as having many different native languages.[39] Similarly, Basil encountered the enslaved people owned by workshop owners, a workman, and a daughter of the emperor, who included a foreman, a woman housekeeper, a household overseer, eunuchs, and a chambermaid.[40]

Byzantine hagiography of the ninth and tenth centuries tended towards biographical portrayals of titular characters with an eye towards framing political and theological issues of the day, and in these two works this trend is apparent in the discussion of slaves' sexual accessibility, a hindrance to salvation for women and men alike.[41] This was an issue not only for enslaved people raped by their owners but also, in the case of Basil's friend Theodora, for those who had been forced to live and produce children with an enslaved partner of their owner's choosing.[42] Although it would have created a self-sustaining household population of enslaved servants, Theodora's past role as a wet nurse suggests other motives for forced pregnancy.[43] As in other parts of Christianised Europe that idealised monogamy, the sexual use and abuse of slaves was typically a side effect of domestic slave ownership rather than its primary function.

Households and workshops appear to have been the most significant consumers of enslaved labour, but it is still visible in other sectors. Agricultural slavery had declined substantially in scale from the Roman period; by the ninth century enslaved people were not deployed in great numbers in this context as preference turned to tenancy, though slaves were probably still common in rural households.[44] References to enslaved agricultural workers disappeared over the course of the eleventh century.[45] Slaves are also visible in imperial construction projects and roadbuilding, and enslaved people may have been sent to labour in imperial mines, as they had in late antiquity.[46] Wealthy urban residents, particularly the imperial family, also used enslaved people in administrative and military contexts. As already mentioned, Andrew was trained as a secretary, and slaves that Basil encountered managed households. Wills from the second half of the eleventh century note armed slaves, implying their use as personal guards or private soldiers.[47] Enslaved eunuchs were present in military and administrative positions at court, but, unlike within the contemporary Islamic world, eunuchs in Byzantium were not all enslaved, though the hagiography discussed here depicts them as such. The early Middle Ages saw an overall shift from the enslaved foreign eunuchs of the late Roman Empire to those who were free and native-born.[48]

Overall, Byzantine sources give the impression that slavery pervaded daily life in urban elite households, and probably also in wealthy rural residences. Narrative and documentary sources alike attest human chattel as a form of wealth alongside land, livestock, cash, clothing, and personal adornments. Individuals disposing of their wealth in testaments could own dozens, hundreds, or – in the exceptional case of a woman named Danelis – thousands of enslaved people.[49] Importantly, these sources concentrate in and around the tenth century. Whereas in the British Isles and the Czech lands this clustering of texts can arguably be the result of source survival, this is not true of the relatively rich Byzantine textual corpus. Slave owning in Byzantium seems to have been especially important as a signifier of affluence in this period, and the continuity of record here suggests that we should take the increased visibility of slavery across Europe in the tenth century at face value.

The regulation of enslavement over the centuries gradually created a situation that relied wholly upon birth rates, captive taking, and sale to replenish the enslaved population. Penal slavery had been outlawed since the sixth century, and the eighth-century *Ecloga* gave Byzantines enslaved elsewhere and sold back to Byzantium the opportunity to ransom themselves, effectively meaning that the unfree status of a Byzantine enslaved abroad would not be recognised.[50] Youval Rotman believes that this second piece of legislation, alongside the development of ransoming and prisoner exchange systems with the Arab world in the ninth and tenth centuries, would have forced serious re-evaluation of the slave supply.[51]

Chronicles and histories correspondingly emphasise captive taking as part of tenth-century Byzantine military successes, particularly against Slavs in the Balkans.[52] Trade privileges were granted to the Rus in the first half of the century and to the Venetians in the second, both of whom were conducting highly visible, and probably high-volume, slave trading at those times.[53] Although Andrew was a fictional saint, the author of his *Life* certainly believed that the purchase of a Slavic boy in Constantinople would be an unobjectionable detail for his audience. There is no explicit connection, but the incidental details all point to an increase in demand for slaves in tenth-century Byzantium, which may have decreased in the eleventh century.

The Viking world

Although Scandinavians were integral to the export of slaves from the British Isles and eastern Europe from the ninth through eleventh centuries, there is little agreement between scholars as to the actual demand for slave labour in Scandinavia itself. Here I address the demand in Norway, Sweden, Denmark, and areas of Scandinavian settlement in northern and eastern Europe. Diaspora communities retained close links with their homelands both politically and culturally, and slaveholding practices in locations such as early Dublin or the Danelaw probably resembled those of the Scandinavian 'home' societies. Even as diaspora groups blended with new neighbouring cultures or diverged from the 'home' culture, they retained attributes closer to those of Scandinavian societies than of their neighbours.[54] Over time these communities may have varied in their slaveholding practices as they adopted local customs, but, in the absence of source material, Scandinavian evidence provides an idea of what demand may have looked like.

Captives were imported to Scandinavia from a range of geographical areas for resale or direct enslavement. The ninth-century *Life of Findan*, an Irish hagiographical work, describes the titular saint's experiences while enslaved aboard several Viking ships. He is resold several times until he ends up as the property of a Norseman intent on returning to Scandinavia, but manages to escape during a stop in the Orkneys.[55] The thirteenth-century Icelandic *Laxdæla Saga* tells of the sale of enslaved women, including an Irish princess, at a seasonal market in Norway in the tenth century. The princess, named Melkorka, who had been enslaved since her capture at the age of sixteen, was purchased by an Icelandic settler to serve as his concubine on the return journey and then as a labourer in Iceland.[56] Rimbert's *Life of Ansgar*, which details the conversion mission to Scandinavia in the middle of the ninth century, provides a contemporary reference to an enslaved population of Christians in Birka, an important market hub in Sweden.[57] These slaves were probably residents rather than merchandise in transit, since they were able to seek out and attend the missionaries' services. Sources likewise indicate slave ownership amongst diaspora groups during the Viking Age. The Treaty of Alfred and Guthrum, dating from *c.* 880–890 within the first generation of Scandinavian settlement in England, prohibited both the West Saxons and the inhabitants of the Danelaw from harbouring each other's fugitive slaves.[58] By the late tenth century the Old Norse word for a male slave, *þræl*, had been adopted in northern England and eventually supplanted the Old English *þeow*.[59] For eastern Europe, the work of Ahmad ibn Fadlān, an Arab envoy from Baghdad, describes slave ownership and the conspicuous consumption of slaves as grave goods by the Rus in 922.[60]

For much of Scandinavia, however, there are no contemporary sources to elucidate how, where, and to what extent foreign slaves were deployed. Archaeology is also largely unhelpful, for, although relative social status is clearly identifiable from housing conditions or supposed 'slave sacrifice' burials, these do not clearly indicate legal status.[61] Provincial law codes surviving from Norway, Iceland, Sweden, Gotland, and Denmark each present a complex challenge, and remnants of an archaic Viking-Age past are mostly inextricable from a twelfth- or thirteenth-century legal context.[62] Slavery still existed at this date, but long-standing customary law had inevitably been altered by Christianisation and the influence of outside legal traditions.[63] Thirteenth-century sagas are likewise problematic as historical sources, despite their attempts to illustrate the early medieval past. They often stereotypically portray slaves in Iceland and Norway as swarthy, foolish, and disposable.[64] Even in the *Rígsþula*, a thirteenth-century poem whose origins may lie in the ninth or tenth centuries, slaves are characterised in terms of these same derogatory tropes.[65]

Nevertheless, the incidental details in these thirteenth-century texts mirror those found in other early medieval sources from northern Europe. Enslaved men were principally associated with outdoor activities that exploited the environment, such as tending crops, herding livestock, and chopping or collecting wood. Enslaved women performed domestic labour by grinding grain, dairying, and acting as servants.[66] As in England and Ireland, there do not appear to have been any tasks unique to unfree status. The Norwegian *Gulaþing* and *Frostaþing* laws also suggest that owners worked alongside their slaves for time-sensitive agricultural tasks such as harvesting.[67] Slaves were given the most arduous and unpleasant work when possible, but their presence was not essential.[68] Enslaved craft workers may also have existed; a runestone from Hørning, near Aarhus in Denmark, was raised after about 1050 by a manumitted slave named Toke the Smith in memory of his former owner, Troels.[69] We do not know if Toke learned his trade before or after manumission, but we can compare him to the enslaved goldsmith in Æthelgifu's will, discussed in Chapter 1.

As elsewhere, enslaved women were generally considered to be sexually accessible to their owners. Pre-Christian Scandinavian societies are thought to have relied on enslaved concubines for polygyny, and anthropological study hints at competition for female sexual partners amongst young men as a motivating factor early viking raids.[70] A number of the provincial law codes of the later Middle Ages indicate that enslaved women provided a means of producing potential heirs so long as the children were recognised as such by their free fathers.[71] Oral sagas written down in the thirteenth century imply strong connections between concubinage and slavery, and many of the children born of extramarital liaisons in sagas had enslaved mothers.[72] Given the varying timeline of conversion in Scandinavia and in diaspora communities, demand for enslaved women in these societies may have remained high through the tenth century, and perhaps to a lesser degree as a folk practice even later.

The extent of demand for slaves, both male and female, in Scandinavia remains a hotly debated subject, with disagreement about the extent to which foreign slaves were imported for labour or for resale along the slave-trading networks of the Baltic and eastern Europe. Proponents of a substantial slave population have placed estimates of between one-fifth and one-third of the total population in Scandinavia during the Viking Age. Tore Iversen, through the analysis of place names suggesting unfree or half-free inhabitants, has argued that large farms were subdivided by landowners to be worked by slaves throughout the first millennium AD, demonstrating a substantial slave population at any given point.[73] Dagfinn Skre has proposed the association of grave mounds on farms with free or high status; small farms lacking grave mounds indicate the lower, possibly unfree status of those operating them.[74] Jørn Sandnes's own high population estimate is based on a provision in the *Frostaþing* law of Norway, in which restitution for blinding a man included providing a new farm along with livestock and three slaves, from which he extrapolated a peak population of 50,000 to 75,000 slaves.[75] Ruth Mazo Karras, however, argues that the *Frostaþing* law probably does not represent the accoutrements of an average farm, since the intention of this restitution was to punish the wrongdoer. The purchase of slaves would have incurred a high cost that ensured a more permanent arrangement than the hiring of free labourers, with more than the average number of enslaved farmhands potentially required to assist the now-blinded farmer.[76] Karras's insistence on a small-scale slavery is situated relative to the millions of enslaved people in early modern Atlantic slave systems, a relativity now taken for granted in early medieval slavery studies, but Stefan Brink has likewise argued against widespread slaveholding due to a lack of explicit evidence for it.[77]

The unremarkable appearance of slavery in contemporary sources and its similarity to that of other regions suggest that the demand for slave labour in Viking-Age Scandinavia and diaspora communities was broadly on a par with that of the British Isles, though visible interest in long-term sexual partners may have created a more elevated population of enslaved women than elsewhere. The extent of slaveholding is impossible to estimate, but the scale of captive taking from the ninth century onwards undoubtedly increased the availability of slaves in Scandinavia. Even if many captives were destined for sale to elsewhere via Scandinavian markets, it is reasonable to assume that raiders returning from abroad would wish to keep slaves when their value as labourers or exotic status symbols exceeded what the market could offer in wealth.

This may also have been true in diaspora communities, especially those in proximity to wealthy urbanised markets such as Dublin and York.

Changing demand in the North Atlantic

Even if the deployment of foreign slaves in Norway, Denmark, and Sweden remained steady during the ninth through eleventh centuries, the settlement of the North Atlantic, principally Iceland, must have prompted dramatic surges in the demand for slaves. Despite their problems as sources, Icelandic sagas indicate a strong connection in the minds of late medieval authors and audiences between the settlement of Iceland, which lasted from *c.* 870 to 940, and 'Celtic' slaves. The twelfth-century Icelandic *Landnámabók* refers several times to freed and enslaved people from Ireland and Scotland being brought to Iceland by the first settlers.[78] The extent of Irish influence in the development of ninth- and tenth-century Iceland has remained contentious, but individuals of British and Irish descent were certainly among the early inhabitants.[79] Large-scale genetic sequencing of the relatively isolated modern population and osteological analysis of ancient skeletons have indicated a significant proportion of British and Irish people in the founding population of Iceland, though this could signal the presence of free wives or people of mixed Anglo- or Hiberno-Norse lineage as much as the importation of slaves.[80] The underrepresentation of women in *Landnámabók* probably obscures the existence of enslaved women whose sons could still become free heirs and respected members of the community.[81] Such is the case in the aforementioned *Laxdæla Saga*, in which Melkorka bears a son, Olaf, to her owner, Hoskuld.[82] Gísli Sigurðsson has also suggested that the paucity of explicit, reliable evidence for Irish influence in Iceland could itself be an indicator of an enslaved population. Irish slaves may have been assigned Scandinavian names, and we can presume that they were forced to learn and communicate in Norse. Slave status would also help to explain the dearth of Insular artefacts from early Iceland, since slaves would have been less able to carry reminders of home with them than free immigrants.[83]

The initial settlement of Iceland lasted only a generation, and slaves were probably imported to resolve early shortages in free labour and livestock.[84] Demand may have been much reduced as farms and multi-generational families were established in the landscape, which would help to explain the rapid decline of slavery in Iceland after 1050.[85] Iceland remains the most extensively studied example of Viking-Age settlement in the North Atlantic, but the potential for brief surges in demand from new settlements in the Faroe Islands (from *c.* 825) and Greenland (from *c.* 985) should be considered, even though the extent of colonisation there was much less. There is little information about the settlement of the Faroes, but Scots in Greenland who may have been slaves were included in a North American expedition (*c.* 1000) according to the *Saga of Erik the Red*.[86] Other enslaved people in Greenland and Newfoundland would have been European, as there is no evidence to suggest that slaves were regularly sourced from indigenous peoples.[87] Contact between the Norse and the Dorset culture in Labrador and Newfoundland appears to have been infrequent, while the Thule, ancestral Inuit peoples in and around Greenland, were predominantly trade partners into the fifteenth century.[88] The settlement of Iceland in the late ninth century and first half of the tenth almost certainly represents the largest surge in demand for slave labour amongst North Atlantic settlements in the early Middle Ages.

Transit zones

For slaves from the British Isles or the Czech lands to reach the Islamic and Byzantine worlds, they had to be transported through areas of Europe where probably only a small proportion of them would have been syphoned off to meet local demand. Peoples from these areas are visible trafficking slaves in the slaving zones, such as Rus and Hungarians in Prague, or are known to have been in control of centres of slave-trading activity, as Frankish rulers were for Verdun and sometimes Venice. Unlike the Islamic world and Byzantium, however, these regions and polities present no clear evidence of a substantial and renewable demand for slave labour within their own borders. They certainly practised slavery, but sources (which are admittedly sparse for Rus and Hungary) give the impression of slaveholding on par with that of the slaving zones: ubiquitous, but small-scale and household-based. The logical conclusion, then, is that these areas predominantly functioned as transit zones for long-distance slave trading from the ninth century onwards. The later emergence of polities in Rus and Hungary means that the consumption of foreign slave labour in the seventh and eighth centuries is visible only in Francia.

Francia

With 'Francia' being a general term for various early medieval polities within what is now France, Germany, Belgium, and the Low Countries, demand for slaves is relevant to both the British Isles and the Czech lands for almost the entirety of the period from the seventh through the eleventh centuries. Irish, British, and English captives appeared at Merovingian markets in the seventh century and earlier, particularly in hagiographical works of the second half of the seventh century, and these people were probably destined for household servitude. This practice was widespread in Merovingian Francia, whereas agricultural labour was performed overwhelmingly by tenants.[89] The purchase and manumission of foreign enslaved captives by high-profile members of the Neustrian courts of Dagobert I and his son, Clovis II, acted as important demonstrations of piety in hagiographical works about Eligius, bishop of Noyon (d. 660), and Balthild, wife of Clovis II (d. 680), as well as in that of their contemporary, Amand (d. *c.* 675), who worked as a missionary in Frisia.[90] All these individuals established the former slaves as tenants and clergy at the numerous religious houses they founded in their careers, but this demand for saleable slaves, as with Bohemian monastic foundations, was unlikely to have been a consistent driver behind Merovingian demand.[91]

Enslaved people from Britain and Ireland are not visible in a Carolingian context in the eighth and ninth centuries. Although household chattel slavery continued to exist, the presence of such people within a home seems to have held less importance as a signifier of power over others.[92] As in the earlier Merovingian period, agricultural production on estates was largely carried out by tenants, most of whom had probably not been purchased as chattel slaves. As mentioned in Chapter 1, the *ancillae* working in textile workshops, *gynaecea*, were probably members of unfree tenant families on estates whose roles could change depending on their marital status and life stage.[93]

Scholarship has nevertheless seen the deployment of unfree Slavs on the estates of ninth- and tenth-century East Francia as both a symptom of and stimulus for slave trading along the frontier. As early as 770, a Bavarian deed from Peigiri to the diocese of Freising includes mention of a slave (*mancipium*) named 'Sasca the Slav'.[94] Charles Verlinden has argued that *sclavus* morphed from exclusively an ethnonym (Slav) into a term of status (slave) in the tenth century in East Frankish charters, with the prevalence of these people serving as evidence of the scale of Frankish slave raiding in Slavic lands. Working backwards from the etymological perspective that modern words in western European languages such as *l'esclavage* derive from *sclavus*, Verlinden believed that, because *sclavus* was used to describe donated individuals amidst others labelled *lidi* and *mancipia*, *sclavus* must therefore have connoted unfree status.[95] Alice Rio has pointed out, however, that special arrangements for free Slavs are known in Frankish charters, and that no diplomatic use of *sclavus* conclusively represents anything other than ethnicity.[96] Verlinden's support primarily comes from narrative material describing slave trading, and there is very little evidence to indicate that Slavs captured in Frankish raids became slaves in Francia.[97] Nevertheless, as we have seen in this chapter and the previous one, there is often very little explicit mention, if any, of connections between captive taking and slave trading, on one hand, and the presence of enslaved people in households or on estates, on the other. Use of the word *sclavus* may have served to distinguish foreign captives from others whose unfree status was hereditary, or, in the case of penal slaves and self-sellers, whose circumstances of enslavement may have set them apart when it came to manumission or resale.[98] We have also seen in the case of *wealh* in English and *saqāliba* in Arabic that the conflation of ethnonyms and status had occurred elsewhere by the tenth century.

There is, nonetheless, very little likelihood of a large population of unfree Slavs on East Frankish estates. Estate management in this period relied on tenancy normally resulting from hereditary status rather than chattel slavery. The donation of *mancipia* could occur independently of land, but could also reflect the relocation of surplus labourers, such as the adult children of tenants, to new lands under cultivation.[99] The declining importance of household slavery in this context also has significant bearing on the scale of foreign-born enslaved labour. Households were the places where slave labour was most easily overseen; if ownership of chattel slaves was no longer essential to displays of prestige, there is little reason to think that there was significant demand for enslaved Slavs in East Francia, and this part of Europe was primarily a transit region for slave trading.

Rus

As Scandinavians settled the area east of the Baltic Sea and formed communities in places such as Staraia Ladoga and Gorodishche in the late eighth century and ninth, it is very likely that they brought Scandinavian-style slaveholding traditions with them.[100] We have very little information about slavery amongst these peoples, however, who were known as Rus by the middle of the ninth century. Even so, long-distance slave trading may have begun as early as the late eighth century along the river systems of eastern Europe and through the Caucasus to the Abbasid Caliphate.[101] What we do know of slave ownership comes from accounts of Islamic geographers and diplomats who travelled in eastern Europe and the Caucasus region, who were keenly interested in the origins of this trade. As such, slave ownership amongst the Rus is portrayed as a side effect of slave trading, with the ownership and use of slaves being an intermediate stage between capture and sale. Ibn Rusta, writing *c.* 903–913 but possibly drawing from a text composed in the second half of the ninth century, notes that the Rus took care to dress and treat their slaves well, because they were, ultimately, considered trade goods.[102] Ahmad ibn Fadlān, who witnessed Rus traders at Bulghar on the river Volga in 922, describes Rus slave dealers in a way that blurs ownership with concubinage; those beautiful women whom a trader offered for sale were also those whom he used for sex.[103]

Ibn Fadlān does provide hints at longer-term slave ownership, with a focus on personal servants and concubinage. This may be due to the author framing foreign practices within or in contrast to his own knowledge of Abbasid slavery, but he nevertheless asserts that the king of Rus had 400 companions, each of whom kept two enslaved women – one a serving girl, the other a concubine. The king himself kept a harem of 40 enslaved concubines.[104] We can glean from this the importance of gendered slavery amongst Rus traders and elites, though this was not to the exclusion of male slaves. In his famous depiction of a Rus chieftain's funeral, Ibn Fadlān notes that the opportunity to die for their owner as part of the sacrificial rituals was offered to both enslaved girls and boys.[105] Although wealthy Rus were undoubtedly slave owners, it is impossible to tell the extent of demand for slaves and slave labour within Rus territory.

As the Rus became increasingly Slavicised through the tenth century and the seat of power shifted to Kyiv, we have to consider that slaveholding traditions also morphed, though what they may have looked like remains a mystery.[106] The earliest law code, the Short Redaction of the *Russkaia Pravda*, which may derive in part from the reign of Iaroslav the Wise in the first half of the eleventh century, records customary laws of the sort related to resident slave populations: what to do when runaway slaves are found in the possession of others, how to punish a slave who strikes a freeman, and the punishments for killing an enslaved tutor or nurse.[107] Nevertheless, the inclusion of provisions for recovering a slave who has been resold as many as four times suggests a high level of transience among local enslaved populations.[108] This is potentially reflected in a birchbark letter from Novgorod, dated *c.* 1100–1120, which appears to relate to the purchase of an enslaved woman in Pskov, her resale, and the subsequent legal issue when someone claimed the woman had been stolen.[109]

With both the earlier, outside evidence and the later, local evidence in mind, demand for slaves amongst the Rus seems to have not necessarily been for their labour. The Rus were undoubtedly slaveholders, but the textual elision of slave ownership and slave trading suggests that slaves acquired in Prague or from trade in Poland or Scandinavia were just as likely to be sold onwards as to become a part of Rus society. There was high demand for slaves by Rus traders, but the source of that demand lay in the networks that connected eastern Europe with Byzantium and the Abbasid Caliphate.

Hungary

Slavery was undoubtedly practised by the Magyars, who arrived in central Europe in the closing decades of the ninth century and who, by the turn of the eleventh century, were settled in the Carpathian Basin and known as Hungarians. The earliest law code, issued during the rule of Stephen I (*c*. 997–1038), suggests the existence here of customary slaveholding practices we have seen already. These laws address problems that could most commonly arise from a settled population of unfree people, such as manumission, the testimony of *servi*, and marriage between free men and *ancillae*.[110] Cameron Sutt has argued that both legislative and charter evidence demonstrate the continued treatment of *servi* and *ancillae* on Hungarian estates as chattel slaves into the thirteenth century, but this is very much an area of ongoing historiographical debate.[111] Nearly all of this discussion has taken place in Hungarian, but it is worth noting that interpretation of unfree labour has mirrored that of Czechoslovakia, with a strong Marxist influence from the middle of the twentieth century onwards.[112]

There was, nevertheless, some demand for foreign slaves at least within the later Hungarian kingdom. Abū Hāmid al-Andalusī al-Gharnātī, a traveller writing about his experiences of living in Hungary from 1150 to 1153, notes that the prices of slaves dropped dramatically during raiding seasons. A Byzantine boy could be purchased for as little as 3 dinars, and al-Gharnātī himself bought an eight-year-old Byzantine girl to serve him. Another girl, 15 years old, who he purchased as a concubine was skilled in cooking, sewing, and embroidery, indicating the types of labour that an enslaved woman might be expected to perform.[113] Canons promulgated a generation earlier in 1092 by Ladislas I demonstrate that this demand was not a later development. The Canons of the Synod of Szabolcs punish a priest who lives with an *ancilla* in place of a wife with the *ancilla*'s sale, which hints at a more common phenomenon of enslaved concubinage.[114] Another canon indicates the existence of internal slave trading by declaring that the Christian wives and slaves of Jews shall be freed and whoever sold them shall lose the profits of the sale.[115]

That religious minority communities could be engaged in different types of slaveholding within a polity is borne out by al-Gharnātī's testimony that the Muslim men serving the Christian king Geza II as soldiers were given special permission to own enslaved concubines, and al-Gharnāṭī himself had a child by the teenage girl he purchased.[116] Even if Christian Hungarian landholders were deploying *servi* and *ancillae* as unfree tenants rather than slaves, Muslim and Jewish communities were still very much interested in domestic chattel slavery by the middle of the twelfth century, which may also have continued to influence the demographics of captives targeted by Christian Hungarian raids. Although there is little information about slavery before the twelfth century, what does survive is enough to hint at a demand for foreign slaves within Hungary and that captives were an important part of Hungarian long-distance trade networks. Like Rus, tenth- and eleventh-century Hungary may have been primarily a transit zone, where some captives were probably syphoned off to meet demand at home with the majority sold onwards.

Slave ownership in Europe and around the Mediterranean operated on vastly different scales. Apart from the Islamic polities and the Byzantine Empire, slavery appears to have existed at a low to moderate levels and to have been dominated by household servitude and farm work. Although we will encounter Rus, Hungarian, and Frankish slavers in subsequent chapters, the evidence from these areas does not depict slaveholding on a level sufficient to create a demand for foreign slaves that would cause changes in the scale of enslavement elsewhere. In Byzantium, the strong Roman legal tradition of chattel slavery and level of economic organisation contributed to an institution that deployed slave labour in ways similar to the British Isles and Scandinavia, but on a much larger scale. This also meant a reliance on slaves in military and administrative roles, as well as in infrastructure projects. In the Islamic world, however, we see a voracious demand for enslaved people caused not only by strictures on the enslavement of Muslims but also by the development of new institutions reliant on enslaved labour, in addition to its casual deployment in highly urbanised societies. This demand in the Islamic world experienced a dramatic increase in the ninth and tenth centuries, with a parallel shift in the northeast Mediterranean hinted at by Byzantine sources, and these both had far-reaching impacts on the economic, military, and administrative developments of the northern and east central slaving zones.

Notes

1 Cristina de la Puente, 'Free fathers, slave mothers and their children: a contribution to the study of family structures in al-Andalus', *Imago Temporis: Medium Aevum*, 7 (2013), 36, 38–9. See also Al-Qudūrī, *Mukhtaṣar*, in Bernard Lewis (ed. and trans.), *Islam from the Prophet Muhammad to the Capture of Constantinople*, 2 vols (Oxford: Oxford University Press, 1987), ii, pp. 238–9.

2 Nadia Maria El Cheikh, 'Revisiting the Abbasid harems', *Journal of Middle East Women's Studies*, 1:3 (2005), 1–19. Nadia Maria El Cheikh, *Women, Islam and Abbasid Identity* (Cambridge, MA: Harvard University Press, 2015), pp. 7–8, 81–2.

3 El Cheikh, 'Revisiting the Abbasid harems', 8.

4 Fuad Matthew Caswell, *The Slave Girls of Baghdad: The Qiyn in the Early Abbasid Era* (London: I.B. Tauris, 2011), p. 265. Dwight F. Reynolds, 'The *Qiyan* of al-Andalus', in Matthew S. Gordon and Kathryn A. Hain (eds), *Concubines and Courtesans: Women and Slavery in Islamic History* (Oxford: Oxford University Press, 2017), p. 112.

5 Caswell, *Slave Girls of Baghdad*, p. 268.

6 Patricia Crone, *Slaves on Horses: The Evolution of the Islamic Polity* (Cambridge: Cambridge University Press, 1980), p. 79.

7 Crone, *Slaves on Horses*, pp. 75–9.

8 Daniel Pipes, *Slave Soldiers and Islam: The Genesis of a Military System* (New Haven, CT: Yale University Press, 1981), pp. 182–3. The *ghilman* of the first half of the ninth century were typically from central Asia and could be either free or enslaved, and these may have held a different position from the enslaved, primarily black African and Slavic soldiers known as mamluks. Étienne de la Vassière, *Samarcande et Samarra: Élites d'Asie central dans l'empire Abbasside* (Paris: Association pour l'Avancement des Études Iraniennes, 2007).

9 Pipes, *Slave Soldiers and Islam*, p. 192.

10 Reuven Amitai, 'The Mamlūk institution, or one thousand years of military slavery in the Islamic world', in Christopher Leslie Brown and Paul D. Morgan (eds), *Arming Slaves: From Classical Times to the Modern Age* (New Haven, CT: Yale University Press), p. 48.

11 David Ayalon, 'On the eunuchs in Islam', *Jerusalem Studies in Arabic and Islam*, 1 (1979), 68–9.

12 Ayalon, 'On the eunuchs in Islam', 70–1.

13 Nadia Maria El Cheikh, 'Servants at the gate: eunuchs at the court of Al-Muqtadir', *Journal of the Economic and Social History of the Orient*, 48:2 (2005), 236. The imbalanced ratio may be explained

by shiftwork and the breadth of eunuchs' duties. David Ayalon, *Eunuchs, Caliphs and Sultans: A Study in Power Relationships* (Jerusalem: Magnes, 1999), pp. 16–17.

14 Matthew S. Gordon, 'Preliminary remarks on slaves and slave labour in the Abbasid Empire', in Laura Culbertson (ed.), *Slaves and Households in the Near East* (Chicago, IL: University of Chicago Press, 2011), pp. 80–1. Kurt Franz, 'Slavery in Islam: legal norms and social practice', in Reuven Amitai and Christoph Cluse (eds), *Slavery and the Slave Trade in the Eastern Mediterranean (c. 1000–1500)* (Turnhout: Brepols, 2017), pp. 90–5.

15 Franz, 'Slavery in Islam', pp. 120–4.

16 Hugh Kennedy, *The Prophet and the Age of the Caliphates: The Islamic Near East from the 6th to the 11th Century*, 3rd edn (London: Routledge, 2015), p. 181. Alexandre Popović, *The Revolt of African Slaves in Iraq in the 3rd/9th Century* (Princeton, NJ: Marcus Wiener, 1999), pp. 153–4.

17 Mohamed Meouak, *Saqaliba: Eunuques et esclaves à la conquête du pouvoir* (Helsinki: Academia Scientiaria Fennica, 2004).

18 Roger Collins, *Caliphs and Kings: Spain, 796–1031* (Chichester: Wiley, 2012), pp. 182–5. Dmitri Mishin, 'The saqāliba slaves in the Aghlabid state', *Annual of Medieval Studies at CEU 1996/97* (1998), 236–7. Ahmad Nazmi, *Commercial Relations between Arabs and Slavs (9th–11th Centuries)* (Warsaw: Wydawnictwo Akademickie Dialog, 1998), pp. 77–80.

19 C. E. Bosworth et al., 'al-Sakāliba', in P. Bearman et al. (eds), *The Encyclopaedia of Islam*, vol. 8, 2nd edn (Leiden: Brill, 1995), pp. 872–81.

20 Ibn Buṭlān, *Shirā al-Raqīq*, in Lewis, *Islam*, ii, pp. 246–7. Cf. Christina de la Puente, 'The ethnic origin of female slaves in al-Andalus', in Gordon and Hain, *Concubines and Courtesans*, pp. 124–42, who argues that enslaved women in al-Andalus were Christian Europeans from northern Iberia and Berbers from north Africa.

21 Caswell, *Slave Girls*, p. 14.

22 Ibn Buṭlān, *Shirā al-Raqīq*, translated in Ayalon, 'On the eunuchs in Islam', 116. 'al-Ğāḥiẓ', in Tadeusz Lewicki (ed. and trans.), *Źródła arabskie do dziejów Słowiańszczyzny*, vol. 1 (Wrocław: Wyd. Polskeij Academii Nauk, 1956), pp. 166–7.

23 al-Qāḍī al-Nuʿmān, *Iftitāḥ al-Daʿwa*, in Hamid Haji (trans.), *Founding the Fatimid State: The Rise of an Islamic Empire* (London: I.B. Tauris, 2006), p. 169.

24 Mishin, 'The *saqāliba* slaves in the Aghlabid state', 238, 243. Shainool Jiwal, 'From slaves to supporters: the role of Slavs in the Fatimid

Mediterranean empire in the fourth/tenth century', *Medieval Studies*, 77 (2015), 103–25.

25 Pascual de Gayangos (trans.), *The History of the Mohammedan Dynasties in Spain*, 2 vols (London: Oriental Translation Fund, 1840–3), i, p. 238. Gayangos's work is an abridged translation of a history of al-Andalus by al-Maqqarī, a north African scholar of the late sixteenth and early seventeenth centuries who drew heavily from earlier source material. El Cheikh, 'Servants at the gate', 236.

26 See p. 182–4.

27 Fanny Bessard, *Caliphs and Merchants: Cities and Economies of Power in the Near East (700–950)* (Oxford: Oxford University Press, 2020).

28 Olivia Remie Constable, *Trade and Traders in Muslim Spain* (Cambridge: Cambridge University Press, 1996), p. 206.

29 Mishin, The *saqāliba* slaves in the Aghlabid state', 236–7.

30 Albeit alongside metaphorical connotations of slavery and freedom (e.g. 'slave of God'). Alexander P. Kazhdan, 'The concepts of freedom (*eleutheria*) and slavery (*duleia*) in Byzantium', in George Makdisi et al. (eds), *La Notion de liberté au Moyen Âge: Islam, Byzance, Occident. Penn–Paris–Dumbarton Oaks Colloquia, IV, session des 12–15 octobre 1983* (Paris: Société d'Édition les Belles Lettres, 1985), pp. 215–26.

31 See p. 19.

32 Noel Lenski, 'Slavery in the Byzantine Empire', in Craig Perry et al. (eds), *Cambridge World History of Slavery*, vol. 2: *AD 500–1420* (Cambridge: Cambridge University Press, 2021), pp. 453–81. For the scale and practice of slavery in late antiquity, see Kyle Harper, *Slavery in the Late Roman World, AD 275–425* (Cambridge: Cambridge University Press, 2011).

33 Günther Prinzing, 'On slaves and slavery', in Paul Stephenson (ed.), *The Byzantine World* (London: Routledge, 2012), p. 92.

34 *Book of the Eparch*, in Edwin Hanson Freshfield (ed. and trans.), *Roman Law in the Later Byzantine Empire* (Cambridge: Bowes & Bowes, 1938), p. 12 (II.8), p. 16 (IV.2), 22 (VI.7), p. 26 (VIII.7), p. 32 (XI.1).

35 *Book of the Eparch*, p. 14 (III.1), p. 24 (VII.3, VII.5).

36 Rotman, *Byzantine Slavery*, p. 99.

37 Rio, *Slavery after Rome*, p. 140.

38 Nicephorus, *The Life of St Andrew the* Fool, ed. and trans. Lennart Rydén, 2 vols (Uppsala: Uppsala University Press, 1995), i, p. 13.

39 Nicephorus, *Life of St Andrew the Fool*, i, pp. 85, 89, 115.

40 *The Life of Saint Basil the Younger*, ed. and trans. Denis F. Sullivan, Alice-Mary Talbot, and Stamatina McGrath (Washington, DC: Dumbarton Oaks, 2014), pp. 281–341 (III.2, 5, 7, 10, 31, 36–8, 41).

41 Stephanos Efthymiadis, 'Hagiography from the "Dark Age" to the age of Symeon Metaphrastes (eighth–tenth centuries)', in Stephanos Efthymiadis (ed.), *The Ashgate Research Companion to Byzantine Hagiography*, 2 vols (Farnham: Ashgate, 2011), i, p. 96.
42 Nicephorus, *Life of St Andrew the Fool*, i, pp. 85, 115. *Life of Saint Basil the Younger*, p. 119.
43 *Life of Saint Basil the Younger*, p. 119.
44 Rio, *Slavery after Rome*, p. 140.
45 Angeliki E. Laiou and Cécile Morrisson, *The Byzantine Economy* (Cambridge: Cambridge University Press, 2007), p. 102.
46 Rotman, *Byzantine Slavery*, p. 103.
47 Rotman, *Byzantine Slavery*, p. 106.
48 Shaun Tougher, *The Eunuch in Byzantine History and Society* (London: Routledge, 2008).
49 Michael F. Hendy, *Studies in Byzantine Monetary Economy c. 300–1450* (Cambridge: Cambridge University Press, 1985), pp. 201–18.
50 *Novellae*, ed. Rudolph Schoell, *Corpus Iuris Civilis*, vol. 3, 6th edn (Berlin: Wiedmann, 1956), XXII.8, p. 152. *The Laws of the Isaurian Era: The* Ecloga *and Its Appendices*, trans. Mike Humphreys (Liverpool: Liverpool University Press, 2017), §8.2, p. 58. Rotman, *Byzantine Slavery*, p. 36.
51 Rotman, *Byzantine Slavery*, p. 56.
52 For chronicles depicting significant captive taking by Byzantine armies, particularly c. 960–980, see Kazhdan, 'The concepts of freedom', p. 222.
53 Rotman, *Byzantine Slavery*, pp. 78, 80.
54 Lesley Abrams, 'Diaspora identity in the Viking Age', *Early Medieval Europe*, 20:1 (2012), 17–38. Judith Jesch, *The Viking Diaspora* (London, 2015), pp. 163–203.
55 *Vita Findani*, ed. O. Holder-Egger, MGH, SS 55 (Hanover, 1887), pp. 503–4.
56 *Laxdæla Saga*, trans. M. Magnusson (London: Penguin, 1969), pp. 24–5, 64–8.
57 Rimbert, *Vita Anskarii*, ed. G. Waitz, MGH, SS rer. Germ. 55 (Hanover, 1884), pp. 72–3.
58 Alfred and Guthrum §5, in Liebermann (ed.), *Die Gesetze*, i, p. 128.
59 David Pelteret, 'Slavery in the Danelaw', in Ross Samson (ed.), *Social Approaches to Viking Studies* (Glasgow: Cruithne, 1991), pp. 183–4.
60 'The Book of Ahmad Ibn Fadlān 921–22', in Paul Lunde and Caroline Stone (eds and trans.), *Ibn Fadlān and the Land of Darkness: Arab Travellers in the Far North* (London: Penguin, 2012), pp. 50–1.
61 Orri Vésteinsson, 'Ethnicity and class in settlement-period Iceland', in John Sheehan and Donnchadh Ó Corráin (eds), *The Viking*

Age: Ireland and the West (Dublin: Four Courts Press, 2010), pp. 494–510. Fontaine, 'Early medieval slave-trading', 483–8.

62 Per Norseng, 'Law codes as a source for Nordic history in the early Middle Ages', *Scandinavian Journal of History*, 16:3 (1991), 137–66. Regarding slavery specifically, see Karras, *Slavery and Society*, pp. 167–78.

63 Elsa Sjöholm, 'Sweden's medieval laws: European legal tradition – political change', *Scandinavian Journal of History*, 15:1/2 (1990), 65–87. Elsa Sjöholm, *Gesetze als Quellen mittelalterlicher Geschichte des Nordens* (Stockholm: Almqvist & Wiksell, 1977), pp. 120–62.

64 Brink, *Thraldom*, pp. 95–6. Their expendability and anonymity may have made slaves a convenient device for later authors; they were easier to insert for plot progression than free people, who required names and genealogies of their own. Karras, *Slavery and Society*, p. 182.

65 For discussion of the critical analysis, see Brink, *Thraldom*, pp. 85–7. For the text, *The Poetic Edda*, vol. 2: *Mythological Poems*, ed. and trans. Ursula Dronke (Oxford: Oxford University Press, 1997), pp. 164–5.

66 Karras, *Slavery and Society*, pp. 76–92. Brink, *Thraldom*, pp. 186–8. These reflected gender divisions for all statuses. Jenny Jochens, *Women in Old Norse Society* (Ithaca, NY: Cornell University Press, 1995), pp. 117, 120.

67 Karras, *Slavery and Society*, p. 79.

68 Janken Myrdal attempts to identify tasks such as grinding grain, tending livestock, and fertilising as slave work, but he admits that free people performed them when there were no slaves. Janken Myrdal, 'Milking and grinding, digging and herding: slaves and farmwork 1000–1300', in Bjørn Poulsen and Søren Michael Sindbæk (eds), *Settlement and Lordship in Viking and Early Medieval Scandinavia* (Turnhout: Brepols, 2011), pp. 296–9, 306.

69 Brink, *Thraldom*, pp. 106–7.

70 Ben Raffield, Neil Price, and Mark Collard, 'Polygyny, concubinage, and the social lives of women in Viking-Age Scandinavia', *Viking and Medieval Scandinavia*, 13 (2017), 179, 182.

71 Karras, *Slavery and Society*, pp. 73–5. These provisions in the Norwegian *Gulaþing* and *Frostaþing* laws, written down in the middle of the thirteenth century at the earliest, are probably representative of much older custom given that the stance is at odds with ecclesiastical perspectives of that time. Ruth Mazo Karras, 'Concubinage and slavery in the Viking Age', *Scandinavian Studies*, 62 (1990), 144–6.

72 Melkorka's role in *Laxdæla Saga* has already been discussed, and, for other examples, see Karras, *Slavery and Society*, p. 75.

73 Tore Iversen, *Trelldommen: Norsk slaveri i middelalderen* (Bergen: University of Bergen, 1994), pp. 213–40. Cited from Dagfinn Skre, 'The social context of settlement in Norway in the first millennium AD', *Norwegian Archaeological Review*, 34:1 (2001), 7–8.

74 Skre, 'The social context', 11–12. For challenges and Skre's rebuttal, see pp. 13–34.

75 Jørn Sandnes, *Ødetid og gjenreisning: Trøndsk busetnings historie ca. 1200–1660* (Oslo: Universitetsforlaget, 1971), p. 86. Jørn Sandnes, 'Bondesamfunnet', in Ingrid Semmingsen et al. (eds), *Norges kulturhistorie*, vol. 1: *Vår fjerne fortid* (Oslo: H. Auschehoug, 1979), p. 50. Jørn Sandnes, '"Tolv kyr, to hester og tre træler": litt om omfanget av træleholdet i Norge i vikingtid og tidlig kristen tid', *Historisk Tidsskrift*, 62 (1983), 81–2. All cited from Karras, *Slavery and Society*, p. 78.

76 Karras, *Slavery and Society*, pp. 78–9. See also Ole Jørgen Benedictow, 'The demography of the Viking Age and the High Middle Ages in the Nordic countries', *Scandinavian Journal of History*, 21:3 (1996), 154.

77 Brink, *Thraldom*, pp. 297–302.

78 *Landnámabók*, trans. H. Pálsonn and P. Edwards (Winnipeg: University of Manitoba Press, 1972), pp. 19–21, 51, 53, 62, 63, 144.

79 Gísli Sigurðsson, *The Gaelic Influence in Iceland* (Reykjavik: University of Iceland Press, 2000), i, regarding slaves specifically, 30 n. 22. For the types of Irish people mentioned in Icelandic sources, see J. Kristjánsson, 'Ireland and the Irish in Icelandic tradition', in H. B. Clarke et al. (eds), *Ireland and Scandinavia in the Early Viking Age* (Dublin: Four Courts Press, 1998), pp. 262–3.

80 A. Helgason et al., 'Estimating Scandinavian and Gaelic ancestry in the male settlers of Iceland', *American Journal of Human Genetics*, 67:3 (2001), 723–37. A. Helgason et al., 'mtDNA and the origin of the Icelanders: deciphering signals of recent population history', *American Journal of Human Genetics*, 66:3 (2000), 999–1016. Kimberly A. Plomp et al., 'The composition of the founding population of Iceland: a new perspective from 3D analyses of basicranial shape', *PLoS ONE*, 16:2 (2021), 1–16.

81 William Sayers, 'Management of the Celtic fact in *Landnámabók*', *Scandinavian Studies*, 66:2 (1994), 139–40.

82 *Laxdæla Saga*, pp. 24–5, 64–8.

83 Sigurðsson, *The Gaelic Influence*, p. 33.

84 Vésteinsson, 'Ethnicity and class', pp. 504–5. For example, *Landnámabók* describes one Hjorleif hitching his slaves to a plough because he has only one ox: p. 20.

85 Karras, *Slavery and Society*, pp. 135–6.

86 *Eirik the Red's Saga*, trans. Keneva Kunz, in Gísli Sigurðsson (ed.), *The Vinland Sagas* (London: Penguin, 2008), p. 41.

87 The capture and baptism of two indigenous (*Skræling*) children in the Vinland sagas was a notable event. *Eirik the Red's Saga*, p. 48.

88 P. D. Sutherland, 'The Norse and native North Americans', in W. W. Fitzhugh and E. Ward (eds), *Vikings: The North Atlantic Saga* (Washington, DC: Smithsonian Institution, 2000), pp. 238–47. H. C. Gulløv, 'Natives and Norse in Greenland', in Fitzhugh and Ward (eds), *Vikings: The North Atlantic Saga*, pp. 318–26. There is little evidence for sustained, direct Norse–Inuit contact in the early medieval period in Greenland. P. Schledermann and K. M. McCullough, 'Inuit–Norse contact in the Smith Sound region', in James H. Barrett (ed.), *Contact, Continuity, and Collapse: The Norse Colonization of the North Atlantic* (Turnhout: Brepols, 2003), pp. 183–205.

89 M.-J. Tits-Dieuaide, 'Grands domaines, grandes et petites exploitations en Gaule mérovingienne', in Adriaan Verhulst (ed.), *Le Grand domaine aux époques mérovingienne et carolingienne: Actes du colloque international, Gand, 8–10 Septembre 1983* (Ghent: Belgisch Centrum voor Landelijke Geschiedenis, 1985), pp. 23–50. Wickham, *Framing the Early Middle Ages*, p. 282. On household slavery, see Rio, *Slavery after Rome*, pp. 156–8.

90 Dado of Rouen, *Vita Eligii ep. Noviomagensis*, ed. B. Krusch, MGH, SS rer. Merov. 4 (Hanover, 1902), pp. 677–8. Eligius freed *Brittani* and *Scotti*, among others, and Balthild redeemed 'de gente sua viros et puellas'. For further discussion of the captives' status as slaves, see Flechner and Fontaine, 'The admission of former slaves', 598–9. *Vita Sanctae Balthildis A*, ed. B. Krusch, MGH, SS rer. Merov. 2 (Hanover, 1888), pp. 494, 677.

91 Flechner and Fontaine, 'The admission of former slaves', 599–601.

92 Rio, *Slavery after Rome*, pp. 159–60.

93 Rio, *Slavery after Rome*, p. 161. Jean-Pierre Devroey, 'Men and women in early medieval serfdom: the ninth-century north Frankish evidence', *Past & Present*, 166 (2000), 25.

94 T. Bitterauf (ed.), *Die Traditionen des Hochstifts Freising*, vol. 1: *744–926* (Munich: Rieger'sche Universitätsbuchhandlung, 1905), no. 38, pp. 65–6.

95 Verlinden, 'L'origine de *sclavus*', 122–3.

96 Rio, *Slavery after Rome*, pp. 166–7.

97 Verlinden, 'L'origine de *sclavus*', 104–22. Rio, *Slavery after Rome*, pp. 165–6.

98 See pp. 78, 81.

99 Mary Sommar, *The Slaves of the Churches* (Oxford: Oxford University Press, 2020), pp. 161–2, believes that *mancipia* donated independently of any land were probably considered chattel.

100 For overviews of Scandinavian material culture in the Rus heartlands, see, for example, Ulf Fransson et al. (eds), *Cultural Interaction between East and West: Archaeology, Artefacts and Human Contacts in Northern Europe* (Stockholm: Stockholm University, 2007) and Fedir Androshchuk, *Vikings in the East: Essays on Contacts along the Road to Byzantium* (Uppsala: Uppsala University, 2013).

101 This is evidenced by the appearance of silver Islamic dirhams along this route and in Rus territory, as well as *saqāliba* slaves in Islamicate texts in the early ninth century. Marek Jankowiak, 'Dirham flows into northern and eastern Europe and the rhythms of the slave trade with the Islamic world', in J. Gruszczynski, M. Jankowiak, and J. Shepard (eds), *Viking-Age Trade: Silver, Slaves and Gotland* (Abingdon: Routledge, 2021), pp. 111–12.

102 'Ibn Rusta on the Rūs 903–913', in Lunde and Stone (eds), *Arab Travellers*, p. 126.

103 'The Book of Ahmad Ibn Fadlān', p. 47.

104 'The Book of Ahmad Ibn Fadlān', pp. 54–5.

105 'The Book of Ahmad Ibn Fadlān', p. 47.

106 For a general discussion of later social stratification, see Janet Martin, *Medieval Russia: 980–1584* (Cambridge: Cambridge University Press, 2007), pp. 64–99.

107 Daniel H. Kaiser (ed. and trans.), *The Laws of Rus': Tenth to Fifteenth Centuries* (Salt Lake City, UT: Charles Schlacks, Jr., 1992), §§11, 16, 17, 27, pp. 16–17. Unlike *Zakon*, the customary law of this code has no apparent Byzantine influence. S. Franklin and J. Shepard, *The Emergence of Rus, 750–1200* (London: Routledge, 1996), p. 221.

108 Kaiser (ed.), *The Laws of Rus'*, §16, p. 16.

109 Jos Schaeken, *Voices on Birchbark: Everyday Communication in Medieval Russia* (Leiden: Brill, 2019), p. 72.

110 'The Laws of King St Stephen I of Hungary (1000–1038)', in J. M. Bak (ed. and trans.), *Online Decreta Regni Mediaevalis Hungariae: The Laws of the Medieval Kingdom of Hungary* (2019). All complete monographs, 4, https://digitalcommons.usu.edu/lib_mono/4 (accessed 22 July 2023), §§I.18, 20, 21, p. 35; §I.29, p. 38; §II.4, p. 47; §II.18, p. 49.

111 Cameron Sutt, *Slavery in Árpád-Era Hungary in a Comparative Context* (Leiden: Brill, 2015), pp. 8–18. See also László Solymosi, 'Liberty and servitude in the age of Saint Stephen', in Attila Zsoldos

(ed.), *Saint Stephen and His Country. A Newborn Kingdom in Central Europe: Hungary* (Budapest: Győző Cholnoky, 2001), pp. 69–79.
112 Summarised in Sutt, *Slavery in Árpád-Era Hungary*, pp. 8–18.
113 'The travels of Abū Hāmid al-Andalusī al-Gharnātī 1130–1155', in Lunde and Stone (eds), *Arab Travellers*, pp. 80–1.
114 *The Canons of the Synod of Szabolcs*, in Bak (ed. and trans.), *Online Decreta Regni Mediaevalis Hungariae*, §2, p. 60.
115 *Canons of the Synod of Szabolcs*, §10, p. 62.
116 'The travels of Abū Hāmid al-Andalusī al-Gharnātī', p. 83. Cameron Sutt, 'Sexual access to slave women: Árpádian Hungary as a case study', in Andrea-Bianka Znorovszky and Christopher Mielke (eds), *Same Bodies, Different Women: Witches, Whores, and Handicapped. 'Other' Women in the Middle Ages and the Early Modern Period* (Budapest: Trivent Publishing, 2019), pp. 152–68.

3

Making slaves

People reduced to slavery could come from within a group or outside it, and not all slaves were considered saleable. This chapter returns to the British Isles and the Czech lands to consider how they could meet the demand for slave labour both from within these regions and, most importantly, from outside them. Slave-trading networks leveraged pre-existing legal and customary mechanisms for creating saleable slaves, and what mattered for supply was the extent to which these mechanisms were elastic, capable of enslaving more or fewer people in response to changes in market demand. Elasticity of slave supply has been studied extensively for Africa both before and during the trans-Atlantic trade, with robust economic models of supply relative to demand and pricing based on forms of statistical analysis that are impossible to replicate in an early medieval context.[1] The lack of information on market prices in northern and east central Europe means that we cannot formally establish elasticity of supply, though we can presume that prices rose as demand for slaves increased, which encouraged individuals to sell more slaves. Even at this rudimentary level, we should consider the ways in which pre-existing processes were capable of meeting demand, questioning when and why methods of enslavement could become strategies of slaving.

Supplying slaves for increased demand depended upon the ability to create slaves as necessary, so this chapter focuses on the enslavement of otherwise free people. The number of those born into slavery, inheriting legal status from one or both parents, could not have fluctuated enough to meet demand. There is very little early medieval evidence for forced procreation, and raising an enslaved person from birth to adulthood, or even just to an age at which they could be exploited for labour, required a considerable investment of time and resources with significant risk due to high rates of infant and child mortality.[2] Those who inherited slave status could be sold as chattel, but these circumstances meant that many recorded examples focus on the sale's justification or exceptionality.

Penal enslavement and direct sale created slaves from within a community, albeit in very different circumstances. People enslaved for judicial reasons were in some ways seen as outsiders, since enslavement broke bonds of community and kinship. Those who sold themselves or were sold by family had done nothing to 'deserve' slavery, but the circumstances of their treatment could vary widely. The enslavement of captives, taken by kidnapping or in war, was by far the most adaptable method, since the subsequent deracination required no legal process and could be achieved by distance alone. Captive taking also allowed for selectivity, with the age, sex, and social background all potentially dictated by market demand. Even in cases of unambiguous enslavement, saleability within each of these categories was neither uniform nor guaranteed, though penal enslavement, child sale, and captive taking all appear to have contributed to the market supply of chattel slaves.

Penal enslavement

Penal slavery was widespread in the early Middle Ages, and, in principle, served to cut someone off from their position and community as punishment for a serious offence. This cause was not always true in practice historically. Some rulers in pre-colonial Africa exploited penal enslavement to suit growing demand for slaves by expanding its application as a punishment.[3] Alice Rio has argued, however, that, although early medieval practices differed by region, offenders here were not enslaved out of any demand for labour.[4] She notes that penal slavery was a flexible institution with means for avoiding the sentence, such as compensation payments, and that manumission may have been a subject of negotiation. Penal slavery therefore operated on the level of local politics and kin groups, since compensation payments were too high to be paid by any one individual; the decision to make such a payment was therefore a communal one. The potential for an inability or unwillingness to make compensation payments means that penal enslavement was closely related to debt slavery, for which there is almost no direct evidence in the early medieval British Isles or Czech lands. Through this process, Rio argues that penal enslavement did not depend on the strength of the governmental apparatus, and, by serving the judicial needs of smaller communities, it existed separately from any market demands for slaves.

Irish and Welsh law appear to adhere to this model. Irish law featured two types of penal unfree status whose treatment varied by circumstance: the *fuidir* and the *muirchrech*. A *fuidir* was in most cases a half-free tenant, and only the lowest class can be linked to penal servitude. In this category, a '*fuidir* of the gallows' served the person who had ransomed them from the death penalty, assuming a gradation of unfree status very like penal servitude, but the *fuidir* was not considered to be a slave and so probably was not saleable.[5] A *muirchrech* was punished for a range of crimes by being set adrift in a boat and was to be enslaved wherever it washed up.[6] This physical removal from a community was reserved especially for women, probably as an alternative to outright execution.[7] If the *muirchrech* washed up on their own shore, they were regarded as a *fuidir*, suggesting that they were viewed differently from chattel slaves. Welsh law describes penal servitude in similar terms for the *lleidr gwerth*, or 'sale thief'. For the price of seven pounds, a thief could either ransom themselves or be purchased by someone else, and, if this sum could not be met, the *lleidr gwerth* faced banishment rather than execution.[8] The 'purchase' of a thief probably reflects collective ransoming by a kin group or by a very wealthy patron, whom, like a *fuidir*, the *lleidr gwerth* may have been expected to serve without the expectation of saleability.[9] Extant examples of penal servitude from throughout the early medieval period illustrate the placement of wrongdoers in service to a monastery rather than their sale.[10]

The question of whether penal slaves in England were eligible for sale appears to have been a more complex one. Offenders could be enslaved for theft and, in the case of Ine's seventh-century West Saxon law (688 × *c.* 694), for working on a Sunday.[11] In a move that may have been novel for the seventh century, Ine also forbade the sale of any person overseas, slave or free, even if they were guilty of a crime.[12] Two pieces of evidence suggest that Ine sought to change the treatment of West Saxon penal slaves and prevent sales that may have until then been acceptable.[13] Bede hints at the existence of justly saleable penal slaves in Northumbria in his *Ecclesiastical History* when he insists that Aidan, the bishop of Lindisfarne, redeemed those who had been 'unjustly' sold.[14] More explicitly, a Kentish law of Wihtred, promulgated *c.* 695, stipulates that a thief caught in the act faced one of three possible punishments: execution, ransom for the price of his wergild, or sale 'overseas'.[15] This law code was probably issued in relation to Ine's, suggesting that Wihtred sought to confirm a more customary approach to the saleability of penal slaves in Kent.

When penal slaves (*witeþeowes*) appear in wills of the tenth and eleventh centuries, they are settled on estates and in most instances are being freed, with others being noted as bequests.[16] Wills in which the testator refers to slaves whose enslavement he or she oversaw attest the local judicial nature of penal enslavement.[17] This may reflect a long-standing custom, as one of Ine's laws releases the free family members of slaves from any obligations of kinship.[18] Sale of penal slaves may have continued, but, until the late tenth century, may have been only occasional. When the practice appears again, in the early eleventh century as part of Archbishop Wulfstan II of York's heavy involvement in royal legislation, it appears to have been practised with some frequency. Prior to the Danish conquest, Wulfstan believed in prohibiting only the sale of innocent (*unforworhte*) people out of England, mentioning it in his homily *Sermo Lupi ad Anglos*, composed and revised multiple times between 1009 and 1014, and in the legislation V and VI Æthelred, the first issued at Enham *c.* 1008 and the second from 1009 as a revised, possibly private, draft.[19]

Like Bede, Wulfstan seems to have perceived guilty people as being eligible for sale, though, by the time he assisted with composing Cnut's Oxford code of 1018, he was inclined to prohibit the sale of all Christians out of the country.[20] Wulfstan repeatedly expressed grave concern for Christian countrymen being sold abroad and to 'heathens', and the saleability of penal slaves would go far to explain his role in reducing the number of enslaveable offences in royal law. II Cnut, authored by Wulfstan and promulgated 1020 × 1021, removed penal enslavement as a punishment for two offences first addressed by Ine more than three centuries previously. Whereas Ine had allowed for the enslavement of freemen who worked of their own volition on a Sunday and families complicit in hiding stolen goods, II Cnut instead prescribed penance and a fine for Sunday labour and forbade the enslavement of infants as accessories to theft.[21] This and Wulfstan's assertion that it was the custom of 'greedy people' to enslave infants may have been in reaction to the exploitation of these practices to create saleable slaves.[22]

Although this English evidence is speculative, for ninth-century Great Moravia the saleability of penal slaves is unequivocal. Almost a half of the clauses in the law tract *Zakon Suydnji Ljudem* involve slavery, with many of those stipulating enslavement as the punishment for crimes ranging from rape to oath breaking to theft. What is especially significant about this text compared to British and Irish ones is that criminals are to be *sold* into slavery.[23] The laws do not always specify what happened to the profits of the sale, though some of these may have gone to ducal coffers or served as compensation for the victim.[24] In the event of rape, the man's property and the proceeds of the sale were to be given to the victim, while, in other clauses, the proceeds of sale into slavery were to be given to the poor.[25] Although no documentary evidence survives to illustrate when, where, to whom, or even how often offenders were sold, the frequency of penal enslavement and sale within the text suggests that a criminal's reduction in status to that of chattel slave must have been relatively common. Whether *Zakon* played an exploitative role through its heavy reliance on penal enslavement is difficult to establish given our lack of understanding of its authorship or how this document operated. The appearance of penal enslavement may be disproportionate, and the compiler may have been particularly interested in slavery. The tentative dating of this text precedes the emergence of substantial demand for slaves from central Europe, suggesting that the comprehensive replacement of the *Ecloga*'s mutilations with penal enslavement has distorted our perception of local custom.

From Přemyslid Bohemia, decrees issued by Břetislav I in 1039 support the idea that penal enslavement was customary in the early medieval Czech lands. Reported by Cosmas as direct speech in his chronicle, the record probably derives from a now lost edict issued by Břetislav on the occasion of the translation of St Adalbert's remains in Gniezno.[26] One decree states that a man or woman who refuses to return to their marriage after a quarrel and separation should not be reduced to slavery in Bohemia as had been a 'rite of our land', but should be taken to Hungary whence they cannot return, nor can they redeem themselves with money. The same was true for women who had extramarital sex and convicted domestic abusers.[27] The latter part of the decree could reference slave trading with Hungary, with a redemption price referring to manumission, but exile is the more likely meaning. The accused was not to be enslaved in the Bohemian custom, and the price was therefore probably a compensation payment. The resolution of domestic disputes and issues of extramarital sex with enslavement indicates that enslavement was justifiable for less serious offences in Přemyslid Bohemia than it was in contemporary England.[28] Břetislav's decree could also serve as further proof for establishing *Zakon* as Moravian by demonstrating the disproportionate references to penal enslavement to be representative of a wider Czech legal context, though it does not clarify the saleability of penal slaves. It is worth noting, however, that this decree came only two decades after Wulfstan's attempts to limit penal enslavement, seemingly in response to exploitation of this practice in a period of high demand for slaves.[29]

Despite a relatively clear-cut situation in Ireland and Wales, societies in England and the Czech lands adopted approaches that left no sharp divide between penal enslavement and slave trading. Czech sources are more difficult to parse, but the English texts very much suggest a situation in which penal slavery was a source of saleable slaves and that this may have been increasingly relied upon during a period of heightened demand. This may also have been the case in the Czech lands, but the difficulties of textual transmission prevent any certainty on our part. Penal enslavement, as a customary judicial practice, did not become more widespread to supply chattel slaves, but a person's fate once enslaved may have depended increasingly upon market demand as much as elite perceptions of penal slavery's role within a community.

Direct sale

Free people could sell themselves or their children into slavery, and, although these sales operated very differently, they shared a perceived relationship to destitution. Self-sale appears largely in literary sources and penitentials from Britain and Ireland but is absent from

Czech texts, which may result from limited source survival, since the practice appears to have existed throughout much of Europe in the early Middle Ages.[30] Self-sale was seen by ecclesiastical authors as an extreme and pitiable measure, and, uniquely, it did not stem from outcast status. As such, it may have carried less stigma than penal enslavement, and certainly less than the enslavement of captives. This factor may have contributed to a negotiability of terms such as freedom for descendants or an increased likelihood of manumission.[31] We may see this in the sole English documentary source for self-sale, a tenth-century manumission in the Durham *Liber Vitae*, in which a woman freed 'all the people whose heads she took for their food in those evil days'.[32] Overall, self-sellers may have been considered off-limits to slave trading when they remained within their community, even if kinship ties were cut by the reduction in status.[33]

Such negotiability and mercy may have been customary, and few overt restrictions were placed upon self-sale. It remains conspicuously absent from secular legislation in Britain and Ireland, and only in the seventh- or eighth-century *Penitential of Theodore* was the minimum age of self-sellers placed at 14.[34] Self-sellers were probably much less likely to end up as saleable chattel slaves than captives or even penal slaves. Crucially, self-sale did not create a supply of slaves that could fluctuate to suit a market demand; demand could determine only how self-sellers were treated. We can presume that numbers of self-sellers increased during times of hardship, such as in the context of viking raids, but these individuals would have entered unfree service to a local lord or ecclesiastical institution. The *domboc* of the West Saxon king Alfred, probably compiled between 893 and 899, includes in its Prologue a modification of Exodus 21:7, in which Alfred proposes that, when the daughter of a man who voluntarily remained in slavery was purchased, she was ideally to be set apart from 'enslaved women and other servile women' and in particular was not to be resold to strangers.[35] Like the laws restricting penal enslavement, the attention here to the treatment of the children of voluntarily enslaved people came at a time of increased demand for slaves from the British Isles, particularly in Iceland. Although this law is folded into a larger treatment of Mosaic law in Old English, its amendments were certainly deliberate.

Another means of direct entry into slavery was the sale of a child by their parent. Like self-sale, the associated forfeiture of kinship and free status would normally have been a sign of severe hardship. The Irish law tract *Gúbretha Caratniad*, possibly composed before the second quarter of the eighth century, allowed parents to sell their children into slavery when they were unable to feed them, and this practice was later recorded in the *Annals of Ulster* during a famine in 965.[36] It may have been the case that parents could sell children locally to ensure that they were cared for and remained close enough for visitation and inclusion in kinship networks. There are indications, however, that these children were less likely to receive this treatment than self-sellers. English penitentials demonstrate a sustained interest in children's age of consent for their own sale. First to address this was the *Penitential of Theodore*, which stipulates that it was not a sin for parents to sell children under the age of seven, but that children older than seven had to give their consent.[37] Unlike his canon on self-sale, however, Theodore's restriction on child sale was repeated in the adapted *Old English Canons of Theodore*, composed sometime between the seventh and eleventh centuries, and in the late ninth-century Old English *Scriftboc*.[38] The *Old English Penitential*, produced after *Scriftboc*, goes even further by banning the practice of selling one's child or any near kin under pain of exclusion from the Christian community until the person sold could be redeemed or another redeemed in their place.[39]

Rather than simply functioning as poor translations and messy compilations of Irish, English, and Carolingian penitential texts, a common assumption in nineteenth- and twentieth-century scholarship, Stefan Jurasinski has convincingly argued that these Old English penitentials were conscious adaptations of earlier material to suit later English contexts, especially regarding slavery.[40] That these texts were written as demand for slaves increased may be especially significant for the role of child sale in the supply of chattel slaves. We know from Gerald of Wales that the Irish purchased English children sold as slaves by their parents to escape hunger and poverty before the Norman invasion in 1169.[41] Alongside Wulfstan's legislation on penal enslavement, Old English penitentials likewise indicate that, in the late ninth through the early eleventh centuries, ecclesiastical figures were becoming increasingly alarmed by the frequency of enslavement, which left people vulnerable to sale. The perception of slavery as an inherently sinful state of being is probably what led to emphasis on the protection of children as innocents.[42]

English texts indicate that children and other close relatives were sold as chattel slaves during the peak of demand in the late ninth, tenth, and early eleventh centuries, with some implication that these people increasingly fell victim to long-distance trade networks. Rarer evidence for this practice in the Czech lands indicates that parents actively responded to external demand. The Old Church Slavonic penitential *Někotoraja Zapověd* survives only in a late form, but is believed to have originated in Bohemia between the ninth and eleventh centuries.[43] One canon in this text prohibits a boy's castration by force or by a parent for the purpose of sale, an idea that is unique in both western and eastern European penitential tradition and that may reflect local ecclesiastical attempts to impose regulations on the Prague slave trade.[44] The canon does not prohibit the sale of one's own children, but it does seek to prevent the sale of a child for obvious financial gain or in conditions that would inevitably lead to non-Christian ownership. As discussed in Chapter 2, enslaved eunuchs were in high demand in the Islamic world and to some extent in Byzantium at the time of this penitential's composition; the *Někotoraja Zapověd* is almost certainly referencing this demand.

A late medieval context may illuminate the impetus behind this otherwise anomalous canon. In the Black Sea region in the thirteenth and fourteenth centuries, impoverished parents and their children were aware of the potential for social mobility and financial success accorded to mamluks in the Mamluk sultanate. Mamluks and eunuchs could rise to positions of wealth and power as they did in the earlier Umayyad and Abbasid Caliphates, sometimes gaining the resources to trace and relocate their families. This was apparently general knowledge in areas where slave traders operated, even at a substantial distance from the sultanate, and some recorded cases indicate that parents and children alike believed success in slavery to be a preferable alternative to freedom in poverty.[45] It is quite possible that information about the fate of slaves in al-Andalus or central Asia reached Bohemia either as rumours spread along trade routes or even via direct visitors such as Ibrāhīm ibn

Ya'qūb, a Jewish traveller from Cordoba who journeyed to Prague in the 960s.[46] This would help to explain parents' willingness to castrate their sons beyond the desire to earn more from their sale.

Slave-trading systems were clearly able to exploit child sale to an extent that they could not for self-sale. Self-sale hinged on the choice of a legally responsible adult and may have yielded preferential treatment amongst slaves or negotiable manumission following a term of service. Child sale, on the other hand, did not legally require the consent of the child, though in England it was considered a moral obligation for older children. The strong suggestion of links between external demand for slaves and the sale of children also indicates that children were far more likely to be treated as chattel, though this group could not have dominated the supply of tradable slaves. The decision to sell a child could not have been something that most families took lightly. We must acknowledge, however, that instances of child sale may very well have increased in response to demand from the late ninth century onwards, or, at least, that the susceptibility of children to long-distance slave-trading networks was great enough to cause a flurry of concern amongst ecclesiastical authors in this period.

Capture

Enslavement from within a society could have contributed only partly to the supply of tradable slaves. Medieval sources suggest that, as in most slaveholding societies, the most successful and consistent means of creating such chattel slaves were through violence: kidnapping and warfare. These captives could either be enslaved outright by their captors or sold into slavery at the earliest opportunity, since their forced removal from their own communities severed social ties and removed support networks. Distance greatly reduced the possibility that kin could ransom them or bring a legal challenge, making captives the perfect candidates for enslavement as chattel. Orlando Patterson has drawn a fine line between capture through warfare, symptomatic of political conflict, and kidnapping, an opportunistic means of acquiring slaves unrelated to war.[47] The reliance on political meaning is somewhat unhelpful in an early medieval context, since, as Chapter 4 argues, political conflict could be manufactured to support slave raiding. We can instead make the distinction that kidnapping was governed wholly by economic, rather than political, considerations. This method involved snatching people from travel routes and stealing free people or slaves to sell them elsewhere, all with little immediate risk or glory for the kidnapper. Often kidnappers appear to have targeted individuals precisely because of the lower risk involved. Captive taking in war, by contrast, involved the public subjugation of an enemy, and was a process heavily imbued with social and political meaning in addition to the economic factors involved.

Kidnapping

As a fundamentally opportunistic means of acquiring captives, often one at a time, kidnapping cannot have been scaled up dramatically in response to increased demand without becoming something indistinguishable from slave raiding. Clear evidence of enslavement through kidnapping survives predominantly from before the tenth century, suggesting that raiding took precedence as the most reliable means of captive taking as the demand for slaves increased. Kidnapping could coexist with captive taking in war, but, as an inconsistent and sometimes extra-legal means of acquiring captives, it would have been unable to provide as reliable a supply of chattel slaves as warfare. Evidence is overwhelmingly British and Irish in origin, which may be due solely to the greater numbers of sources, though it is predominantly visible only until the early ninth century.

Perhaps the most famous kidnapping victim in the British Isles is Patrick, who was snatched by pirates as a child in Britain and subsequently sold as a slave in Ireland in the first half of the fifth century.[48] The perils of travel appear in Eddius Stephanus's seventh-century *Life of St Wilfrid*, in which Wilfrid and his companions narrowly escape capture by pagans after their ship is beached in Sussex by a storm. Opportunists attack the party in the hope of seizing both the ship and its passengers, and are driven off only by an act of God.[49] The story is probably exaggerated, turning what appears to be a party looking to retrieve flotsam into a vast army bent on destroying the Christian companions, but it demonstrates that kidnapping was a known danger to travellers, especially for men whose high status and accompanying wealth must have made them attractive targets.

Even Vikings, often thought of as quintessential raiders, preyed on travellers in their search for quick profit. The ninth-century Irish *Life of Findan*, like the *Life of Wilfrid*, frames kidnapping as a pagan threat to Christians. At one point the saint was captured by Northmen while on his way to ransom his sister, she herself having been captured in an earlier raid. In this instance Findan was released, because his captors feared that preventing a ransom payment by kidnapping the ransomer would set a bad precedent.[50] A later episode also demonstrates the role that kidnapping could play in disputes. Findan's father had become embroiled in a feud that ultimately led to his death, and, although the matter was settled with a compensation payment, the rival later contracted Findan's kidnapping. Having been invited to dine under the guise of setting aside differences, Findan was surprised by the sudden arrival of Northmen, who carried him off into slavery.[51] It was following this second capture that Findan was sold numerous times between Northmen ships around the British Isles, events we return to in detail in Chapter 5.

Law codes also imply a connection between kidnapping and disputes. English laws greatly concerned themselves with the 'binding' of free and unfree people.[52] The 'stealing' of free men is perhaps clearer in its implications, with a Kentish law issued by Hlothhere and Eadric (679 × 685) laying out the legal procedure for cases in which a stolen free man returned to accuse his kidnapper.[53] Ninth-century laws were more explicit in the connections between kidnapping and enslavement. Alfred's Prologue includes provisions against the theft and sale of freemen, though punishment for binding 'an unsinning ceorl' in the body of his code seems more closely aligned with kidnapping as part of a dispute.[54] It is likewise in a ninth-century legal context that we find the only reference to kidnapping for enslavement in the Czech lands. *Zakon Syudji Ljiudem* dictates that anyone who enslaved or sold a free person was to be themselves enslaved in the same manner.[55] These laws probably addressed real concerns, especially in England; the hagiography of St Swithun, written in the late tenth century, includes the story of an enslaved northern girl who is stolen from her owner and carried south to be sold in Winchester.[56]

There are a number of possible explanations as to why kidnapping becomes more difficult to discern from the tenth century onwards. Authors may have seen fewer reasons to distinguish between opportunistic kidnapping and the events of war when both funnelled into a large-scale slave trade. Christianisation in northern Europe also limited opportunity for the kidnapping of Christians by pagans, and so these events disappear from hagiography. Increasing administrative control in England may also have made the theft of people within the kingdom more difficult and not worth the risk of punishment.[57] As the demand for slaves increased, those looking to profit may also have turned to organised raiding, which allowed them to capture more people in one expedition than they could by lying in wait for unsuspecting travellers. There is no reason to believe that kidnapping disappeared in later centuries, and it probably contributed to opportunistic slave trading so long as buyers existed.

Capture in war

Captive taking was a normal part of warfare, accompanied by the taking of livestock and portable wealth and the destruction of crops and buildings. The complete subjugation of people in this way held various social, political, and economic meanings, all of which served as part of what Joseph C. Miller has argued to be the historical strategy of slaving, with the capture and enslavement of enemies demonstrating slavers' superiority over rival groups within a society and enhancing their own economic potential.[58] The idea of a universal goal of dominance and prestige through enslavement holds true for the early Middle Ages, when, as with most pre-modern societies, captives were trophies representing a victory perfected through the shame and degradation of one's enemies. Captive taking thus conveyed power by creating a lower stratum of captives whom captors could dominate and by increasing the number of people within the captor's oversight.[59] For the defeated, enslavement symbolised the utter failure of a lord to protect his or her own people.

Early medieval raiding and its associated captive taking thus appear frequently within the context of political conflict, and these challenges to an authority also had inherent economic aspects.

Raiding removed or destroyed produce, and, even more importantly, the means of production. Killing or capturing labourers ensured the severity of an enemy's defeat by crippling their ability to rebuild. The impact of this strategy can be seen in the *Anglo-Saxon Chronicle*, which reports that, in 1065, Northmen destroyed houses and grain in Northampton and captured hundreds of men, 'so that shire and other neighbouring shires were worse for it for many winters'.[60] Enslaving captives guaranteed a rise in the raiders' own economic status through the acquisition of slave labour, which increased their own production capabilities, while, alternatively, selling captives supplied goods or cash.[61] Looking back on Brian Boru's campaigns against the Dublin Norse in the late tenth and early eleventh centuries, the *War of the Gaedhil with the Gaill* glorifies the economic benefits of Brian's captive taking, noting that no Irish man or woman needed to do any work, because they had so many Norse slaves to do it all for them.[62] This is even before we consider that some raids were conducted specifically to procure merchandise. Bernold of Constans insisted that, during Henry IV's campaign in Swabia in 1077, the Bohemian troops specifically targeted people in their raids rather than livestock, because the people could be raped and sold.[63]

David Wyatt has focused on the role of masculinity in the enslavement and sexual abuse of men and women, with slavery holding greater cultural significance as a symbolic state of subjugation than as a functional socio-legal status; rape was a tool for making slaves and humiliating people to the point of being *like* slaves.[64] This strategy supported the warrior class and upheld ideas of 'hypermasculinity', as demonstrated in part by the use of graphic sexual imagery in Warner of Rouen's eleventh-century poem *Moriuht* to emphasise the titular character's abject humiliation by his captors and complete 'emasculation' via rape.[65] Rape was a reality for enslaved people, but, as noted in Chapter 1, slaves also played crucial roles in domestic and agricultural production, which suggests at least some economic incentive behind violent enslavement. Slave status could and did function separately from sexual abuse, and, although this expression of dominance may have been foundational for slaveholding in early medieval Britain and Ireland, abuse is not essential for defining slavery and could not have been the driving factor behind elastic means of enslavement.

The limitations of early medieval sources mean that raiding is often framed in a particular way, most frequently in annals concerned with elite politics, which makes raiding seem almost exclusively the result of cross-border political warfare. This does not mean that raiding never occurred within a polity, merely that such events remain largely invisible. Depending on the time and region in which the source was written, a focus on raiding by pagans against Christians could make similar raiding activities by Christians hard to distinguish. This is the case for Irish sources, which are very concerned with the capture of Christians by pagan vikings in the ninth and early tenth centuries, but by the second half of the tenth and into the eleventh century the most frequently recorded raids were those undertaken by Christian Irish kings against other Christian Irish kingdoms. Similarly, although ninth-century Frankish annals record raids by the pagan Polabian Slavs across Frankish borders, they simultaneously devote a considerable amount of space to raids conducted by Christian Moravians. Raiding by non-Christians was a concern, but not as great as was the disregard for political borders and the failure this represented to rulers. It was more often when the ownership and sale of slaves came into play that religious outrage peaked. Even with these limitations, enslaved captives must have formed the bulk of tradable chattel slaves in the British Isles and the Czech lands during the early Middle Ages. Unlike enslaved insiders, captives came with no communal ties, these having been severed by the captives' violent removal from their homes, nor could they negotiate the terms of their own enslavement. The transition from captive to chattel slave was probably easy, and the potential to source war captives in large numbers ensured not only that raiding remained the largest source of tradable slaves but that it persisted as the method of enslavement most sensitive to fluctuations in demand.

The profile of an enslaved captive

Raiders and kidnappers could target individuals for slavery based on factors such as age, sex, and specialised labour, and, even in instances of more indiscriminate captive taking, not all captives were eventually enslaved. Social status and luck played a role in determining who was ransomed, enslaved to their captor, sold into slavery, or executed. Examining the process of enslavement allows us to determine the ways in which both internal and external demand could influence the types of people captured. Captive taking appears to have faced similar operational problems and decision-making processes throughout the early medieval period, and changes in response and targeting over time are less visible, less important, or both. The potential for shifts in types of victims and their treatment is highlighted here as appropriate, but the most important chronological change was in scale, which is the focus of Chapter 4.

Individuals were primarily targeted for enslavement by sex and age. Depictions of slaves at markets usually note their youth, as in Bede's story of Pope Gregory I seeing 'angelic' Anglian slaves for sale in Rome, or that of the boys purchased for baptism by Wenceslas in tenth-century Prague.[66] This may be a cliché, but older people would have been less able to carry out much of the physically demanding labour attested for slaves in the source material, and so were not worth the logistical difficulties of capture and transport.[67] Older men and women had fewer years left to spend in slavery, making them an overall poor return on investment for slave owners.[68] This would explain the portrayal of a raid in the Greek *Life of Clement* from *c.* 1100, itself based upon a lost Slavonic text, about St Clement of Ohrid, a priest who began his career as a member of Cyril and Methodius's mission in Great Moravia in the second half of the ninth century. The text describes how, following Methodius's death in 885 and the Franks' replacement of Rastislav with his relative Svatopluk as duke, already fraught political tensions escalated. Perhaps caving in to Frankish pressure, which sought authority over the Moravian church, the duke Svatopluk seems to have repudiated the Byzantine mission. Men under the direction of Wiching, bishop of Nitra, plundered Methodius's churches and attacked priests, with young students being killed or captured and taken to Venice for sale and elderly men left in the wilderness.[69]

Different types of sources have led to opposing conclusions amongst historians regarding just which sex raiders targeted, since, where prices are listed, women tend to be valued more highly than men.[70] Some have taken this to signify that female slaves were scarcer than their male counterparts, with the implication that men were the primary targets of raiding.[71] Female scarcity is plausible, but demand also explains the higher valuation of enslaved women; people pay more for things that are desirable. In addition to sexual accessibility and the potential for producing heirs, demand for enslaved women may have derived from labour needs. In precolonial Africa, women were more highly valued than men as slaves because gendered divisions of labour meant they performed a greater variety of tasks and worked longer hours. Enslaved women shared agricultural labour with men in addition to completing domestic work, which was considered outside the male sphere.[72] This is not incongruent with much of the early medieval slave labour outlined in Chapters 1 and 2. On the other hand, we must consider that the demand for eunuchs and slave soldiers in the Islamic world caused an increase in the proportion of men and boys who were enslaved, but only through the peak of this demand in the tenth century.

John Gillingham has refuted the arguments in favour of early medieval female scarcity by looking at twelfth- and thirteenth-century narrative sources from northern Europe, which portray women and children as the intended targets of raiding while men, deemed less useful and less available for sexual exploitation, were killed outright.[73] Gillingham has also pointed out a past reluctance, especially for English evidence, to translate non-gender-specific terms such as *homo* (Latin) and *manna* (Old English) as such; when these would probably signify 'people', they were often translated by nineteenth- and twentieth-century commentators as 'men'.[74] The same can be said for the masculine plural forms of Latin words such as *captivus*, which can denote either men alone or mixed groups of men and women. That *cumal*, the Old Irish word for a female slave, had come to denote a unit of currency in Ireland by the seventh century suggests the prevalence of enslaved women at an early date.[75] Women and children were the primary targets of capture and subsequent enslavement, but adult men were not excluded from the process. The *Penitential of Theodore* makes it clear that both men and women were taken as captives by setting down how long either sex must wait to remarry after their spouse is captured with no hope of ransom.[76] The early tenth-century Raffelstetten customs tariff placed a higher tax on enslaved women transported down the Danube, but their male counterparts were still taxed at a considerable rate, the same as a mare.[77] Ultimately, enslaved women were universally more sought after, but enslaved men also contributed to the idea of economic superiority.

By capturing individuals of both high and low status, raiders could increase their chances of receiving ransom payments for some while enslaving the others, with outcomes depending upon the will of the captor. There probably was not much delineation between captives for ransom and captives for enslavement, and which outcome each captive faced may not have been immediately obvious. Captives were available for ransom should the money be forthcoming and were enslaved when it was not. *Zakon* suggests that this was the case in Great Moravia, stating that captives who were ransomed after purchase should be released. It also borrows the *Ecloga*'s ruling that unransomed captives could labour towards a set redemption price.[78] In other times and places, enslavement would be the next logical step for unransomed captives. Their captors would be unlikely to simply free them or kill them outright when a more profitable option was available or when the execution of a high-status captive was not worth the trouble it would provoke. Enslavement or sale would ensure at least minimal financial gain, and higher-status captives would have even held political value as trophies.

High-status captives, secular and ecclesiastic, were more likely to be successfully ransomed, if only because they had the means and connections to secure the payment. It is thus unsurprising that we find Olaf Sitricson, the king of Dublin, ransomed from the Irish in the same year as his capture, and that Muirchertach son of Niall, the king of Ailech, was even able to ransom himself.[79] Such circumstances were by no means the rule, and there are indications that high-status captives could not always rely on their connections. The abbot of Killeigh must not have been confident in his own ransom following his capture in 937, as he drowned the following year near Dalkey Island while fleeing vikings who were probably his captors.[80] Enslaved women of high-status origin likewise indicate some instances of unsuccessful ransoming. Between 709 and 731 Brihtwold, archbishop of Canterbury, attempted to secure the ransom of a girl held captive by Abbot Beorwold of Glastonbury. Brihtwold's appeal to Forthhere, bishop of Sherborne, was prompted by Beorwold's continued refusal of 300 shillings from the girl's family, the highest wergild value in Kent. We do not know the outcome of Brihtwold's petition, but until her release the girl remained 'in the sorrow of slavery'.[81] The thirteenth-century *Laxdæla Saga* also tells of Melkorka, the Irish princess for sale with other slave women in Norway, though we should not put excessive faith in a story about the enslaved mother of a saga hero who just happens to be royalty.[82]

Just as high status did not guarantee a captive's ransom, lower status did not guarantee their enslavement. For example, when Kildare was raided in 964, almost all of the clergy members were ransomed as an act of charity by Niall ua Eruilb.[83] Similarly, when the Bohemians captured a number of Henry III's soldiers during an attack in 1040, Henry ransomed them himself the following year.[84] In such instances, the ransomed captives tended to be part of a mixed-status group – perhaps one reason such events were recorded. They also appear only when they were paid for or conducted by a particularly important person, obscuring the frequency of lower-status ransoming. The ransoming procedure must have been customary from an early date, since even in sixth-century Ireland the *Penitential of Finnian* punished ecclesiastics for the theft of church funds under the pretence of redeeming captives.[85]

Meeting a market demand for slaves also required captors to respond to captive mortality, accidental or deliberate, as well as to escape attempts and rescues. That Étgal of Scelec starved to death in 824 while being held by vikings may reflect either the harsh conditions of captivity or the deliberate deprivation of a notable figure.[86] Captors may have accepted a high degree of loss, but death meant neither ransom payments nor profit from sale. High-status captives also faced politically motivated execution and maiming. The son of a king of Leinster was executed by vikings following his capture in 980, which might be related to the Irish sack of Dublin that same year.[87] Maiming served a similar political purpose; a ruler could effectively eliminate a rival by reducing that rival's perceived capacity to lead. In 870, when the Moravian duke Rastislav was captured, Louis the German had him blinded, effectively removing the duke from the political scene.[88] If captors wished to send a message, some high-status captives may never have been eligible for ransom, nor at risk of enslavement. Political hostages also do not appear to have faced enslavement in the face of a broken agreement, and instead were executed or maimed.[89]

The most significant impact of captive mortality may have been felt in the enslavement of Slavic boys for the purpose of their sale into the Islamic world as eunuchs. These castrations were probably performed by specialist surgeons who, through experience, might be able to reduce the risk of death. Even so, mortality rates were almost certainly high due to risks of traumatic haemorrhaging and blockage of the urethra, a fact attested by contemporaries and in the high prices of eunuchs.[90] Pre-pubescent boys were typically the targets of this mutilation, as they were more likely to survive than teenagers and adults, but far more Slavic boys would have had to be enslaved than ultimately ended up in servitude – circumstances that must have influenced the targets of raiding in the ninth, tenth, and early eleventh centuries in east central Europe. Such a shift may also have been felt in the British Isles; viking raids on monasteries there must have created a significant number of male slaves of all ages.[91]

Less common were the problems caused by escape and rescue, though these still hindered the enslavement of captives. According to the *Life of Findan*, the titular saint was able to elude his captors in the Orkneys when they stopped to rest on their way to Scandinavia.[92] Domhnall Claon, the king of Leinster, was captured by vikings in 979 but liberated by the Irish the following year, along with Irish hostages, during a sack of Dublin.[93] Thietmar of Merseburg likewise tells of how, in 1017, the Margrave Henry liberated Bohemians who had been recently taken captive by the Moravians and brought them home.[94] Like ransom, escape and rescue enabled captives to return to their own society as free people. These must have been very sporadic events, however, and the losses they caused to captors could not have factored greatly into the scale and targets of their raiding.

In summary, capture did not guarantee enslavement, but captive taking was by far the most flexible means of creating chattel slaves. Factors for targeting captives such as age and sex had to be weighed against the status and notability of the individual. With all this in mind, the enslavement of many captives was probably a drawn-out process with no clear consequence from the outset. For those captives enslaved even in a known location, ransom could still take years to materialise.[95] Captives were typically young and female, though numbers of captive men may have increased in the second half of the ninth century in response to external demand for eunuchs and soldiers. These men, women, and children would normally have been of lower-status backgrounds, unable to source a ransom payment, and less at risk of political execution or maiming. These are the multitude of individuals who remain nameless in early medieval sources, but who must have formed the bulk of slaves sold in the British Isles and the Czech lands.

Although violent raiding is the most visible means of enslavement, it was not the only one. Penal slavery and child sale contributed to the supply of tradable slaves, but we have only a very small window onto these processes. They were pre-existing methods of enslavement, designed to fulfil specific legal and social purposes, but the victims were not always insulated from external demand for slave labour. Kidnapping certainly created chattel slaves, but the opportunistic nature of this activity means that it could not have been the most successful means of supply. Raiding, on the other hand, served as the largest and most continuous source of saleable chattel slaves. Enslavement offered a means of further denigrating captives in a process that symbolised personal defeat and political failure and also served to remove an enemy's labour resources in a process with inherently economic significance. Additionally, raiding severed the social ties of captives, making them eligible for enslavement and sale, often without the possibility of ransom or negotiated terms – unlike penal slaves and self-sellers. By considering slave raiding alongside other means, however, it becomes clear that enslavement, and especially the creation of chattel slaves, was not a static process for the early medieval period in either the British Isles or the Czech lands. Fluctuations in demand held substantial sway over the sort of people who were enslaved and the ways in which this was achieved.

Notes

1 For example, E. Philip LeVeen, 'The African slave supply response', *The African Studies Review*, 18:1 (1975), 9–28. Paul E. Lovejoy, 'The impact of the Atlantic slave trade on Africa: a review of the literature', *Journal of African History*, 30:3 (1989), 365–94.

2 D. Alexandre-Bidon and D. Lett, *Children in the Middle Ages: Fifth–Fifteenth Centuries* (Notre Dame, IN: University of Notre Dame Press, 1999), pp. 32–6.

3 Svend E. Holsoe, 'Slavery and economic response among the Vai (Liberia and Sierra Leone)', in Suzanne Miers and Igor Kopytoff

(eds), *Slavery in Africa: Historical and Anthropological Perspectives* (Madison, WI: University of Wisconsin Press, 1977), pp. 293–5. Martin A. Klein, 'Servitude among the Wolof and Sereer of Senegambia', in Miers and Kopytoff (eds), *Slavery in Africa*, p. 343.

4 Alice Rio, 'Penal enslavement in the early Middle Ages', in A. Lichtenstein and C. de Vito (eds), *Global Convict Labour* (Leiden: Brill, 2015), pp. 79–107. For a specifically English context, see Rio, *Slavery after Rome*, pp. 67–70.

5 Rudolf Thurneysen (ed. and trans.), *Irisches Recht* (Berlin: Verlag der Akademie der Wissenschaften, 1931), pp. 66, 77 n. 3. Thurneysen links this to the example of Librán, a man ransomed from a death charge by a wealthy kinsman, who is thereafter obliged to serve that relative. *Adomnán's* Life of Columba, p. 154. See also Kelly, *Guide to Early Irish Law*, pp. 33–5.

6 The *Cáin Adomnán* §45 notes being set adrift as the punishment for a woman who commits murder or arson or breaks into a church. *Cáin Adamnáin: An Old-Irish Treatise on the Law of Adamnan*, ed. and trans. Kuno Meyer (Oxford: Oxford University Press, 1905), p. 31. See also Mary E. Byrne, 'On the punishment of sending adrift', *Ériu*, 11 (1932), 97–102.

7 Kelly, *Guide to Early Irish Law*, pp. 219–20.

8 *The Law of Hywel Dda*, pp. 164–5. T. M. Charles-Edwards, 'The Welsh law of theft: Iorwerth versus the rest', in Charles-Edwards and Russell (eds), *Tair Colofn Cyfraith*, p. 119.

9 Dafydd Jenkins, 'Crime and tort and the Three Columns of Law', in Charles-Edwards and Russell (eds), *Tair Colofn Cyfraith*, p. 9.

10 Lifris of Llancarfan, *Vita Cadoci*, in W. J. Rees (ed.), *Lives of the Cambro British Saints* (London: Longman, 1853), p. 66. Evans, *Text of the Book of Llan Dâv*, p. 220. See also Davies, *The Llandaff Charters*, no. 218, p. 120.

11 Wihtred §26, in Liebermann (ed.), *Die Gesetze*, i, p. 14. II Edward §6, in Liebermann (ed.), *Die Gesetze*, i, p. 144. Ine §3.2 and §7.1, in Jurasinski and Oliver (eds), *Laws of* Alfred, pp. 372–3, 376–7.

12 Ine §11, pp. 378–9.

13 On Ine's law code as otherwise innovative and representative of active law making, see Patrick Wormald, '"Inter cetera bona genti suae": law-making and peace-keeping in the earliest English kingdoms', in Patrick Wormald (ed.), *Legal Culture in the Early Medieval West: Law as Text, Image and Experience* (London: Bloomsbury, 1999), p. 188.

14 'qui iniuste fuerant venditi', *Bede's Ecclesiastical History*, p. 228.

15 'ofer sæ', Wihtred §26, p. 14.

16 Pelteret, *Slavery in Early Mediaeval England*, pp. 120–30. Rio, 'Penal enslavement', pp. 99–100.
17 *Anglo-Saxon Wills*, ed. Whitelock, especially the wills of Archbishop Ælfric, p. 54; Ætheling Æthelstan, p. 56; and Wynflæd, p. 12.
18 Ine §74.2, pp. 343–5.
19 Wulfstan of York, *Sermo Lupi*, pp. 51–2. V Æthelred §2, in Liebermann (ed.), *Die Gesetze*, i, p. 238. VI Æthelred §9, in Liebermann (ed.), *Die Gesetze*, i, p. 250. On the dating of *Sermo Lupi*, see Simon Keynes, 'An abbot, an archbishop, and the viking raids of 1006–7 and 1009–12', *Anglo-Saxon England*, 36 (2007), 203–13.
20 A. G. Kennedy, 'Cnut's law code of 1018', *Anglo-Saxon England*, 11 (1982), 74. Wulfstan may have had in mind slaves who had been convicted of a crime, but the language covers penal slavery. For the former interpretation, see Jurasinski, *Old English Penitentials*, pp. 98–9. For the latter, see Rio, *Slavery after Rome*, p. 67.
21 Ine §3.2 and §7.1, pp. 372–3, 376–7. II Cnut §45.1 and §76.2–3, in Liebermann (ed.), *Die Gesetze*, i, pp. 342, 364.
22 'gitseres', II Cnut §76.2, p. 364. See further discussion in Janel M. Fontaine, 'Archbishop Wulfstan and the slave trade', in Toplak, Østhus, and Simek (eds), *Viking-Age Slavery*, pp. 147–64.
23 The meaning of the phrase 'da prodastь sę' is contested, with possible translation as 'sale into slavery' or the 'sale of property for compensation'. *Zakonъ sudnyi ljudьmъ*, MMFH, iii, pp. 147–98, esp. 185 n. 32. 'Sale into slavery' better fits most contexts in the code. For example, §28 states that, in the third offence of stealing livestock, the wrongdoer should be punished 'da prodastь sę', following flogging for the first and exile for the second. As the sale of property for compensation only after the criminal has already faced exile does not seem a logical progression, penal enslavement is the better interpretation.
24 *Zakon Sudnyj Ljudem*, §26, 28–29, p. 21.
25 *Zakon Sudnyj Ljudem*, §11–12, p. 13; §1, p. 5; §4, p. 9.
26 Cosmas of Prague, *Chronicle of the Czechs*, p. 163. On Cosmas's source, see Lisa Wolverton, *Hastening toward Prague: Power and Society in the Medieval Czech Lands* (Philadelphia, PA: University of Pennsylvania Press, 2001), pp. 115, 323 n. 21. On oral proclamations, see M. Bláhová, 'Verschriftlichte Mündlichkeit in der Böhmischen Chronik des Domherrn Cosmas von Prag', in A. Adamska and M. Mostert (eds.), *The Development of Literate Mentalities in East Central Europe* (Turnhout: Brepols, 2004), p. 338.
27 'secundum ritum nostre terre', Cosmas of Prague, *Chronicle of the Czechs*, pp. 156–8.

28 Sexual misconduct was also punishable by enslavement in Lombard and Visigothic law. Rio, *Slavery after Rome*, pp. 58, 63.
29 See pp. 174–5.
30 See the various documentary and normative examples in Alice Rio, 'Self-sale and voluntary entry into unfreedom', *Journal of Social History*, 45:3 (2012), 661–85.
31 Rio, 'Self-sale', 666–7, 676.
32 'Ealle þa men þe heo nam heora heafod for hyra mete on þam yflum dagum', Walter de Gray Birch (ed.), *Cartularium Saxonicum*, 3 vols (London: Whiting & Co., 1893), iii, no. 1254, pp. 358–9.
33 Ine's law regarding kinship obligations suggests that family were not responsible for *any* member who became a slave and does not specify the means of enslavement. Ine §74.2, pp. 434–5.
34 *Poenitentiale Theodori,* II.xiii.2, p. 202. This text is a compilation of canons allegedly issued by Theodore while archbishop of Canterbury (668–690).
35 'ne sie hio ealles swa ðeowu swa oðru mennenu', Alfred's Prologue §12, in Jurasinski and Oliver (eds), *Laws of Alfred*, pp. 234–5. This passage has traditionally been interpreted as referring to a daughter sold by her father due to an assumed manuscript error. Previous editors altered *bebyccge* (buy) to *gebyccge* (sell), but Jurasinski and Oliver argue convincingly for the reading of the text provided above: p. 235 n. 24. For discussion of the Prologue's changes to the biblical material, see Pelteret, *Slavery in Early Mediaeval England*, p. 83.
36 *Gúbretha Caratniad*, in Rudolf Thurneysen (ed.), 'Aus dem irischen Recht III', *Zeitschrift für Celtische Philologie*, 15 (1925), §30, 339–40. AU, s. a. 965, p. 405.
37 *Poenitentiale Theodori*, iii, II.xiii.1, p. 202.
38 *Das altenglische Bussbuch*, XV.18.c, p. 183. *The Old English Canons of Theodore*, §133, p. 14.
39 *Die altenglische Version des Halitgar'schen Bussbuches*, ed. Josef Raith (Hamburg: H. Grand, 1933), IV.21, p. .
40 Stefan Jurasinski, 'The Old English penitentials and the law of slavery', in S. Jurasinski, L. Oliver, and A. Rabin (eds), *English Law before Magna Carta: Felix Liebermann and* Die Gesetze der Angelsachsen (Leiden: Brill, 2010), pp. 97–118.
41 Gerald of Wales, *Expugnatio Hibernica*, ed. and trans. A. B. Scott and F. X. Martin (Dublin: Royal Irish Academy, 1978), pp. 68–9.
42 Sinfulness was an idea stemming from late antiquity. Gregory, *Moralia in Iob*, 21.14–15, drawing from Augustine, *De Civitate Dei*, 19.15. Adam Serfass, 'Slavery and Pope Gregory the Great', *Journal*

of Early Christian Studies, 14:1 (2006), 79–80. Alexandre-Bidon and Lett, *Children in the Middle Ages*, pp. 21–31.

43 Josef Vašica, 'Církevněslovanský penitenciál českého původu', *Slavia*, 29 (1960), 31–2.

44 *Někotoraja zapověd*, ed. Vašica, 'Církevněslovanský', 45. For connection to the Prague slave trade, Petr Charvát, *The Emergence of the Bohemian State* (Leiden: Brill, 2010), pp. 156–7.

45 Hannah Barker, *That Most Precious Merchandise: The Mediterranean Trade in Black Sea Slaves, 1260–1500* (Philadelphia, PA: University of Pennsylvania Press, 2019), p. 127.

46 'Ibrāhīm ibn Ya'qūb on northern Europe 965', in Lunde and Stone (eds), *Arab Travellers*, pp. 164–5.

47 Orlando Patterson, *Slavery and Social Death* (Cambridge, MA: Harvard University Press, 1982), pp. 106–22.

48 *The Book of Letters of Saint Patrick the Bishop*, ed. D. R. Howlett (Dublin: Four Courts Press, 1994), p. 52.

49 *The Life of Bishop Wilfrid by Eddius Stephanus*, ed. and trans. Bertram Colgrave (Cambridge: Cambridge University Press, 1985), pp. 26–8.

50 *Vita Findani*, p. 503.

51 *Vita Findani*, pp. 503–4.

52 Æthelberht §88, p. 8. Alfred §35, pp. 328–9. II Cnut §42, pp. 340–1.

53 Hlothhere and Eadric §5, in Liebermann (ed.), *Die Gesetze*, i, p. 9.

54 'Gif mon cierliscne mon gebinde unsynnigne', Alfred §15 and §36, in Jurasinski and Oliver (eds), *Laws of Alfred*, pp. 238–9, 328–9. Alongside §36 are six compensation payments owed for physical injury and humiliation, but scourging and the cutting of hair were both potentially linked to slave status. On physical punishment for slaves, see Pelteret, *Slavery in Early Mediaeval England*, p. 87. Long hair appears to have been connected to free status in early Kentish law: Æthelberht §73, p. 7.

55 *Zakon Sudnyj Ljudem*, §31, p. 21.

56 Lantfred, *Translatio et Miracula Sancti Swithuni*, pp. 302–3. Wulfstan of Winchester, *Narratio Metrica de S. Swithuno*, in Lapidge (ed.), *Cult of St Swithun*, p. 496. By Lantfred's telling, the girl is stolen by 'greedy traders' ('ab auidis mangonibus'), whereas Wulfstan attributes the crime to a lone thief. The story probably dates from the late 960s to mid-970s, and Michael Lapidge speculates a more precise date of late 971 or early 972: p. 217.

57 See pp. 210–11.

58 Miller, *The Problem of Slavery as History*, pp. 100–18.

59 Catherine M. Cameron, *Captives: How Stolen People Changed the World* (Lincoln, NE: University of Nebraska Press, 2016), pp. 78–90.
60 'swa þæt seo scir 7 þa oðra scira þæ ðærneah sindon wurdan fela wintra ðe wyrsan', ASC D, s. a. 1065, p. 78.
61 Cameron, *Captives*, pp. 85–8. The need for labour may have been the primary motivation for some slave raids. Robert Bartlett, *The Making of Europe: Conquest, Colonization and Cultural Change 950–1350* (Princeton, NJ: Princeton University Press, 1994), pp. 118–20.
62 *War of the Gaedhil with the Gaill*, p. 115.
63 Bernold of Constans, *Chronicon*, ed. I. S. Robinson, MGH, SS rer. Germ. N.S. 14 (Hannover, 2003), p. 414. Bernold may have been mistaken in his assertion that the Swabians were sold to be eaten by dog-headed men (*cinocephalis*), but there is no reason to doubt that the victims of raids were enslaved.
64 Wyatt, *Slaves and Warriors*, pp. 173–242.
65 Wyatt, *Slaves and Warriors*, pp. 169–71, 229–36, 395.
66 *Bede's Ecclesiastical History,* pp. 132–4. *Legenda Christiani*, ed. and trans. Jaroslav Ludvíkovský (Prague: Vyšehrad, 1978), pp. 66–8.
67 Even men and women in their 30s and 40s could suffer from diseases such as osteoarthritis, which would limit mobility. Shannon Lewis-Simpson, 'Old age in Viking-Age Britain', in Shannon Lewis-Simpson (ed.), *Youth and Age in the Medieval North* (Leiden: Brill, 2008), pp. 246–8.
68 In late medieval Venice and Genoa, a slave's price declined steadily from approximately age 26. Barker, *That Most Precious Merchandise*, pp. 107–8.
69 *Βίος Κλήμεντος*, MMFH, ii, p. 227. McCormick, *Origins of the European Economy*, p. 766.
70 For example, a female slave for sale was taxed at one *tremissis*, but a male slave was taxed at only one-twelfth of a *solidus*, or one-quarter of that of a female slave in the *Inquisitio de thelonis Raffelstettensis*, ed. A. Boretius and V. Kraus, MGH, Capit. 2 (Hanover, 1897), §6, p. 251. A female slave was worth 24 *solidi*, while a male was worth only 12 in the *Lex Baiwariorum*, ed. E. de Schwind, MGH, Leges 3 (Hanover, 1926), §XIII.9, p. 316.
71 McCormick, *Origins of the European Economy*, p. 248. Charles Verlinden, 'Slavery, slave trade', in J. Strayer (ed.), *Dictionary of the Middle Ages*, 13 vols (New York, NY: Charles Scribner's Sons, 1982–1989), xi, p. 336.
72 Meillassoux, *Anthropology of Slavery*, pp. 110–11.
73 Gillingham, 'Women, children, and the profits of war', pp. 61, 71.
74 Gillingham, 'Women, children, and the profits of war', pp. 68–9.

75 See p. 41, n. 44.
76 *Poenitentiale Theodori*, II.xiii.20 and 22, p. 200.
77 *Inquisitio de thelonis Raffelstettensis,* §6, p. 251.
78 *Zakon Sudnyj Ljudem*, §21, p. 19.
79 AU, s. a. 1029, p. 467. The reference to Muirchertach being taken to a fleet of ships implies that the raid was a viking one. AU, s. a. 939, p. 390.
80 AFM, s. a. 938, p. 639. The abbot may have been brought there to await sale in Dublin when ransom was not forthcoming. Holm, 'The slave trade of Dublin', 328.
81 'in servitutis tristitia', Brihtwold to Forthhere, in Haddan and Stubbs (eds), *Councils and Ecclesiastical Documents*, iii, p. 284. For the wergild, see Hlothhere & Eadric §1, p. 9.
82 *Laxdæla Saga,* pp. 24–5. Corroborating genealogical evidence from the twelfth-century *Landnámabók* may link this story with a long-standing oral tradition. Kristjánsson, 'Ireland and the Irish', p. 274.
83 AU, s. a. 964, p. 495.
84 Herman of Reichenau (Contractus), *Chronicon*, ed. G. H. Pertz, MGH, SS 5 (Hanover, 1849), s. a. 1041, p. 123.
85 *Penitentialis Vinniani,* §30, p. 84.
86 AU, s. a. 824, p. 281.
87 AU, s. a. 980, p. 417.
88 AF, s. a. 870, p. 70.
89 Ryan Lavelle, 'The use and abuse of hostages in later Anglo-Saxon England', *Early Medieval Europe*, 14:3 (2006), 292–5. Adam Kosto argues that there is little evidence for mistreatment of hostages when agreements were broken. *Hostages in the Middle Ages* (Oxford: Oxford University Press, 2012), p. 64. For an Irish context, see Robin Chapman Stacey, *The Road to Judgment: From Custom to Court in Medieval Ireland and Wales* (Philadelphia, PA: University of Pennsylvania Press, 1994), pp. 82–111.
90 Jan S. Hogendorn, 'The location of the "manufacture" of eunuchs', in Miura Toru and John Edward Philips (eds), *Slave Elites in the Middle East and Africa* (London: Kegan Paul International, 2000), pp. 51–2.
91 Valante, 'Castrating monks', pp. 174–87.
92 *Vita Findani*, p. 504.
93 AT, s. a. 979–80, i, pp. 340–2.
94 *Thietmari Merseburgensis episcopi chronicon*, ed. R. Holtzmann, MGH, SS rer. Germ. N.S. 9 (Berlin, 1935), p. 475.
95 Adomnán was sent to ransom Irish captives in Northumbria two years after they had been taken. AT, s. a. 684, i, p. 208; s. a. 686, i, p. 210. See discussion on p. 109.

Part II

Logistics and strategies of slaving

4

Warfare and enslavement

Captive taking and plundering were crucial to the logic of early medieval warfare, visible in the aftermath of highly organised battles and sieges as well as in small-scale, opportunistic raids. People could serve as loot in the same manner as did luxury items and precious metals, to be distributed by leaders to their followers in recognition of skill, service, and the success of the campaign itself. Stripping personal freedom and kinship ties from the losing side resulted in their total subjugation and humiliation while simultaneously enhancing the prestige of the victors with human plunder that could supplement the productive capability of their holdings or be otherwise 'liquidated' through ransom payments or sale.[1] The enslavement or sale of captives could function as a performative aspect of masculinity in medieval warrior cultures as well as a direct means of amassing wealth, and both these motivations contributed to endemic warfare.[2]

Despite the clear connection between warfare and enslavement, the path from captivity to slavery is only explicitly referenced in a handful of texts. The sale or immediate enslavement of captives is usually mentioned only when the author felt there was particular significance in the circumstances, such as the barbarism or paganism of the enslavers. There are hints that enslavement was a more common fate for captives than the sources directly acknowledge; they portray the ransom or killing of all or most captives regardless of status or gender as atypical. In exploring the social and political motivations for captive taking and its relationship with enslavement, Chapter 3 acknowledged that establishing a ratio of the number of enslaved captives to the number of those ransomed or killed is unfeasible. This makes meaningful quantitative analysis of enslavement via warfare impossible, even if we accept the suspect numbers of captives recorded occasionally in annals and chronicles.

Although relationships between outcomes of captive taking remain ambiguous, we can identify some broad changes over time, notably fluctuations in captive taking in warfare, a trend visible not only during periods of increased or decreased raiding but also in the scale of the raids themselves. In Irish annals especially, we catch a glimpse of how this impacted the numbers of captives being taken. These changes map very clearly onto the shifts in demand for slaves outlined in Chapter 2, with captive taking increasing dramatically in the late ninth and tenth centuries and declining sharply by the second half of the eleventh century. These trends strongly imply a direct correlation between the scale of slave trading and the extent of enslavement via warfare.

This connection served as the crux of Poul Holm's 1986 article on the Dublin slave trade in the Viking Age, in which he argues for a direct link between slave trading and the large numbers of captives taken by the Irish (as opposed to the Hiberno-Norse) in the eleventh century. Through close reading of the Irish annals, he theorises that the Irish learned the value of slave raiding from the Dublin Norse, thus turning endemic conflicts between kingdoms into large-scale slaving expeditions.[3] Despite the lack of attention to this sort of phenomenon elsewhere in Europe, there has nevertheless been substantial interest in the close relationship between warfare and enslavement. The scholarship on medieval slavery has regularly explored captive taking as not only an essential means of sourcing people in any numbers but also a key component in the deracination and humiliation of enslaved people.[4] Although military historians of the Middle Ages have long appreciated the role of pillaging in challenging enemies and rewarding followers, they have paid considerably less attention to the function of human plunder. Often this scholarship downplays the potential role of loot as a motivation for warfare, especially on the eastern Frankish frontier.[5]

The works of John Gillingham and Matthew Strickland, however, have made substantial contributions to our understanding of connections between violent conflict and slaving. Gillingham's work has demonstrated the widespread enslavement of Christians by fellow Christians, and he has also argued convincingly that raiding most frequently targeted women and children for enslavement.[6] Strickland's focus on the introduction of chivalry in England with the Norman Conquest of 1066 has very clearly indicated that this shift ended the English practice of enslaving captives, as the new Anglo-Norman nobility exclusively relied on ransom or execution.[7] Although Holm's article argues that we should view the scale of raiding within the context of slave trading, Gillingham and Strickland pose the question of how the tactics and mentalities of warfare itself could contribute to or prevent slaving. This chapter seeks to bring together these two strands of enquiry, utilising the slaving zones of the British Isles and east central Europe as case studies to examine how the scale and methods of warfare enabled rulers, warriors, and their wider societies to meet the fluctuating demand for slaves outside these two geographic regions. The result is two identifiable periods of change: the tenth century, in which raiding was scaled up and tactics altered to facilitate captive taking; and the mid- to late eleventh century, in which captive taking diminished in scale and frequency. These shifts coincided with the peak and decline of external demand for foreign slaves. Slave-trading networks in Europe and the Mediterranean, therefore, fundamentally altered the landscape of warfare in the early Middle Ages.

The British Isles before the Vikings

To illustrate what these changes in captive taking were and why they matter, we first have to establish its place in the warfare of earlier centuries. For the Czech lands, this is limited to the ninth century, the period in which our earliest textual sources emerge and in which we can glimpse warfare before the changes effected by Magyar raids in the early tenth century. For Britain and Ireland, Viking warfare in the ninth century likewise constituted a significant point of change, but the extant evidence base for preceding centuries in terms of sources and their chronology allows us to explore some of the key thematic elements of how authors presented captive taking. Normative and narrative sources are crucial, and sporadic references across genres, locations, and centuries indicate that capture was standard practice in cross-border raiding throughout the British Isles during a period of limited source survival.[8]

The authors of these texts were primarily members of the Christian clergy, for whom captive taking posed problems of a spiritual or ecclesiastical nature, and these issues are detectable even in the earliest post-Roman evidence. Thus, a fifth-century letter sent by the bishop (and later saint) Patrick to a Briton named Coroticus denounced Coroticus's capture of recently baptised Christians in Ireland and their subsequent sale to pagans in Britain.[9] Ecclesiastics across Europe perceived pagan ownership of Christians as a threat to slaves' eternal souls, not only because of the vulnerability of slaves to sin at the command of their owners but also because of the potential for a lapse of faith. Patrick himself had been enslaved in pre-Christian Ireland following his capture by pirates near his family home in Britain as a child.[10] Similar fears surrounding the threat of pagan slave ownership were also documented in the sixth century by Gildas's apocalyptic sermon *On the Ruin of Britain*, which lamented the enslavement of Christian Britons by pagan Germanic settlers.[11] Gildas's work is singular in its survival from this period, but it reflects what may have been a common anxiety, given that raiding by Germanic settlers on Ireland is documented as early as the fifth century.[12]

Sixth- and seventh-century penitential texts and canon law from Ireland attest the continuation of captive taking there and offer a pragmatic response to the problems it posed for ecclesiastical oversight in increasingly Christianised societies. The sixth-century *Penitential of Finnian* encouraged Christians to make charitable contributions for ransoming captives, but also advocated a full year of penance for those who stole from monasteries and churches under the guise of collecting these contributions.[13] These canons were repeated in the seventh-century *Penitential of Cummean*, and they hint at established ransoming procedures including communal fundraising.[14] The legal text *Heptads*, composed in the seventh or eighth century, suggests that warfare remained the primary means of creating these captives, since ransom payments were due in full for any man captured during a battle, but only half for one captured after the fighting.[15] The Irish penitentials in turn served as partial inspiration for the earliest penitential in England, that of Theodore, archbishop of Canterbury from 668 to 690. This text likewise implies frequent captive taking through the adoption of conditions for remarriage should a spouse be captured or enslaved far away. Theodore sought to establish not just the time a spouse had to wait before remarrying but also guidelines should the first spouse return to find a new husband or wife in residence.[16]

These normative texts are supplemented by rare contemporary records of captive taking in annals and chronicles, and one episode clarifies that the scarcity of information results from omission rather than infrequency. We know from Irish annals that Adomnán, abbot of Iona, secured the ransom of 60 Irish captives from Northumbria in 687 and another group in 689.[17] These captives were probably taken during a Northumbrian raid in 685, but laconic annals for this year do not always mention captives.[18] Bede, who records Adomnán's diplomatic mission to Northumbria in his *Ecclesiastical History*, likewise omits mention of captives, focusing instead on the Irish abbot's acceptance of the Roman calculation of Easter.[19] The seizure of captives and Adomnán's trip as a venue for ransoming negotiations do not seem to have held great importance to our authors. For Irish annalists, this captive taking by co-religionists did not matter until a politically significant outcome had been achieved by an important ecclesiastical figure, and it is probably no coincidence that the annals for these years were probably first recorded at Adomnán's own monastery of Iona.[20] For Bede, captive taking did not fit in with his primary narrative goal, so it could be omitted entirely.

This episode highlights two significant points. The first is that, when captive-taking events were perpetrated by co-religionists, authors of historical narratives often left it to be inferred as the normal aftermath of war, its inclusion redundant. The second is that even sparse records of captive taking can hint at processes and logistics of enslavement. Following the raid on Brega, a period of two to four years elapsed in which these people remained identifiable for ransom in Northumbria – a detail that points to this captive taking as a political message rather than fuel for slave trading. The Irish captives may have been enslaved until the ransom was paid, since, in other historic cultures, control over captives' labour was a key expression of captors' power and dominance.[21]

Bede provides a handful of references to captive taking in warfare in late seventh-century Britain, though his willingness to exclude it means that we should always be cautious of his intent. The Northumbrian raid in 685 appears to have been part of a larger push to secure the king's interests against the Picts and their allies.[22] In that same year the king Ecgfrith was killed on a disastrous campaign into Pictish territory that led to the death and enslavement of much of the retreating Northumbrian army.[23] For Bede, a king's inability to take counsel led to the enslavement of his own men, meaning that enslavement was symptomatic of Ecgfrith's failure as a ruler, underpinning Bede's narrative of declining Northumbrian power.

Bede also includes the more anomalous story of the enslavement of an individual war captive that ultimately led to that man's sale, though slave trading here is framed as the solution to a problem arising from very specific circumstances and is included solely for its relation to a miracle story. Asserting the reliability of his oral sources, Bede informs us that an injured Northumbrian thegn named Imma was captured by Mercians on the battlefield, probably in 679. Although he disguised himself as a peasant, Imma's ruse was short-lived. His mannerisms soon betrayed his high status, and his captor, a high-ranking Mercian nobleman (*comes*), promised Imma safety should he reveal his identity. Imma relented, and the Mercian became frustrated that his own promise prohibited him from killing Imma to avenge his slain kinsmen. To remove Imma from the equation without causing bodily harm, the *comes* sold Imma to a Frisian in London, who allowed the thegn to negotiate his own ransom by the king of Kent, the nephew of the Northumbrian queen whom Imma served.[24] Bede's interest was not in Imma's captivity or sale, of which he offers no critique, but in his repeated miraculous unchaining throughout these events. Imma's brother, a priest named Tunna, believed Imma to have been killed in the battle and said daily masses for his soul, at which time Imma's shackles would fall off.[25]

We return to Imma's sale again in the next chapter, but here our focus remains on the circumstances of his capture. Even in Bede's story, told with clear motivations, we can surmise that high-status combatants were normally killed by Mercians as part of a bloodfeud; killing enemy combatants served justice for slain fellows. This was probably also a Northumbrian and a wider English practice given Bede's own lack of criticism and his assumption that the audience would understand the context. Imma seems to have disguised himself because people of low status, perhaps those supporting an army on campaign, were more likely to be captured than executed. Following the discussion in Chapter 3 of how status influenced outcomes for captives, it seems likely that those of low status were more often enslaved than ransomed.[26]

Though sparse, the evidence of capture and enslavement in the British Isles before the Viking Age demonstrates that these processes were hidden rather than non-existent. Specific events were normally omitted from annals and chronicles unless the author perceived the captive taking to have significance. For the most part, this method of enslavement was taken for granted as a facet of warfare that included raiding and pitched battles. Captive taking appears most frequently either in response to the problems it posed to these newly Christian societies, spiritually and institutionally, or when it served the author's narrative purposes. These are themes that recur throughout the early Middle Ages, and understanding their role in seventh- and eighth-century contexts helps us contextualise the fundamental changes to captive taking that occurred in the later centuries.

The Czech lands in the ninth century

The earliest evidence of captive taking in Bohemian and Moravian warfare survives from the late eighth and early ninth centuries, and, despite a steady increase in its visibility through the ninth century, the sources remain overwhelmingly Frankish in origin. This situation creates difficulty in assessing captive taking that is portrayed almost exclusively from an outsider perspective, since this process is narratively linked to the authors' negative opinions of Slavic rulers' challenges to Carolingian authority. Authors' objections to the paganism of Slavic groups in earlier decades also contributed to the visibility of their raiding, but this became less important as the century progressed. Moravian and Bohemian elites had converted to Christianity by the middle of the ninth century, but a degree of Byzantine influence in Great Moravia contributed to ongoing political conflicts with East Francia.[27] For Carolingian rulers keenly interested in exerting hegemony over their eastern neighbours, records of Slavic violence could serve as explication for Frankish military campaigns across the border. These attempts to crush

Bohemian and Moravian autonomy could in turn prompt further raids, thereby creating a cycle of endemic warfare and captive taking motivated principally by high politics rather than slave trading.

This violence has received considerable attention for its role in Carolingian politics and military strategy and its proposed contribution to sustained slave trading. Scholarship by Bernard Bachrach and David S. Bachrach especially has sought to downplay the need for plunder as having fuelled Carolingian expansion eastwards, principally in response to Timothy Reuter's article arguing just that.[28] Michael McCormick's works have re-emphasised plunder as an essential motivator of Carolingian warfare, however, by focusing on slavery, arguing that the sale of captives to traders in the Mediterranean drove Francia's rapid economic growth.[29] Although his belief in substantial slaving has encouraged lively debate regarding Frankish warfare, McCormick's core argument runs counter to the available evidence in stating that large-scale slave raiding along the eastern Frankish frontier in the eighth and ninth centuries chiefly victimised Slavs. Subsequent scholarship has noted the lack of direct evidence for these raiding operations, though the case of early British and Irish material lends credence to McCormick's assertion that the vast majority of captive-taking events were not recorded.[30] More important, however, is McCormick's lack of attention to Slavic raiding on Frankish settlements – events that are fairly well documented thanks to the extent of surviving Frankish material and that indicate that Slavs such as the Bohemians and Moravians took captives.[31]

The scope of Frankish evidence also allows us to consider questions such as how the style of warfare contributed to or hindered captive taking and what this can reveal about the scale of enslavement. What emerges from this line of enquiry is a picture of military tactics that could not support enslavement on any substantial scale. We must, of course, acknowledge that captive taking may have been recorded only when it held particular political significance, especially given our reliance on royally focused Frankish annals. Some raiding and plundering by both Franks and Slavs undoubtedly remain invisible. A great deal of raiding by Slavs appears to have been considered a political challenge, however, so slave raiding and captive taking are depicted as retaliatory measures by Carolingians designed to subdue Bohemian or Moravian unrest or by western

Slavs to challenge Frankish hegemony, from the earliest appearance of such raiding in Frankish sources to the beginnings of Magyar encroachment in the last decade of the ninth century.

Mention of the Bohemians and Moravians first occurs in the context of Carolingian attempts to establish a tributary buffer of Slavic territories beyond the rivers Elbe and Danube.[32] The earliest reference to Bohemians, a diploma of Charlemagne from 799 or 800, notes their captive taking in Frankish territory, which provides some background for Charles the Younger's successful campaigns there in the first decade of the ninth century.[33] The tribute extracted by Charles must have been satisfactory, as there is an apparent lack of military interest in the Czech lands until Louis the German ascended to the East Frankish throne in 843. Louis's campaigns into Moravia and Bohemia from 846 onwards were prompted by Mojmir's and his heirs' consolidation of power in Moravia and apparent Bohemian discontent with Frankish overlordship, perhaps under Mojmirid influence. In these conflicts, which also encompass the earliest references to Moravians, plunder is not recorded.[34] Louis's campaigns in 846, 848, and 849 had clear political motivations, as Carolingian expansion eastwards brought new Slavic neighbours, who tested the limits of Frankish control over their frontier.

The western Slavs' response to Louis's campaigns was to construct fortifications not just in Bohemia and Moravia but also in lands controlled by the Wends, Sorbs, and other groups east of the Elbe.[35] This defensive tactic seems to have reduced Frankish opportunities for plunder, as people could withdraw into the strongholds with their valuables, forcing East Frankish campaigns to become prolonged sieges that razed the countryside until the ensconced Slavic ruler submitted.[36] Regarding the Bohemian defeat in 848 and the Frankish defeat at Bohemian hands the following year, the *Annals of Fulda* record hostage exchanges rather than captive taking.[37] These tactics continued in subsequent decades, with Louis forced to besiege fortifications and pillage the countryside in 855 and 864.[38] Although Louis's capture of Slavitach's *civitas* in Bohemia in 857 may have resulted in captive taking, the Fulda annalist, like Bede and the Irish annalists, seemingly left this for readers to extrapolate.[39] Captives may not have been of substantial interest to Carolingian armies at this point, however; during Louis's son's campaigns in Great Moravia in 869, Carloman reportedly killed everyone he came across, and Charles the Fat's only loot was what his army found hidden in the woods and fields.[40]

Sheltering within strongholds preserved lives and goods, but destruction of the countryside by Frankish armies presented a challenge to lordship, particularly in Moravia, where Mojmir's descendants were steadily gaining power and influence both within their own territory and over neighbouring groups such as the Bohemians. It is no surprise that Mojmir's successor, the duke Rastislav, and Rastislav's nephew, Svatopluk, eventually sought to meet the Frankish challenge directly, and it is in this context that we can discern captive taking.[41] In 869 the *Annals of Fulda* attest raiding by Bohemians who were probably in alliance with Great Moravia across the Bavarian border, in which *villae* were burned and women carried off.[42] Captive taking by Moravians first appears in 872, when Rastislav attacked the Bavarian army, taking prisoner all the men whom he did not kill.[43] It may be that the change in warfare reflected a direct desire to capture slaves at a time when power consolidation in Moravia led to an intensification of land use to feed urban populations, thereby increasing the need for dependent labourers.[44] It was also a time when a rising elite social class desired expensive imports from the Mediterranean, such as silk and glass, and, as we will see in the following chapter, Moravians may well have sold slaves to obtain them.[45]

We do, however, have to situate increasingly visible captive taking within the push-and-pull context of political relations on the East Frankish frontier to assess whether enslavement was the motivation for this change in warfare or a side effect of it. Unlike later centuries, raiding at this point appears to have been exclusively related to the East Frankish desire to exert political control over Great Moravia and its allies and to force Slavic rulers into paying tribute. These political tensions are apparent not just in the royal Frankish perspective of annals but in the other documents reporting ecclesiastical politics. It was these policies that led to Rastislav's invitation of a Byzantine mission to Moravia, the later Frankish imprisonment of the missionary bishop Methodius, and, ultimately, the mission's expulsion following Svatopluk's shift in allegiance. Captive taking may have increased because of more frequent and more destructive raids, open battles, and even the desire to maximise the humiliation of an enemy, but not necessarily due to an increased demand for slaves.

There were several factors that also changed the landscape of our source material in the middle of the ninth century, which could have affected the record of captive taking by making an invisible activity suddenly detectable. The *Annals of Fulda*, a principal witness to these frontier politics, shifts in style from 869 through 887, probably due to a change in authorship, and the general increase in detail may have lent itself to greater attention to captive taking.[46] Texts also emerge in association with the Byzantine mission to Great Moravia, which arrived in the early 860s, and these all suggest that captive taking was a regular component of warfare before the 870s. Laws including penal enslavement and captive taking in *Zakon* adapt the Byzantine legal source material to what may have been a local practice. The *Life of Constantine* also attests a captive population in Great Moravia via its mention of the 900 captives that Rastislav granted to Cyril.[47]

Some raiding may remain entirely invisible due to the nature of the source material. Frankish annalists were not interested in any raiding conducted by Bohemians and Moravians on Slavs such as the Poles and Bulgars, who were not already tributary to, and therefore allies of, East Francia. Sparse Moravian texts and the Frankish focus of the annals also obscure any enslavement resulting from internal conflict. References to decreasing numbers of dukes in Bohemia throughout the ninth century make it clear that power consolidation by a few families, of which the Přemyslids would become foremost, was well under way.[48] In Moravia, the Mojmirids had amassed substantial control by the arrival of the Byzantine mission, and the earliest lives, the *Life of Naum* and *Life of Clement*, name Svatopluk as being complicit in the enslavement of Moravians and Byzantine missionaries to further his own political agenda. In these accounts, enslavement was nevertheless a tool for removing the problematic missionaries, whose alignment with Byzantium challenged Frankish ecclesiastical influence over the eastern frontier. The ninth-century Old Church Slavonic *Life of Naum* along with the Greek *Life of Clement* indicate that Svatopluk's support led to the enslavement of priests associated with Methodius's mission and their sale to Jewish merchants, who brought the clerics to Venice to be sold onwards.[49]

McCormick takes this event to be indicative of otherwise invisible slaving by the Franks on western Slavs even though the circumstances were exceptional and motivated primarily by an ongoing power struggle.[50] Even as raiding increased in visibility throughout the second half of the ninth century, captive taking and plundering appear to have maintained their targeted nature as refutations of Frankish influence in central Europe. In 880 the Bohemians allied with the Sorbs and Daleminzi to plunder those Slavs around the river Saale loyal to the Thuringians, and Svatopluk's army also took captives while on campaign in Pannonia in 884 in a major assault against Frankish hegemony.[51] In 893 the Moravians laid ambushes for Arnulf's army all along his return to Bavaria following a campaign against Svatopluk.[52] Such raiding may have been a regular part of relations between Great Moravia and especially Frankish Pannonia; a letter from Theotmar, archbishop of Salzburg, to Pope John IX in 899 accused the Moravians of burning churches, taking prisoners, and enslaving Christians from Pannonia.[53] It may be that Great Moravian slave trading gained greater regularity during these decades, with enslaved captives exchanged for luxury items in this seemingly coinless society. It is worth noting, however, that these major military operations were all at least four years apart – hardly the systematic, large-scale raiding necessary to sustain a substantial slave trade – and that Moravian success in this regard was, as we shall see, short-lived.

Generic references to plunder taken by Frankish armies probably disguise the presence of Slavic captives who could have been enslaved.[54] We do have to consider, however, that East Frankish armies continued to be less successful in captive taking than their adversaries. In the final decades of the ninth century royal campaigns were continually forced to raze the countryside, with no mention of plunder.[55] Even if the most effective slave raids were small, quick strikes across the border and not part of the royal campaigns on which annals were most keenly focused, the delicate political relationships with Bohemian and Moravian rulers would surely have been impacted by recurrent attacks. East Frankish rulers continually sought pacified and tributary Slavic neighbours, especially Great Moravia, and so it seems unlikely that these rulers turned a blind eye to Slavic raids in periods of peace.[56]

Captive taking in both directions across the East Frankish border could not have been part of a large-scale operation designed primarily to source slaves. It was instead a consequence of the conflict between Carolingian rulers' desire for hegemonic control of their Slavic neighbours and the increasingly powerful Bohemian and Moravian dukes. The scale of warfare and captive taking amongst Slavic groups is far less certain. Mojmirid influence within the Czech lands, especially under Svatopluk, doubtless brought the Moravians into conflict with Slavs to the west, north, and east in whom East Frankish annalists were not interested. Even if the major raids against the East Franks in the 880s and early 890s temporarily increased the availability of enslaved captives, substantial changes soon altered the landscape of raiding along the East Frankish frontier. Svatopluk's death in 894 and the division of power between his heirs weakened any Great Moravian threat, and the increasingly powerful Přemyslid family in Bohemia subsequently aligned itself with East Francia when two nobles, including the son of the Přemyslid duke Bořivoj, arrived in Regensberg in 895 to offer allegiance.[57] Perhaps most significantly, the first Magyar raid across the Danube is recorded in 894, and subsequent attacks only increased in intensity during the first decade of the tenth century. With Great Moravia already weakened by internecine warfare between Svatopluk's sons, the Magyar raids proved overwhelming, and the political entity had disintegrated by 907, along with its military challenge to East Francia.[58]

The Viking Age

The Viking Age in Britain and Ireland, like the ninth century in the Czech lands, is an era dominated by one-sided accounts of raiding and warfare, which obscure the motives and intent of the participants. The important distinction between these two, however, is that textual evidence from Britain and Ireland was exclusively produced by the raided, and authors make it clear that viking attacks created captives from their earliest days. Alcuin's letter to Higbald regarding the devastation at Lindisfarne in 793 acknowledges that monks were carried off.[59] An attack on Howth (Étar) in Ireland in 821 likewise resulted in the capture of many women.[60] Viking raids soon engulfed all parts of the British Isles, from coastal attacks to increasingly inland incursions, and, within decades, raids were accompanied by settlement and then by the creation of autonomous polities through conquest and threat of violence.[61] Set battles became more important as these armies sought political victories, but raiding remained a defining feature of the Viking Age in the British Isles.

Although raids are recorded everywhere, captive taking is most often noted in Irish annals. This is unlikely to indicate a discrepancy in styles of warfare between locations given that the same raiders moved between them, and, instead, stems from the varying interests of our sources' authors. Irish annals were composed with an ecclesiastical focus, and so their attention to raids concentrates on the institutions despoiled and Christians captured. In the ninth century this attention is primarily on raiding by pagan vikings; the Irish certainly targeted churches and monasteries in their own raids, but the lack of attention to captives by the annalists may be due to the lack of a perceived spiritual threat to these victims. By contrast, the manuscripts of the *Anglo-Saxon Chronicle* comprise a series of vernacular texts focused primarily on the royal court of Wessex and then of England. Recording raids and warfare illustrated the adversity faced by these kings and highlighted their military achievements.[62] Captive taking, therefore, is recorded much less frequently for England, despite the substantial record of viking activity there.

Early viking raids were quick strikes that carried off people and portable wealth either immediately to Scandinavia or to island staging points, where plunder and captives accumulated until the end of the raiding season.[63] The number of high-status people captured during the first few decades of the ninth century indicates the importance of ransoming, and some of these individuals' deaths were recorded decades later, presumably because they had been ransomed and returned to their normal lives.[64] This situation did not last, however, and in Ireland the frequency of raiding and captive taking increased correspondingly with overwintering, first detectable in a Christmas raid in Southern Brega in 836, and the establishment of more permanent raiding bases called longphorts, beginning with one at Lough Neagh in 840, which would have provided fortified locations for holding captives following periods of extensive raiding.[65] Substantial raids into Ireland launched from

Scotland around this time suggest that captives could also have been transported within the British Isles, and alliances between Irish and Norse groups also serve as a reminder that many captives may have been ransomed from or enslaved by the Irish themselves.

Vikings' increasing involvement in secular politics appears to have led to a period of reduced raiding in Ireland from the mid-840s through the 870s, with an emphasis instead on plundering pre-eminent religious centres such as Armagh and Kildare.[66] Plundering continued elsewhere, however, and, when the warlords Olaf and Ivar returned with their armies to Dublin in 871 after capturing Dumbarton in Strathclyde, they carried with them British, English, and Pictish captives on as many as 200 ships.[67] This particular endeavour, along with Olaf's capture of around 1,000 people from Armagh in 869, may indicate Olaf's strategic use of slave raiding as a means of reinforcing his role as a leader following several setbacks, including the killing of his son Karl by the king of the Uí Néill in 867, and as a means of retaining followers with plunder.[68] The scale of predation inflicted by the Great Army in England from 865 is not well attested textually, but the growing assemblage of finds from the site of the 872–73 winter camp at Torksey provides ample evidence of seized portable wealth, such as English dress accessories, and the tools necessary for enacting high-value exchanges, such as receiving ransoms or selling slaves in the forms of weights, ingots, and hackmetal.[69]

A more perceptible and consistent change in raiding towards an interest in enslavement emerged in the final two decades of the ninth century, when Irish annals record a series of raids with staggering numbers of captives. Although the numbers should be viewed sceptically, annalists certainly wished to convey the scale of the events when they recorded 280 prisoners taken from Kildare in 886 and 710 people seized at Armagh by Glún Iarainn's Dubliners in 895.[70] These annals stand out amidst a period of intensified raiding that endured until the Irish sack of Dublin in 902, matched by increased raiding in England and Wales in the 890s, and a higher proportion of captive taking recorded for viking raids in Francia between 873 and 896.[71] These decades correspond to the intensification of settlement in Iceland, and discussion in Chapter 2 noted the seeming importance of enslaved British and Irish people in this process, the majority of whom may have been enslaved directly by Norse raiders seeking their fortune in war before staking their claim in the North Atlantic.[72] Such a scenario would simultaneously explain the lack of a visible large-scale slave trade in the British Isles at this point and the clear interest in slave raiding evident in the Irish annals.

Colmán Etchingham has argued that evidence for the demand for slaves from within Ireland and in Scandinavia does not support the idea of captive taking for the primary purpose of enslavement, and that ransoming remained foremost through at least the tenth century.[73] Raiders may well have remained open to ransoming attempts within a certain time frame, but this argument does not account for the escalation in numbers of captives in the late tenth century, nor does it consider demand for slaves beyond agricultural production in northern Europe. Ransoming certainly continued through this period, but, as discussed in Chapter 3, it was probably the reserve of the wealthy and powerful. The Irish annalists' shock at the scale of captive taking suggests that raiding practices were moving beyond the capacity of local ransoming towards the export of enslaved captives.

It is around this time, in the late ninth century and into the first half of the tenth, that slaving also becomes regularly visible in the warfare of Irish, English, and Scots combatants. Alfred's West Saxon army plundered the Viking fortification at Benfleet in 893, taking the women and children to London.[74] Records of Edward the Elder's campaigns and raiding against Viking armies in the subsequent two decades are likewise marked by their attention to captive taking, with West Saxons and Mercians seizing both men and property from the raiding army in 909 and from Tempsford in 920, amidst substantial raiding campaigns by the Vikings and West Saxons throughout lowland Britain and Wales.[75] Conflicts prompted by English expansionism meant that royal English campaigns raided the Scots in 933, Cumbria in 945, and Viking Northumbria in 948, while the king of Scots, Malcolm I, seized captives and cattle from the English north of the river Tees in 950.[76] Some of this visibility may be due to the circumstances of their recording; the *Anglo-Saxon Chronicle* documented the deeds of West Saxon kings contemporaneously from 891, and scribes may have perceived captive taking as being more immediately relevant to their narrative than it had been for the retroactive accounts of previous generations' warfare. Nevertheless, this coincides with an increase in recorded captive taking by the Irish alongside a continued escalation by Viking armies. The Irish took up to 1,600 captives from Dublin in 948, a decade after Vikings had seized around 1,000 people from Kilcullen in 938, and Gothfrith of Dublin allegedly captured as many as 3,000 people in his raids on various religious institutions in 951.[77] This parallel shift in English and Irish records suggests we are witnessing an actual change in practice, not merely one of perspective.

It is probably not a coincidence that this escalation in captive taking also corresponded to a period of political expansionism. The West Saxon royal house claimed kingship of England from 927 onwards, while, in northern Britain, the Alpin dynasty of Dál Riada gradually gained power over Pictish kingdoms in the ninth and tenth centuries to become kings of Alba. The sharp increase in captive taking that accompanied the first decades of settlement in Iceland may have informed those rulers seeking to consolidate their power of the value of slave raiding, certainly in its contribution to rewarding followers with plunder and as a revenge tactic against enemies, but perhaps also in the financial resources that the sale of enslaved captives provided to rulers seeking to construct new fortifications, finance campaigns, and display their wealth personally and through gift giving. The political conflicts visible in our sources through the middle of the tenth century may not have been manufactured specifically to create saleable slaves, but this must have been perceived as an advantage of them.

By the second half of the tenth century raiding appears to have taken on new levels of frequency and destruction, in a pattern that suggests that slaving played a central role within it. Semi-independent war bands conducted increasingly frequent raiding around the Irish Sea from the 970s, including a raid on Anglesey that, allegedly, resulted in 2,000 captives, and along the southwest coast of England from 980 to 982.[78] England confronted successive raiding armies from Scandinavia, beginning in 991 with Olaf Trygvasson's attacks and lasting until Swein's conquest of England in 1014 and his son Cnut's coronation in 1016. The scribe of the E manuscript of the *Anglo-Saxon Chronicle*, eager to demonstrate the failings of Æthelred II, 'the Unready', provides substantial detail regarding these armies' geographic ranging and scope of plundering, though the scribe reserves mention of captives for his particular horror at the events of 1011, when Thorkell the Tall's army sacked Canterbury and seized all the ordained men and women.[79] Contemporary attempts by Wulfstan, archbishop of York, to reduce the legitimate avenues for enslavement and to further restrict the categories of slaves who could be sold overseas strongly suggest that the Danish armies moving throughout England in the first 16 years of the eleventh century did their plundering alongside a flourishing slave trade. That Wulfstan's most programmatic outline of these strictures did not appear until 1020 or 1021, in the ordinances of II Cnut, suggests that these ideas were more readily accepted by Cnut and the Anglo-Danish elites once the stability of his kingship had drastically reduced the supply of captives within England.[80] Although viking raids continued through the eleventh century in Wales, England never experienced the same scale of raiding after 1016.[81]

In Ireland, the declining political power of the Dubliners in the 970s and 980s may explain why the Hiberno-Norse did not engage in substantial raids themselves, though any slave trading in market hubs such as Dublin may have been supplied by the more indiscriminate activities of the semi-independent raiders active around the British Isles.[82] There was certainly enough high-value trade emanating from this market to merit the first issue of silver coinage in Ireland at Dublin *c.* 997. This indirect involvement became direct from the turn of the eleventh century, when Brian Boru's victories in 999 established Dublin's tributary status. As part of this new alliance, Dublin raiders resumed targeted attacks on Brian's rivals while other raiding armies engaged in widespread plundering in England. Numerous episodes of large-scale captive taking in the first and second decades of the eleventh century indicate that this practice had become an important part of Irish political conflicts and was no longer enacted primarily across Irish-Norse lines.[83]

The British Isles experienced two peaks of slave-raiding activity during the Viking Age. The first of these, in the late ninth century and early tenth, coincided with the initial settlement of the North Atlantic, most noticeably Iceland. The second, more substantial peak emerged in the late tenth century and early eleventh and coincided with the expansion of slave trading throughout Europe. In England this peak fed by the Danish conquest ended rather abruptly with the creation of an Anglo-Danish kingdom, and in Ireland slave raiding endured for decades, with the Irish surpassing the Norse settlers as prolific slave raiders. Raiding generally appears in annals to have maintained a veneer of political motivation, with captive taking ostensibly serving the social and economic prestige brought about by the destruction of one's enemies. The scale of plundering – and, in Irish sources, captive taking – nevertheless reveals the alternative motives of raiders. It is unlikely that they attempted to ransom or directly enslave hundreds of captives at a time, and so must have taken these people with the intent of selling them onwards, probably over some distance. Slave trading must have fuelled this second peak, thereby fundamentally changing the aftermath of war.

The rise of Přemyslid Bohemia

Although the identification of raiders and raided in the British Isles in the tenth century remains relatively clear, the contemporary situation in the Czech lands is more obscure. Following the collapse of Great Moravia in the first decade of the tenth century, power in the Czech lands shifted to Bohemia, particularly to the Přemyslid family. These dukes ruled from their seat in Prague, where slave trading was a regular feature of the growing economy.[84] The *Legenda Christiani*, a hagiographical work about the Přemyslid duke Wenceslas, tells us that he was able to purchase pagan boys for baptism during his rule (*c.* 921–935).[85] By the 960s, the Cordoban traveller Ibrāhīm ibn Ya'qūb likewise reported Prague to be a place where slaves were sold, and the sale of Christians to Jews during Adalbert's tenure as the second bishop of Prague (982–997) caused him great consternation.[86] The clear evidence of slave trading in sources related to tenth-century Bohemia has nevertheless proved difficult for historians to reconcile with the near-silence regarding contemporary Bohemian raiding. In arguing for the growth of a substantial slave export system in the tenth century, Dušan Třeštík insists that raiding must have been widespread, albeit textually invisible.[87] More recent works by Martin Ježek and Ivo Štefan have argued that we should not presume that frequent large-scale raids were systematically hidden or overlooked by medieval authors, and Ježek favours the idea of a smaller-scale, internal slave market.[88]

The seeming regularity of slave trading in Prague in the tenth century alongside the growth in external demand for slaves discussed in Chapter 2 means that we ought to expect frequent raids with high numbers of captives. Their absence from the source material may be in part due to our continued reliance on Frankish authors, who, as in the ninth century, were most interested in conflicts with implications for Bohemia's tributary status. The Přemyslid family's intensified efforts at power consolidation and state building in the vacuum left by Great Moravia's collapse probably means that violence was deployed to subjugate internal rivals, a scenario hinted at by the mass burial excavated at the stronghold of Budeč, which may reflect the suppression of Wenceslas's supporters following his murder by his brother and successor, Boleslav I.[89] This process remained outside the attention of Frankish authors, but chroniclers' continued interest in the eastern frontier in the tenth century means that we should not simply disregard the absence of cross-border Bohemian raiding. This is especially true in light of the substantial evidence of large-scale raiding by other parties in east central Europe, notably the Magyars, Ottonian rulers, and Frankish marcher lords, to the point that Přemyslid-sanctioned raiding may not have been necessary to facilitate the growth of slave trading in central Bohemia.[90]

There can be no doubt that the Magyars enslaved the captives taken on their near-annual raids into Frankish territory between 907 and 926.[91] Ibn Rusta suggested that raiding by Magyars in the late ninth and early tenth centuries was principally undertaken to source slaves for long-distance trading, with raiders carrying Slavic captives to the Byzantine port of Kerch on the Black Sea to exchange them for Byzantine textiles and other goods.[92] It also seems likely that diplomatic connections between the Magyars and Bohemians enabled raiders to attack Thuringia and Saxony during these early decades by allowing Magyars to move through Bohemian territory unopposed.[93] In facing a return journey of hundreds of miles, raiders may have sought to offload some of their captives, who required not only a means of transport but also shelter and food on the return journey. Similar circumstances may explain the purported sale of a Swabian count's daughter by Magyars in Worms following her capture.[94] The period of intensive Magyar raiding in the early tenth century and their alliance with Bohemians may have been crucial to Prague's development as a noted centre for slave trading.

This political arrangement and its consequences for slave raiding could only have been temporary. The peace agreement negotiated between Henry I of East Francia and the Magyars in 926 seems to have paused raiding, and Wenceslas's submission to East Frankish overlordship around 929 would have ended any ducally sanctioned Bohemian raiding on the Franks. When Henry I stopped tribute payments to the Magyars in 932, their subsequent military defeat by the Franks the following year meant that the Magyars never regained their prominence as raiders before their final defeat at Lechfeld in 955, and this shift in political dynamics would have substantially upset any slave trading in Prague sustained by Magyar raiding. It is in this context that, following the peace agreement of 926, Henry I launched his campaigns against the Elbe Slavs. Although these campaigns generally continued the long-standing East Frankish policy of establishing a band of tributary Christian Slavic polities along the eastern border, Henry also had an undeniable interest in taking captives – a focus that sits in stark contrast to the warfare of his Carolingian predecessors.[95] Widukind of Corvey's portrayal of these events suggests that the captives' treatment was unusual in its brutality. For instance, following the seizure of the Hevelli fortification of Brandenburg, Henry's armies besieged the Daleminzi at Gana in 929, where the royal army slaughtered all the adults before carrying off the boys and girls into slavery.[96] In his attack on the Redarii at Lenzen, Henry had all the captives beheaded rather than ransomed or enslaved, and, following his battle with the Magyars in 933, Henry's armies, not the Magyars, were the one to take captives.[97] Rodolphe Keller has argued that this ruthlessness exhibited towards captives on these campaigns is indicative of royal revenge against the Magyar-allied Slavs.[98] Although the fate of these captives and slaves is not clear, it may be significant that the victories at Brandenburg and Gana immediately preceded Henry's march to Prague, which forced Wenceslas's submission in 929. As such, the capture of Hevelli, Daleminzi, and Magyar people by Bohemia's new Frankish allies feasibly coincided with Wenceslas's alleged purchase of pagan boys for baptism.

With Otto I's ascension to the East Frankish throne in 936, Widukind of Corvey, our principal source for frontier captive taking, turned his attention inwards, and we therefore perceive little of border conflicts with the western Slavs, including the wars between Otto I and Boleslav I, until after 950.[99] Plunder was still important to the aftermath of war, however, since, immediately following his 950 victory at Nymburk in Bohemia, Otto prevented his soldiers from looting the fortification so as to prevent any harm from coming to them while distracted.[100] Up to this point Frankish captive taking had occurred within the royal political desire to subdue Slavic neighbours and exact tribute. There was certainly scope for substantial captive taking during this period by Magyar raiders and royal Frankish armies, with both groups having access to Bohemian markets during various periods of alliance. Successive waves of captives created by political conflicts may have surged onto the east central European slave market, a situation that would have done much to solidify this region's status as a slave supplier.

The establishment of powerful marcher lords along the eastern Frankish frontier by the middle of the tenth century appears to have impacted the scope of raiding by shifting focus away from royal campaigns. Rodolphe Keller has argued that the relative autonomy of lords such as the Margrave Gero allowed them to pursue their own plundering expeditions with unclear justifications, such as Gero's seizure of 'vast plunder' from the Ukrani in 954.[101] Thiadric's raid against the rebelling Obodrites in 954 likewise resulted in captives.[102] This did not supplant the role of human plunder in occasional royal campaigns, as evidenced by Otto's capture of Obodrites the following year, nor did it reduce Slavic raids against the Franks and their allies, as was the case when Obodrites took a number of women and children in 955 from the Cocarescemi, a Frankish-allied Slavic group who probably lived east of the Elbe.[103]

In the second half of the tenth century, however, we are increasingly confronted with evidence of alliances and conflicts in east central Europe precipitated by these marcher lords, seemingly outside royal oversight.[104] Victories over Slavic groups east of the Elbe furthered Ottonian desires for tribute and the reorganisation of these territories according to the Frankish model of fortress districts, *burgwarde*, but they involved Bohemian fighters directly in plundering expeditions through the use of ethnically diverse war bands and created captives within reach of the Bohemian and Baltic trading networks.[105] It is probably this context that influenced one al-Andalusi author, who wrote towards the end of the tenth century that the Franks and Byzantines both took Slavic captives.[106] The Frankish rebel Wichmann the Younger took plunder following a battle with the Polish ruler Mieszko I (d. 992) in 963 and a Bohemian alliance with the Poles fought against Wichmann and the Wolin Slavs in 967.[107] Sometime in the 970s the Thuringian count Dedi led a group of Bohemians who raided a church at Zeitz, around the same time that Bohemians ravaged as far as the river Tanger and defeated an army of Bavarians near Plzeň.[108] Boleslav II's plundering and burning of Frankish lands in 986 stood out to Thietmar of Merseburg because the Bohemians unusually left the people of the region unharmed.[109] There can be no doubt that raiding escalated in the second half of the tenth century due to the combination of Ottonian warfare and individual interests of marcher lords. It may have been in reaction to this escalation that Henry II forbade the sale of Christians to 'the heathen' at a synod in 1006.[110] Although Frankish slave raiding disappeared from this point, participation by Slavic groups continued and appears to have been exacerbated by rivalries between the Ottonians, the Přemyslids, and the Piasts.

The circumstances of captive taking suggest two significant shifts: that Bohemians appear to have become actively interested in supplying their own slave trading; and that Piast rulers in Poland were now engaged in their own slaving operations. Amidst successive campaigns by the emperor Henry II, the Piast ruler Bolesław Chrobry, and the Přemyslid duke Oldřich, Thietmar alleges that 3,000 Saxon captives were taken by Poles from Mugeln in 1003, over 1,000 Saxon men, women, and children were captured by Oldřich from Biesnitz in 1015, and numerous Bohemian captives were seized by Mieszko III in 1017.[111] Cosmas of Prague, writing over a century later, believed that the multitude of captives taken by Oldřich on a campaign into Polish-controlled Moravia were sold into the kingdom of Hungary and beyond.[112]

Even when conflict was motivated by political issues, such as a revolt against Frankish hegemony or the quest for dominance within east central Europe, there is a perceptible shift in the tenth century to a style of warfare more intensely interested in taking captives. This is a striking difference from Carolingian warfare of the ninth century, which effectively sought the same outcome as Ottonian warfare – the creation of a tributary Slavic border – but which had decidedly less interest in and opportunity for enslaving captives. Slave raiding undertaken by Magyars and then Ottonians in the first half of the tenth century may well have kick-started Prague's position as a slave-trading centre of east central Europe. By the second half of the century, however, Bohemians appear to have been capable of supplying their own market demands, either through ducally sanctioned warfare or via warriors' involvement in the campaigns of Frankish lords. The lack of identifiable Bohemian raiding earlier on speaks to the importance of political and trade networks in central Europe for the growth of slaving activity. Whether the Přemyslids were able to build their Prague market by being in the right place at the right time or if there was conscious political manoeuvring involved, we may never know. Either way, interest in slave trading seems to have had a profound effect on the aftermath of war in east central Europe by the close of the tenth century.

Declining slave raiding

From a high point in the second half of the tenth century and early eleventh, the second half of the eleventh century saw the decline of slave raiding in the British Isles and east central Europe alike. Political developments in both regions reduced the opportunities for raiding, but, even though the scope of this warfare diminished overall, it did not disappear. Changes in the mentality of warfare also contributed to a decline in slaving activity. The introduction of chivalry to England via the Norman Conquest of 1066 and its growing importance in the Holy Roman Empire meant that captive taking focused on the ransom of noble combatants and the slaughter of others, and enslavement was no longer an outcome of warfare. By the middle of the eleventh century captive taking no longer sustained large-scale, long-distance slave-trading networks, and, even where enslavement remained a feature of warfare, there was a visible reduction in the scale of slave-raiding activity.

The British Isles

The starkest area of decline in enslavement was in England, which experienced two conquests in the eleventh century that fundamentally altered the mentalities of warfare and associated captive taking. Cnut's coronation in 1016 established a unified kingdom of England, Denmark, and Norway, and this political development was directly responsible for the cessation of visible Scandinavian raiding on English coasts for much of the next three decades. When raiding re-emerged in the *Anglo-Saxon Chronicle*, it had an opportunistic and sporadic character that more closely resembles the raiding of the seventh and eighth centuries than that of the tenth and early eleventh. Captive taking was related to very specific political grievances, such as Godwin's capture and sale of the *ætheling* Alfred's men in 1036, the raiding undertaken by Godwin and his son Harold during their return from exile in 1052, or Earl Alfgar's raid on Hereford in protest against his exile in 1055.[113] Viking attacks still produced captives, such as raids by Lothen and Erling on Sandwich and Essex in 1046 or Harald Hardrada's campaign in England in 1066, but these raids were likewise intermittent.[114] Lothen and Erling took their captives for sale to Normandy, indicating the continued operation of overseas slave-trading networks, but English captives could not have made up as substantial a proportion of raiding victims as they had at the turn of the century.

This decline in slave raiding was cemented by the Norman Conquest of 1066, which introduced a new ruling class to England – one that did not enslave captives as part of warfare. By the late eleventh century Norman interest in captive taking focused on ransoming as part of the developing chivalric culture of war, which also eschewed the slaughter of high-status enemy combatants.[115] October 1066 was not a sharp cut-off point in the style of warfare, and raiding by the sons of Harold Godwinsson in 1067 and the armies supporting the *ætheling* Edgar in 1069 may well have enslaved captives. Like the episodes noted above, however, these events were not indicative of a constant supply of slaves. By 1070 William I's power was assured, and the systematic replacement of the English nobility with an Anglo-Norman one ended the creation of slaves through warfare in England.

This decline was not replicated elsewhere in the British Isles until the extension of Norman power in the twelfth century, and the enslavement of captives remained a part of Welsh and Scots warfare throughout the eleventh century. The *Anglo-Saxon Chronicle* notes this sort of raiding to have been a key part of Malcolm III's campaigns into northern England, and the hagiographer of Malcolm's wife, Margaret, noted that, as part of her virtuous behaviour, this granddaughter of Edmund Ironside took it upon herself to redeem English captives held by the Scots.[116] Welsh warfare likewise continued to take captives, seemingly with enslavement in mind. The author of the *Life of Gruffudd ap Cynan* attests the importance of seizing women and children as part of conflicts between Welsh kingdoms and of taking captives from Anglo-Norman armies in the late eleventh century, though the latter may well have been to extract ransoms from nobility willing to pay.[117] Despite the continued importance of raiding and captive taking in these areas, the episodes share the sporadic nature that we see in English material, suggesting that captives were no longer being taken to meet an external demand for slave labour.

The greater availability of source material for Ireland allows us to see greater nuance in this declining interest in slave raiding. The late tenth- and early eleventh-century escalation in captive taking in Ireland mirrors the contemporary situation in England, but, whereas the establishment of an Anglo-Danish kingdom seems to have abruptly diminished the frequency of raiding in England, in Ireland the period of high-volume captive taking extended well into the middle of the eleventh century and was dominated by the Irish themselves. It may be that reduced raiding in England created a market shortage for slaves, and, in the wake of Dublin's waning power, Irish kings and raiders sought to meet it. This may also have been true of Welsh and Scots rulers such as Gruffudd ap Cynan and Malcolm III, though it is a phenomenon best attested in Ireland. In 1031 Aed ua Néill took 1,200 captives and 3,000 cows from the territory of a certain son of Eochaid, and over the next two decades wars by the Leinster kings allegedly created hundreds of captives.[118] In the decade before 1063 the Cenél nEógain in the north were also visibly engaged in substantial captive-taking activity, resulting in hundreds or thousands of captives alongside even higher numbers of cattle.[119] In addition to political clashes between increasingly powerful over-kings, captive taking is also visible as a major part of opportunistic raiding that sought people, plunder, and cattle by the middle of the eleventh century. A record of the 1056 raid by the Uí Chairpre of West Meath on the Dal nAraide of Ulster, seizing 200 cows and 60 captives, provides what may be representative numbers for similar major raids, which occurred on a near-annual basis.[120]

Following the Cenél nEógain's 1062 raid on Connaught, which resulted in around 1,000 captives, there is an unmistakable decline in the annals' records of captive taking. Only a handful of episodes appear in the final four decades of the century, despite the continued importance of plunder and cattle.[121] Captive taking resumed its regularity in the first two decades of the twelfth century, and Poul Holm has taken this to reflect a continuance of slave-raiding practice through the second half of the eleventh.[122] The majority of captives recorded in these decades are of high status, however – lords, kings, and their sons – who were almost certainly intended for ransom rather than enslavement. This, alongside the heavy emphasis on stealing cattle, suggests that the fervour of slave raiding had ended by the mid-1060s, and that subsequent episodes of captive taking reflect a return to small-scale, internal, and opportunistic slave trading. The years 1109 to 1116 did see a flurry of captive-taking activity, but the brevity of this period in the context of reduced demand in a wider European context can only be seen as a blip, fuelled by escalating retaliatory raids, the last of which resulted in the release of the captives as a pious offering to God and St Flannán.[123] This act may be related to the famine recorded in that same year, which annalists noted led to an increase in the sale of children by their parents for food and the depopulation of Leinster; in the face of potential food shortages and a rapid rise in the availability of slaves for sale, maintaining large numbers of captives may not have been feasible.[124] Captive taking remained a part of Irish warfare well into the twelfth century, but it never again matched its peak of the late tenth and early eleventh centuries.

East central Europe

Slave raiding in east central Europe experienced a similar pattern of decline in the mid- to late eleventh century, despite notable gaps in our available source material. Following Bolesław Chrobry's and the Moravians' campaigns in Bohemia in 1017 and Thietmar of Merseburg's death in 1018, there is little information about captive taking in east central Europe during the following two decades.[125] When Břetislav I returned to Prague from his campaign in Poland in 1039 with a convoy of captives to be sold, it was the last major slaving operation in the region. This act, along with the unsanctioned translation of St Adalbert's relics from Gniezno to Prague, was considered so disgraceful that the pope demanded that Břetislav build a monastery in atonement.[126] This decline in slave raiding coincided with the probable collapse of demand for Slavic slaves from the Umayyad Caliphate, which disintegrated in 1031 into the successive unstable Taifa states and which disrupted al-Andalus's status as a slave-trading hub of the Islamic Mediterranean. Whether it was the papal chastisement, the lack of demand for slaves, or – as is most likely – a combination of both, Břetislav's capture of numerous soldiers in 1041 during a botched campaign by the Salian king Henry III led not to their enslavement but to their ransom.[127]

For the remainder of the century raiding was recorded with some frequency, but in circumstances that suggest a return to the more opportunistic captive taking that had been common until the ninth century. As previously mentioned, Frankish captive taking no longer appeared in relation to enslavement following Henry II's ruling against the sale of Christians to the heathen in 1006. It is clear, however, that, even as slave raiding declined in scale and frequency in east central Europe, it remained an important part of Slavic warfare, particularly for the Přemyslid and Piast armies. When Bohemian raiding reappears in Frankish sources, albeit for the final time, it was as a tactic deployed by Henry IV via his mercenaries to humiliate and demoralise his political rivals in Swabia. Both Bernold of Constans and Berthold of Reichenau were appalled by the brutality of these campaigns in 1077 and 1078, with the former claiming that Bohemians were more interested in seizing people than cattle because people could be raped and sold.[128] The twelfth-century chroniclers Cosmas of Prague, his continuator the Canon of Vyšehrad, and Gallus Anonymus also indicate the continued role of enslavement in Přemyslid and Piast cross-border warfare – against each other and the Pomeranians – well into the twelfth century, and the presence of enslaved servants amongst Bohemian Jews by 1124 certainly suggests the continuance of at least a small-scale trade in slaves, probably fuelled by raiding.[129] Never again, however, do we see the scale of slave raiding as in Oldřich's attack on Biesnitz in 1015 or Břetislav I's campaign into Poland in 1039, and by the close of the eleventh century the enslavement of captives appears to have returned to a small-scale operation.

Conclusion

Captive taking in warfare was fundamental to early medieval slavery, serving as the primary means for creating a supply of deracinated subject peoples regardless of whether slave trading operated at a local, opportunistic level or as part of a large-scale, long-distance network. Also visible throughout the entirety of this period are themes that remained important to the ecclesiastical authors of the annals and chronicles. The enslavement of Christians to non-Christians remained a perceived threat to souls across a changing religious landscape and applied directly to pagan populations in the British Isles before and during the Viking Age, as well as to pagan Slavs along the eastern Frankish frontier. Jewish and Muslim buyers at the end of the supply chain also appear to have contributed to these fears during peak periods of slave raiding, as is explored more fully in Chapter 6. Some authors also did not feel the everyday aftermath of war to be worth recording, while others felt captive taking to be essential for establishing the success of a campaign or the barbarity of an enemy. The inconsistency in its appearance means that we should not generalise about this activity's pervasiveness or absence without careful scrutiny of sources and their contexts.

Even within these thematic and contextual limitations, there are obvious patterns in the scale of enslavement through warfare in both the British Isles and east central Europe. Although there is drastic variation in the expansion of slave raiding in the ninth and tenth centuries, the overall chronology of escalation, peak, and decline is striking. Through most of the ninth century, viking raids undoubtedly increased the scope of raiding in the British Isles, but this was not necessarily the case for the scale of enslavement. The first few decades focused on ransoming, and beyond that raiding was shaped by political alliances; there is no evidence that viking raiders or armies were primarily interested in slaves until the end of the ninth century, when greater numbers of captives coincided with the settlement of Iceland by the Norse. By contrast, armies and raiders in the ninth century in east central Europe appear to have remained less interested in captive taking, the result of not only the royally focused lens through which we must view this warfare but also the Slavs' strategic reliance upon fortifications. Warfare necessarily centred on prolonged sieges and razing of the country-side after any potential captives had taken shelter behind walls and palisades.

Drastic change occurred in both parts of Europe in the tenth century. Along the east Frankish frontier, the rapid escalation of Magyar raids and their Bohemian alliances resulted in what must have been substantial numbers of Frankish and Slavic slaves within a few decades and positioned the developing urban centre of Prague at the crux of a raiding and slave-trading network. The adoption of a slave-raiding strategy by the Ottonians may have been in reaction to these trends, both in terms of revenge upon non-Frankish raiders and as an attempt to participate in the increasing wealth being generated by slave trading just beyond the eastern Frankish frontier. The shifting political landscape and the subsequent end of Magyar raids may have driven Bohemians to begin their own slave-raiding activities in the second half of the tenth century to satisfy increasing external demand. In England and Ireland, native armies and raiders demonstrated growing interest in captive taking, initially against viking raiders, but soon native and Viking alliances show enslavement to have been the pursuit of all combatants. For England, Danish efforts at conquest appear to have brought about another peak in slave raiding, while, in Ireland, slave raiding reached a fever pitch amongst the Irish themselves. Even if the high numbers of captives are exaggerated, they suggest that people were the most valuable plunder, hinting at a situation in which political conflict may have been manufactured so as to support the slave trade.

High-volume slave raiding in east and west continued into the first two decades of the eleventh century, except in England, where it apparently declined quickly with the Danish conquest. England also saw a sudden change in warfare with the Norman Conquest 50 years later, which abruptly shifted attention from the enslavement of captives to the ransoming of elites. Slave raiding appears to have disappeared from Frankish warfare on its eastern frontier much earlier, possibly as early as the first decade of the eleventh century, though the withdrawal of Frankish participants seemingly did not impact the scale of slave raiding. These changes certainly represent major shifts in the mentalities of warfare in both regions, and they must have substantially decreased the slave supply at a time when external demand appears to have been waning. For most of the peoples residing in the British Isles and east central Europe, though, captive taking continued, with the available evidence suggesting that these victims were destined for enslavement. By the middle of the eleventh century, however, captive taking in warfare appears to have become sporadic, with numbers so greatly reduced as to indicate a return to ninth- or even eighth-century levels of slave trading.

Notes

1 For an overview of historiographical and anthropological study of plundering, see Rodolphe Keller, 'Prédation et sociétés de l'Antiquité tardive au Moyen Âge', in Rodolphe Keller and Laury Sarti (eds), *Pillages, tributs, captifs: Prédation et sociétés de l'Antiquité tardive au haut Moyen Âge* (Paris: Éditions de la Sorbonne, 2018), https://books.openedition.org/psorbonne/39926 (accessed 2 August 2023). For plundering as a means of self-promotion, see Guy Halsall, 'Predatory warfare: the moral and the physical', in Keller and Sarti (eds), *Pillages, tributs, captifs*, http://books.openedition.org/psorbonne/39940, para. 27 (accessed 2 August 2023).

2 On masculinity, see Wyatt, *Slaves and Warriors*, generally and Karras, 'Desire, descendants, and dominance', pp. 16–29. On the profitability of warfare, see Reuter, 'Plunder and tribute', 75–94. For endemic warfare in an early medieval context, see Guy Halsall, 'Anthropology and the study of pre-conquest warfare and society: the ritual war in Anglo-Saxon England', in Sonia Chadwick Hawkes (ed.), *Weapons and Warfare in Anglo-Saxon England* (Oxford: Oxford University Press, 1989), pp. 155–77.

3 Holm, 'The slave trade of Dublin', 317–45.

4 For example, Rio, *Slavery after Rome*, pp. 19–41; and Wyatt, *Slaves and Warriors*, pp. 61–172.

5 Guy Halsall, *Warfare and Society in the Barbarian West, 450–900* (London: Routledge, 2003), p. 91. David S. Bachrach, *Warfare in Tenth-Century Germany* (Woodbridge: Boydell, 2012), pp. 170–3.

Bernard S. Bachrach, *Early Carolingian Warfare: Prelude to Empire* (Philadelphia, PA: University of Pennsylvania Press, 2001), pp. 49–50. These works respond to the emphatic centring of plunder in Carolingian warfare in Reuter, 'Plunder and tribute', 75–94.

6 Gillingham, 'Christian warriors', pp. 237–56. Gillingham, 'Women, children, and the profits of war', pp. 61–74.

7 Strickland, 'Slaughter, slavery or ransom', pp. 41–59. Strickland, *War and Chivalry*, pp. 313–17.

8 Pelteret, 'Slave raiding and slave trading', 99–114.

9 Patrick, *Epistola ad Milites Corotici*, in Bieler (ed.), *Libri Epistolarum Sancti Patricii Episcopi*, p. 98

10 Patrick, *Confessio*, p. 56.

11 *Gildas: The Ruin of Britain and Other Works*, ed. and trans. Michael Winterbottom (London: Philimore, 1978), p. 98.

12 AU, s. a. 434, p. 39; s. a. 471, p. 49.

13 *Penitentialis Vinniani*, §30, p. 85; §32, p. 86.

14 *Poenitentiale Cummeani*, IX.14, p. 126.

15 AL, v, p. 149.

16 *Poenitentiale Theodori*, II.xiii.20, II.xiii.22, p. 200.

17 AT, s. a. 686, i, p. 210; s. a. 688, i, p. 211.

18 AT, s. a. 684, i, p. 208. For the connection between the raid and Adomnán's ransoming see, for example, FA, s. a. 687, pp. 36–7; and AFM, s. a. 684, pp. 290–3. These later texts probably draw from lost early material.

19 *Bede's Ecclesiastical History*, pp. 504–7.

20 Alfred P. Smyth, 'The earliest Irish annals: their first contemporary entries, and the earliest centres of recording', *Proceedings of the Royal Irish Academy*, 72 C (1972), 1–48.

21 Cameron, *Captives*, 82–3.

22 James E. Fraser, *From Caledonia to Pictland: Scotland to 795* (Edinburgh: Edinburgh University Press, 2009), p. 201.

23 *Bede's Ecclesiastical History*, p. 428.

24 *Bede's Ecclesiastical History*, pp. 400–4.

25 This is a common trope of early medieval miracle stories and derives from the biblical story of Paul's miraculous unchaining in Acts 16. Pelteret, *Slavery in Early Mediaeval England*, p. 58.

26 See pp. 92–3.

27 For the political context, see Milan Katuninec, 'The mission of the Thessaloniki brothers in Great Moravia: between Constantinople and Rome', *Hiperboreea*, 8:2 (2021), 159–83. Maddalena Betti, *The Making of Christian Moravia (858–882): Papal Power and Political Reality* (Leiden: Brill, 2014).

28 See pp. 135–6, n. 5.
29 McCormick, *Origins of the European Economy*, pp. 738–52. McCormick, 'New light on the "Dark Ages" ', 17–54.
30 McCormick, *Origins of the European Economy*, p. 772. See critiques in Joachim Henning, 'Slavery or freedom? The causes of early medieval Europe's economic advancement', *Early Medieval Europe*, 12:3 (2003), 272–3; and Rio, *Slavery after Rome*, pp. 24–8.
31 Galuška, 'O otrocích na Velké Moravě', pp. 75–86.
32 Eric J. Goldberg, *Struggle for Empire: Kingship and Conflict under Louis the German, 817–876* (Ithaca, NY: Cornell University Press, 2006), pp. 119–20.
33 Edumund E. Stengel (ed.), *Urkundenbuch des Klosters Fulda*, vol. 1 (Marburg: Elwert, 1913; repr. 1958), no. 274, p. 396. ARF, s. a. 805, p. 120; s. a. 806, p. 122. Later evidence of payments and the presence of Bohemian envoys in Francia indicates that this tributary status continued until sometime before 840, when Bohemians harried Louis the German's army as it crossed their territory. Dušan Třeštík, 'The baptism of the Czech princes in 845 and the Christianisation of the Slavs', *Historica*, 2 (1995), 31–4.
34 AF, s. a. 846, p. 36; s. a. 848, p. 37; s. a. 849, p. 38.
35 Joachim Henning and Matthias Ruttkay, 'Frühmittelalterliche Burgwälle an der mittleren Donau im ostmitteleuropäischen Kontext: ein deutsch–slowakisches Forschungsprojekt', in Machaček and Ungerman (eds), *Frühgeschichtliche Zentralorte*, pp. 259–88. Hajnalka Herold, 'Fortified settlements of the 9th and 10th centuries AD in central Europe: structure, function and symbolism', *Medieval Archaeology*, 56 (2012), 75.
36 Goldberg, *Struggle for Empire*, pp. 122, 127–9. The importance of Slavic fortifications to East Frankish interests is heavily implied by their enumeration in a list compiled in the middle of the ninth century by the so-called Bavarian Geographer: *Descriptio civitatum et regionum ad septentrionalem plagam Danubii*, in Erwin Herrmann (ed.), *Slawisch–germanische Beziehungen im südostdeutschen Raum von der Spätantike bis zum Ungarnsturm* (Munich: R. Lerche, 1965), pp. 212–21. See also Maddalena Betti, 'La *Descriptio civitatum et regionum ad septentrionalem plagam Danubii*: lo spazio oltre il "*limes*" nel IX secolo', *Mélanges de l'École française de Rome – Moyen Âge*, 125:1 (2013), https://doi.org/10.4000/mefrm.1078 (accessed 3 October 2023).
37 AF, s. a. 848, p. 37; s. a. 849, p. 39.
38 AF, s. a. 855, pp. 45–6; s. a. 864, p. 62.
39 AF, s. a. 857, p. 47.
40 AF, s. a. 869, p. 67.

41 For the implications of harrying for lordship, see Halsall, *Warfare and Society*, p. 140.
42 AF, s. a. 869, p. 67.
43 AF, s. a. 872, p. 76.
44 At Břeclav-Líbivá, a settlement site about 3.5 miles from the stronghold of Pohansko, researchers excavated a grouping of large grain silos dating to the Great Moravian period that were probably used to store grain for the nearby urban centre. Macháček, *Rise of Medieval Towns*, pp. 57–60.
45 J. Poulík, 'Svědectví výzkumů a pramenů archeologických o Velké Moravě', in Bohuslav Chropovský and Josef Poulík (eds), *Velká Morava a počátky Československé státnosti* (Prague: Academia, 1985), pp. 9–80. Luděk Galuška et al., 'The glass of Great Moravia: vessel and window glass, and small objects', *Journal of Glass Studies*, 54 (2012), 65–7.
46 Timothy Reuter (trans.), *The Annals of Fulda* (Manchester: Manchester University Press, 1992), p. 8.
47 '*Life* of Constantine', p. 71.
48 Bohemia was reportedly governed by at least 14 'princes' in 845, but by the turn of the eleventh century there was only one. Třeštík, 'The baptism of the Czech princes', 7–59.
49 *Βίος Κλήμεντος*, p. 227. *Žitije Nauma,* MMFH, ii, p. 178.
50 McCormick, *Origins of the European Economy*, p. 766.
51 AF, s. a. 884, p. 113.
52 AF, s. a. 880, pp. 94–5; s. a. 893, p. 122.
53 *Epistola Theotmari episcopi*, ed. Fritz Lošek MGH, *Studien und Texte* 15 (Hanover, 1997), p. 152.
54 AF, s. a. 898–9, p. 132.
55 AF, s. a. 892, p. 121; s. a. 893, p. 122; s. a. 900, p. 134.
56 Peace treaties were agreed between East Frankish rulers and the Moravians in 874, 885, 890, and 901. Timothy Reuter, *Germany in the Early Middle Ages 800–1056* (London: Longman, 1991), p. 83.
57 AF, s. a. 895, p. 126.
58 Evidence from the north suburb church cemetery at Pohansko suggests cultural continuation into the middle of the tenth century. Jiří Macháček, Petr Dresler, and Renáta Přichystalová, 'Das Ende Großmährens: Überlegungen zur relativen und absoluten Chronologie des ostmitteleuropäischen Frühmittelalters', *Praehistorische Zeitschrift*, 93:2 (2018), 307–48. Political instability and economic decline are visible in the mortuary archaeology of the late ninth century through poorer jewellery workmanship and a shift to shallow, unaligned burials without coffins. Pavel Kouřil, 'The Magyars and their contribution to the collapse and fall of Great Moravia: allies, neighbours, enemies', in Jiří Macháček and Martin Wihoda (eds), *The*

Fall of Great Moravia: Who Was Buried in Grave H153 at Pohansko near Břeclav? (Leiden: Brill, 2019), p. 68.

59 Alcuin to Higbald, ed. E. Dümmler, MGH, Epistolae 4 (Hanover, 1895), pp. 57–8.

60 AU, s. a. 821, p. 277.

61 Peter H. Sawyer, *Kings and Vikings* (London: Routledge, 1982), pp. 78–112.

62 The main exception is the Mercian Register in MSS B, C, and D, which focuses on Mercian rulers from 902 to 924.

63 Emer Purcell, 'The first generation in Ireland, 795–812: viking raids and viking bases?', in Howard B. Clarke and Ruth Johnson (eds), *The Vikings in Ireland and Beyond* (Dublin: Four Courts Press, 2015), pp. 41–54.

64 Colmán Etchingham, *Viking Raids on Irish Church Settlements in the Ninth Century* (Maynooth: Department of Old and Middle Irish, 1996), p. 40.

65 Etchingham, *Viking Raids*, p. 17. See also the detailed overview in Ó Cróinín, *Early Medieval Ireland*, pp. 252–6.

66 Etchingham, *Viking Raids*, p. 56.

67 AU, s. a. 871, p. 327. For examples of raiding in Scotland, see AU, s. a. 866, p. 321; ASC D, s. a. 875, p. 26.

68 AU, s. a. 869, p. 325. Holm, 'The slave trade of Dublin', 320–1.

69 Dawn Hadley et al., 'The winter camp of the Viking Great Army, AD 872–3, Torksey, Lincolnshire', *The Antiquaries Journal*, 96 (2016), 23–67.

70 AU, s. a. 895, p. 349. CS, s. a. 886, p. 143. The 'many' captured from the oratory of Ciannán in 881 should also be included. AU, s. a. 881, p. 337.

71 *Annales Cambriae AD 682–954: Texts A–C in Parallel*, ed. and trans. David N. Dumville (Cambridge: Department of Anglo-Saxon, Norse, and Celtic, 2002), s. a. 893–4, pp. 14–15. ASC A, s. a. 893, p. 57; s. a. 894, p. 58; s. a. 896 p. 59. Holm notes that, of the 26 instances of viking captive taking in Francia from 834 to 896, more than a half (15) occurred between 873 and 896. Holm, 'The slave trade of Dublin', 325.

72 See also discussion in Holm, 'The slave trade of Dublin', 322–4.

73 Etchingham, 'Slavery or ransom?', pp. 117–45.

74 ASC A, s. a. 893, p. 57.

75 ASC A, s. a. 909, p. 63; s. a. 917, p. 67.

76 ASC A, s. a. 933, p. 70; s. a. 945, p. 74. ASC D, s. a. 948, p. 44. Benjamin T. Hudson, 'The Scottish Chronicle', *The Scottish Historical Review*, 77:204 (1998), 158.

77 AU, s. a. 951 p. 397; s. a. 948, p. 393. On increased records of captive taking by the Irish, see Holm, 'The slave trade of Dublin', 328–9.

78 BT, s. a. 986, pp. 9–10. For wider raiding context, see Holm, 'The slave trade of Dublin', 331–2. For connections between enslavement and war bands, see Wyatt, *Slaves and Warriors*, pp. 61–166.
79 ASC E, s. a. 1011, pp. 68–9.
80 Fontaine, 'Archbishop Wulfstan', pp. 156–63.
81 BT, s. a. 1000, p. 11; s. a. 1037, 1040, p. 13; s. a. 1071, p. 16; s. a. 1089, p. 18.
82 There were enough enslaved Irish in Dublin for it to be notable when they were freed by the king of Meath, Máel Sechnaill. AU, s. a. 980, pp. 415–17.
83 AT, s. a. 1003, p. 355. AFM, s. a. 1005, p. 755. AU, s. a. 1011–13, pp. 443–7. CS, s. a. 1015, p. 219. Hiberno-Norse and other viking groups continued captive taking as a tactic against the Irish. AT, s. a. 1002, p. 355. AFM, s. a. 1013, p. 773. AI, s. a. 1015, p. 187.
84 The strength of Přemyslid control may be an illusion of source survival, since many of our texts were written either to celebrate members of that dynasty, such as the hagiography of Sts Wenceslas and Ludmila, or after the Přemyslids had eliminated their rivals, as in the case of Cosmas of Prague's very pro-Přemyslid *Chronicle of the Bohemians*.
85 *Legenda Christiani*, pp. 66–8.
86 'Ibrāhīm ibn Ya'qūb', p. 165. *Life of Saint Adalbert Bishop of Prague and Martyr*, ed. and trans. C. Gaşpar, in G. Klaniczay (ed.), *Saints of the Christianisation Age of Central Europe (Tenth–Eleventh Century)* (Budapest: Central European University Press, 2013), pp. 124–7.
87 Třeštík, ' "Veliké město Slovanů jménem Praha" ', p. 54.
88 Ježek, 'A mass for the slaves', p. 636. Ivo Štefan, 'Slavery and slave trade in early medieval Bohemia: archaeology of slavery or slavery of archaeology?', in Biermann and Jankowiak (eds), *The Archaeology of Slavery*, pp. 127–40.
89 Ivo Štefan, Petra Stránská, and Hana Vondrová, 'The archaeology of early medieval violence: the mass grave at Budeč, Czech Republic', *Antiquity*, 90:351 (2016), 759–76.
90 For political overviews of these wars, see Bachrach, *Warfare in Tenth-Century Germany*, pp. 14–69; and Reuter, *Germany*, pp. 137–74.
91 Adalbert of Magdeburg, *Continuatio Regionis*, ed. F. Kurze, MGH SS rer. Germ. 50 (Hanover, 1890), 154–8, s. a. 907–926. The Annals of Corvey state that men and women were taken captive in Saxony by Magyars in 919. *Annales Corbeienses*, ed. G. Pertz, MGH, SS 3 (Hanover, 1839), s. a. 919, p. 4. Regino of Prüm, in adapting the eighth-century text of Paul the Deacon, claimed of the ninth-century Magyar raiding that, '[b]ecause Germany is so populous, often innumerable crowds of captives are taken and sold away to southern peoples for

a price'. Author translation from Regino of Prüm, *Chronicon*, ed. F. Kurze, MGH SS rer. Germ. 50 (Hanover, 1890), s. a. 889, p. 132.

92 'Ibn Rusta on the Magyars 903–913', in Lunde and Stone (eds), *Arab Travellers*, pp. 122–3.

93 Bernhard Friedmann, *Untersuchungen zur Geschichte des abodritischen Fürstentums* (Berlin: Duncker & Humblot, 1986), pp. 180–1.

94 Lantbert, *Vita Herberti Archiep. Coloniensis*, ed. G Pertz, MGH SS 4 (Hanover, 1841), p. 741.

95 Henry I also sought tighter control over these peoples, especially the Sorbs, to create a buffer against Hungarian raids. Bachrach, *Warfare in Tenth-Century Germany*, pp. 25–30.

96 'captivitati servatae', Widukind of Corvey, *Res Gestae Saxonicae*, ed. H. E. Lohmann and Paul Hirsch, MGH, SS rer. Germ. 60 (Hanover, 1935), p. 50.

97 Widukind of Corvey, *Res Gestae Saxonicae*, pp. 51–2. Adalbert of Magdeburg, *Continuatio Regionis*, s. a. 934, p. 159.

98 Rodolphe Keller, 'Pillage et pouvoirs aux marges orientales de la Germanie ottonienne (919–1024)', in Feller and Rodríguez (eds), *Objets sous contrainte*, https://books.openedition.org/psorbonne/26844, para. 12 (accessed 2 August 2023).

99 Sverre Bagge, *Kings, Politics, and the Right Order of the World in German Historiography c.950–1150* (Leiden: Brill, 2002), p. 28.

100 Widukind of Corvey, *Res Gestae Saxonicae*, pp. 108–9. Cf. David S. Bachrach, who believes this indicates Otto's lack of interest in plunder. *Warfare in Tenth-Century Germany*, pp. 170–3.

101 'Preda inde ingens ducta', Keller, 'Pillage et pouvoirs', paras. 13–15. Widukind of Corvey, *Res Gestae Saxonicae*, p. 122.

102 Widukind of Corvey, *Res Gestae Saxonicae*, p. 126.

103 Widukind of Corvey, *Res Gestae Saxonicae*, pp. 131–2, 135.

104 For political overviews of this period, see Jerzy Strzelczyk, 'Bohemia and Poland: two examples of successful western Slavonic state-formation', pp. 514–35; and Eckhard Müller-Mertens, 'The Ottonians as kings and emperors', pp. 233–66, in Timothy Reuter (ed.), *The New Cambridge Medieval History*, vol. 3: *c. 900–1024* (Cambridge: Cambridge University Press, 1999).

105 On territorial reorganisation, see Bachrach, *Warfare in Tenth-Century Germany*, pp. 59–60; Keller, 'Pillage et pouvoirs', paras. 19–20.

106 *El 'Ḏikr al-Aqālīm' de Isḥāq ibn al-Ḥasan al-Zayyāt*, ed. and trans. Fransisco Castelló (Barcelona: University of Barcelona, 1989), p. 258.

107 Widukind of Corvey, *Res Gestae Saxonicae*, pp. 141, 143–4. The Polish ruler Mieszko I was at this point married to Boleslav I's daughter. See also raids as part of the Liutzi confederation's rebellion against the Holy Roman Empire in 982/3 in *Thietmari Merseburgensis*,

pp. 120–2. A Polish–Frankish alliance raided Polabian Slavs in 986. *Annales Quedlinburgenses*, ed. M. Giese, MGH, SS rer. Germ. 72 (Hanover, 2004), s. a. 986, p. 476.

108 *Thietmari Merseburgensis*, p. 20.

109 *Thietmari Merseburgensis*, p. 146.

110 *Thietmari Merseburgensis*, p. 308.

111 *Thietmari Merseburgensis*, pp. 262, 420–1, 472–3.

112 Cosmas of Prague, *Chronicle of the Czechs*, p. 138. The date of this event is unclear, though Cosmas places it before 1021.

113 ASC C, s. a. 1036, p. 106; s. a. 1055, p. 116. ASC E, s. a. 1052, p. 83.

114 ASC E, s. a. 1046[a], pp. 78–9. ASC D, s. a. 1065, p. 78.

115 Strickland, 'Slaughter, slavery or ransom', pp. 41–59.

116 ASC E, s. a. 1079, p. 92. Turgot, *Life of St Margaret*, p. 57.

117 *Vita Griffini Filii Conani: The Medieval Latin Life of Gruffudd ap Cynan*, ed. and trans. Paul Russell (Cardiff: University of Wales Press, 2005), pp. 68–71, 74–7.

118 AU, s. a. 1031, p. 469; s. a. 1041, p. 481; s. a. 1044, p. 483. AFM, s. a. 1035, p. 831; s. a. 1040, p. 839; s. a. 1048, p. 855; s. a. 1053, p. 865.

119 AU, s. a. 1059, p. 497; s. a. 1062, p. 499.

120 Holm, 'The slave trade of Dublin', 336. AU, s. a. 1056, pp. 493–5. See also unspecified numbers of captives taken in raids in AFM: s. a. 1053, p. 865; s. a. 1055, p. 869; s. a. 1060, p. 879.

121 AI, s. a. 1073, p. 231; s. a. 1088, p. 241. AFM, s. a. 1080, p. 915. CS, s. a. 1089, p. 255. On cattle raiding, see Lucas, *Cattle in Ancient Ireland*, pp. 125–9.

122 Holm, 'The slave trade of Dublin', 337.

123 AT, s. a. 1116, p. 37.

124 CS, s. a. 1116, p. 271.

125 *Thietmari Merseburgensis*, pp. 472–5. The Annals of Hildesheim attest Polish capture of Saxons and Thuringians in 1028. *Annales Hildesheimenses*, ed. G. Waitz, MGH, SS rer. Germ. 8 (Hannover, 1878), s. a. 1028, p. 35.

126 Cosmas of Prague, *Chronicle of the Czechs*, p. 174.

127 Herman of Reichenau, *Chronicon*, s. a. 1041, p. 123.

128 Bernold of Constans, *Chronicon*, p. 414.

129 Cosmas of Prague, *Chronicle of the Czechs*, especially Book III. Gallus Anonymus, *Gesta Principium Polonorum*, ed. and trans. Paul W. Knoll and Frank Schaer (Budapest: Central European University Press, 2003), see Books II and III.

5

Small-scale slave trading

Opportunistic slave trading consisted of the ad hoc sale of enslaved people designed to meet specific circumstances, often connected to domestic or even high politics, and these types of sales are visible from the seventh through even the twelfth centuries in northern and east central Europe. The people sold could still be caught up in long-distance and commercial networks, but this was not the initial impetus for their sale. Before the steep increase in external demand and escalation of slave raiding in the tenth century, however, ad hoc sales were the most common form of slave trading. This chapter and the next explore slave trading trends chronologically, beginning with what these smaller-scale operations looked like in the seventh, eighth, and ninth centuries, before moving on to subsequent high-volume slave trading in Chapter 6. Discussion of small-scale slave trading for the moment focuses on the reasons slaves were commonly sold and how these sales linked up with existing trade networks in the period before substantial demand arose in the Islamic world.

Reasons for sale

Motivations for sale could vary greatly, but surviving examples indicate that both newly enslaved individuals and those enslaved from birth were often sold in direct response to problems presented by the enslaved themselves. These could be simple issues, such as ensuring peace within the home, or larger concerns, involving ecclesiastical ideals or political conflict. As each case demonstrates, the distance over which a person was sold or the effort expended by the slave owner to make a sale was dictated by the urgency of removing the enslaved from a particular community. Of those long-distance sales that are visible before the tenth century, sellers appear to have sought out this distance to prevent the enslaved person from returning to cause problems.

The power dynamics of slavery encouraged sexual relationships, most of which were probably non-consensual, and the sale of enslaved women appears frequently as a means of discouraging polygyny before the tenth century in both normative and narrative ecclesiastical texts.[1] The earliest penitential texts from Ireland, the sixth-century *Penitential of Finnian* and the seventh-century *Penitential of Cummean*, both prescribed the manumission of the enslaved woman if she had borne her owner's children and her sale if she had not.[2] These canons had a wide reach in Europe due to the transmission of Irish penitentials, and the idea likewise appears in the eighth- or ninth-century *Penitential of Merseburg*, a Frankish text based on that of Cummean which could have reached Bohemia in the ninth or tenth centuries given Prague's close ecclesiastical connections with Francia.[3] The *Zakon Suydnji Ljudem*, a law tract probably composed in an ecclesiastical context in the ninth century, advised that the enslaved woman had to be sold out of the territory while the man had to fast for seven years, and the proceeds of the sale were to be given to the poor.[4] Although the sexual use of enslaved women was probably ubiquitous, there is little about these morally driven, idealistic prescriptions that evince a connection to a market demand for slaves. This is borne out by the ninth-century Irish *Vita Prima Sancti Brigitae*, in which the titular saint was the child of Dubthach, a lord in Leinster, and his slave Broisech. Dubthach's wife, who had borne only sons, feared that a beloved daughter would compete with her own children, and she pressured Dubthach to sell Broisech until he relented.[5] Broisech was sold first to a passing poet, who took Broisech to his own region in Uí Néill territory, but soon sold her again to a visiting druid. It is also clear that Broisech's unborn child remained Dubthach's property regardless of where Broisech was sold, and there remained the expectation that someday Brigit would return to her father as his slave.[6] We have little detail regarding these sales, but both imply that they took place locally to travelling men, which implies that slave sales could be a relatively private affair away from markets and day-to-day exchange in a process that minimised expenses for the seller.

It is only in eleventh-century sources that we see any indication that sales related to the sexual abuse of enslaved women were linked consistently with commercial slave trading. In contrast to earlier ecclesiastical nonchalance about the woman's subsequent ownership, Wulfstan of York drew from English penitential tradition for an ordinance in the law code II Cnut that required a man who fornicated with his own female slave to forfeit her, which implies her transfer to ecclesiastical or royal ownership rather than sale.[7] This may have been in response to a problem that Wulfstan had identified in his *Sermo Lupi ad Anglos*, in which women were purchased by groups of men to be gang-raped and resold to 'enemies'.[8] The *Life* of Wulfstan of Worcester also depicts the sale of pregnant women from Bristol to Ireland as a regular part of commercial slave trading.[9] As we have seen in relation to penal enslavement and the sale of kin in Chapter 3, a greater demand for slaves from the tenth century onwards may have impacted the fate of any slave, regardless of the circumstances of their enslavement.

Reasons for ad hoc sales in the earlier centuries extended well beyond normative attempts to prevent fornication, with the practicalities of feeding and caring for another person playing an important role. In desperate times, this could lead to selling oneself or one's children into slavery, with the latter more likely to end up as chattel or in chattel-like circumstances.[10] More casual transactions are depicted in the mid-ninth-century *Life of Findan*, in which Findan was sold three times between Northmen around the British Isles, with the first sale taking place after his owner decided he was not returning to Scandinavia and therefore had no need of a slave.[11] This may have been a common attitude amongst vikings active in the British Isles in the ninth century; when Findan escaped his final owner in Orkney, he had been en route to Scandinavia. Sales were also prompted by misbehaviour on the part of the enslaved or their owner. The *Vita Prima* describes how, after Brigit returned to her father's household, Dubthach attempted to sell her to the king because he viewed her charitable gifts to the poor as the theft of his property – an offer the king, unsurprisingly, declined.[12] The story may hold some truths of ninth-century Irish slave trading, especially if we consider that a king would have had disposable wealth for purchasing a slave, and there may have been political motivation in Dubthach offering his daughter for the king's service, particularly given the role of enslaved women in producing children. As discussed in Chapter 3, *Zakon* included sale as part of punishment for those individuals whose criminal offences merited enslavement, similarly indicating that sale could function to remove troublesome people from a particular setting in Great Moravia.[13]

Misbehaviour by an enslaved person or that resulted in a person's enslavement could be resolved by removing the offender from their immediate situation, with problems overcome locally through sale into another household. When slaves were acquired through questionable means such as kidnapping or theft, however, the sellers were forced to offload their slaves at greater distances to avoid getting caught. The seventh-century Kentish laws of Hlothhere and Eadric established a procedure should a man who had been illicitly sold away return to accuse his kidnapper, with similar circumstances appearing in the tenth-century *Narratio Metrica de S. Swithuno* by Wulfstan of Winchester, which tells the story of a northern girl who was stolen from her owner and taken to Winchester, the royal seat of Wessex and a substantial town.[14] There the thief promptly sold the girl, presumably because he and his stolen goods were unlikely to be recognised.

Travel to distant markets could occur in licit circumstances as well, but such a journey required a reason that the enslaved could not be sold locally. In Bede's story of Imma, the sale of a Northumbrian thegn to a Frisian in London by his Mercian captor was motivated by high politics directly linked to Imma's status and royal connections.[15] In this story, recorded by Bede because of its exceptionality, sale into slavery served to resolve a problem created by the customs of seventh-century England. Having promised not to kill the thegn, the Mercian nobleman could not receive satisfaction for his own slain kin. Leaving Imma alive and within reach of Northumbrian nobility also risked Imma's ransom, which would pre-empt the Mercian's revenge. Selling Imma to a foreigner, especially one likely to operate along long-distance trade networks, would serve to remove Imma from the reach of kin and community. Removal of a politically important person via enslavement required planning, and this likewise appears to have been the case for Findan in ninth-century Ireland, when a rival contracted his kidnapping by Northmen.[16] As in Imma's case, Findan's enslavement was arranged with non-Christian foreigners who would ensure that Findan remained forever beyond the reach of his kin.

Opportunistic slave trading occurred throughout the early Middle Ages, and most recorded sales in the seventh, eighth, and ninth centuries were in response to very specific circumstances, even those involving a merchant with implicit or explicit long-distance trade links. Only in the case of sexually exploited women do we see intentional commercial links, and even then only in the eleventh century. The implication of our sources is that earlier sales, long-distance or otherwise, stemmed from problems created by the enslaved person's presence, be that jealousy within the home, the risk of illicit activity, or political tension. There was nothing to prevent problematic captives from being sold abroad, but local sales enabled slave owners to remove the issue from their households without the expense of travelling to large market centres. Imma was the main exception to this, since his status created a problem that required a drastic solution – one mirrored by the hired raid that carried off Findan nearly two centuries later. Imma's story also indicates that the presence of merchants dealing in slaves does not necessarily signify large slave-trading operations.

Long-distance and commercial trade

Ad hoc sales were driven by circumstances unique to each enslaved person and seller; local sales were convenient, but even opportunistic sales could become linked with commercial activities and long-distance trade networks. The English kingdoms before the tenth century and Great Moravia in the ninth and early tenth centuries serve as case studies that illustrate how commercial slave trading may have operated at this time. There is ample archaeological evidence for long-distance trade in Ireland, Wales, Scotland, and Bohemia, but few or no texts that situate slave trading in this context. Material evidence is essential to discussion of the networks utilised by slave trading, but slave status is difficult to see archaeologically, meaning that we are reliant upon written sources to conclusively prove its presence.[17] The interconnectedness of these areas via trade, political alliances, ecclesiastical communication, and raiding suggests that slave trading out of England and Moravia was closely linked with geographic neighbours, but this remains speculative. Each case study examines: slave traders, exploring whether these merchants dealt predominantly in people or whether they appeared only as party to ad hoc sales; markets, to determine where slave trading occurred; and destinations, to glean some clues as to the frequency of long-distance slave trading and the circumstances that led to it.

Early English kingdoms

There has been very little formal study of slave trading in the early English kingdoms before the arrival of vikings. David Pelteret has established that it did occur, and depicts a system dominated by Frisian slave merchants, maritime traders originating from the Low Countries who facilitated an English supply of slaves to Continental markets.[18] Michael McCormick has likewise presumed that slave trading in England was the domain of Frisian merchants and operated on a considerable scale, but other studies of slavery in England have not assessed this claim.[19] Frisians were certainly heavily involved in the prosperous North Sea trade networks of the seventh and eighth centuries. They operated along a network of *emporia*, also known as *wics*, which were trading settlements normally located in border or frontier areas and under the direct oversight of a lord, usually the ruler.[20] There is little evidence to suggest that they monopolised slave trading or even dominated this sphere, though this may be due to the general scarcity of source material from the English kingdoms and as yet illiterate Frisian society. As such, it is important to establish the role of Frisians in long-distance trade out of Britain, since they operated along the same routes that we know English slaves to have moved and included the only known foreign slave trader in the early English kingdoms: Bede's Frisian.

Frisian involvement in commercial slave trading on the Continent is hinted at in a Frankish text, the ninth-century *Miracles of St Goar*, which tells of a Frisian merchant's boat being towed up the Rhine by slaves, though their role as merchandise or as personal property is unclear.[21] Bede's story of Imma is the only source for Frisian slave trading in England, but textual and archaeological evidence indicates substantial Frisian presence in English *emporia*, to a degree that would make it hard to rule out the existence of commercial slave trading activity. The *Life of Liudger* describes how Liudger, a Frisian who had come to study at York with Alcuin, was forced to flee in 773 alongside other Frisians to avoid becoming victims of a feud when a noble's son was killed by a Frisian merchant.[22] The most widely distributed form of pottery in England at this time, Ipswich ware, was probably produced by Frisians in England in imitation of their own native type of pottery and dispersed to markets and settlements throughout the southeast via internal trade.[23] Even if Bede's Frisian buyer is an early eighth-century cliché, the idea of a Frisian purchasing a slave at a trade centre must have seemed realistic to a contemporary audience.

The introduction of silver coinage in both England and Frisia in the late seventh century is also indicative of increased trade between these regions. For the seventh and eighth centuries, English *sceattas* have been found with some frequency in continental areas dominated by Frisian trade: largely northern France, northwest Germany, the Rhine valley, and the Netherlands.[24] The Frisian coins of Series E, also known as the 'porcupine' types, seem to have been minted specifically for the importation of English goods. More Frisian coins ended up in England than vice versa, suggesting an explosion of silver export to England and a substantial trade imbalance.[25] This does raise questions about the sorts of merchandise being traded, but, rather than pointing to a high-volume slave trade out of England, silver pennies may have gained rapid popularity for a range of social and economic reasons that impacted England earlier than the Low Countries. These include relative political stability and the network of *emporia* facilitating the movement of smaller transactional amounts around the North Sea, as well as Christianisation requiring elite redistribution of wealth via almsgiving in smaller quantities and more frequently than gold coinage would allow.[26]

Southeast England, particularly the kingdom of East Anglia, also had very close connections with Merovingian Francia, as evidenced by the movement of people, coins, and dress accessories. Frankish merchants, as was often true of Christian merchants across Europe throughout the early Middle Ages, are not mentioned in relation to slave trading. They were nevertheless present at *emporia* in lowland Britain, with burials from Ipswich, Hamwic, and London yielding assemblages of grave goods that consistently point to their origins, and very likely that of their wearers, in what is now northern France, the Netherlands, or northwestern Germany.[27] Gold Merovingian coins, *tremisses*, circulated via North Sea trade in the seventh century, demonstrating high-value transactions.[28] The absence of any Frankish slave trading in our texts may be due to the dearth of sources more generally, as well as to the Franks' more established status as Christians, since conversion did not begin in Frisia until the seventh century. After all, as noted in Chapter 2, captives from the British Isles were available with some frequency in Merovingian Francia in the second half of the seventh century. We also cannot rule out the involvement of English traders in transporting slaves across the Channel.

Slave trading appears to have occurred in England at locations that attracted trade generally, such as *wics* and other types of royal settlements in Northumbria and Wessex, all of which argue against any specialised slave market sites. *Wics*, as focal points of trade, must have offered substantial opportunity for securing buyers, and it is no surprise that London featured as the location of Imma's sale.[29] The flow of luxury goods and long-distance trade through London and other *wics* at that time certainly suggests that commerce was booming enough to support the sale and purchase of such expensive items as slaves.[30] Other royal settlements housed concentrations of elites, which may have created a high demand for domestic labour in locations where more people would have been able to afford slaves. According to the life of Aidan in Bede's *Ecclesiastical History*, this bishop of Lindisfarne was known for regularly redeeming people for sale and setting them up as members of the clergy, and, although Bede does not say where these transactions occurred, Aidan frequently travelled around Northumbrian royal estates (*villae regiae*), with Bamburgh and Yeavering in easy reach of Lindisfarne.[31] Raiding, such as the attack on Brega in 695 that brought Irish captives to Northumbria, probably fulfilled much of the demand for enslaved labour, but ransoming would have created some turnover, and captives would have been less available in times of peace. High-status settlements may have played an important role outside England as well, since in the *Vita Prima* Dubthach took Brigit to a king in his attempt to sell her. Even with a regular demand for labourers at or near royal residences, however, there must have been a saturation point, and the demand for household slaves could not have been consistent even if it was high compared to other locations.

As liminal ports of trade with connections to long-distance trade routes, *wics* probably facilitated the sale of people out of England more so than other royal settlements. Though opportunistic in nature, long-distance slave trading occurred often enough in the late seventh century that Ine, the king of Wessex, promulgated a law prohibiting the sale of anyone, slave or free, 'overseas' even if they were guilty of an offence.[32] The contemporaneous decision by Wihtred to allow the sale of Kentish criminals 'overseas' as one of three possible outcomes is, again, suggestive of ad hoc sales decided on a case-by-case basis.[33] The contemporaneous *Penitential of Theodore* also acknowledged the complications that could ensue when a person returned from slavery abroad to a spouse who had remarried.[34] The evidence for Frisian and Frankish trade on the east coast of England indicates that enslaved people were often removed to these areas of the Continent, most likely disbursed via coastal *emporia* such as Quentovic and Dorestad.

There is frequent attestation of English slaves abroad during these earlier centuries, particularly in Merovingian Francia, though how they got there is never made explicit. A letter from Pope Gregory I in 595 instructed the priest Candidus to purchase English boys aged 17 or 18 in Gaul for baptism and training as clergymen, probably for their use as translators and cultural ambassadors in the Augustine mission to Kent two years later.[35] Seventh-century Merovingian hagiography also refers to enslaved people from Britain and Ireland available for purchase on the Continent, as in the Lives of Eligius, Balthild, and Amand.[36] Amand's redemption of 'captives or boys from across the sea' took place during missionary work in Frisia in the middle of the seventh century, and the language that mirrors the 'overseas' of West Saxon and Kentish law implies England or the wider British Isles as their probable origin.[37] Balthild herself was an English woman who may have come to Neustria as part of this trade. Her hagiographer similarly describes her as a Saxon 'from regions overseas' who rose from slavery in the household of Erchinoald, a mayor of the palace, to become queen.[38] Balthild may well have been the victim of a politically motivated sale, and, although her hagiographer implies that her rise in status was a reward for her virtue and piety, she had probably been born into a very prominent East Anglian family and thus was considered eligible to become the wife of a king.[39] As in Imma's case, long-distance commercial slave trading may have been a convenient means of removing a problematic captive, though we also have to consider the role of Erchinoald's own potential connections to the southeast of England in his receipt of this high-status girl as his slave.[40]

Two eighth-century English lives of Pope Gregory I present a similar picture of English slaves being sold in continental Europe. The version produced by an anonymous author at Whitby is the first evidence of Gregory's often cited encounter with English boys for sale in Rome. Upon seeing these youths from the Northumbrian kingdom of Deira, Gregory was inspired by their fair complexion and some clever puns (*Angli/angeli*, or Angles/angels, for example) to convert their people to Christianity.[41] There is no evidence for a factual origin to this story, which may have been inspired by Gregory's letter to Candidus.[42] Several prominent Northumbrians such as Benedict Biscop and Wilfrid did make trips to Rome in the seventh and early eighth centuries, and they may have encountered English slaves there. The story was believable enough to an early eighth-century audience that Bede included it in his own *Ecclesiastical History* not long afterwards.[43]

Slave trading in England before the Viking Age was capable of utilising long-distance trade networks. The evidence presented thus far probably reflects some degree of commercial slave-trading activity, but cross-Channel raiding may also have been a contributing factor. As discussed in Chapter 4, raiding overseas was normal within the British Isles from an early date, and examples of captive taking in sources related to St Patrick in the fifth century indicate that the people taken on raids across the Irish Sea could be sold upon the raiders' return home. The Britons and Saxons purchased by Eligius and those 'from across the sea' redeemed by Amand hint at cross-Channel raiding practices at least through the seventh century, and we know that this did happen in the reverse direction; Filibert, abbot of Jumièges, sent monks across the sea, presumably to England, to redeem captives sometime in the seventh century.[44] Gregory's enslaved boys in Rome or those whom Candidus purchased in Gaul likewise could have been the victims of raids that served to feed slave-trading networks in western Europe.

There are very few absolutes to be gleaned from the source material regarding the forms of slave trading in the early English kingdoms. A number of sales appear to have been opportunistic and ad hoc, with long-distance trade serving to facilitate the removal of a politically important individual. The regularity of people from Britain and Ireland appearing for sale in certain Merovingian hagiography does hint at commercial activities, but references to captive taking and ransoming in these contexts likewise indicate that a significant proportion of the people sold in Francia may have been taken directly by slavers rather than sold out of the British Isles. This means that slave trading in the seventh and eighth centuries was not exclusively the domain of middlemen – Frisian, Frankish, or English – who relied on warfare within the British Isles to create the merchandise they then sourced from locals. Although there seems to have been a sustained demand for British and Irish slaves in Francia, the context of raiding in this period, as examined in Chapter 4, does not suggest that enslavement was the primary goal of conflict. That Filibert could travel across the Channel to ransom captives from Francia, probably in the second half of the seventh century, suggests a context similar to what we have seen regarding the Irish captives in Northumbria whom Adomnán ransomed in the 680s. Although slave-trading networks were certainly a part of cross-Channel raiding and commercial exchange, they were not a significant driver of economic and military change before the Viking Age.

Great Moravia

The scale of slave trading in east central Europe, and especially in Great Moravia, in the ninth century has been extensively discussed in scholarship, often with the conclusion that slaves were exclusively exported from this region. The idea was first presented as part of the Soviet-era Marxist work by Matúš Kučera, who has argued that there is no evidence of unfree labour contributing to local production.[45] Oldřich Tůma has surmised slaves to have been a principal export, forming a large-scale slave-trading system facilitated by links with Venice – a conclusion reached independently by Michael McCormick some years later.[46] For any study of slave trading in or near Great Moravia, however, there are major evidentiary hurdles to overcome, including the paucity of relevant textual and archaeological sources. Even though substantial excavation has been undertaken at Great Moravian sites since the middle of the twentieth century, the near-absence of any coinage begs the question of how slave trading with the coin-based economies of Francia or the Mediterranean could have operated on a significant level.[47] This situation, considered alongside the surviving material evidence of long-distance trade, has led Lumír Poláček to argue that slave trading out of Great Moravia could not have been large-scale in nature, though the case for large-scale slave trading has nevertheless found support from Jiří Macháček.[48] The aim of this case study, then, is to reassess the evidence in light of the previous chapter's conclusions about captive taking, namely that it was certainly a feature of Moravian–Frankish warfare in the ninth century, but that the strategies of military campaigns themselves were not conducive to large-scale slave raiding of the type we see in Ottonian campaigns and Magyar raids of the tenth century. As in the case of early English kingdoms, slave trading could and did connect with long-distance commerce, but this did not amount to the large-scale export of slaves from Great Moravia.

In arguing for large-scale slave trading, scholars point to Jewish merchants whose visibility dealing slaves in Great Moravia and elsewhere in central Europe has been taken as an indicator of their role as the primary slave traders of the time. Charles Verlinden first proposed a Jewish monopoly on slave trading in his monumental works on medieval slavery published in the middle of the twentieth century, though his conclusions were largely focused on the later Middle Ages. Extending this assessment, Tůma has asserted that, in the ninth century, the 'inland slave trade was practiced above all by the Jews'.[49] We must consider, however, that the visibility of Jewish merchants is due, first, to their status as non-Christians, and only secondarily because of their far-ranging trade connections or their importance in slave trading. Michael Toch has argued extensively for the reframing of available written evidence, pointing to ecclesiastical injunctions against the sale of slaves to Jews or non-Christians as being evidence of slave ownership, not slave trading.[50] He has also highlighted the lack of slave trading in Hebrew sources from central Europe that survive from the tenth century onwards, which Verlinden did not examine.[51]

The key texts behind the assumption of Jewish slave merchants in Moravia are the Bulgarian *Life of Naum* and *Life of Clement*, which provide accounts of the destruction of Methodius's church after the bishop's death in 885 and the subsequent sale of the clergy to Jewish merchants, who then brought the clerics to Venice.[52] The enslaved priests were rescued by a Byzantine bureaucrat, who, upon recognising them, purchased the clergymen and brought them back to Constantinople, with Naum and Clement eventually travelling to Bulgaria as missionaries.[53] These hagiographical works describe a monumental political event, but they have nevertheless been taken to reflect a norm in which Jewish slave merchants drove caravans of Slavic slaves from Moravia directly to Venice.[54] McCormick has further linked these Jewish merchants to the 'Radhanites' mentioned by the Arab geographer Ibn Khurradādhbih, possibly drawing from a mid-ninth-century source. These multilingual Jewish merchants allegedly operated trade routes by land and sea between the Mediterranean and east Asia, and transported slaves alongside other goods from Francia to Egypt and to Baghdad via Antioch.[55]

The overt political and ecclesiastical implications of these events, however, are inherently linked to the role of the Jewish merchants, who may well have been sought out for the task. The ousting of the Byzantine-led mission was a turn against eastern Christianity and an expression of the political tensions that forced a shift in the Moravian elite's alignment from Constantinople to Francia. The enslavement of priests was itself a strong statement against the mission, but their sale to Jews doubtless added insult to injury – one that later hagiographers felt it was important to highlight. As in Imma's case, foreign (and here, obviously, non-Christian) merchants were crucial to the circumstances of the sale. Imma's captor knew that the thegn's high connections were likely to lead to his ransom, and this would have been the case for attackers charged with disposing of missionary clergy with links to Rome and the Byzantine court. In both cases, powerful connections are precisely what led to successful ransoming at the eleventh hour. Other evidence for slave trading in central Europe names diverse participants, even over longer distances. The Raffelstetten customs tariff, a Frankish document recording levies on goods transported through Raffelstetten via the Danube in the first decade of the tenth century, notes that Jews and other merchants were subject to tolls on slaves as on other goods, and also references Bavarian, Rus, and Bohemian merchants dealing in slaves.[56] It makes sense that a diverse range of traders moved enslaved people alongside a variety of other items within this significant trade corridor, and mention of Bavarian and Bohemian merchants underlines the point that people who traded Christian and pagan slaves in the early Middle Ages were often Christians themselves.

Even small-scale slave trading out of Great Moravia, however, was clearly linked with the long-distance networks that brought silks, glass, Byzantine jewellery, and Baltic amber to elite settlement sites.[57] The remains of donkeys excavated from the fortified elite settlements at Mikulčice and Uherské Hradiště may indicate more direct trans-Alpine connections, though not necessarily commercial ones.[58] Venetians were singled out in our sources for their role in slave trading as early as the middle of the eighth century, when their business of selling Christians to Muslims in Africa led Pope Zacharias to shut down their operation in Rome, which may give some indication of the intended destination for Naum and his companions.[59] The same is true of a treaty between Lothar I and the Venetians from 840, in which the Venetians made promises to cease the sale of Christians to 'pagans' and stop castrations.[60] Similar legislative attempts were made throughout the second half of the ninth century, apparently with little to no success, so that, by the time the missionaries from Moravia were captured, Venice and its merchants were seen as a definitive means of removing problematic clergy in the late ninth century.[61] Any commercial slave trading that did occur with Great Moravia may have been a factor in these Adriatic and wider Mediterranean connections, and was more likely to have been linked with eastern Mediterranean trade than that of al-Andalus.[62]

Closer trade associations with Francia also supplied 'everyday' materials, such as quern stones, salt, and building supplies, all of which could have served as exchange items for slaves. The Raffelstetten tariff refers to a 'market of the Moravians', though current scholarship interprets this as a wide economic zone including many 'proto-urban' and high-status sites rather than as a single focal point, such as Mikulčice.[63] There is no direct evidence for the locations of any slave sales, however, and even the mention of the Moravian market refers predominantly to salt trading in the preceding ordinance.[64] Moravian fortified sites could have had multiple functions, as high-status residences as well as urbanised *emporia*-like settlements, and it may be that these locations held a similar function for slave trading as did *wics* in England.[65]

There is also a lack of evidence for Moravian people enslaved abroad, since references to Slavic slaves tend to be generalised without reference to their ethnic or geographic origin. There are no unambiguously enslaved people with Slavic names listed in Bavarian charters from the late ninth or early tenth centuries, which may well support the idea of limited captive taking, but we cannot discount the possibility that non-local unfree labourers had their names changed by their lord as an expression of dominance.[66] Although *Zakon* suggests that penal slaves were saleable, it does not necessarily point to the creation of slaves for sale out of Great Moravia. Only one of the clauses that stipulates sale into slavery requires sale abroad, in which a female slave must be sold away if her master has had sex with her.[67] The clear penitential intent of this ruling, along with the requirement that the sale profits be given to the poor, is not indicative of enslavement for export.

Archaeological evidence likewise makes it difficult to envisage a large-scale commercial trade in slaves operating via Great Moravia. The lack of stray coin finds from the ninth century has already been mentioned, but it must be noted that there has as yet been no published lead isotope study of Great Moravian silver jewellery that might pinpoint the ore's origin, as has been done for ornaments and coins in northern Europe during the Viking Age.[68] Jiří Macháček has argued that no other known exports from Great Moravia – horses, honey, and wax – would have been sufficient to account for the volume of silver jewellery at these sites, but this supposition will need to be corroborated by silver analysis.[69] Strontium isotope analysis of the remains of 123 individuals buried within the central fortified 'acropolis' at Mikulčice identified only one non-local male out of 25 male skeletons, all presumed to be individuals of lower status due to the absence of grave goods or a coffin.[70] Non-local people who might have been victims of long-distance slave trading may instead have been buried further outside the settlement, but the results of this study do not initially support the idea of a large numbers of foreign male slaves being trafficked through this proto-urban site. Of the 27 non-elite female skeletons examined, four or five were deemed to be non-local, possibly because most trafficked people in this time and place were women, but marriage practice can also account for non-local origins. As discussed in Chapter 1, osteological assessment also suggests that enslaved servants were not common enough to reprieve wealthy urban women from strenuous physical labour.[71] In these contexts, it is very difficult to envisage the sustained movement of foreign slaves through Great Moravian sites on any substantial scale.

Archaeological study may eventually support the hypothesis of large-scale Moravian slave trading, but the combined factors of current archaeological, bioanthropological, and textual evidence point to small-scale slave trading similar to that of seventh- and eighth-century England. This is unsurprising given the raiding evidence presented in Chapter 4; politically motivated raiding and royal campaigns unable to take large numbers of captives did not create a situation conducive to sustained enslavement on a substantial scale. The following chapter on large-scale trading systems further highlights how the Great Moravian evidence for long-distance trade pales in comparison to tenth- and eleventh-century Přemyslid contexts, which do coincide with substantial textual evidence for captive taking. Future archaeological studies may greatly enhance our understanding of long-distance trade in Great Moravia and perhaps further elucidate these networks' role in forced migration, but slave trading in and out of this region was probably not the focus of commercial enterprise in the ninth century.

Conclusion

The early English kingdoms and Great Moravia participated in long-distance trade networks that served to move enslaved people as was necessary, with sources offering little indication that slave trading was the focus of high-volume commercial operations before the late ninth and tenth centuries, respectively. The examples of Frisian and Jewish merchants demonstrate that we cannot take the presence of foreign, non-Christian traders to be indicative of a foreign, non-Christian monopoly on slave trading, nor can we assume that evidence of these merchants transporting slaves along long-distance routes reflected anything more than opportunistic or occasional sales. Focus on these highly visible 'outsider' merchants also risks our overlooking a key theme of early medieval slave trading, which is the general invisibility of Christian, or 'insider' merchants. Close examination of opportunistic sales and slave trading through case studies makes it possible to formulate ideas of how small-scale slave trading might have looked in the early medieval period. Slaves were a by-product of warfare, acting primarily as symbols of political and economic defeat. Visible sales were symptomatic of problems caused by ecclesiastical regulation, domestic discord, or political conflict. Commercial slave trading over long distances could and did happen, but it was not a primary driver of economic or political development before the Viking Age in the British Isles and before the tenth century in the Czech lands.

Notes

1 Sexual abuse was probably a significant part of subjugating slaves and expressing dominance in the early Middle Ages. Karras, 'Desire, descendants, and dominance', pp. 20–1.

2 Sources focus on male owner/enslaved woman relationships, but we can presume that some enslaved men were exploited by their owners. The early eleventh-century poem *Moriuht* describes the sexual abuse of an enslaved man by his viking captors in Britain. Warner of Rouen, *Moriuht*, ed. and trans. Christopher J. McDonough (Toronto: Pontifical Institute of Medieval Studies, 1995), pp. 229–36. *Penitentialis Vinniani,* §39, p. 88; §40, p. 88. *Poenitentiale Cummeani*, §26–7, p. 116.

3 *Poenitentiale Merseburgense*, in F. W. H. Wasserschleben (ed.), *Die Bussordnungen der abendländischen Kirche* (Halle: Ch. Graeger, 1851), p. 397. Bohemia was overseen by the diocese of Regensburg until 974 and, with the establishment of a bishopric in Prague, became suffragan to the archdiocese of Mainz from 976 until 1344. The Old Church Slavonic penitential *Zapovědi svętyichъ otьcь* was adapted for Great Moravia from a Latin text very similar to the *Penitential of Merseburg*, however, and here the enslaved woman was to be manumitted. *Zapovědi svętzichъ otьcь*, MMFH, iii, p. 144.

4 *Zakon Sudnyj Ljudem,* §4, p. 9.

5 *Vita Prima Sanctae Brigitae*, pp. 118–19.

6 *Vita Prima Sanctae Brigitae*, p. 119. This may be related to the importance of female slaves in providing offspring, an idea that was phased out through Christianisation, but that probably still held sway in

mid-fifth-century Ireland. Karras, 'Desire, descendants, and dominance', p. 19. It may be equally significant as a political statement that Brigit lived with her enslaved mother in Munster, Connacht, and Uí Néill territory, but was herself never enslaved to owners in those lands.

7 II Cnut §54, p. 348.

8 Wulfstan of York, *Sermo Lupi*, pp. 57–8.

9 William of Malmesbury, *Vita Wulfstani*, in *William of Malmesbury: Saints' Lives: Lives of ss. Wulfstan, Dunstan, Patrick, Benignus and Indract*, ed. and trans. R. M. Thompson and M. Winterbottom (Oxford: Oxford University Press, 2002), p. 100.

10 See pp. 81–4.

11 *Vita Findani*, p. 503.

12 *Vita Prima Sanctae Brigitae*, p. 120. For Dubthach as a Leinsterman, see *Vita Prima Sanctae Brigitae*, p. 118.

13 See p. 79.

14 Hlothhere & Eadric §5, pp. 9–10. Wulfstan of Winchester, *Narratio Metrica de S. Swithuno*, p. 496.

15 *Bede's Ecclesiastical History*, pp. 400–4.

16 *Vita Findani*, pp. 503–4.

17 Fontaine, 'Early medieval slave-trading', 466–88.

18 Pelteret, 'Slave raiding and slave trading', 102–6. Medieval sources also refer to Frankish merchants operating out of Frisian territory as Frisians. Stephàne Lebecq, 'Use of the word 'Frisian' in the 6th–10th centuries written sources: some interpretations', in S. McGrail (ed.), *Maritime Celts, Frisians and Saxons* (London: Council for British Archaeology, 1990), p. 89. Pelteret hypothesises Jewish slave traders, but later work demonstrates that Jews were not present in Anglo-Saxon England. Andrew P. Scheil, *In the Footsteps of Israel: Understanding Jews in Anglo-Saxon England* (Ann Arbor, MI: University of Michigan Press, 2004).

19 McCormick, *Origins of the European Economy*, p. 739. Alice Rio discusses slave trading only in the Viking Age: *Slavery after Rome*, pp. 29–34. David Wyatt, *Slaves and Warriors*, is not interested in slave trading.

20 Stephàne Lebecq, 'Long distance merchants and the forms of their ventures at the time of the Dorestad heyday', in H. Sarfatij et al. (eds), *In Discussion with the Past: Archaeological Studies Presented to W. A. van Es* (Zwolle: Amersfoort, 1999), p. 235. The classic, albeit dated, study of North Sea *emporia* is Richard Hodges, *Dark Age Economics: The Origins of Towns and Trade, AD 600–1000* (London: Duckworth, 1982).

21 Wandalbert of Prüm, *Miracula Sancti Goaris*, ed. W. Wattenbach, MGH, SS 15.1 (Hanover, 1887), p. 370.
22 Altfrid, *Vita Liudgeri episcopi Mimigardefordensis*, ed. G. H. Pertz, MGH, SS rer. Merov. 2 (Hanover, 1879), p. 407.
23 Paul Blinkhorn, *The Ipswich Ware Project* (Dorchester: Medieval Pottery Research Group, 2012), pp. 66–8.
24 Rory Naismith, *Medieval European Coinage with a Catalogue of Coins in the Fitzwilliam Museum, Cambridge*, vol. 8: *Britain and Ireland c. 400–1066* (Cambridge: Cambridge University Press, 2017), pp. 63–110.
25 M. Metcalf and W. Op Den Velde, 'Series E reconsidered', in T. Abramson (ed.), *Studies in Early Medieval Coinage*, vol. 2: *New Perspectives* (Woodbridge: Boydell, 2011), p. 110. Naismith, *Medieval European Coinage*, p. 87.
26 Naismith, *Medieval European Coinage*, pp. 106–8.
27 Tim Pestell, 'The kingdom of East Anglia, Frisia and Continental connections, c. AD 600–900', in John Hines and Nelleke Ijessennagger-van der Pluijm (eds), *Frisians and Their North Sea Neighbours: From the Fifth Century to the Viking Age* (Woodbridge: Boydell, 2017), pp. 199–202. These are burials that contain multiple foreign objects, which means they are less likely to have been acquired by locals as singular gifts or purchases.
28 Pestell, 'The kingdom of East Anglia', p. 208.
29 *Bede's Ecclesiastical History*, p. 404. London may not have been under Mercian control *c.* 679, which emphasises either the lengths the nobleman undertook to be rid of Imma or Bede's use of London as a narrative device. J. R. Maddicott, 'London and Droitwich, c. 650–750: trade, industry and the rise of Mercia', *Anglo-Saxon England*, 34 (2005), 22.
30 Derek Keene, 'London from the post-Roman period to 1300', in D. M. Palliser (ed.), *The Cambridge Urban History of Britain*, vol. 1: *600–1540* (Cambridge: Cambridge University Press, 2000), pp. 188–9.
31 *Bede's Ecclesiastical History*, p. 262. Aidan often stayed at a church about half a mile from the early medieval royal residence at Bamburgh.
32 Ine §11, pp. 378–9.
33 Wihtred §26, p. 14.
34 *Poenitentiale Theodori*, II.xii.24, p. 201.
35 *S. Gregorii Magni Opera: Registrum Epistularum Libri I–VII*, ed. Dag Norberg (Turnhout: Brepols, 1982), pp. 378–9.
36 See p. 60.
37 'captivos vel pueros transmarinus', *Vita Amandi Episcopi I*, ed. B. Krusch and W. Levison, MGH, SS rer. Merov. 5 (Hanover, 1910), p. 435.

38 'de partibus transmarinis', *Vita Sanctae Balthildis*, p. 482.
39 Paul Fouracre and Richard A. Gerberding, *Late Merovingian France: History and Hagiography 640–720* (Manchester: Manchester University Press, 1996), pp. 98–9.
40 Fouracre and Gerberding, *Late Merovingian France*, pp. 103–4.
41 *The Earliest Life of Gregory the Great*, ed. B. Colgrave (Lawrence, KS: University of Kansas Press, 1968), p. 90.
42 Dorothy Whitelock (ed. and trans.), *English Historical Documents*, vol. 1: *500–1042* (Oxford: Oxford University Press, 1955), p. 790.
43 *Bede's Ecclesiastical History*, pp. 132–4. Colgrave and Mynors attribute the two variations to a Northumbrian oral tradition: p. 133 n. 2. Mediterranean trade links in early Anglo-Saxon England are suggested by single finds of lower-value Byzantine coins. C. Morrison, 'Byzantine coins in early medieval Britain: a Byzantinist's assessment', in M. Allen, R. Naismith, and E. Screen (eds), *Early Medieval Monetary History* (Farnham: Ashgate, 2014), p. 215.
44 *Vita Filiberti Abbatis Gemeticensis et Heriensis*, ed. B. Krusch and W. Levison, MGH, SS rer. Merov. 5 (Hanover, 1910), p. 596.
45 Kučera, *Slovensko po páde Velkej Moravy*, p. 273.
46 Tůma, 'Great Moravia's trade contacts', 67–77. McCormick, *Origins of the European Economy*, pp. 765–6.
47 Only five coins are currently known from Great Moravian sites, none of whose deposition obviously relates to trade. Jiří Macháček and Jan Videman, 'Monetisation of early medieval Moravia in light of new archaeological discoveries in the Lower Dyje region (Czech Republic)', in Bogucki and Rębkowski (eds), *Economies, Monetisation and Society*, p. 183.
48 Lumir Poláček, 'Ninth-century Mikulčice: the "market of the Moravians"? The archaeological evidence of trade in Great Moravia', in Joachim Henning (ed.), *Post-Roman Towns, Trade and Settlement in Europe and Byzantium*, 2 vols (Berlin: De Gruyter, 2007), i, p. 510. Jiří Macháček, 'Slave trade in Great Moravia: reality or fiction?', in Biermann and Jankowiak (eds), *The Archaeology of Slavery*, pp. 113–26.
49 Tůma, 'Great Moravia's trade contacts', 68.
50 Michael Toch, 'Jews and commerce: modern fancies and medieval realities', in S. Cavaciocchi (ed.), *Il ruolo economico delle minoranze in Europa: Secc. XIII–XVIII* (Florence: Instituto Francesco Datini, Prato, 2000), pp. 43–58. Michael Toch, 'Was there a Jewish slave trade (or commercial monopoly) in the early Middle Ages?', in S. Hanβ and J. Schiel (eds), *Mediterranean Slavery Revisited (500–1800)* (Zurich: Chronos, 2014), pp. 421–44. Michael Toch, *The Economic History of European Jews* (Leiden: Brill, 2013), pp. 177–99.

51 Toch, 'Was there a Jewish slave trade', p. 434.
52 *Βίος Κλήμεντος*, p. 227.
53 *Žitije Nauma*, p. 178.
54 Tůma, 'Great Moravia's trade contacts', 67. McCormick, *Origins of the European Economy*, p. 766.
55 'Ibn Khurradādhbih on the routes of the Rādhānīya and the Rūs c. 830', in Lunde and Stone (eds), *Arab Travellers*, pp. 111–12. McCormick, 'New light on the "Dark Ages"', 49. The accuracy of Ibn Khurradādhbih's description has been debated, and he may have lumped many groups of merchants and trade routes into a single category. For a 'maximalist' interpretation, see Moshe Gil, 'The Rādhānite merchants and the land of Rādhān', *Journal of the Economic and Social History of the Orient* 17 (1974), 299–328.
56 *Inquisitio de thelonis Raffelstettensis*, §9, p. 252; §6, p. 251. Toch has argued that the separation reflects the insider/outsider dichotomy between Christians (who authored the text) and non-Christians. Whereas Christian merchants would be distinguished in a Christian society by their vocation, Jewish merchants were primarily identified by their religion. Toch, 'Was there a Jewish slave trade', p. 435.
57 Poláček, 'Ninth-century Mikulčice', pp. 508–9.
58 Macháček, *Rise of Medieval Towns and States*, p. 459.
59 *Le Liber Pontificalis*, ed. L. Duchesne, 2 vols (Paris: E. Thorin, 1886), i, p. 433.
60 *Pactum Hlotharii I*, ed. A. Boretius and V. Krause, MGH Capit. 2 (Hanover, 1897), no. 233, §3, p. 130; §33, p. 135.
61 McCormick, *Origins of the European Economy*, pp. 765–8.
62 The late ninth century was a period of political instability in al-Andalus, which probably affected demand for slaves. Manzano Moreno, 'Circulation de biens et richesses', para. 38. The Christian eastern Mediterranean was also not closely connected with al-Andalus, probably due to direct access to goods via eastern Islamic trade. Constable, *Trade and Traders*, p. 38.
63 Dušan Třeštík, 'Trh Moravanů – ústřední trh Staré Moravy', *Československý časopis historický*, 21 (1973), 890. Poláček, 'Ninth-century Mikulčice', p. 520.
64 *Inquisitio de thelonis Raffelstettensis*, p. 252. It refers back to the previous ordinance.
65 Jiří Macháček, 'Early medieval centre in Pohansko near Břeclav/Lundeburg: *munitio*, *emporium*, or *palatium* of the rulers of Moravia?', in Henning (ed.), *Post-Roman Towns, Trade*, i, p. 488.
66 See the excerpts regarding slaves translated in Hammer, *A Large-Scale Slave Society*, pp. 95–129.

67 *Zakon Sudnyj Ljudem*, p. 11.
68 For example, XRF analysis of silver from Scotland has identified the reuse of dirhams in jewellery and ingots following their importation via trade networks through Scandinavia and eastern Europe. S. Kruse and J. Tate, 'XRF analysis of Viking Age silver hoards in Scotland', in J. Graham-Campbell (ed.), *The Viking-Age Gold and Silver of Scotland, AD 850–1100* (Edinburgh: National Museums Scotland, 1995), p. 75.
69 Macháček, 'Slave trade in Great Moravia', pp. 116–17.
70 Zdeněk Vytlačil et al., 'Residential mobility in Great Moravia: strontium isotope analysis of a population sample from the early medieval site of Mikulčice-Valy (ninth–tenth centuries)', *Archaeological and Anthropological Sciences*, 13:8 (2021), 8. Burials within or close to the church structure often contained luxury items and/or coffins, and so the researchers deemed these items to be strong indicators of elite status.
71 Havelková et al., 'Entheseal changes', 249.

6

High-demand systems

Slave trading as a flexible and sometimes commercialised means of exchanging human chattel is present in the earliest texts related to the British Isles and east central Europe. This activity was not introduced from outside by foreign raiders or hegemonic powers and by all accounts functioned as a normal part of each slaveholding society. Nevertheless, the ninth and tenth centuries saw significant external demand for slaves and increases in the raiding that created them. This chapter examines the connections between areas of demand and supply to further explore the context of the rise, peaks, and denouement of slave trading out of our two slaving zones. It is impossible to reconstruct these networks in their entirety, even for the tenth and eleventh centuries, when increased source survival and vocal opposition to some slaving make it more visible than in previous centuries. Time and distance ultimately made precise geographic origins of the enslaved irrelevant to captors, so they became known only by their identity in the broadest sense, such as 'Christian' or 'Slav'. The networks sketched in this chapter are likely only the core routes that radiated outwards from the British Isles and the Czech lands. People may have been trafficked to other parts of Europe, north Africa, and western Asia, but discussion here extends only to the furthest distances through which we can evidence the movement of enslaved people from our two regions.

As is the case throughout this study, the question of scale is relative rather than quantifiable. Some scholars have attempted to estimate the number of enslaved people trafficked across Europe in the ninth and tenth centuries by working backwards from rare market prices and redemption values or from the vast quantities of Islamic silver buried in eastern Europe and Scandinavia.[1] Precise quantification emphasises the importance of slave trading for formative economies and polities, but there is potentially greater importance in elucidating the intermediary stages of slaving networks, the middlemen involved, and the multitude of branching routes and destinations. This chapter, therefore, takes a broad logistical and qualitative approach.

Maritime networks in northern Europe

In terms of slave trading, the Viking Age brought profound changes to the British Isles through the introduction of new and more extensive trade routes, which created increased demand for British and Irish captives even as old systems such as *emporia* declined. This gradual change from small- to large-scale slave trading is illustrated by the evidence for raiding, which suggests a complex operation that went beyond the transportation of captives to farms in Scandinavia or the North Atlantic, or even to estates in England. We have already seen that, even in times of smaller scale slave trading, the archipelago of the British Isles was already well connected internally and to the western European continent by networks of trade and communication along which people were trafficked. The expansion of 'Viking' trade networks in a new cultural milieu meant that these connections continued, even intensified, as the British Isles were integrated into the system known in academic scholarship as the 'northern arc'.[2] From the Baltic, Scandinavian and later Rus traders moved goods along the river systems of eastern Europe to the Caspian Sea, where they sold wares to traders operating out of the Abbasid Caliphate and Samanid Empire. Travel accounts from the Islamic world attest high-volume trade in items that are difficult to trace archaeologically: furs, honey, wax, timber, and slaves. The return routes funnelled goods from Asia, such as silks, beads, gemstones, spices, and silver, into northern Europe. Piecing together both textual and archaeological evidence for slave trading in the British Isles and beyond illustrates not only who may have dealt in slaves commercially and where this trading took place, but also how slave trading in the British Isles contributed to a vast network of overland, maritime, and riverine trade routes stretching across the European continent.

Expansion of 'Viking' slave trading

The networks introduced to the British Isles through viking raiding and Scandinavian settlement in the early and mid-ninth century were not immediately focused on commercial slave trading. Pagan and foreign vikings are the most visible raiders, and their tactics, like those of the English and Irish, appear to have focused as much on extracting ransom payments from local populations as on creating slaves. Findan's two captures illustrate this well, the first when he was taken and released while en route to ransom his sister, the second (and three subsequent sales amongst Northmen) giving the impression of self-contained 'Viking' slave trading that relied heavily on local or chance encounters and operated alongside a primary system of ransoming.[3] Findan's sales were driven by convenience, and he was initially sold because his owner did not wish to immediately return to Scandinavia. The establishment of both temporary and permanent raiding camps in Britain and Ireland may have facilitated this sort of dual system by providing venues for exchanging large payments for ransoms or sales with other raiders, traders, and the local populace. Metal detecting and surveying of the Great Army's 872–73 winter camp at Torksey has yielded hackgold, hacksilver, dirham fragments, and over 350 weights, with a similar array of items excavated from Woodstown, a viking raiding base known as a longphort, near Waterford in Ireland.[4] High-value transactions in Scandinavian England, particularly by the Great Army, appear to have led to the introduction of a limited gold bullion economy, perhaps partly made possible by the receipt of ransom payments in gold.[5]

Findan's story also suggests that removal to Scandinavia was an important part of acquiring slaves in this period, and that keeping enslaved people on a ship as personal property was worthwhile only if they could be sold or taken back home. He was able to escape captivity in Orkney on a break in the journey to Scandinavia, implying that Findan had been sold onwards until he ended up with someone intent on returning.[6] The monk Rimbert describes in his *Life of Ansgar* what appears to be a resident population of enslaved Christians at Birka in Sweden in the middle of the ninth century, which Rimbert had witnessed as part of his and Ansgar's mission there.[7] These outsiders in an otherwise pagan society were probably the victims of raids in the British Isles and Francia, and their presence corroborates the demand for slaves hinted at by Findan's circumstances. These sources also uphold the testimony of the twelfth-century Icelandic *Landnámabók*, which mentions the removal of Irish slaves directly to Norway by raiders.[8] By the middle of the ninth century Scandinavian markets may have served as slave-trading hubs, which could explain some of the interest in transporting captives from the British Isles across the North Sea. Captives taken cheaply in raids or purchased at lower prices in the British Isles could potentially have been sold for profit in places such as Birka, as well as Kaupang in Norway and Hedeby in Denmark. These maritime trade connections were critical to the political and economic success of what Tom Horne has described as the 'Uí Ímair network kingdom', the Scandinavian polities ruled by Olaf, Ivar, and Ivar's sons that encompassed a substantial portion of the British Isles from the middle of the ninth century through the middle of the tenth.[9] The routes that transmitted communications and commodities are detectable in the distribution of weights, silver ingots and jewellery, dirhams, silk, and amber, along with other Scandinavian-influenced items. Major markets such as Hedeby, Kaupang, Dublin, and York served as pre-eminent nodal points that directed the flow of goods between east and west. York and Dublin were initially connected via a coastal route around Scotland, and later, following the conquests of the Great Army, across northern England. Horne's two 'primary nodal highways' and any secondary routes probably facilitated the growth of enslavement and slave-trading operations in the second half of the ninth century and first half of the tenth.

From Scandinavia, enslaved people may well have been carried farther afield, along the trade routes illustrated in Map 3. Recent analysis of silver ingots and rings deposited in hoards on the Baltic islands of Gotland and Öland has demonstrated Baltic connections with fur- and slave-trading networks in eastern Europe from an early date, since the objects were comprised of a high proportion of Sasanian and Islamic dirhams minted in the first half of the ninth century.[10] The appearance of gemstones and glass beads from central Asia in Scandinavia and the British Isles can also be attributed to the extension and escalation of trading at this time.[11] Dirham hoarding in Gotland reached a peak in the 860s and 870s, and this has been linked to intensification of fur and slave trading south and east along the river Volga, where these goods were exchanged for silver, silk, and spices.[12] There is no direct evidence that captives from the British Isles were caught up in this trade, which principally relied on people sourced from the Baltic and eastern Slavic lands, but there was a contemporaneous escalation in raiding both in England and in the Carolingian domain.[13] Routes eastwards were not unknown in the British Isles, as demonstrated by the alleged account of Wulfstan, an English traveller whose report to Alfred of Wessex is preserved in the Old English *Orosius*. Wulfstan claimed that from Hedeby he was able to sail to Truso on the Baltic coast in seven days, and from there past Gotland to the Vistula estuary.[14] This sort of interlinkage allowed luxury items and coinage from the Islamic world to reach the British Isles, and it seems quite plausible that enslaved captives were transported in the reverse direction. Such connections did not need to be direct to be effective; Søren Sindbæk has argued that Scandinavian networks operated on what network theory calls a 'small world' model, in which participants such as merchants traversed sections of the conglomeration of routes that made up a full network.[15] This would mean that slave trading was undertaken in stages, as Wulfstan's journey was, with sales in Scandinavian trade hubs serving to disburse enslaved people locally and among traders operating on different routes. This would explain why only a single English coin, that of Æthelwulf of Wessex dating to 845 x 848, was recovered during excavations at Truso.[16] It also sits well with the variation of routes and staging made possible by Scandinavian and Rus navigation by river systems in eastern Europe. The multitude of potential paths between the Baltic and the Black, Caspian, and Mediterranean Seas that were probably exploited to avoid customs houses also may have served to disperse enslaved people to buyers throughout this region.[17]

The settlement of Iceland from the 870s until *c.* 940 appears to have driven a noticeable shift in enslavement patterns in the British Isles during what may have been a lull in the flow of dirhams to Gotland between the 870s and 950s.[18] The escalation of captive taking by vikings in the British Isles and Francia in the second half of the ninth century may well be linked to a desire for enslaved labour on new farms in Iceland. Although these people were normally taken for direct enslavement rather than for sale, we have seen in the previous chapter that opportunistic captive taking and enslavement could lead to ad hoc sales regardless of the scale of contemporary slave trading operations. Even though we may never know the answer, it is worth pondering the extent to which the Icelandic settlement period and the redirection of British and Irish slaves to the North Atlantic related to the reduced importation of dirhams into Gotland. The lull from *c.* 877 was probably caused by political upheaval in the Abbasid Caliphate and the collapse of the Rus Khaganate around this time, and the disruption of eastern networks may have reduced financial incentive for raiders to sell their captives when those interested in claiming land in Iceland could deploy the cheap labour themselves. A redirection of traffic may also explain the possible presence of unfree Slavs at Sviegakot in Iceland, as indicated by the discovery of sunken-feature buildings at a marginal site with a low-status archaeological assemblage.[19]

The settlement of Iceland lasted only 70 years, and concurrent developments set the stage for more widespread and commercialised slave trading involving a diverse range of participants. We have seen in chronicles and annals that intensified raiding and captive taking by viking armies seem to have prompted a reactive change in English and Irish warfare, which likewise emphasised captive taking. Despite the implied diversification of large-scale captive taking in these texts, there is very little direct evidence of large-scale slave trading in the tenth century, either by vikings or other groups. This absence becomes even more glaring when we consider the contemporary economic developments that would have fostered the sale of enslaved people in high volumes and across long distances. Old English penitentials composed between the late ninth and early eleventh centuries strongly suggest cross-cultural slave-trading links in their repeated injunctions against the sale of Christians to 'heathens'. As discussed in Chapter 3, these texts were probably adapted from their continental source material to suit a contemporary English context, and the growing concern with delimiting acceptable bounds of slave trading very probably reflects a reaction to ongoing practices.

The tenth century also saw the rise of towns in Britain and Ireland, which functioned as hubs for long-distance trade and as gathering points for wealthier members of society, and it is perhaps in the context of a nearby urban market that we should view the decision of Alfred's army to remove the captured women and children of Benfleet to London in 893.[20] There is a similar implication in the hagiography of St Swithun, composed in the 970s, which highlights the presence of an enslaved population in Winchester. The miracle story relating to the northern slave girl who was stolen and brought to the town for sale indicates that even those who acquired slaves illicitly could count on sufficient demand in Winchester to sell these people onwards without difficulty. Already in the reigns of Edward the Elder and Æthelstan we find ordinances restricting trading to towns under the oversight of the king's port-reeves, who could extract taxes, with slaves probably having fallen under these ordinances as high-value goods.[21]

Viking towns such as Dublin likewise experienced a boom in the tenth century, facilitated not only by their long-distance connections but also through trade relationships with neighbouring peoples. Mapping of silver hoards undertaken by Michael Kenny illustrates their high concentrations within an arc of 30 to 70 miles around Dublin in Irish territory. Deposition dates do not correspond to known raids on Dublin, implying that the hoard contents are the result of trade or other political connections.[22] Mary Valante has likewise mapped finds of imported luxury items such as amber and jet in Ireland deposited between 934 and 1014, which are also concentrated in the Irish-controlled Dublin hinterland.[23] At a time of intensified captive taking by the Irish and reduced raiding by the Dubliners, the Irish must have played a key role in supplying slaves to Dublin in exchange for valuable imports by the end of the tenth century. Slave trading in tenth-century Ireland was no longer predominantly a viking or Norse activity, but a commercial enterprise that linked Irish and Hiberno-Norse communities.[24] The flourishing of these networks is attested by the foundation of a Dublin mint in 997 that relied upon imported silver to produce the first coinage in Ireland.[25] Dirham finds in Ireland and throughout the British Isles attest the 'northern arc' as an important component of this activity. XRF analysis has also demonstrated the presence of Arab silver in Viking-Age ingots from Scotland, suggesting that eastern trade connections were even more significant than dirham survival rates would indicate.[26] The cessation of dirham deposition in England *c.* 927, probably a result of expanding West Saxon control over areas such as York, means that northern arc links are more difficult to identify, though the consolidation of royal control in this period may have led to a more rigorous programme of dirham recycling.[27]

Other trade centres doubtless played a role in slave-trading networks, even if they themselves lacked substantial urban slave-owning populations. Llanbedrgoch in Anglesey, originally a Welsh site on the Irish Sea, grew in wealth during the Viking Age, having yielded a Scandinavian artefact assemblage including hacksilver, coins, and a variety of weights suggesting exchange on a scale comparable to Woodstown and Torksey.[28] Five contemporaneous burials in the settlement ditch, including two adult males with their hands tied, have recently been interpreted as evidence of late ninth- or tenth-century captive taking, if not slave raiding.[29] A similar site has yet to be identified in Scotland, but evidence for Viking trade, settlement, and looting in the Clyde, Nith, and Annan river valleys (including the significant Galloway hoard) suggests that further research and excavation will eventually uncover camps or permanent settlements.[30] Adrián Maldonado has highlighted the unusually heavy inset weights discovered in Dumfries and Galloway as signifiers of very high-value transactions, as well as the scatter of Samanid dirham fragments from the Scottish west coast and islands that are a characteristic of the 'northern arc'.[31]

Although permanent settlements must have been foci for slave trading, these locations were not essential. Sales may have taken place on or near a ship wherever it landed, and it is likely that seasonal fairs and encampments attracted sellers and buyers.[32] The thirteenth-century *Laxdæla Saga*'s story of Melkorka begins with one such seasonal fair, at which she was offered for sale along with 11 other women by a professional merchant named Gili the Rus, whom the author claims was distinguishable not only by his reputation for wealth but also by his Rus-style hat.[33] The story itself may be a later fabrication, but the core elements match well with textual and archaeological evidence of the tenth century. Captives sourced from the British Isles were sold at markets in Scandinavia, which attracted merchants and buyers from across the Viking world, and the presence of a Rus trader hints at slave-trading networks that extended even farther east. Even if the details of the people involved are literary rather than factual, they appear to preserve a cultural memory of early medieval slave trading.

Al-Andalus, an undisputed centre of slave demand in western Europe, does not appear to have been directly connected with the slave-trading networks of the British Isles. Mention by the Irish

Fragmentary Annals of enslaved 'blue men' from Mauretania brought to Ireland by Dubliners in 867 does indicate a north African connection, but the scribe's implication that this was an unusual event refutes the idea of a regular trade network.[34] The dating and predominantly central Asian mints of those dirhams that reached the British Isles reflect patterns seen in Scandinavia and Rus, confirming that eastward connections dominated the slave trading of the British Isles in the ninth and tenth centuries.[35] Significantly, there are as yet no archaeological indications that Scandinavians travelled to Iberia for trade, or even settlement.[36] We cannot completely discount indirect links with al-Andalus, however. Agobard of Lyon decried the capture of Christians in Arles and Lyon by Jews for sale to al-Andalus in 826 or 827, suggesting a trade route down the Rhône, and Liutprand of Cremona attested in the middle of the tenth century that merchants of Verdun ran an operation that castrated enslaved boys for export to Iberia.[37] These routes are often connected with the transport of slaves from east central Europe, but we should also consider that the boys captured from monasteries and settlements throughout the tenth century and into the eleventh may have been transported across the Channel rather than the North Sea. Mary Valante has argued that frequent viking raids on Irish monasteries would have sourced the literate and educated boys who were in high demand as eunuchs in al-Andalus.[38] We know from the evidence discussed in the previous chapter that English slaves had historically moved along this trade corridor. Although there is little explicit evidence for continuance in the tenth century, the poem *Moriuht*, composed by Warner of Rouen possibly *c.* 1026, features the titular Irishman and his wife being sold along trade routes that connected Ireland and north-east England with Saxony and Normandy.[39] The *Anglo-Saxon Chronicle* also notes that, in 1046, the vikings Lothen and Yrling raided Sandwich and Essex before selling both captives and plunder in Flanders.[40] If cross-Channel slave trading can be documented both before and after the peak of demand for slaves in al-Andalus in the middle of the tenth century, it is very probable that such networks continued to function throughout this period. Some dirhams minted in al-Andalus and Africa have been discovered in France, but slave trading across the Channel cannot have been direct or of high enough volume for these coins to work their way north.[41]

Nevertheless, an indirect connection would be sufficient to explain the unusual and often disregarded statement in the tenth-century geographical text *Ḥudūd al-'ālam* that Britain was an *emporium* of Byzantium and al-Andalus.[42]

Evidence of increased raiding and captive taking paired with more circumstantial evidence of trade suggests an overall escalation of slave trading in the British Isles throughout the tenth century. Although the settlement of the North Atlantic, particularly Iceland, drove an increase in captive taking in the late ninth and early tenth centuries, this activity was probably directed towards sourcing labour for new farms by the landholders themselves, and it is unlikely that slave trading saw a parallel expansion. Through the middle and second half of the tenth century, however, slave trading took on more expansive cross-cultural dynamics that saw English and Irish raiders tapping into long-distance trade hubs regardless of who oversaw them. Scandinavia appears to have been the principal destination of British and Irish slaves, either for settlement or for transit through the markets that supported networks extending through the Baltic, eastern Europe, and the Caspian Sea (see Map 4). Connections to opportunistic trading in the North Atlantic and to staged trade routes through Frankia to al-Andalus may also have siphoned captives away from this eastward trade. These networks radiating outwards from the North and Irish Seas would remain the intensive focus of English and Irish authors well into the eleventh century.

Eleventh-century reactionism

The information with which we can reconstruct slave-trading networks in the tenth century is often circumstantial, but, for England in the eleventh century, slave trading becomes highly visible due to both royal and ecclesiastical attempts to control it. This vocal reaction emerges as a systematic campaign to introduce slave-trading regulations by Wulfstan, archbishop of York, and to reduce the number of people who could be considered saleable.[43] One of Wulfstan's chief concerns was to ensure a holy and ordered society, to which fluidity of status was antithetical.[44] Wulfstan did not oppose slavery or slave trading, only those conditions that led to the enslavement or sale of the 'wrong' people.[45] When the boundary between free and slave status became blurred, undeserving people would be exposed to sin. Wulfstan's polemic reflects his anxieties about a millenarian apocalypse, but the effect of his writings is to depict ubiquitous and profitable slave trading coinciding with increased raiding activity.

Wulfstan's opinions on slave trading are expressed most clearly, and perhaps most personally, in his *Sermo Lupi ad Anglos*, a sermon that is part homily and part programme for reform. Written in English for an undoubtedly English audience, Wulfstan railed against the sale of poor, free Christians out of this land to foreigners, despite their innocence of any crime.[46] That family members would likewise sell each other to foreigners, circumstances that horrified Wulfstan, is probably linked to the poor harvests and destructive Danish raids that he mentions elsewhere.[47] By the time Wulfstan composed the latest surviving revision, version C, he had included the example of women purchased jointly by gangs of men for sex and then sold onwards.[48] In each of these examples, the English were the perpetrators, selling both family and countrymen indiscriminately to a pool of readily available buyers – a theme that also appears in laws that Wulfstan drafted for Æthelred and later Cnut that attempted to prohibit the sale of people 'to the heathen' or 'into heathendom'.[49]

The Danish campaigns that culminated in Swein Forkbeard's conquest of England in 1014 suggest that Wulfstan's foreigners and heathens were either Danes or their trade partners. In the *Gesta Regum Anglorum*, initially completed in 1125, William of Malmesbury relates a story in which Cnut's sister was responsible for shipping attractive (and thus highly valuable) young girls to Denmark.[50] The later date of William's writing and his assurance that she was punished for her actions by being struck by lightning make the tale dubious, but it preserves a folk memory of common and profitable slave trading only a century beforehand.[51] The Danish conquest certainly provided a basis for political links between England and eastern Europe; Swein's wife and the mother of Cnut is believed to have been a daughter of the Polish duke Mieszko I and sister to Bolesław I Chrobry (r. 992–1025), while Cnut's sister Estrith may have been briefly married to a Rus prince.[52] These political connections may well have been mirrored in trade, if not enabled by it, and, although there is no direct evidence of slaves from the

British Isles being carried along these routes, Adam of Bremen attested slave-trading connections between Danish Zealanders and the Baltic coast in the 1070s.[53]

Slave trading in the first half of the eleventh century also contributed to the networks that continued to connect the British Isles internally and with markets in Francia. The connections illustrated by Warner of Rouen's *Moriuht* have already been discussed, but it is worth emphasising that the events described in this insult poem rely upon the understanding that Scandinavian networks could feasibly see captive men and women trafficked between the British Isles and the Continent. Moriuht's buyers, nuns and later a widow, serve as punchlines for the character's promiscuity, but these sorts of people may not have seemed out of place as slave owners in the early eleventh century.[54] This cross-Channel slave trading is also corroborated by the aforementioned raiding by Lothen and Yrling, who sold English captives in Flanders in 1046. Tolls were levied in London on locals and those foreigners bringing goods from France, Lotharingia, and the Holy Roman Empire in the early eleventh century, and these routes continued to import items such as silk, ivory, quern stones, and wine to the British Isles.[55] Some commercial slave trading along the Rhine may have remained active through the middle of the eleventh century; a set of tolls from Koblenz, copied down in the second half of the eleventh century, charged Jewish traders four *denarii* for each slave (*sclavo*) they purchased there, implying that Christian buyers may not have faced a specific slave-trading tax.[56]

In the second half of the eleventh century the focus of slave trading appears to have shifted westwards to the Irish Sea (see Map 5). This may be related to a number of political factors, such as the dissolution of a united kingdom of England, Denmark, and Norway following the death of Harthacnut in 1042. If captives from the British Isles did filter through slave-trading networks to al-Andalus via France, such trade would also have been crippled by the decline and collapse of the Umayyad Caliphate by 1031. Closer to home, waning interest in slave labour on English estates and in Normandy, combined with a decrease in slave raiding within England, may also have helped to reorient slave trading westwards, where prolific raiding indicates that slaves were still in demand and where close trade connections continued with slaveholding societies in Scandinavia and the North Atlantic. The *Life of Wulfstan*, a Latin translation by William of Malmesbury of an earlier, lost Old English text by Coleman, describes this Irish Sea slave trading operating out of Bristol. The text laments lines of young men and women chained together awaiting sale, including women sold by their owners who had made them pregnant and people sold into slavery by their kin.[57] Despite efforts by Wulfstan, bishop of Worcester, and Lanfranc, archbishop of Canterbury, to persuade William the Conqueror to end slave trading out of England, this Irish Sea trade appears to have endured illicitly for some time. William issued a law forbidding the sale of anyone out of the country before his death in 1087, but Gerald of Wales's *Expugnatio Hibernica* describes a Council of Armagh, held in 1169, in which the Irish deemed it was their purchase of English slaves 'from merchants, robbers, and pirates' that had caused God to punish them with the Norman invasion.[58]

Regardless of destination, however, these sources all suggest that the British Isles played a significant role in northern European slave trading operations in the eleventh century and even into the twelfth. This perspective is partly due to our skewed source material, which is largely English in origin and was either written or heavily influenced by churchmen who viewed the practices of their countrymen as amoral. It is important, however, that the authors consistently point to the English as perpetrators and to external outlets as crucial for driving slaving practices. Annalistic records of raiding in Ireland and Wales suggest that the pool of saleable people was supplemented with captives from these areas. Raiding by the Scots in northern England and by vikings in the Western Isles, Man, and Wales in the last three decades of the eleventh century also prompts speculation about the role of these regions in slave-trading operations when the peoples of the British Isles were otherwise so closely interlinked.[59] Although the evidence of raiding suggests that enslavement declined in the second half of the eleventh century, slave trading continued, albeit probably on a much-reduced scale. Importantly, it adapted to meet changes in demand politically and geographically.

The Viking-Age slave trade in the British Isles was more than simply a viking operation. Raiders from Scandinavia initiated the process of expansion towards large-scale slave trading by incorporating the archipelago into wide-ranging trade networks in which the raiders were also the traders. The peoples of the British Isles became heavily involved in this trade, from the creation of slaves to their sale and transport. The number of references to Scandinavian merchants and raiders is misleading, since in many cases their non-Christian status obscures the presence of Christian buyers and sellers who, in the eyes of ecclesiastical authors, did not pose a threat to the welfare of Christian slaves. Organising the sale and transport of slaves within this region was a complex operation that involved the participation of people from a variety of ethnicities and statuses. The export of enslaved people likewise relied on a range of trade networks, both within the British Isles and beyond. Although it is impossible to know how many people were trafficked, we can assume numbers to have been relatively high throughout the late ninth, tenth, and early eleventh centuries based on the evidence of raiding. Viking trade networks instigated a change from slave trading as an ad hoc solution to a situation in which slaves were goods with predominately economic, not symbolic, associations. Vikings did not introduce slave trading, but the changes they initiated were of enormous significance whose impacts could be felt on networks well into the eleventh century.

Slave trading and Prague

Our perception of Prague as a focal point of slave trading in early medieval Europe results from relatively plentiful contemporary references to such activities there and in the lands under Přemyslid control. The rise of this ducal family in the ninth century and their consolidation of power, accompanied by territorial expansion from the tenth century onwards, facilitated the development of Prague as an administrative centre and market hub. Great Moravia's collapse during the escalation of slaving activity in central Europe may well have created a gap in the market that Přemyslid Bohemia sought to fill. Although evidence of slave trading is fragmentary, when combined with a wealth of circumstantial evidence, Prague and the Přemyslid domain emerge as a bustling regional hub of slaving that probably peaked in the second half of the tenth century but continued through the eleventh.

We know from the Raffelstetten customs tariff that Bohemians were trading slaves on the Bavarian border regularly in the first years of the tenth century. The evidence presented in Chapter 4 suggests that these slaves were probably the victims of smaller-scale raiding against political neighbours rather than any substantial slave-taking operations, but the early date of the text demonstrates that large-scale slave trading did not appear in a vacuum. Prague's market of Malá Strana on the western bank of the river Vltava was only beginning to develop at that time, so merchants dealing in slaves may have found more or wealthier buyers for their wares at the markets along the Danube.[60] Within two to three decades, however, slave trading is visible in Prague, which is unsurprising given the connections between high-status sites and the availability of slaves that we have seen elsewhere.[61] According to a late tenth-century hagiographical text known as the *Legenda Christiani*, the Přemyslid duke Wenceslas was known to purchase boys from the market in Prague for Easter baptisms when no catechumens were readily available; non-Christians such as Polabian Slavs must have been for sale at a moment's notice.[62] A similarly casual reference appears in Ibrāhīm ibn Ya'qūb's account from his visit to Prague from Cordoba in the mid-960s. Ibn Ya'qūb's reason for travel is unclear, but his keen interest in commerce meant that he records slaves for sale alongside horses and gold, and notes that Rus, Hungarian, and other Slavic traders all came to Prague to buy slaves, tin, and furs.[63]

Further sources likewise portray Prague as a growing town in which long-distance slave trading was a known and common practice. The *Crescente fide*, a hagiographical work written before 983, includes a miracle story in which a prisoner was sold to foreign pagans after Wenceslas's intercession freed him from his shackles.[64] This story deploys a recurring trope of Wenceslas as a freer from chains and the pagan buyers feature as a spiritual threat, but the text's date may correspond closely to Ibn Ya'qūb's account, which could serve as corroboration for the literary source. By the final two decades of the tenth century the purchase of Christian slaves by Jews was regular enough to frustrate the second bishop of Prague, Adalbert (982–997).[65] Boleslav II, who was allegedly complicit in these sales to Jews, also issued a charter granting 'decimum hominum captivum' to Břevnov monastery in 993, with this unusual donation suggesting that slave trading was a profitable enterprise in which the Přemyslid dukes themselves had a substantial stake.[66] An eleventh-century rabbinic *responsum*, discussed in more detail below, likewise demonstrates that Jews themselves could be sold as slaves in Prague in the eleventh century to buyers with trade connections as far as Constantinople.

As discussed in Chapter 4, Prague appears to have gained its prominence in slave trading by acting as a market hub for neighbouring slaving operations, which increased in scale and frequency through the tenth century. Archaeological evidence likewise indicates a flow of goods and silver between Bohemia and Poland and Hungary.[67] By the eleventh century, when Bohemians began to engage in their own targeted enslavement operations, there are surprisingly few mentions of slave trading. Captives taken in 1021 and 1039 were explicitly bound for sale into slavery, and by 1077 the Bohemians had some notoriety as slavers, but there are no references to slave trading in Prague such as we see in the tenth century.[68] This may be symptomatic of our surviving sources. Tenth-century hagiography includes slave trading as a facet of life that intersected with ecclesiastical concerns and attempts to sanctify members of the Přemyslid family. These appear alongside unique texts, such as Ibn Yaʿqūb's travelogue and an anomalous charter. For the eleventh century, we are principally reliant on Cosmas's early twelfth-century chronicle, meaning we are beholden to one man's narrative decisions. It is therefore extremely difficult to determine the duration of lucrative slave-trading activities in Prague or in Bohemia more generally, but the eagerness with which Bohemian raiders seem to have pursued captive taking throughout the eleventh century suggests continued links to slaving networks.

Prague's place in these networks, particularly in the tenth century, has been reimagined several times. Josef Šusta, writing in 1899, envisaged a Bohemian slaving system centred on Prague that was primarily export-based through the middle of the tenth century, later becoming an import system when the coalescence of the Czech state and the development of estates necessitated slave labour.[69] František Graus, writing in the 1950s under the Czechoslovak Communist regime, could not ignore the evidence for Prague's involvement in slave trading, despite a strict Marxist interpretation that necessitated the complete disappearance of slavery and the rise of serfdom well before the tenth century. Graus's solution was to attribute this traffic in people to an export system that declined with the development of a Přemyslid state, an idea that dominated studies of unfree labour in the Czech lands until the twenty-first century.[70] Independently of this Czech-language tradition, Charles Verlinden's *L'Esclavage dans l'Europe médiévale* likewise perceived the tenth-century evidence as indicative of an export system monopolised by Jewish merchants moving pagan Slavs west and south into Christian Francia and Byzantium. Enslaved people were then transported to buyers across Europe and into the Middle East by merchants seeking to make a profit selling pagan slaves to non-Christians – a model adapted by Michael McCormick to the ninth century.[71]

Dušan Třeštík took this further, arguing that the income from slave trading in Prague, perpetrated by trans-continental Jewish merchants operating out of the Islamic world, allowed the Přemyslid dukes to consolidate their power and lay the foundation of the Czech state.[72] Constant warfare in the early tenth century prompted by territorial expansion created a steady supply of pagan captives for Jewish merchants, which attracted further trade, so that, by the time of Ibrāhīm ibn Ya'qūb's visit in the 960s, Prague was a booming market town.[73] It has been noted that Třeštík's model is somewhat circular, since a strong ducal retinue would have been necessary to conduct the warfare that created slaves, but slave trading was necessary to support the provisioning and expansion of a ducal retinue.[74] Třeštík also presumed that the supply of slaves preceded the demand, but does not explain why raiders might take so many captives if they did not deploy them on their own lands and there were not yet many buyers.[75] Since Třeštík's publication, however, there has been greater interest in Prague's role for providing slave labour within Přemyslid Bohemia, with Martin Ježek arguing for the likely use of slave labour in iron production in the Prague Basin and Tomáš Petráček remaining open to the presence of slaves on Bohemian estates before the eleventh century in his study of donated people.[76] Chapter 1 has also outlined both direct and circumstantial evidence for the use of enslaved labour on monastic lands and in urban households, which suggests that we cannot overlook the potential role of internal demand in the development of slave trading.

Because most surviving textual evidence relates to the tenth century, any discussion of slave-trading networks in relation to Bohemia is chronologically limited. Historiography has been most interested in connections with the Islamic world in the tenth century, especially with al-Andalus, but there is sufficient evidence to suggest that Prague was well connected to trade routes that radiated outwards in all directions and over a much longer period. Prague served as a central point of exchange on the European continent, as illustrated in Map 4, connecting to neighbouring polities such as Hungary and Poland as well as farther-flung locations such as Iberia, Rus, and Constantinople.

From Bohemia to al-Andalus

We know that al-Andalus used *saqāliba* slaves extensively within its bureaucratic structures in the tenth century, engaging these individuals as high- and low-level administrators, domestic servants, concubines, and soldiers.[77] Czech historians, following Verlinden, have remained confident that westward trade from Prague fed the significant demand for Slavic slaves in al-Andalus.[78] This sort of trade route was acknowledged by Ibn Hawqal, an Arab geographer writing in the late tenth century, when he recorded that Andalusian raiders obtained these slaves from the northern parts of the Slavic lands.[79] Ibn Hawqal was clearly not well informed about who supplied slaves, but he shows that connections between al-Andalus and central Europe were known to contemporaries in other parts of the Islamic world.[80] The penitential *Někotoraja Zapověd* suggests that connections with al-Andalus influenced slave trading in Prague, given its punishment for the castration of children for sale.[81] The raiding of churches and monasteries, such as the one on Zeitz in 977, could also hint at links to the Islamic world; the literate, educated boys who lived there were precisely the kind of slaves most highly sought after, especially after castration.

The imagined logistics of such trans-European slave-trading routes are tied up with discussions of the merchants who might have facilitated them. Verlinden places the responsibility squarely on the shoulders of far-ranging Jewish merchants, an idea that has featured heavily in subsequent historiography based on mention of Jewish merchants in Ibn Ya'qūb's account from the 960s and in the

Life of Adalbert's reference to Jewish buyers several decades later. Třeštík has gone so far as to label these as Radhanites, but these enigmatic merchants known from eighth- and ninth-century texts may not have operated in Europe by the time of Ibn Ya'qūb's trip to Prague.[82] Michael Toch's arguments regarding Jewish involvement in trans-European slave trading have already been touched on for Great Moravia, and they are certainly relevant to tenth- and eleventh-century Bohemia. Most early medieval sources used to prove a heavy Jewish involvement in slave trading have been misinterpreted or have nothing to do with Jews.[83] Verdun has classically been seen as a key location in Jewish slave trading to al-Andalus based on a claim by Liutprand of Cremona that boys were castrated in Verdun by merchants for sale to Spain, but Clément Venco's re-evaluation of ninth- and tenth-century evidence clearly demonstrates that visible Verdun merchants moving through this Islamic polity were Christians and that there was not even a Jewish community in Verdun until the twelfth century.[84] Enough Christian slaves were purchased by Jews in Prague in the late tenth century for Adalbert to see such trading as a grave concern, but this episode exemplifies the Church's extreme distaste for such transactions on any scale, akin to Wulfstan's polemic on the sale of Christians to heathens only a few years later. It is not clear whether Jewish buyers were always the career merchants mentioned by Ibn Ya'qūb; a small Jewish community existed in Prague in the tenth century, meaning that Jewish purchasers probably included those seeking household servants.[85] This seems to have been the context for the events of 1124 as related by Cosmas, in which the duke Vladislav redeemed all Christians enslaved by Jewish owners.[86] Adalbert's complaint, therefore, should not be taken as proof that Jews were the predominant slave traders in Prague.

We should not place the responsibility for trans-European slave-trading networks on the shoulders of Jewish merchants, but there were certainly long-distance connections facilitated by Jewish communities across the continent. The correspondence of Hasdai ibn Shaprut and Joseph, king of Khazaria, indicates the role of prominent Jewish men in linking east central Europe and al-Andalus diplomatically, and rulers in central and eastern Europe seeking to communicate with powerful Islamic states may have found it easier to identify a local Hebrew translator than an Arabic one.[87] Ibn

Shaprut, a rabbi and administrator at the court of ʿAbd al-Rahmān III in the middle of the tenth century, relied on the assistance of two Jewish messengers from the king of *Gebalim* to take his letter to their king, who would see it carried to Hungary and onwards until it reached Khazaria.[88] *Gebalim* has not been conclusively identified, but Dušan Třeštík has made a strong case for it being Prague based on both Hebrew and central European toponymic traditions in the early Middle Ages and geographical information provided by Ibn Shaprut.[89] This possible connection hints that Ibrāhīm ibn Yaʿqūb's visit to Prague in the 960s may have been for the purpose of shoring up diplomatic and trade connections with a known polity. Such a motivation would speak to Prague's rapid growth into a significant market in less than 50 years and the explosion of slaving activity in east central Europe. It may also not be a coincidence that the collapse of the Umayyad Caliphate in al-Andalus in the first half of the eleventh century corresponds not only to the disappearance of Slavic slaves there but also to a decline in Jewish merchant activity.[90]

Discussion of a Prague–Cordoba slave trading route has often relied upon the assumption that merchants, usually Jewish, moved large caravans of enslaved people and other goods overland across the European continent via Verdun to al-Andalus.[91] Liutprand of Cremona's mention of castration operations in Verdun does not specify Jews or Slavs, only that the boys could be sold at great profit.[92] There are no surviving mentions of such slave caravans moving across Europe, just as there are no records of the slave revolts that would surely accompany the movement of large groups of enslaved people across thousands of miles of roads and rivers in areas with a substantial textual record.[93] Viking trade along the 'northern arc' suggests that, even when the archaeological footprint of long-distance trade is highly visible, as with dirhams, it does not illustrate a direct, continuous route – only corridors of greater and lesser importance. We should consider that slave trading from Prague followed similarly branching patterns in which groups of people operating in smaller trading spheres ultimately distributed enslaved people to major urban or market hubs as well as regional points of lesser demand.

In re-evaluating these networks, it is worth examining who exactly traded slaves in Prague. We know from Ibrāhīm ibn Yaʿqūb's account that the market was frequented by merchants from central and eastern Europe: Rus and Slavs (*saqāliba*) from Cracow, and Hungarians, Jews, and Muslims from Hungary.[94] Cracow was, at this date, a Přemyslid town bordering Piast territory, and recent scholarship has emphasised the mounting circumstantial evidence for slave-trading connections between the increasingly powerful Piast state in the second half of the tenth century and Přemyslid Prague. By the 960s the Piasts may have already been heavily involved in slave trading eastwards; dirham hoards in Greater Poland indicate that inflows of silver began in earnest in the 930s and ballooned in the 940s, coinciding with the depopulation of areas around the river Obra, just west of the core Piast territory, and the destruction of hill forts that have been dendrochronologically dated to the middle of the tenth century.[95] Such slave-trading activity may have been the source of Mieszko's impressive wealth in the mid-960s, as described by Ibn Ya'qūb, but a reliance on such a precarious source of silver means that, as eastern imports of dirhams dwindled through the 960s and 970s, the Piast ruler must have desperately sought new outlets for obtaining and selling captives.[96]

As we have seen in Chapter 4, around this time Mieszko began to engage in serious raiding and captive taking northwards towards the Baltic and across the river Oder into Frankish and Frankish-allied territory. In 965 he married Dobrava, the daughter of the Přemyslid duke Boleslav I, and sometime between the mid-960s and the 970s either Boleslav I or his son Boleslav II began minting silver coins. The earliest examples of these coins are found not in Bohemia but in Greater Poland and Silesia, alongside German coinage that probably travelled to the Piast realm via Bohemia. This has led Marek Jankowiak to hypothesise that Přemyslid coinage was minted in response to the demand from silver-hungry Piasts already accustomed to receiving money in exchange for enslaved people via eastern trade networks.[97] It seems very likely that Piast followers were included amongst Ibn Ya'qūb's *saqāliba* traders who exchanged their captives in Prague, and that these captives were *saqāliba* who ultimately ended up in al-Andalus. This mid-tenth-century network of slaving, then, did not start in Bohemia but, rather, to the east and northwest, with the capture of Slavs by Piast raiders.[98] The substantial numbers of Bohemian deniers minted in the second half of the tenth and first half of the eleventh centuries that were deposited in hoards in Gotland and Scandinavia, as well as one of Boleslav II in Iceland, raise the questions of whether Polish slaving was exclusively sustained by raiding, and whether a tributary of the northern arc might have diverted some British and Irish slaves into central Europe via Baltic networks.[99] Certainly, English coinage believed to be related to Danegeld payments in the late tenth and early eleventh centuries has been found in substantial quantities along the Baltic coast.[100]

Ibn Yaʿqūb does not include western merchants in his description of the Prague market, which may be a consequence of their obviousness to him given that he had managed to travel to Prague from the Holy Roman Empire. Their absence is curious, however, in the context of his interest in the people trading goods so highly valued in al-Andalus and in the rarity of German coins in Bohemia before the 960s.[101] Any Frankish merchants in Prague must have been trading predominantly with goods rather than cash, and they may not have been seeking out slaves there in significant numbers. Slave trading may have largely bypassed East Francia through the first half of the tenth century, focusing instead on routes that moved eastwards towards Kyiv and southeast along the Danube. This is consistent with Eduardo Manzano Moreno's argument that al-Andalus was not supplied with enormous numbers of Slavic slaves until the middle of the tenth century, when new trade routes opened across western Europe.[102] We should also consider that Bohemia may have had trade links with Venice that operated along routes similar to those from Moravia in the ninth century, since this port remained a hub of trans-Mediterranean slave trading in the tenth century and later.[103] The Samanid coins that Ibn Yaʿqūb found so astonishing in Mainz do indicate some eastward trade links, but without providing evidence of any more concrete connections to slave trading in Prague or elsewhere.[104]

It may be that slaves moved westwards from Prague through Verdun, which was seen in western historiography as a primary 'castration centre', and thus a staging point for long-distance slave trading. Another centre was known, however, close to Pechina near the southern coast of al-Andalus, and allegedly operated by Jewish merchants.[105] The *Někotoraja Zapověd* and those ninth-century treaties from Venice mentioned in the previous chapter indicate that other major market centres provided venues for castration. One eleventh-century author attributed operations on the frontier with the Christian kingdoms of northern Iberia to both Jews and Muslims, and Venetian and Bohemian sources as well as Venco's work on Verdun suggest active Christian involvement in castrations.[106] Authors writing in Arabic in the ninth and tenth centuries agree that most *saqāliba* eunuchs entered the rest of the Islamic world via al-Andalus, emphasising the critical importance of Iberian connections to central Europe.[107] Nevertheless, for slave trading via Verdun in the tenth century, it may be worth considering riverine connections northwards to the British Isles. The locations of other castration centres indicate that sea routes probably also played a role in the importation of slaves from east central Europe. Venice had closer links to the slave-trading networks of the eastern Mediterranean, but other ports in Italy and Francia probably served as the points of direct connection with al-Andalus.[108]

Any further claims about westward overland routes in the second half of the tenth century or the eleventh would require heavy speculation. Prague probably fed into a trade network made up of numerous stages, as Alice Rio has similarly argued for slave trading on the Carolingian frontier in the ninth century.[109] This would account for the scarcity of dirhams in the Czech lands and explain why slave caravans are invisible in the source material. If overland routes did exist, shorter distances would have meant merchants could make trips more frequently and with fewer enslaved people alongside a variety of other goods. Such a scenario still situates Bohemia, Přemyslid power, and the Prague market within the larger narrative of European slave trading and the relationship between Christendom and the Islamic world without taking the evidence (or lack thereof) for granted. Slavic slaves filtering westwards through numerous markets would also mirror the evidence for northern Europe in the Viking Age and suggest that early medieval slave trading tended not to rely on long-haul caravans operated by a select group of merchants. It seems more likely that Prague, or Přemyslid Bohemia more generally, was a bottleneck in east–west slave-trading routes rather than the starting point of a direct route.

All roads lead to Prague

The primacy of a Prague–Cordoba slave-trading route in the historiography has tended to obscure connections between Přemyslid territory and other focal points of demand. There is, in fact, more direct evidence that Prague slave trading fed into major eastern European networks than there is for westward trade. This is not to argue against the importance of east central Europe in supplying the enslaved Slavs of the Islamic world, albeit via routes that are frustratingly unclear. Rather, the evidence of eastward trade emphasises the importance of Přemyslid Bohemia in the operation of several major slave-trading corridors in the tenth and eleventh centuries.

Unlike his vague mention of *saqāliba* traders in Prague, Ibrāhīm ibn Ya'qūb is very clear about the presence of the Rus from Cracow there, which may have been their nearest staging point on a longer trade route. The route between Prague and Kyiv had also been opened no more than a decade before this, which would have facilitated travel for those looking to purchase slaves in either location.[110] The overland movement of slaves eastward into Rus may not have been substantial, however. Initially written in the early twelfth century, the *Russian Primary Chronicle* recalls valuable items moving down the Danube from Bohemia to Pereyaslavec (also Presthlavitza), a town in present-day Romania. In reported speech, the ruler Svyatoslav referred to the Rus trade:

> I do not care to remain in Kiev, but should prefer to live in Pereyaslavets on the Danube, since that is the centre of my realm where all riches are concentrated: gold, silks, wine, and various fruits from Greece, silver and horses from Hungary and Bohemia, and from Rus furs, wax, honey, and slaves.[111]

The *Primary Chronicle* would have us believe that this description should be placed in 969, but the prosperity the author describes is more likely to reflect the situation after 1000.[112] If slaves were included among the goods moving eastwards to Kyiv from Prague, they were not remembered in significant numbers, and may represent only a minor tributary of Rus slave trading. The flow of goods down the Danube by Bohemian merchants echoes the traffic attested in Raffelstetten customs tariff in the early tenth century, which did include slaves.[113] Shackles discovered in the lower Danube region have been taken as evidence for the movement of Bohemian slaves, but this would have been only one potential reason for their use, and perhaps not even the most likely.[114] Samanid dirhams continued to make their way to Rus in substantial quantities through the 980s and thence to Greater Poland, suggesting a continued interest by the Rus in sourcing western Slavic slaves for eastern Islamic markets until the inflow stopped between *c.* 985 and 1000.[115] Prague slave trading may well have been connected by Rus traders to the Caspian Sea; this would have been a short-lived enterprise of only a few decades, but that would have been long enough to aid in boosting Prague's economy and renown as a slave-trading hub.

If a slave-trading connection with Rus was broken in the late tenth century, where might traders have trafficked the slaves purchased in Prague in the late tenth and eleventh centuries, when the Bohemians themselves were becoming deeply invested in slaving? Ibn Yaʿqūb's account also suggests a route operating between Prague and Hungary that involved a range of traders.[116] These merchants are difficult to trace archaeologically for the tenth century and earlier, since coins were not minted until the early eleventh century under the rule of Stephen, the first king of Hungary. Instead, Hungarians probably purchased their slaves with largely untraceable livestock and consumables or long-distance items such as Byzantine silk and precious metals. Moravia's location on the border of Hungarian territory and connections to the Danube via the river Morava suggest that it may have been an important region for slave trading, either under Přemyslid oversight from the second half of the tenth century or during its period of Piast control in the first decades of the eleventh century. The discovery of a tenth- and eleventh-century market at Kostice-Zadní hrúd, Czech Republic, underlines the importance and volume of trade between the Přemyslid and developing Hungarian polities as Přemyslid influence in Moravia grew. The site is located along the Morava, and the coin finds, more than 100, include a great many single finds reflecting incidental loss. The coins date from 950 onwards and represent mints in Bavaria, Hungary, Austria, Bohemia, and Moravia.[117] Additionally, enormous amounts of lead, fragments of silver and bronze, and even a fragment of a Scandinavian-style folding balance have been discovered in recent excavations, clearly establishing Kostice's role as a trading settlement and hinting at the non-monetary items that may have been exchanged for slaves.[118] Jiří Macháček believes that

Kostice may represent a customs house along a trade route from Regensburg along the rivers Danube and Morava. This route, and Kostice along with it, would have developed with the pacification of this area following the Battle of Lechfeld in 955 and the later formation of the Hungarian kingdom.[119] It may have been Kostice or other undiscovered sites like it that enabled the episode noted by Cosmas in which Poles in Moravia were captured during the Přemyslid reconquest of that territory before 1021 and then sold into Hungary and beyond.[120] We should also consider the potential for slave trading in developing Moravian towns such as Brno, Znojmo, and Olomouc, which were key to Přemyslid administration in the region.

Hungary's own use of enslaved labour and its connections with the Mediterranean may have played a role in continued captive taking by Přemyslid and Bohemian raiders well into the middle of the eleventh century, when demand for Slavic slaves in Iberia had declined and royal interests in the Holy Roman Empire had already begun to eschew slave trading.[121] They may also have been the motivation behind Břetislav's capture of Poles on his campaign in 1039, whose sale as 'brute animals' was condemned by the papal Curia, as well as the captive taking noted by Bernold of Constans during the Bohemian campaign in Swabia in 1077 at the behest of Henry IV.[122] Magyar and Rus trade connections seem to have been established in the second half of the tenth century and were certainly in place in the eleventh, and Rus merchants may have travelled through the Carpathian Basin to reach Prague.[123] These links may well have supported the bulk of Bohemian slave trading as westward demand declined, then collapsed, in the first third of the eleventh century.

Slave-trading connections between Byzantium and Prague, albeit with unidentified intermediaries, is also attested by an eleventh-century rabbinic *responsum* that preserves the story of two Jewish brothers from Przemysil in Poland, sent by relatives to stay with a 'non-Jew' in the countryside during a period of civil unrest.[124] When peace was restored, the relatives sought to track down the boys, only to be told that one had died. The living brother returned to Przemysil, married, and died soon afterwards. Only after his death was it discovered that the other brother was alive in Constantinople, having been sold to a Greek or Byzantine Jew in

Prague by the non-Jew tasked with caring for the boys. It is worth highlighting that someone in Poland knew they could easily sell a boy in Prague, and that a Jewish person was sold by a (probable) Christian. Direct connections between Byzantium and Bohemia also throw further light on the *Nekotoraja Zapověd*'s prohibitions on castration, given than enslaved eunuchs were still in demand in Constantinople, albeit to a lesser degree than in the Islamic world.

Archaeological evidence of connections between the Czech lands and Byzantium is not common, suggesting that contacts were more often indirect. Finds of Byzantine coins in the Czech lands from the tenth and eleventh centuries are rare, but chance finds of two tenth-century gold coins from the hill fort of Kozojedy-Dřevíč and near the Slavnikid seat at Libice, as well as a bronze follis dated 970–1092 from Týnský dvůr in the Old Town area of Prague, all suggest ongoing diplomatic and trade links.[125] These may have operated at least partly via Hungary, since the Libice coin is clipped – normally only a feature of Byzantine coins found in the Carpathian Basin.[126] Connections between Hungary and Byzantium and Rus attested in art and archaeology of the late tenth and eleventh centuries may have served to link Bohemian slave trading with demand in these polities.[127] Despite their scarcity today, Byzantine coins must have been familiar enough to the Přemyslids and their immediate trade partners for the dukes Boleslav II and Jaromir to imitate the iconography of contemporary Byzantine gold coins on their own silver issues.[128] Four fragmentary silver coins were also included in a hoard deposited near Kelč in the northern part of Moravia in the eleventh century. The hoard included substantial numbers of coins from across the known world: principally German territories, but also Italy, Hungary, France, central Asia, and even five English pennies of Æthelred II.[129] Numismatic evidence is supported by finds of Byzantine silk in Bohemian elite inhumation burials, attesting the importance of high-value transactions.[130] Routes that operated via Hungary to Rus and Byzantium are probably what sustained slaving in Přemyslid territory well beyond the collapse of the Umayyad Caliphate in Iberia.

Prague therefore appears to have been a key node in slave-trading networks that crossed the European continent in multiple directions. Most of the evidence establishes trade connections with neighbouring peoples, but there are indications that Prague's linkages extended further afield. Long-distance slave trading that funnelled central European slaves via Prague to the Islamic world may have been fuelled by Prague's connections with other major trade hubs in Francia, Constantinople, and Rus, rather than by any direct links over thousands of miles. Prague was undoubtedly a significant staging point for the movement of slaves; it may have been the gateway through which captives taken by Polish and Bohemian raiders entered core trade routes in western Europe, along the Danube corridor, and even into Rus. Like any network node, however, Prague owed its success to its position within a constellation of market hubs and to the diverse traders who moved between them. It was not driven exclusively by far-ranging Jewish merchants, as has previously been claimed, and, as also evidenced by the raiding practices discussed in Chapter 4, did not exist solely to traffic non-Christian slaves to the Islamic world. As in the British Isles, a wide range of people participated in slave trading, which resulted in equally diverse origins of those slaves.

Notes

1 Třeštík, '"Veliké město Slovanů jménem Praha"', p. 62 (30,000 to 35,000 sold in Prague during the reign of Boleslav I alone). Marek Jankowiak, 'Tracing the Saqaliba: slave trade and the archaeology of the Slavic lands in the tenth century', in Biermann and Jankowiak (eds), *The Archaeology of Slavery*, p. 166 (100,000 captives in the ninth and tenth centuries). For a more conservative approach, see McCormick, *Origins of the European Economy*, pp. 772–5.

2 McCormick, *Origins of the European Economy*, pp. 606–13.

3 *Vita Findani*, p. 503.

4 Hadley and Richards, 'Winter camp', 36–42. John Sheehan, 'The *longphort* in Viking Age Ireland', *Acta Archaeologica*, 79:1 (2008), 287.

5 Jane Kershaw, 'Gold as a means of exchange in Scandinavian England', in Jane Kershaw and Gareth Williams (eds), *Silver, Butter, Cloth: Monetary and Social Economies in the Viking Age* (Oxford: Oxford University Press, 2018), pp. 245–6.

6 *Vita Findani*, p. 503.

7 Rimbert, *Vita Anskarii*, pp. 72–3.

8 *Landnámabók*, §6, p. 19.

9 Tom Horne, *A Viking Market Kingdom in Ireland and Britain* (London: Routledge, 2021), espec. chaps 6–8. On the crucial but invisible role of slavery, pp. 238–40.

10 Jane Kershaw et al., 'The scale of dirham imports to the Baltic in the ninth century: new evidence from archaeometric analyses of early Viking-Age silver', *Fornvännen*, 116 (2021), 185–204.

11 Matthew C. Delvaux, Transregional slave networks of the Northern Arc, 700–900 CE (PhD thesis, Boston College, 2019), pp. 158–82. For glass production in the Islamic world, see Julian Henderson, 'The politics of production, glass provenance and social context on the early Islamic silk roads', *Journal of Islamic Archaeology*, 8:2 (2021), 203–37.

12 See recent discussion in Gruszczyńsky, Jankowiak, and Shepard (eds), *Viking-Age Trade*; and in Biermann and Jankowiak (eds), *The Archaeology of Slavery*.

13 For a summary, see Sawyer, *Kings and Vikings*, pp. 85–91.

14 *The Old English History of the World: An Anglo-Saxon Rewriting of Orosius*, ed. and trans. Malcolm Godden (Cambridge, MA: Harvard University Press, 2016), pp. 44–5.

15 Søren Michael Sindbæk, 'The small world of the Vikings: networks in early medieval communication and exchange', *Norwegian Archaeological Review*, 40:1 (2007), 59–74.

16 Andrzej Buko, '"Tribal" societies and the rise of early medieval trade', in Henning (ed.), *Post-Roman Towns, Trade*, i, p. 437.

17 Csete Katona, *Vikings of the Steppe: Scandinavians, Rus', and the Turkic World (c. 750–1050)* (London: Routledge, 2022), pp. 69–72.

18 Jankowiak, 'Dirham flows', pp. 116–22. The use of hoarded dirhams as chronological markers of exchange is complicated by possible large-scale silver recycling in Scandinavia. Kershaw et al., 'The scale of dirham imports', 198–9.

19 Vésteinsson, 'Ethnicity and class', pp. 506–7. Sunken-feature buildings dated by volcanic layers to *c.* 870–940 were also discovered at the nearby site of Hrísheimar. Thomas H. McGovern and Orri Vésteinsson, 'The peopling of Iceland', *Norwegian Archaeological Review*, 45:2 (2012), 211.

20 See p. 39, n. 74.

21 I Edward §1–1.1, in Liebermann (ed.), *Die Gesetze*, i, pp. 156–7. II Æthelstan §12 and 13.1, in Liebermann (ed.), *Die Gesetze*, i, pp. 156–8. George Molyneaux, *Formation of the English Kingdom in the 10th Century* (Oxford: Oxford University Press, 2015), p. 106.

22 Michael Kenny, 'The geographical distribution of Irish Viking-Age coin hoards', *Proceedings of the Royal Irish Academy*, 87C (1987), 514–15. For the association between hoard depositions and political alliances between the Irish kingdoms and Viking Dublin, see Emer Purcell and John Sheehan, 'Viking Dublin: enmities, alliances

and the cold gleam of silver', in D. M. Hadley and Letty ten Harkel (eds), *Everyday Life in Viking-Age Towns: Social Approaches to Towns in England and Ireland, c. 800–1100* (Oxford: Oxbow, 2013), pp. 35–60.

23 Valante, 'Dublin's economic relations', pp. 69–83.

24 This has been demonstrated for the eleventh century by Ellis, 'Perceptions of the slave trade in Britain and Ireland'.

25 Kenny, 'Geographical distribution', 514.

26 Richard Hall, 'A check-list of Viking-Age coin finds from Ireland', *Ulster Journal of Archaeology*, 36/37 (1973/74), 71–86. Kruse and Tate, 'XRF analysis', p. 75.

27 Rory Naismith, 'Islamic coins from early medieval England', *The Numismatic Chronicle*, 165 (2005), 206. David Metcalf believed that the comprehensive reuse of dirhams was probably responsible for drastically changing the composition of the stock metal in the second half of the tenth century: 'The monetary history of England in the tenth century viewed in the perspective of the eleventh century', in M. A. S. Blackburn (ed.), *Anglo-Saxon Monetary History: Essays in Memory of Michael Dolley* (Leicester: Leicester University Press, 1986), p. 136.

28 Mark Redknap, 'Viking-Age settlement in Wales and the evidence from Llanbedrgoch', in J. Hines et al. (eds), *Land, Sea and Home* (Leeds: Maney, 2004), pp. 139–75.

29 Katie A. Hemer, 'To tread the paths, and traverse the moors: investigating slavery in early medieval western Britain', in Biermann and Jankowiak (eds), *The Archaeology of Slavery*, pp. 45–6.

30 Courtney Helen Buchanan, 'Scandinavians in Strathclyde: multiculturalism, material culture and manufactured identities in the Viking Age', in Anna Ritchie (ed.), *Historic Bute: Land and People* (Edinburgh: Scottish Society for Northern Studies), pp. 17–32. Adrián Maldonado, *Crucible of Nations: Scotland from Viking Age to Medieval Kingdom* (Edinburgh: National Museums Scotland, 2021), pp. 86–90.

31 Maldonado, *Crucible of Nations*, pp. 89, 131. He also notes that nearly all Scottish dirham finds, single and hoarded, were minted 895/6–941/2.

32 Raffield, 'The slave markets of the Viking world'.

33 *Laxdæla Saga,* pp. 63–6.

34 FA, s. a. 867, p. 121. Ann Christys argues that this episode is quasi-historical given the nature of the Fragmentary Annals, but I see no reason to doubt that such an event occurred. Ann Christys, *Vikings in the South: Voyages to Iberia and the Mediterranean* (London: Bloomsbury, 2015), p. 57.

35 Naismith, 'Islamic coins', 198–9.

36 Christys, *Vikings in the South*, p. 6.

37 Agobard of Lyon to Louis the Pious, ed. E. Dummler, MGH, Epistolae 5 (Hanover, 1899), pp. 183–5. Liutprand of Cremona, *Antapodosis*, ed. J. Becker, MGH, SS rer. Germ. 41 (Hanover, 1915), pp. 155–6. Trade between Verdun and al-Andalus is attested in a number of other sources: Clément Venco, 'Par-delà la frontière: marchands et commerce d'esclaves entre la Gaule carolingienne et al-Andalus (VIIIe–Xe siècles)', in Sébastien Gasc et al. (eds), *Las fronteras pirenaicas en la Edad Media (siglos VI–XV)* (Zaragoza: University of Zaragoza, 2018), pp. 12–13.

38 Valante, 'Castrating monks', pp. 174–87.

39 Warner of Rouen, *Moriuht*, pp. 76–7, 82–3, 90–1. Moriuht may have been a real literary rival to Warner: F. P. C. de Jong, 'Rival schoolmasters in early eleventh-century Rouen with special reference to the poetry of Warner of Rouen (fl. 996–1027)', *Anglo-Norman Studies*, XXXIX (2016), 45–63.

40 ASC E, s. a. 1046[a], pp. 78–9.

41 Naismith, 'Islamic coins', 198–9.

42 Constable, *Trade and Traders*, p. 42 n. 91.

43 Fontaine, 'Archbishop Wulfstan', pp. 156–63.

44 Andrew Rabin (ed. and trans.), *The Political Writings of Archbishop Wulfstan of York* (Manchester: Manchester University Press, 2015), p. 43.

45 Pelteret, *Slavery in Early Mediaeval England*, pp. 89–101. Jurasinski, *The Old English Penitentials*, pp. 109–17. For discussion of Wulfstan's acceptance of other forms (and victims) of slave trading, see Jurasinski, 'Old English penitentials and the law of slavery', pp. 110–12.

46 Wulfstan of York, *Sermo Lupi*, pp. 51–2.

47 Wulfstan of York, *Sermo Lupi*, pp. 53–5.

48 Wulfstan of York, *Sermo Lupi*, pp. 57–8.

49 V Æthelred §2, p. 238. VI Æthelred §9, p. 250. VII Æthelred §5, in Liebermann (ed.), *Die* Gesetze, i, p. 261. II Cnut §3, p. 310.

50 William of Malmesbury, *Gesta Regum Anglorum*, ed. R. A. B. Mynors, R. M. Thomson, and M. Winterbottom, 2 vols (Oxford: Oxford University Press, 1998), i, p. 362.

51 William also appears to have thought of Cnut as a poor Christian early in his reign, which may have influenced the inclusion of this scandalous story. Elaine Treharne, *Living through Conquest: The Politics of Early English, 1020–1220* (Oxford: Oxford University Press, 2012), pp. 38–40.

52 Timothy Bolton, *Cnut the Great* (New Haven, CT: Yale University Press, 2017), pp. 32–3.

53 Adam of Bremen, *Gesta Hammaburgensis Ecclesiae Pontificum*, ed. Bernhard Schmeidler, MGH, SS. Rer. Germ. 2 (Hanover, 1917), pp. 233–4.
54 Warner of Rouen, *Moriuht*, pp. 78–9, 82–5.
55 IV Æthelred §2–2.8, in Liebermann (ed.), *Die Gesetze*, pp. 232, 234. Stéphane Lebecq and Alban Gautier, 'Routeways between England and the Continent in the tenth century', in David Rollason, Conrad Leyser, and Hannah Williams (eds), *England and the Continent in the Tenth Century: Studies in Honour of Wilhelm Levison (1876–1947)* (Turnhout: Brepols, 2010), pp. 17–34. Valante, 'Dublin's economic relations', pp. 69–83.
56 *Die Urkunden Heinrichs IV*, part 3, ed. Alfred Gawlik, MGH, Diplomata (Hanover, 1978), p. 751.
57 William of Malmesbury, *Vita Wulfstani*, p. 100.
58 'a mercatoribus quam predonibus atque piratis', Gerald of Wales, *Expugnatio Hibernica*, p. 70. For William's law, see Ten Articles of William I §9, in Liebermann (ed.), *Die Gesetze*, i, p. 488. The text is probably a twelfth-century compilation of decrees issued by William: Patrick Wormald, *The Making of English Law: King Alfred to the Twelfth Century* (London: Blackwell, 1999), pp. 402–3.
59 ASC E, s. a. 1079, p. 92; s. a. 1091, p. 102; s. a. 1093, p. 103. *Cronica Regum Mannie and Insularum*, ed. and trans. George Broderick, 2nd edn (Douglas: Manx National Heritage, 1995), s. a. 1056 for 1079, f. 33r. BT, s. a. 1089 for 1091, p. 18.
60 Charvát, *Emergence of the Bohemian State*, p. 139. Prague became the Přemyslids' primary seat only in the late ninth century. V. Huml, Z. Dragoun, and R. Novy, 'Der archäologische Beitrag zur Problematik der Entwicklung Prags in der Zeit vom 9. bis zur Mitte des 13. Jahrhunderts und die Erfassung der Ergebnisse der historisch-archäologischen Erforschung Prags', *Zeitschrift für Archäologie des Mittelalters*, 18/19 (1990), 37–8.
61 See p. 150.
62 *Legenda Christiani*, pp. 66–8. Twentieth-century studies hotly debated the dating of this text, but many scholars now accept a tenth-century date of authorship. David Kalhous, *Anatomy of a Duchy: The Political and Ecclesiastical Structures of Early Přemyslid Bohemia* (Leiden: Brill, 2012), pp. 185–93. David Kalhous, Legenda Christiani *and Modern Historiography* (Leiden: Brill, 2015).
63 'Ibrāhīm ibn Ya'qūb', pp. 164–5.
64 Jaroslav Ludvíkovský, 'Nově zjištěný rukopis legendy *Crescente fide* a jeho význam pro datování Kristiána', *Listy Filologické*, 81 (1958), 62.
65 *Life of Saint Adalbert*, pp. 124–7.

66 CDB I, no. 375, p. 348. The unusual donation may itself indicate authenticity of the gift. Petr Charvát, *Boleslav II: Sjednotitel českého státu* (Prague: Vyšehrad, 2004), p. 82.
67 J. Machula, 'Foreign items and outside influences in the material culture of tenth-century Bohemia', *Annual of Medieval Studies at the CEU*, 8 (2002), 65–88. Jankowiak, 'Two systems of trade', pp. 143–4.
68 Cosmas of Prague, *Chronicle of the Czechs*, pp. 138, 174. Bernold of Constans, *Chronicon*, p. 414.
69 Šusta, 'Otroctví a velkostatek v Čechách', 77.
70 Graus, *Dějiny venkovského lidu*, i, pp. 186–7.
71 Verlinden, *L'Esclavage dans l'Europe médiévale*, i, pp. 211–25. McCormick, *Origins of the European Economy*, pp. 759–77.
72 This idea was first exposited, albeit briefly, by Josef Žemlička, 'Das "Reich" der bohmischen Boleslavs und die Krise an der Jahrtausendwende', *Archeologické Rozhledy*, 47 (1995), 270–1.
73 Třeštík, '"Veliké město Slovanů jménem Praha"', p. 54.
74 Štefan, 'Slavery and slave trade', p. 137.
75 Třeštík, '"Veliké město Slovanů jménem Praha"', p. 54.
76 Ježek, 'A mass for the slaves', pp. 623–42. Petráček, *Power and Exploitation*, pp. 52–3.
77 Crone, *Slaves on Horses*, pp. 74–81.
78 Verlinden, *L'Esclavage dans l'Europe médiévale*, pp. 220–1. Třeštík, '"Veliké město Slovanů jménem Praha"', p. 62. Žemlička, 'Das "Reich" der bohmischen Boleslavs', 270–1.
79 'Ibn Hawqal on the trade in eunuchs 988', in Lunde and Stone (eds), *Arab Travellers*, pp. 173–4.
80 See also Mas'ūdī, writing from Egypt in 956, who attests the movement of furs from far northeastern Europe to Francia and al-Andalus, and from there to the Maghrib: 'Mas'ūdī on the fur trade 956', in Lunde and Stone (eds), *Arab Travellers*, pp. 160–1.
81 *Někotoraja zapověd*, §41, p. 45.
82 Třeštík, '"Veliké město Slovanů jménem Praha"', pp. 52–3. Nazmi, *Commercial Relations*, p. 128.
83 See pp. 162–3, nn. 50–51.
84 Venco, 'Par-delà la frontière', pp. 12–15.
85 Peter Hilsch, 'Die Juden in Böhmen und Mähren im Mittelalter und die Ersten Privilegien', in F. Seibt (ed.), *Die Juden in den böhmischen Ländern* (Munich: R. Oldenburg Verlag, 1983), p. 15.
86 See p. 44, n. 94.
87 Norman Golb and Omeljan Pritsak (eds), *Khazarian Hebrew Documents of the Tenth Century* (Ithaca, NY: Cornell University Press, 1982), pp. 83–4.

88 Joseph, king of Khazaria, to Hasdai ibn Shaprut, trans. J. R. Marcus (ed. and trans.), *The Jew in the Medieval World: A Sourcebook, 315–1791* (Cincinnati: Hebrew Union College Press, 1999), p. 256. A. Kaplony, 'Routen, Anschlussrouten, Handelshorizonte im Brief von Hasdāy b. Šaprūt an den hazarischen König', in P. Charvát and J. Prosecký (eds), *Ibrahim ibn Ya'qub at-Turtushi: Christianity, Islam and Judaism Meet in East-Central Europe, c. 800–1300 AD* (Prague: Czech Academy of Sciences, 1996), pp. 140–68. For some discussion of logistics, see Norman Golb, *The Caliph's Favourite: New Light on Manuscript Sources of Hasdai ibn Shaprut of Cordova* (Chicago, IL: Oriental Institute of the University of Chicago, 2011), pp. 1–13.

89 Třeštík, '"Veliké město Slovanů jménem Praha"', pp. 56–8.

90 Olivia Remie Constable, 'Spain and Mediterranean slavery: the medieval slave trade as an aspect of Muslim–Christian relations', in Scott L. Waugh and Peter D. Diehl (eds), *Christendom and Its Discontents: Exclusion, Persecution, and Rebellion, 1000–1500* (Cambridge: Cambridge University Press, 1996), pp. 268–9.

91 Verlinden, *L'Esclavage dans l'Europe médiévale*, i, pp. 222–3. Třeštík, '"Veliké město Slovanů jménem Praha"', p. 52.

92 Liutprand of Cremona, *Antapodosis*, pp. 155–6.

93 For the better-documented and much larger-scale trans-Atlantic slave trade, 392 revolts were recorded aboard slave ships over two centuries. David Richardson, 'Shipboard revolts, African authority, and the Atlantic slave trade', *The William and Mary Quarterly*, 58:1 (2001), 73.

94 'Ibrāhīm ibn Ya'qūb', p. 164.

95 Jankowiak, 'Dirham flows', p. 121.

96 Roach, 'The people-trafficking princes', 137–9.

97 Jankowiak, 'Two systems of trade', pp. 143–5.

98 Jankowiak has also proposed that the enormous fortifications constructed in the tenth century in southern Poland, Bohemia, and Ukraine were holding points for the vast numbers of captives en route to market, since these hill forts would have been difficult to defend, and excavation has not ruled out a transient population in the outer levels. Jankowiak, 'Tracing the Saqaliba', pp. 170–4.

99 Kateřina Tomková, 'Bohemian coins in the tenth-to-twelfth-century silver hoards', in Charvát and Prosecký (eds), *Ibrahim ibn Ya'qub at-Turtushi*, pp. 82–3.

100 Stanisław Suchodolski, 'Change of transcontinental contacts as indicated by coins in the Baltic zone around 1000', in Przemysław Urbańczyk

(ed.), *Europe around the Year 1000* (Warsaw: Wydawnictwo DIG, 2001), pp. 92–3.

101 Jankowiak, 'Two systems of trade', pp. 141–2.

102 Manzano Moreno, 'Circulation de biens et richesses', paras. 40–3.

103 Romney David Smith, 'The business of human trafficking: slaves and money between western Italy and the House of Islam before the Crusades (*c.* 900–*c.* 1100)', *Journal of Medieval History*, 45:5 (2019), 523–52.

104 'Ibrāhīm ibn Ya'qūb', p. 163.

105 al-Muqaddasī, *Aḥsan al-Taqāsīm fī Ma'rifat al-Aqālīm*, translated in Ayalon, *Eunuchs*, p. 219.

106 Constable, *Trade and Traders*, p. 206.

107 For examples translated into English, see Ayalon, 'On the eunuchs in Islam', 104–5. Gaiser, 'Slaves and silver', 41–70, argues that this slave trading underpinned political relationships between al-Andalus and the Maghreb.

108 Constable, *Trade and Traders*, pp. 16–17, 38–9.

109 Rio, *Slavery after Rome*, pp. 24–8.

110 Jankowiak, 'Two systems of trade', p. 142. For an English-language overview of research on Rus trade networks, see Jonathan Shepard, 'Back in Old Rus and the USSR: archaeology, history and politics', *English Historical Review*, 131:549 (2016), 390–401.

111 *The Russian Primary Chronicle: Laurentian Text*, trans. S. H. Cross and O. P. Sherbowitz-Wetzor (Cambridge, MA: Medieval Academy of America, 1953), p. 86. For political context, see Franklin and Shepard, *Emergence of Rus*, pp. 145–9.

112 Charvát, *Emergence of the Bohemian State*, p. 145.

113 *Inquisitio de thelonis Raffelstettensis*, §6, p. 251.

114 For example, as cited in Henning, 'Gefangenenfesseln im slawischen Siedlungsraum', 403–26. Cf. Fontaine, 'Early medieval slave trading', 467–73.

115 Jankowiak, 'Dirham flows', pp. 122–3.

116 This part of the manuscript could read either 'Muslim merchants from the land of the Turks' or 'while from the country of the Turks and of the Muslims come to them Jews and Turks'. Tadeusz Lewicki, 'Opis Pragi w arabskim słowniku geograficznym al-Himjarīego (XV wiek)', *Archeologia Polski* 16 (1971), 698–9. This could indicate Iberian Muslims, but there are few Islamic coin finds in Bohemia, and Ibn Ya'qūb did not mention Muslims from al-Andalus in the Frankish towns he visited. Petr Charvát believes that archaeological finds from Prague indicate a broader interpretation than simply 'Hungarian',

in ‘Who are Ibrahim’s “Turks”? (a discussion note)’, in Charvát and Prosecký (eds), *Ibrahim ibn Ya’qub at-Turtushi*, pp. 72–3.
117 Macháček and Videman, ‘Monetisation of early medieval Moravia’, p. 190.
118 A. Balcárková et al., ‘Archeologický výzkum raně středověkého sídliště Kostice Zadní hrúd v letech 2009–2011’, *Archeologické Rozhledy*, 65 (2013), 763–5, 768–9.
119 Macháček and Videman, ‘Monetisation of early medieval Moravia’, pp. 191–2.
120 Cosmas of Prague, *Chronicle of the Czechs*, p. 138.
121 *Thietmari Merseburgensis*, p. 308. A diploma of Conrad II from 1027 denounced the sale of *mancipia* by the church in Verden ‘like brute animals’. *Die Urkunden Konrads II*, ed. H. Bresslau, MGH, Diplomata (Hanover, 1909), p. 176.
122 Cosmas of Prague, *Chronicle of the Czechs*, p. 174. Bernold of Constans, *Chronicon*, p. 414.
123 Katona, *Vikings of the Steppe*, pp. 80–93.
124 Frantiszek Kupfer and Tadeusz Lewicki (eds and trans.), *Źródła Hebajskie do Dziejów Słowian I Niektórych Innych Ludów Środkowej I Wschodniej Europy* (Warsaw: Polish Academy, 1956), pp. 36–7.
125 Naďa Profantová, ‘Byzantine coins from the 9th–10th century from the Czech Republic’, in Marcin Wołoszyn (ed.), *Byzantine Coins in Central Europe between the 5th and 10th Century* (Cracow: Polish Academy of Arts and Sciences, 2009), pp. 586–8.
126 Jiří Militký, ‘Nový pohled na zlatou byzantskou minci z Libice nad Cidlinou’, *Numismatický sborník*, 21 (2006), 125–36.
127 Katona, *Vikings of the Steppe*, pp. 70–1. Petr Balcárek, *Byzantium in the Czech Lands (4th–16th Centuries)* (Leiden: Brill, 2023), pp. 214–23.
128 Profantová, ‘Byzantine coins’, p. 588.
129 Taťána Kučerovská, ‘Kelčský nález’, *Folia Numismatika*, 8/9 (1993), 63–187.
130 Profantová, ‘Byzantine coins’, pp. 591–2. Nina Bažantová, ‘Romanesque and early Gothic silk textiles from Czech sources’, in Charvát and Prosecký (eds), *Ibrahim ibn Ya’qub at-Turtushi*, pp. 93–102.

7

Slaving and power

Secular rulers and Christian ecclesiastics alike continuously problematised slaving, their chief concerns being the moral and judicial questions of why and how people could be enslaved and who ought to be ineligible for sale. They dedicated their energies to establishing the boundaries of enslavement within a society often by placing limitations on penal enslavement or by affirming circumstances in which people could sell themselves or their children. Long-distance slave trading prompted backlash in both secular and ecclesiastical law that sought to exclude members of a Christian political or religious community from the risks of sale abroad to non-Christians or beyond hope of ransom. Expansion of networks from the ninth century onwards meant that rulers simultaneously sought to capitalise on the wealth generated by the slave trade by levying taxes, expanding their own captive-taking operations, and generally seeking to hold greater control over slave-trading networks in their realms. This chapter's focus remains primarily on the most centralised polities of this study, England and Bohemia, since little to no relevant textual evidence survives from the other areas. Welsh and Scottish law, both ecclesiastical and secular, survives only in much later forms and does not address slaving, while Irish law deliberately gives the appearance of being static beyond the seventh century, which obscures the reactions of authority figures to contemporary slavery-related problems such as we see in English and Czech texts.

The historiography of control

Discussion of any control over slave trading in the historiography of western Europe has long focused on the role of Christianity in restricting and ultimately ending slavery. Foundational works by Marc Bloch and Pierre Bonnassie supposed that the spread of ideas regarding equality before God prohibited the enslavement of fellow Christians through warfare, meaning that, as this religion expanded into northern and eastern Europe, the pool of enslaveable pagans gradually decreased; slavery ended because access to slaves dwindled over time and Christian thought promoted the humanisation of chattel slaves.[1] Conversely, in writing about Christian European and colonial attitudes to slavery over a nearly 2,000-year period, David Brion Davis argued that, despite the humanisation of individuals, there was no trend amongst medieval clerical authors towards the perception of institutional slavery as indefensible or even amoral.[2] Drawing from Bloch and Bonnassie, David Pelteret has argued that, although Wulfstan of York did not reject slavery altogether, he did internalise Christian views of equality, leading him to advocate more humane treatment of slaves and equal legal protection for them.[3] Jeffrey Fynn-Paul has proposed the delineation of 'no-slaving zones' within early medieval Europe, areas in which the taboo against Christian enslavement of Christians entirely prevented enslavement. The rise of Islam and the caliphate's demand for non-Muslim slaves meant that the pagan peripheries of eastern and northern Europe remained the primary sources of slaves. Meanwhile, the 'no-slaving zones' were enforced though prohibitions on the sale of Christians made by increasingly powerful states and the Church and expanded through the conversion of pagans. Fynn-Paul places the end of this process in the eleventh and twelfth centuries, when the 'no-slaving zones' were 'perfected', and the enslavement of Christians came to a halt.[4]

Fynn-Paul's ideas have had a mixed reception amongst historians of slavery, and a volume edited by Fynn-Paul and Damian Alan Pargas offers a range of scholarly assessments of 'no-slaving zones' in a global context. Its studies of late antique and late medieval Europe tend to agree that, although general 'slaving zones' can be established based on geography and religion, slaving taboos were far more nuanced and complex than Fynn-Paul's original argument suggested.[5] The establishment of a 'perfect no-slaving zone' was theoretical rather than practical. For the early Middle Ages, Alice Rio has argued that notions of Christian equality existed within societies that depended upon its Christianised, hierarchical institutions. Benevolent attitudes towards enslaved people were practically applied only when encouraging lords and masters towards the merciful treatment of their inferiors; they were never intended to overthrow slavery as an institution. Hagiography denouncing the violent treatment of slaves was designed to illustrate proper restraint on the part of lords and masters, thereby bolstering their legitimacy as slave owners.[6] David Wyatt has also directly challenged David Pelteret's arguments for England, pointing out that the early medieval Church never called for slavery's abolition in Britain and Ireland, and that slavery was perceived by contemporaries as part of the natural order.[7] Stefan Jurasinski's close study of Old English penitentials has indicated that canons regarding enslavement became increasingly complex in the tenth century, not to stop the creation of slaves but to protect free people from being enslaved on technicalities.[8]

Similarly, the evidence presented in earlier chapters of this book demonstrates that the enslavement and sale of Christians by Christians persisted long after Christianisation. For example, slavery in England survived almost five centuries of Christianisation and a major regime change before slave trading was banned outright in the late eleventh century. The Irish continued to own and enslave Christians as late as the middle of the twelfth century, and the English certainly had few qualms about selling their fellows in Bristol in the late eleventh century. In Bohemia, no prohibitions regarding the sale of Christians even to non-Christians were put in place until 1124. These scenarios are all covered by Fynn-Paul's assertion that a 'perfect no-slaving zone' did not exist until at least the twelfth century, but it seems unlikely that religious conversion alone was the driving force behind these changes.

The counter-argument to the influence of Christianisation in the demise of slave trading is encapsulated in Joseph C. Miller's deep history of slaving, which argues that participation in this activity was a strategy by which individuals, particularly rulers, could consolidate wealth and power to their own benefit.[9] The historiography of slaving in east central Europe has increasingly served to support this argument by arguing for rulers' interest in sustaining, not hindering, slaving practices. It was Dušan Třeštík's belief that regulation of the slave trade and the development of a Czech 'state' were inherently interlinked, with the sale of war captives providing Přemyslid dukes with the wealth to consolidate their power from their heartland in the Prague Basin.[10] This expansion could not be maintained indefinitely, and around the turn of the eleventh century, following loss of territory in Poland and dynastic crisis, the retinue-based power structures supported by tribute and war booty collapsed. Forced to rely on new means of consolidating their control, the Přemyslids turned to bureaucratic institutions funded by taxation. Works by Marek Jankowiak, Matthias Hardt, and Andrew Roach similarly link Piast power consolidation and territorial expansion in Poland to slaving. This involvement allowed Mieszko I and his descendants to amass the wealth necessary for attracting and keeping followers and maintaining visible symbols of authority such as luxury goods and building projects.[11] These studies of early medieval central Europe discuss rulers as agents who promoted and benefited directly from slave trading, at least during the tenth century, and maintain that slaving contributed directly to dynastic power in Bohemia and Poland.[12]

The difference in historiographical focus between east central and western Europe may stem in part from differences in source survival and focus. Numerous secular legal texts survive from England throughout the early Middle Ages that detail changes in who could be enslaved or sold and under what circumstances, but there is nothing from Bohemia beyond Cosmas's reported edicts of Břetislav I. Penitentials that provide an expressly ecclesiastical perspective on slavery are also far rarer in Bohemia. The result of this discrepancy is that historians of, for example, England and Francia can assume a more top-down perspective on slaving that emphasises the restrictions placed on it by rulers and bishops. Such evidence does not exist for Bohemia, which may have encouraged historians to focus on the evidence that indicates rulers' participation in slaving.

Bohemian sources also hint at an ongoing struggle between ecclesiastical ideals and the activities of the populace and the Přemyslids themselves. Adalbert of Prague's objection to the sale of Christians to Jews is one such example, and Cosmas reports that, in the time of Břetislav I, folk traditions still included polygamy and burial outside church cemeteries.[13] When Břetislav I issued his edicts at Adalbert's tomb in Gniezno, they included a ruling on penal enslavement amongst other decrees intended to bring Bohemian society in line with ecclesiastical mores. This suggests that the Přemyslids were far less interested in creating the closely entwined royal and ecclesiastical policy visible in the interplay between English law codes and penitentials. Despite these differences, as rulers of coalescing polities with ever-strengthening central authority, English kings and Bohemian dukes pursued similar tactics for controlling and exploiting slaving.

Limitations on slaving

Secular rulers were expected to demonstrate some interest in controlling slaving activity regardless of the extent of administrative infrastructure, indicating that oversight of legal status and related decisions regarding who could be enslaved or sold and in what circumstances were all important to a ruler's authority. In ideological terms, rulers desired to be perceived as the upholders of social order, and, in practical terms, to oversee trade via taxation and the granting of rights and protections to merchants.[14] The clergy were responsible for the welfare of Christians' eternal souls, and it was thus their duty to protect individuals from unjustly falling into slavery – a status long associated with sin. Pope Gregory I, writing in a sixth-century context heavily influenced by Roman legal approaches to slavery, argued that the hierarchy of legal status mirrored a hierarchy of sinfulness, and thus a slave's place in society was the will of God.[15] Later ecclesiastical writings, concerned with the ways in which captive taking and hardship made anyone potentially enslaveable, perceived a substantial risk of sin in a slave's complete subjection to their lord. This did not mean that the clergy opposed slavery as an institution, only that ecclesiastical authors feared outcomes such as a lapse of faith for those Christians enslaved to non-Christians or the adultery attributed to both enslaved women and their owners. The unfree were held no less accountable for their sins in western European canon law than free people, but limiting sharp reductions in status could protect certain people from an inherently more sinful way of life.[16]

Early problems of enslavement

Attempts to restrict paths into slavery appear in some of our earliest normative sources and demonstrate that rulers and ecclesiastics alike were driven by a sense of social responsibility to delimit status reduction even before the expansion of slave trading. Examples mostly survive from the English kingdoms of Kent, Wessex, and England as it later emerged from West Saxon conquest, suggesting that rulers and ecclesiastics there held a particular interest in codifying who from within a political or religious community could be made saleable and how, perhaps in reaction to small-scale commercial trading with the Continent. There are hints from the Moravian code *Zakon Suydnji Ljudem* that these questions were important there as well. Secular law codes and penitential canons affirm their authors' perception that enslavement should not be indiscriminate. Stripping the status of a freeborn individual required justification, and both rulers and ecclesiastics sought to provide at least nominal oversight of this process to prevent the 'wrong' people from becoming slaves.

Having been initially introduced as the transcription of oral law with Ætherberht's Kentish code promulgated *c.* 600, written English codes gained increasing complexity over time and appear to reflect the introduction of new law in writing rather than orally, though the act of oral promulgation may still have played a crucial role in establishing the authority of the texts' contents.[17] With surviving codes spanning four and a half centuries before the Norman Conquest, these documents demonstrate an increasing expression of royal power through lawmaking, as well as the expression of focuses and goals unique to the circumstances in which each code was issued.[18] They indicate a concern for protection and peace within a kingdom, as well as the extent to which that protection and peace could be guaranteed by a king.[19] As a result, they regularly legislate on matters regarding enslavement and slave trading, particularly the ways in which subjects could be judicially enslaved and who was eligible for sale.

Our understanding of Great Moravian rulers' interests, by contrast, is obscured by a lack of evidence. Even if the frequent references to penal enslavement in *Zakon* are representative of customary legal tradition, we have no indication as to how this law was guaranteed. *Zakon* is similar to early English codes in that it appears to have been issued as an ideological statement of the ruler's authority and the centrality (perceived or desired) of Christianity in Great Moravian society. Although some form of ecclesiastical hierarchy existed, the penitential character of *Zakon* may have found application only amongst Great Moravian elites, given that all the churches discovered thus far have been primarily associated with elite settlement.[20]

Despite these complications and underlying motives, early law codes from both England and Moravia concerned themselves with when and why reduction in status could occur via two types of regulations. The first limited the privilege of enslavement by a third party to the ruler themselves, and the second stipulated the conditions of that enslavement. These restrictions would have applied only to people within a realm and did not impact the enslavement of outsiders through warfare. Regardless of how the regulations were used or the extent to which they were enforced, laws regarding enslavement helped shape and solidify the ruler's position as law-giver, peacemaker, and protector.

The legislation of penal enslavement allowed rulers to assert their authority to legitimately enslave others within a wider community or to have others enslaved in their name. Penal enslavement must have been a long-standing aspect of customary law, and thus could be enacted and overseen by any judge or legal representative. We catch glimpses of custom in Czech tradition through the large-scale replacement of the *Ecloga*'s mutilations with enslavement in *Zakon* and through Břetislav's eleventh-century adjustment of the terms of judicial enslavement. Customary tradition may also be reflected in the use of penal enslavement as punishment for theft in both eighth-century Kent and Wessex.[21] Rulers also leveraged enslavement in new laws, especially to reinforce Christian religious observance. Ine punished free men who worked on a Sunday with enslavement, and *Zakon* did likewise for theft from the Church and grave robbing.[22] Edward the Elder codified a procedure for those judicially enslaved for theft in the very late ninth century or early tenth, which was doubtless an early part of West Saxon kings' attempts to extend greater royal authority over the law of theft.[23] Although the Peace of Edward and Guthrum is an eleventh-century forgery by Wulfstan, archbishop of York, Wulfstan invoked royal precedent to claim that freemen caught working on a church festival should face enslavement.[24]

We cannot know the extent to which Ine ascribed new powers to himself regarding penal enslavement, but Ine and his councillors, the *witan*, clearly felt that the king had the authority to make rulings on what constituted enslaveable offences. This may have established a precedent exploited by Edward a century later, and may also have been the attitude of whoever composed *Zakon*. In Ine's case, his prohibition of sale overseas for anyone, slave or free, might be connected to his extension of authority over penal enslavement, since sale would have prevented the offender's opportunity for redemptive punishment within their community. Ine's interest in royal oversight of penal enslavement set an important precedent that later West Saxon and English kings would draw upon, as is shown below. He seemingly linked customary and new reasons for judicial enslavement to the king's authority, and in doing so may have restricted such enslavement to a limited number of offences.

This indicates that royal and ducal law sought to prevent indiscriminate enslavement, a position underlined by interest in prohibiting the binding or theft of free men. Æthelberht's code prohibited the 'binding' of a free man – a charge that must have included kidnapping and imprisonment as well as enslavement.[25] The Kentish laws of Hlothhere and Eadric elaborated on this in the late seventh century, outlining the number of witnesses necessary should a stolen man return to lay charges against his kidnapper.[26] Nothing similar appears again until the West Saxon king Alfred issued his *domboc*, in which the new code included punishments for whoever 'binds an unsinning ceorl' along with six additional compensation payments owed for physical injury and humiliation caused.[27] These illustrate a situation more akin to kidnapping as part of a dispute, but scourging and the cutting of hair, punishable by payments of 20 and 10 shillings, respectively, were both potentially linked to slave status.[28] The roughly contemporary *Zakon* is more explicit about this connection, with enslavement prescribed for any kidnapper who enslaves or sells an otherwise free person.[29]

Two non-royal law tracts from tenth- and eleventh-century England confirm that later, local lawmakers were also concerned with the kidnapping or 'theft' of both free and enslaved people. The *Dunsæte Ordinance* suggests that enslaved people were commonly stolen in the Welsh borderlands along the river Wye in the tenth or early eleventh centuries.[30] This law tract functioned as an agreement primarily focused on theft and homicide between neighbouring Welsh and English communities, and included ‘a person’ valued at one pound amongst the compensation payments for livestock.[31] *Forfang*, an anonymous code dated to the second half of the tenth century, offered a reward of 15 pence to any man who retrieved a stolen man or horse.[32] Both *Dunsæte* and *Forfang* hint that royal laws related to enslavement were more than just elite posturing. Although *Dunsæte* probably operated where neither English nor Welsh law held ultimate jurisdiction, *Forfang* suggests a communal need to address the theft of people and that royal influence in this area may have been insufficient during the escalation of slave-trading activity.

Limitations on enslavement via direct sale – both self-sale and the sale of one’s children – first appear in the age restrictions set down in the *Penitential of Theodore* in the late seventh or early eighth century. These canons appear to have established penitentials as the venue for exploring the morality of consent to enslavement, with Theodore stipulating minimum ages of consent for self-sellers and children sold by a parent.[33] These canons became popular in Latin and vernacular penitentials throughout Europe in the ninth and tenth centuries, emphasising that ecclesiastical regulations on enslavement through penitentials applied to any Christian community and were not tied to a particular kingdom or ruler. In England, they appear in the late ninth-century Old English *Scriftboc* and the *Old English Canons of Theodore*, written sometime between the seventh and eleventh centuries.[34] As noted previously, these later texts were not simply translations but conscious adaptations of earlier penitential material to suit later contexts. The repetition suggests not only that the sale of children was an ongoing issue but that there was real concern regarding unwilling participants, particularly given the perception of children as innocents.[35]

It may be indicative of what the clergy saw to be an ongoing problem that these restrictions on direct sale were repeated during the period of escalation in slaving. The *Old English Penitential*, produced after the *Scriftboc*, took the particularly hard line that sale of one’s children or kin was entirely sinful and risked excommunication; atonement was possible only if the sold person was purchased back and freed or another was freed in their place.[36] The escalation of punishment suggests that ecclesiastical figures were growing increasingly concerned about how traders obtained saleable slaves. Fluidity of status in the context of sale to foreigners was also a concern in the Czech lands in this period, with the penitential *Někotoraja Zapověd* ruling that the castration of boys by their parents or for sale was a sin.[37] By labelling certain behaviours as deserving of physically and mentally taxing penance, penitentials must have influenced ideas of what was acceptable or reflected contemporary ways of thinking about these issues. Secular law never sought to address direct sale, and the close connections between law codes and penitentials may also have meant that its treatment in one genre was deemed sufficient.[38] In England at least, royal law and penance were closely interconnected, and bishops played a part in enforcing both.[39] Even if ecclesiastics did not have the authority or the desire to prevent these practices, they were disconcerted by the contexts in which such sales occurred.

Responses to changes in scale

The tenth century in England saw fundamental changes in the extension of royal authority through law and judicial apparatuses, all of which may have had a noticeable impact on kings' ability to exert control over enslavement practices within their realm. Throughout his career James Campbell argued extensively for the existence of an early medieval English 'state' characterised by strong central authority, bureaucratic institutions, and clear borders and unified by a common language, church, and sense of identity, all developments which occurred over course of the tenth century.[40] Such a state would have been capable of ensuring the administrative enforcement of any restrictions on slaving. This idea has been intensively debated by such scholars as Patrick Wormald, Paul Hyams, and Tom Lambert, with feud and communal enforcement serving as test cases for the existence of a centralised legal system.[41] Alice Taylor has also argued that law in England, as well as in Wales and Scotland, was governed by the need for communal enforcement, and therefore the presence of state structures was irrelevant in the local carriage of justice.[42] If this was indeed the case, it would mean that attempts to regulate slaving served to bolster the appearance of rulers as protectors regardless of their efficacy, and that such laws may have merely extended royal support to sentiments already present at a local level. In either case, written law regarding slaving allows us to view changing perceptions over time as to how the management of status fell under a ruler's purview.

If law codes were primarily inspired by ideological perceptions of kingship and the result of otherwise oral promulgation, this did not necessarily lessen their practical value.[43] Wormald and Campbell believed that the growing aspirations for control expressed by law codes of the tenth century onwards indicate that power structures must have been capable of backing up those claims. Royal concern for safeguarding the Christian realm also demonstrates how enslavement and slave trading fitted within contemporary ideas regarding sin and legal wrongdoing.[44] Contemporaries certainly took law codes seriously, and close reading of individual laws has suggested that later English codes held importance as guides for local officials that could be revised and adapted.[45] Despite this and the vocalness of penitential authors in tenth- and eleventh-century England, kings offered few protections or caveats against enslavement during this period. Litigious kings of the tenth century such as Æthelstan and Edgar were silent about it, which may be due to the perceived efficacy of previous rulings or a lack of interest. Given the ongoing concerns of contemporary penitential authors, however, it is possible that these kings made a conscious choice not to restrict enslavement further in written law at a time when this activity was on the rise.

It is probably not a coincidence that the next secular limitations after those of Alfred were authored by Wulfstan of York, who may even have helped to write the *Old English Handbook for the Use of a Confessor*.[46] Wulfstan believed that God's displeasure at fluidity of status was responsible for the devastating viking raids of the late tenth and early eleventh centuries that were the harbingers of the millenarian apocalypse.[47] His *Sermo Lupi ad Anglos*, composed and revised during the devastating campaigns of Thorkell the Tall and Svein Forkbeard that preceded the Danish conquest of England, details the ways in which unsanctioned changes in status perverted the natural order. Slaves who ran away and became vikings could kill or enslave their rightful owners, and lords could be compelled to pay a thegn's wergild for offences committed against such a runaway but receive nothing for offences committed against themselves.[48]

In writing the ordinances known as I and II Cnut, Wulfstan sought to tackle his concerns about enslavement in the king's voice. The structuring of these codes was inspired by Alfred's *domboc*, which drew from and amended earlier codes – a methodology that allowed Wulfstan to impose further limitations by reworking Ine's laws regarding enslavement for working on a Sunday and for family members considered to be accessories to theft.[49] In addressing the former, enslavement was changed to penance, and, in the latter, Wulfstan clarified that wives could not prevent their husbands from bringing home stolen goods, though they were responsible for anything kept under their lock and key.[50] Wulfstan also introduced a law against the enslavement of infants as perpetrated by 'greedy people', implying that there were individuals who sought to maximise the number of people enslaved by judicial means.[51] It is probably relevant to this law that penal slaves, including infants, were probably considered saleable. In a manner similar to penitential authors, Wulfstan sought to restrict enslavement in a way that prevented all but the most deserving offenders from becoming potential victims of slave trading.

It may not be a coincidence that Břetislav's decrees of 1039 revoked enslavement as punishment for refusing to reconcile a marital dispute less than two decades later. The attitudes of these lawmakers in disparate parts of Europe may reflect a reactionary trend in areas of high-volume slave trading that sought to provide greater protections against enslavement. There are few indications, however, that Bohemian dukes were as capable as English kings were of enforcing such limitations. It is probably significant that Břetislav proclaimed the law in the presence of the bishop of Prague and the nobles who had accompanied him on campaign, since Bohemian lords may have held direct control within a certain radius of their strongholds.[52] Legal cases were dealt with almost entirely by the nobility through the thirteenth century, with the duke intervening only when they involved secular lords and clergy.[53] Břetislav's decrees attest the existence of lower courts under the jurisdiction of *comites*, but this may reflect the twelfth-century world in which Cosmas recorded them, and it is unknown how these courts were linked to ducal authority.[54] Rather than appointing representatives, as English kings did with reeves, Bohemian dukes and kings must have relied heavily on their nobles to enforce new law within their own domains in accordance with the decisions of assemblies. This does not mean that Břetislav's decree on penal enslavement was any more or less effective than limitations on enslavement in contemporary England, only that ducal intervention was less direct.

Both secular and ecclesiastical law regarding enslavement attempted to delimit changes in status that could result in saleability. Rulers sought through the legislation of penal enslavement to restrict the how and why of that enslavement to a select number of offences. At least in theory, the law whose authority and legitimacy derived from the ruler could not justify indiscriminate enslavement, either for legal offences or by kidnapping otherwise free people. The two non-royal codes from England also reveal that this was a priority not just for kings but also for local communities, though prerogatives may have differed as slave trading escalated. Direct sale was also probably overseen communally, operating within increasingly strict moral parameters corresponding to a growing risk of sale away. Regardless of their enforcement, these attempts to control enslavement almost certainly reflected wider sentiments and a perceived divide between those enslaved from within a community via legal and customary mechanisms and those enslaved from outside.

Slave trading

Restrictions on slave trading broadly sought to protect particular groups, especially by keeping Christian slaves out of non-Christian hands or, as in some secular laws, by preventing sale beyond political or cultural borders. Surviving evidence of slave-trading regulation is heavily skewed towards English sources, but we must consider that decisions made in ecclesiastical councils in other areas, such as Francia, may have been adopted by clergymen in the British Isles and the Czech lands without leaving overt traces. The sale of Christians to non-Christians was a significant issue for secular rulers, since kings were tasked with the spiritual and physical protection of their people.[55] This issue had long been a concern for Christian rulers in Europe, but in English and Czech documents it becomes visible only during periods of large-scale slave trading.

Earlier records may not have survived, but the evidence does suggest a correlation between concern for regulating the sale of Christians and an increase in the demand for slaves by non-Christians.

England

In England, the earliest limitations on slave trading in secular law imply the importance of political borders as much as religious ones. Ine's code prohibited the sale of any man overseas, which, as discussed in Chapter 3, contrasts with Wihtred's contemporary law allowing penal slaves to be sold away at the king's discretion. A similar issue arises in Alfred's *domboc*, whose prologue adapted Mosaic law to emphasise that the daughters of men who remained enslaved voluntarily should not be sold to foreigners.[56] The *domboc* also appended Ine's code and reaffirmed any laws that Alfred did not directly contradict, which includes Ine's rulings on penal enslavement and the prohibition of selling enslaved or free people overseas. Edward the Elder's procedure for penal enslavement does not mention sale, but it suggests a scenario without it; a man without the support of kin, who offered himself up, was required to do the appropriate slave-work.[57]

As discussed above, eleventh-century laws in the form of Břetislav's edict and II Cnut may have sought to restrict the sorts of people made saleable by penal enslavement. We have very little information about the wider legal context of Břetislav's 1039 decrees, but the changes enacted by Wulfstan were part of his bigger programme of protecting Christians from non-Christian buyers, believing such sales to be 'hateful to God'.[58] The wording and intent of Wulfstan's laws remained broadly the same through most of the codes he drafted, and it appears from the outset in Æthelred's ordinances promulgated at Eynham in 1008 (V Æthelred):

> And the decree of our lord and his witan is that no one sell Christian and innocent people out of this land, especially not to heathen people, but carefully protect them, so that no one destroy the souls which Christ bought with his own life.[59]

This was the most emphatic denunciation of slave trading in royal law to date, but it retained loopholes. It did not address the sale of people within England or the sale of non-Christians overseas, and it appears to countenance the sale of penal slaves even before Wulfstan drafted legislation that limited the number of enslaveable offences.

Æthelred's later codes recycled the language of this ordinance with subtle yet significant changes over time. The penitential code issued at Bath in 1009 in response to the arrival of the viking army (VII Æthelred) prohibited the sale of *anyone* out of the country, perhaps seen as a necessary step in desperate times, and it was ultimately scaled back.[60] Cnut's Oxford code of 1018, also drafted by Wulfstan, decreed only that Christian people should not be sold out of the country 'all too often', which may have been a compromise for the practicalities of enforcement, both in terms of scale and the identities of the perpetrators.[61] William of Malmesbury's allegation that Cnut's own sister had been struck dead by lightning for her role in selling slaves to Denmark implicates the Anglo-Danish elites in high-profile slave trading, and these are precisely the sort of people in the king's council and at court who would have been able to advocate for sufficient legal ambiguity to continue their enterprise.[62] This language appears again in II Cnut, and may provide context for Wulfstan's careful reform of penal enslavement, perhaps to reduce the creation of saleable slaves.[63]

Royal benefits from slave trading are discussed below, and it may be that financial rewards and court pressure were sufficient incentive to keep open legal avenues for exporting slaves eastwards to Scandinavia and the Baltic, across the Channel to Normandy and the Rhine, and westwards to Ireland. No further legislation on slave trading appeared in England until the reign of William I, in which Article 9 of the Ten Articles of William I prohibits the sale of people out of the country.[64] The law may represent William's response to Wulfstan of Worcester's and Lanfranc's calls to end the slave trade out of Bristol, and so would have been issued between Lanfranc's appointment to the see of Canterbury in 1070 and William's death in 1087. The law does not refer to heathens or heathendom, probably reflecting the Christianisation of Scandinavia as well as Christian Irish (or Hiberno-Norse) demand. The final English prohibition on slave trading was a complete one: the Council of Westminster forbade the sale of people like brute animals in 1102.[65]

The Czech lands

In the Czech lands, limitations on slave trading are more difficult to discern in the sparse documentary record. *Zakon* gives no indication as to whether those in power considered the sale of Moravians to foreigners or non-Christians to be a problem. Přemyslid Bohemia offers more information, since we have evidence of ecclesiastical disapproval for the sale of Christians to non-Christians and the attempt to prevent castration for sale in the *Někotoraja Zapověd*.[66] This penitential does not impose any direct restrictions on slave trading but it does seek to lessen the prospect of sale to Muslim or Byzantine buyers. The oddly specific canon is in keeping with a general lack of interest by Bohemian secular elites in restricting the slave trade to protect Christians, despite the regular participation of Muslims and Jews. In the late tenth century Adalbert was unable to convince the Bohemians, including the duke, Boleslav II, that Christians should not be sold to Jews, but we know from Břetislav I's decree that, within a few decades, dukes were capable of exercising some authority over slavery.[67] Despite this and the development of a centralised government by the twelfth century, the earliest surviving restriction on the slave trade dates to 1124, when Vladislav outlawed the sale of Christians to Jews. The evidence suggests that limitations on slave trading were within the ruler's prerogative, though indications that Přemyslids exerted this power before 1124 are conspicuously absent. It may be that they do not survive and were primarily oral, but we should also consider that such decrees never existed.

That Boleslav II appears to have ignored Adalbert without repercussions does not say much for episcopal authority in Bohemia in the late tenth century. Adalbert may also have been at a personal disadvantage as a member of the rival Slavnikid family, and Boleslav may not have been inclined to encourage the expansion of the see's influence. The *Někotoraja Zapověd* may indicate an attempt by senior clergy to restrict slave trading in a manner eschewed by the Přemyslids. Outside Prague, secular lords could use 'private' churches to protect and promote their own interests, and the priests and archpriests present in their strongholds by the eleventh and twelfth centuries were responsible to the steward rather than a bishop.[68] This suggests that penitentials and other limitations on slaving could be enforced at a local level, but only if they did not negatively impact the interests of local lords.

English kings appear to have been more interested than their Moravian and Bohemian counterparts in leveraging slaving restrictions, particularly in writing, to test the limits of their jurisdictional power. It is nevertheless a crucial aspect of this process that neither kings nor the clergy, not even the litigious Wulfstan, sought to eliminate slave trading altogether. Royal promulgations continued to leave gaps allowing certain people to be sold to certain buyers. This demonstrates that, despite different legal traditions and contexts of textual survival, early medieval rulers were concerned with restricting slave trading only to a point, and few had any interest in eliminating it altogether.

Slaving as power

We must now turn to the question of how and why these legal loopholes regarding permissible slave trading were important. The discussion of historiography at the start of this chapter and of captive taking in Chapter 3 have laid the groundwork by establishing that slaving allowed individuals the potential to amass labour resources directly while simultaneously destroying those of an enemy and provided opportunities for accumulating wealth and prestige through the sale of people and the acquisition of exoticised foreigners. These cultural attitudes underpinned practical legal strategies and political aims, from the collection of tolls to captive-taking campaigns, all of which worked together to exert control over slaving networks.

Taxes and tolls

There are indications that tolls levied on slave trading could constitute significant sources of income for rulers, though only two direct references survive from the British Isles and the Czech lands. From Bohemia, we have the alleged foundation charter in which Boleslav II granted a tenth of captives to Břevnov monastery in 993 alongside a tenth of the ducal income from the Prague market and a tenth of the ducal income from the courts, which implies that the duke already held monopolies on these revenue streams.[69] Eleventh-century charters for monastic foundations similarly granted rights to tolls along riverine and overland trade routes, indicating that these were important sources of income with mechanisms in place to collect the goods and cash. The foundation at Litoměřice received from Spitihněv II in 1057 the right to collect tolls from passing local and foreign vessels on the river Elbe.[70] Spitihněv's brother, Otto, granted to Hradiště in 1078 a portion of the tolls from the river Olšava and the bridge at Břeclav castle, both in southern Moravia, and those from the road to Poland at Hradec castle while he controlled the Olomouc principality.[71] As Lisa Wolverton has pointed out, these tolls cover several major trade arteries that directly connected Prague with Meissen via the Elbe and linked Moravia with Cracow and Hungary.[72] These eastward routes from Moravia correspond to what we know of slave trading from Ibn Ya'qūb's account of the buyers in Prague a century earlier, and further suggest that Bohemian slaving in the eleventh century served to supply southeastern European markets.

It is unclear at what point the Přemyslid dukes developed the ability to extract tolls and seemingly hold a monopoly over them, but such mechanisms were in place by the latter years of the slave-trading peak. Dušan Třeštík believes that such tolls contributed as much as 10 million deniers to ducal coffers in the tenth century, though the calculation was based on compensatory redemption values for unfree people rather than market prices for chattel slaves and is thus unlikely to be accurate.[73] The underlying assertion, however, that the Přemyslids received substantial financial benefits from allowing – even encouraging – slave trading in their realm must be true, and would explain the seeming lack of interest by rulers and most ecclesiastics in promulgating limitations on slaving. Boleslav II's lack of interest in Adalbert's attempts to stop the sale of Christians to Jews is particularly telling in this context; revenues from these sales supported not only the duke and his growing administrative structures but also the maintenance of churches and monasteries. Adalbert's frustration may have been partly caused by his own monks and priests turning a blind eye to the practice.

Similar self-interest may have played a part in English legislation on slave trading. According to William of Malmesbury, Wulfstan of Worcester and Lanfranc had difficulty convincing William the Conqueror to stop the slave trade out of Bristol because he was partial to the taxes he collected from it.[74] An entry for Lewes, Sussex, in *Domesday Book* suggests that the amount was as much as eight pence per sale: four from the seller and four from the buyer.[75] The appearance of this amount in two manumission documents of the eleventh and twelfth centuries has led David Pelteret to suggest that the Domesday entry is representative of a kingdom-wide tax on 'manumissions and quittances'.[76] From a coastal market town such as Bristol, where Irish Sea demand drove regular slave trading, the income from taxes must have been considerable.

As in Bohemia, we cannot know for certain when this sort of toll was introduced, though there is an extensive documentary record of trade-related tolls in the English kingdoms extending back to the seventh century. In discussion akin to that of slave-trading revenue in Bohemia, J. R. Maddicott has argued that tolls on salt from Droitwich were critical to the Mercian kings during the period known as the 'Mercian supremacy', in the second half of the seventh century and first half of the eighth. Profits from a particular type of trade allowed the ruler to engage in military expansion and further centralise their power. It may not be a coincidence that London flourished as a Mercian *wic* while Mercian kings were levying and granting the revenue from salt trading.[77] Imma's sale by a Mercian nobleman to a Frisian in London at this time encourages us to ask whether tolls on slave trading were also in place at this early date. By the early tenth century the collection of tolls on expensive transactions within markets was the responsibility of royal officials known as port-reeves.[78] Slave sales were almost certainly included, providing kings with direct revenue streams from slave trading, though this was not without complications, as rogue traders and unscrupulous reeves alike could seek to dodge royal oversight.[79]

Direct evidence of taxation on slave sales is scarce, but it is sufficient to raise our suspicions regarding rulers' interest in this form of trade. In both late tenth-century Bohemia and late eleventh-century England, the appearance of such taxes coincided with the ruler's reluctance to impose further limitations on slave trading. This itself indicates that the income from such tolls was not negligible, as does the donation of a tenth of this income to a newly founded monastery in Bohemia. We can conclude that rulers themselves, despite their attempts to legislate on enslavement and slave trading, had a vested financial interest in their continuance. This goes far to explain the precision of codified limitations and even the paucity of such sources from Bohemia.

Control of the networks

Taxation on slave trading yielded financial benefits to rulers in the same way that any high-value trade did, and it is worth reframing some of the arguments in previous chapters to examine the extent to which rulers were active participants in and beneficiaries of slaving operations. This is a topic of serious discussion for east central Europe regarding the centralised polities that emerged in the ninth and tenth centuries, one that has been addressed in previous chapters for Great Moravia and Přemyslid Bohemia. Here I focus on the paradigms developed for the early Piast state in Poland in the second half of the tenth century. Silver coinage in Poland shifted from Abbasid dirhams to Bohemian silver deniers in the 960s and 970s as political upheaval in the Abbasid Caliphate caused dirham sources to dry up.[80] The rapid redirection of trade that resulted in this change of silver sources indicates that the Poles under Mieszko I were offering items consistently in high demand in both the east and the west, enough that the revenue stream could recover quickly from the near-total collapse of a primary trade route. The most plausible goods that would enable such flexibility and generate such cash flows are slaves, and we have already seen that this chronology maps onto the escalation of Piast raiding and the political alliance of Mieszko I and his Přemyslid counterparts.[81]

Andrew Roach, in arguments similar to those of Dušan Třeštík, has focused on the importance of this accumulated silver for the Piast rulers themselves, particularly Mieszko and his son, Bolesław I Chrobry. Not only did it create immense personal wealth, but it also raised the funds necessary to attract and retain followers and to maintain warriors and their families in comfort. Roach has also highlighted the precarity inherent in dependence on slaving revenue, since it required endemic warfare as a prerequisite for enslavement and a reliance on highly changeable demand, best exemplified by the collapse of eastward trade routes in the second half of the tenth century due to upheaval thousands of miles away.[82] His work with Alex Marshall has identified parallels with the violence and unpredictability of the modern drugs trade, but with the obvious caveat that early medieval slaving was perfectly licit.[83] Matthias Hardt has also asserted the importance of silver acquired via slave trading for the Slavic rulers of east central Europe, which gave them the disposable income to secure their power bases.[84] Most recently, Alice Rio has argued that the political fragmentation of northern and eastern Europe and the resultant dependence on cash as a means to power helped make these areas of Europe into the principle slaving zones of the ninth and tenth centuries, in contrast to the Frankish world, which had come to depend on land as the principal basis of wealth.[85]

These models probably function better to associate slaving and power in central Europe in the second half of the tenth century than they would in contemporary England, which, unlike the coalescing polities of that region, already possessed a strong centralised government, a powerful dynastic family, and a sophisticated monetary system. There is some room to consider that slaving may have played a role in West Saxon territorial expansion in the first half of the century, given that the *Anglo-Saxon Chronicle* suggests that Edward may have been more interested in captive taking than his father in his campaigns against the Danes. It was Edward and his tenth-century successors who were decidedly uninterested in royal limitations on slaving. Alice Rio has also suggested that the pressing need by the English to acquire enough silver to make Danegeld payments in the latter part of the tenth century may have prompted more intensive involvement in slaving, which would also help to explain Wulfstan's accusations and reactionary legislation in the early eleventh century.[86] Discussion of kingship and wealth in Ireland and Scotland would also benefit from analysis via the central European framework to better understand how slave trading related to power consolidation by tenth-century figures such as Brian Boru in Ireland and Kenneth Mac Alpin in Scotland. Poul Holm has already proposed that substantial slave raiding by the Viking warlord Olaf in 869 and 871 may have been intended to secure his power and retain followers in a precarious political situation.[87] As in Poland, the influx of silver to Ireland via Dublin offers the potential to better understand concentrations of wealth and political power alongside datable coinage. In Scotland, for which there are even fewer written sources than for Greater Poland, examination of material wealth may likewise aid in interrogating the accumulation of power and territory by the kings of Alba. Each of these lines of enquiry, being substantial research questions themselves, are beyond the scope of this book, but they do establish the need for further study into the role of slave trading in early medieval power structures.

Apart from the elusive, high-level mechanisms of power consolidation, direct involvement in slaving offered rulers practical control over networks and supply. Pre-emptive or even retaliatory cross-border raiding not only sourced slaves who could be sold and taxed or distributed directly to followers as plunder but also allowed rulers to dictate the identity of the people flooding the markets. This theoretically enabled the targeting of non-Christians where there were still pagan populations, but it was more probably intended to prevent rulers' own subjects from ending up as chattel slaves. In other words, the primary motivations for slaving during peak periods may have been financial, but these were set against a backdrop of constant threats from outside in a period of fierce competition for human chattel, akin to the Piast precarity proposed by Roach and Marshall. The raiding evidence from central Europe suggests that the Přemyslids were initially content to sit back and let captives come to them, but that this lasted only until a flourishing Prague slave trade demonstrated the wealth to be gained by full control over slaving networks, from capture to taxation and sale. This interest is most visible in the period of large-scale slave trading but need not be exclusively linked to it. Captives taken on any royal or ducal campaigns could be moved to trade locations where rulers exerted the most control; the sale of captives in *emporia* in English kingdoms and Great Moravia would have enabled rulers to enforce any limitations on sale while extracting tolls.

Conclusion

Rulers had substantial involvement in slaving with the ability to maximise their financial benefits via taxation and control of local networks. The full effects of this seem to have been felt by the end of the tenth century, but there may well have been substantial impact from earlier, small-scale trading. In England, rulers seem to have perceived escalated slaving activity not only as an opportunity to gain wealth and exert military dominance over rivals but also as an avenue for extending legal and administrative jurisdiction. The lack of evidence from Bohemia gives the impression that dukes took a hands-off approach to oversight of slaving beyond the collection of tolls. Although this income is likely to have prompted Bohemian involvement in large-scale slaving operations, it also probably made dukes unwilling to reduce the new flow of wealth by legislative means. There is no direct evidence that points to the adoption of either method in Ireland, Wales, and Scotland, but the escalation of slaving by Irish kings and the contemporary centralisation of power in Alba means that we should consider whether slaving became a ubiquitous tool for ambitious rulers in politically fragmented areas of Europe in the tenth and eleventh centuries. In the two areas for which we do have appropriate surviving evidence, slaving and political power were inextricably linked. Active participation in slaving enabled rulers to amass the wealth and prestige to expand their influence, which ultimately allowed them to enact controls that shaped slaving to their desired effect. This further enhanced a ruler's wealth and power, creating a cycle that seemingly continued until the cessation of slave trading in the twelfth century, meaning that early medieval slaving was a driver of centralising power.

Notes

1 Bloch, 'Comment et pourquoi finit l'esclavage antique', 38–40. Bonnassie, *From Slavery to Feudalism*, pp. 32, 37.
2 Davis, *The Problem of Slavery in Western Culture*, pp. 91–106.
3 Pelteret, *Slavery in Early Mediaeval England*, pp. 89–101.
4 Fynn-Paul, 'Empire, monotheism and slavery', 4–5, 24, 26.
5 See the contributions by Jennifer A. Glancy, Hannah Barker, Viorel Achim, and William D. Phillips Jr. in Jeffrey Fynn-Paul and Damian A. Pargas (eds), *Slaving Zones: Cultural Identities, Ideologies, and Institutions in the Evolution of Global Slavery* (Leiden: Brill, 2018).
6 Rio, *Slavery after Rome*, pp. 227–9.
7 Wyatt, 'The significance of slavery', 337.
8 Jurasinski, *The Old English Penitentials*, p. 112. Jurasinski, 'Old English penitentials and the law of slavery', p. 108.
9 Miller, *The Problem of Slavery as History*, pp. 36–72.
10 Třeštík, '"Veliké město Slovanů jménem Praha"', pp. 49–70. For the importance of the Prague basin, see J. Sláma, 'Poznámky k problému historického významu některých raně středověkých hradišť

ve středních Čechách', *Archeologické rozhledy*, 29 (1977), 60–79. Archaeology has confirmed the expansion of fortifications in the territory surrounding Prague during Boleslav I's rule: I. Boháčová, 'Prague, Budeč, and Boleslav: the reflection of state formation in early medieval archaeological sources', in Macháček and Ungerman (eds), *Frühgeschichtliche Zentralorte*, pp. 371–95.

11 Jankowiak, 'Two systems of trade', p. 143. Hardt, 'The importance of the slave trade', pp. 81–93. Roach, 'The people-trafficking princes', 132–56.

12 For further historiography and analysis of this model specifically in relation to Miller's arguments, see Alice Rio, *Slaving and the Funding of Elite Status in Early Medieval Europe (ca. 800–1000 AD)* (Berlin: EB Verlag, 2024).

13 Cosmas of Prague, *Chronicle of the Czechs*, pp. 162–4.

14 Barbara Yorke, *Kings and Kingdoms of Early Anglo-Saxon England* (London: Routledge, 1990), pp. 17–18. Nora Berend, Przemysław Urbánczyk, and Przemysław Wiszewski, *Central Europe in the High Middle Ages: Bohemia, Hungary and Poland c. 900–c. 1300* (Cambridge: Cambridge University Press, 2013), p. 185. Peter Sawyer, 'Kings and merchants', in Peter H. Sawyer and Ian N. Wood (eds), *Early Medieval Kingship* (Leeds: University of Leeds, 1977), pp. 139–58.

15 See, IL, n. 42.

16 Rio, *Slavery after Rome*, pp. 223–4.

17 Patrick Wormald, '*Lex scripta* and *verbum regis*: legislation and Germanic kingship from Euric to Cnut', in Wormald (ed.), *Legal Culture*, pp. 37–8. Wormald, '"Inter cetera bona genti suae"', pp. 197–8.

18 Wormald, '"Inter cetera bona genti suae"', pp. 179–99.

19 John Hudson, *The Oxford History of the Laws of England: 871–1216* (Oxford: Oxford University Press, 2012), pp. 19–20.

20 Luděk Galuška, *Slované doteky předků: O životě na Moravě 6.-10. století* (Brno: Moravské Zemské Muzeum, 2004), pp. 117–20, 125–7. Comparison with Frankish and early English ecclesiastical organisation provides some possible interpretations for Great Moravia. David Kalhous, 'Graves, churches, culture and texts: the processes of Christianisation in the early Middle Ages and their social and cultural context', in Macháček and Wihoda (eds), *The Fall of Great Moravia*, pp. 110–29.

21 See p. 151.

22 Ine §3.2, pp. 372–3. *Zakon Sudnyj Ljudem,* §30, p. 21; §29, p. 21.

23 II Edward §6, p. 144. Tom Lambert, 'Theft, homicide and crime in late Anglo-Saxon law', *Past and Present*, 214 (2012), 3–43.

24 Edward and Guthrum §7.1, in Liebermann (ed.) *Die Gesetze*, i, p. 132. Wulfstan must have had a change of heart, since he 'revoked' the law later. II Cnut §45, pp. 342–4. On Wulfstan's authorship, see Dorothy Whitelock, 'The so-called laws of Edward and Guthrum', *English Historical Review*, 56 (1941), 1–21.

25 Æthelberht §24, p. 4.

26 Hlothhere & Eadric §5, pp. 9–10.

27 'Gif mon cierliscne mon geminde unsynnigne', Alfred §35, pp. 328–9.

28 See p. 99, n. 54.

29 *Zakon Sudnyj Ljudem,* §31, p. 21.

30 For dating, see George Molyneaux, 'The *Ordinance concerning the Dunsæte* and the Anglo-Welsh frontier in the late tenth and eleventh centuries', *Anglo-Saxon England*, 40 (2011), 249–72.

31 *Dunsæte Ordinance*, in Liebermann (ed.), *Die Gesetze*, i, p. 378.

32 The language here, specifically the word *forfang*, could potentially refer to the retrieval of a man who has been stolen or of a fugitive slave. It holds both meanings in Ine's law code – e.g. §53 and §72. Runaway slaves in English law were considered thieves, having stolen property (themselves) from their lord. Janel M. Fontaine, 'Slave resistance in early medieval England', *Anglo-Saxon England*, 49 (2022), 260.

33 *Poenitentiale Theodori*, II.xiii.1–2, p. 202.

34 See p. 98, n. 38.

35 Alexandre-Bidon and Lett, *Children in the Middle Ages*, pp. 21–31.

36 *Die altenglische Version des Halitgar'schen Bussbuches*, IV.21, p. 57.

37 *Někotoraja Zapověd*, §41, p. 45.

38 John Hudson, 'Kings and crime: ideology and practice in the tenth and twelfth centuries', in P. Chassaigne and J. Genet (eds), *Droit et société en France et en Grande Bretagne (XIIe–XXe siècles)* (Paris: Éditions de la Sorbonne, 2003), pp. 19–21.

39 Molyneaux, *Formation of the English Kingdom,* pp. 109–17. Hudson, 'Kings and crime', pp. 19–21.

40 James Campbell, 'The late Anglo-Saxon state: a maximum view', in James Campbell (ed.), *The Anglo-Saxon State* (London: Hambledon, 2000), p. 10. For debate on the dating of these developments, see David Pratt, 'Written law and the communication of authority in tenth-century England', in Rollason, Leyser, and Williams (eds), *England and the Continent in the Tenth Century*, pp. 331–50. Molyneaux, *Formation of the English Kingdom*, pp. 116–94. Tom

Lambert, *Law and Order in Anglo-Saxon England* (Oxford: Oxford University Press, 2017), pp. 163–201.

41 Patrick Wormald argues that later kings sought to restructure the system of justice so that communal enforcement was ultimately managed by royal authority: 'Giving God and king their due: conflict and its regulation in the early English state', in Wormald (ed.), *Legal Culture*, pp. 341–2. By contrast, Paul Hyams insists that feud remained the primary means of resolving legal disputes well beyond the Norman Conquest: Paul Hyams, 'Feud and the state in late Anglo-Saxon England', *Journal of British Studies*, 40:1 (2001), 1–43. Tom Lambert has reconsidered this idea, identifying what he believes to be two separate jurisdictions in later English law: kings' ideological, harshly punitive response to theft; and their regulatory, but not prohibitive, response to homicide. The gradual extension of royal protections over various locations increasingly brought homicide under the king's authority, meaning that the role of feud was neither unchanging, nor swiftly suppressed in the tenth century. Lambert, 'Theft', 41–2.

42 Alice Taylor, '*Lex scripta* and the problem of enforcement: Anglo-Saxon, Welsh and Scottish law compared', in F. Pirie and J. Scheele (eds), *Legalism: Community and Justice* (Oxford: Oxford University Press, 2014), pp. 47–75.

43 Simon Keynes, 'Royal government and the written word in late Anglo-Saxon England', in R. McKitterick (ed.), *The Uses of Literacy in Early Mediaeval Europe* (Cambridge: Cambridge University Press, 1990), p. 243

44 Lambert, *Law and Order*, pp. 216–24.

45 Levi Roach, 'Law codes and legal norms in later Anglo-Saxon England', *Historical Research*, 86 (2013), 465–86.

46 The handbook was a product of Wulfstan's close circle, if not his own work. Roger Fowler, 'A late Old English handbook for the use of a confessor', *Anglia*, 83 (1965), 6–12.

47 Malcolm Godden, 'Apocalypse and invasion in late Anglo-Saxon England', in Malcolm Godden, Douglas Gray, and T. F. Hoad (eds), *From Anglo-Saxon to Early Middle English: Studies Presented to E. G. Stanley* (Oxford: Oxford University Press, 1994), pp. 130–62.

48 Wulfstan of York, *Sermo Lupi*, pp. 58–9. Harbouring runaways was forbidden by the treaty of Alfred and Guthrum from the late ninth century and Æthelred's treaty with the vikings (*c.* 994). Alfred and Guthrum §5, p. 128. II Æthelred §6.2, p. 224.

49 Wormald, *Making of English Law*, pp. 352–5, 361.

50 II Cnut §76.1, pp. 362, 364.

51 II Cnut §76.2, p. 364.

52 Cosmas of Prague, *Chronicle of the Czechs*, pp. 162–4. Jan Mařík, 'Hinterlands of early medieval central places in Bohemia: archaeological and historical sources', in Machaček and Ungerman (eds), *Frühgeschichtliche Zentralorte*, p. 402. Dukes were obliged by the twelfth and thirteenth centuries to abide by the consensus of lords at regular assemblies, but Bak and Lukin believe that no reliable examples exist before the thirteenth century and are sceptical of Břetislav's decrees. J. Bak and P. Lukin, 'Consensus and assemblies in early medieval central and eastern Europe', in P. S. Barnwell and M. Mostert (eds), *Political Assemblies in the Earlier Middle Ages* (Turnhout: Brepols, 2003), pp. 98–100.

53 Libor Jan, 'Zrod zemského soudu v Čechách', in A. Barciak (ed.), *Kultura Prawna w Europie Środkowej* (Katowice: Instytut Górnośląski, 2006), p. 237.

54 Cosmas of Prague, *Chronicle of the Czechs*, pp. 162–4.

55 Francis Oakley, *Kingship: The Politics of Enchantment* (Malden, MA: Blackwell, 2006), espec. chap. 4.

56 See p. 98, n. 35.

57 II Edward §6, p. 144.

58 Wulfstan of York, *Sermo Lupi*, p. 57.

59 Author translation of V Æthelred §2, p. 238.

60 VII Æthelred §5, p. 261. Simon Keynes argues that this later Latin text is a translation of a lost Old English original and is probably close to what was promulgated at Bath, unlike the Old English text VIIa Æthelred, which may be a draft. Keynes, 'An abbot, an archbishop', 180.

61 'ealles to swiðe', Kennedy, 'Cnut's law code of 1018', p. 74.

62 William of Malmesbury, *Gesta Regum Anglorum*, i, p. 362.

63 II Cnut §3, p. 310.

64 For dating, see p.196, n. 58.

65 Dorothy Whitelock, M. Brett, and C. N. L. Brooke (eds), *Councils and Synods with Other Documents Relating to the English Church*, vol. 1: *871–1204* (Oxford: Oxford University Press, 1981), §28, part ii, p. 678.

66 *Někotoraja Zapověd*, §41, p. 45.

67 *Life of Saint Adalbert*, pp. 124–7.

68 On private churches, see Petr Sommer, *Svatý Prokop: Z počátků českého státu a církve* (Prague: Vyšehrad, 2007), pp. 28–9. Cf. David Kalhous, 'Problémy formování církevní správy v českých zemích v ránem středověku', *Studia Mediaevalia Bohemica*, 7 (2015), 7–36. On the secular oversight of priests, see Josef Žemlička, *Čechy v Době Knížecí (1034–1198)* (Prague: NakladatelstvíLidové noviny, 1997),

p. 180. Petr Sommer, 'České křestanství doby knížete Václava', in Petr Kubín (ed.), *Svatý Václav na památku 1100: Výročí narození knížete Václava Svatého* (Prague: Charles University, 2010), pp. 66–8.

69 CDB I, no. 375, p. 348. The grant of a tenth share of royal tax revenues is attested across Europe. Charters issued by Otto I in the 960s gave these funds to several German monasteries, meaning that the tenth of captives in this Bohemian charter more likely refers to toll revenue rather than the captives themselves. Neil Middleton, 'Early medieval port customs, tolls and controls of foreign trade', *Early Medieval Europe*, 13 (2005), 327–8.

70 CDB I, no. 55.

71 CDB I, no. 79.

72 Wolverton, *Hastening toward Prague*, p. 26.

73 Třeštík, '"Veliké město Slovanů jménem Praha"', p. 62.

74 William of Malmesbury, *Gesta Regum Anglorum*, pp. 496–8.

75 *Domesday Book*, vol. 2: *Sussex*, ed. John Morris (Chichester: Phillimore, 1976), pp. 1, 12.

76 Pelteret, *Slavery in Early Mediaeval England*, p. 156. For the texts, see Thorpe, *Diplomatarium Anglicum*, p. 627 (Bodmin Gospels, *c.* 1075), p. 646 (Exeter Book, *c.* 1133).

77 Maddicott, 'London and Droitwich', 51.

78 See p. 193, n. 21. Reeves may have had royal lawbooks to hand as part of their duties. Catherine Cubitt, 'As the lawbook teaches: reeves, lawbooks and urban life in the anonymous Old English Legend of the Seven Sleepers', *English Historical Review*, 124 (2009), 1044–7.

79 There was probably constant communication between kings and trade centres via reeves, who had to be informed of royal decisions and changes in the law. Keynes, 'Royal government', pp. 226–57. Attempts by kings to limit trade to ports and burhs under reeves' jurisdiction, coupled with the repetition of punishments for reeves who failed to carry out their duties, suggests that kings struggled to completely control trade. Molyneaux, *Formation of the English Kingdom*, p. 109. Simon Keynes, 'Crime and punishment in the reign of King Æthelred the Unready', in Ian Wood and Niels Lund (eds), *People and Places in Northern Europe 500–1600: Essays in Honour of Peter Hayes Sawyer* (Woodbridge: Boydell, 1991), pp. 69–70.

80 Jankowiak, 'Dirham flows', pp. 123–4.

81 The other major component of this trade was fur, but Andrew Roach has argued that fur revenue cannot have been enough to justify the quantities of silver present in Poland, since it does not result in comparable wealth elsewhere. Roach, 'The people-trafficking princes', 134. Cf. James Howard-Johnston, 'The fur trade in the early Middle

Ages', in Gruszczyńsky, Jankowiak, and Shepard (eds), *Viking-Age Trade*, pp. 57–74.

82 Roach, 'The people-trafficking princes', 132–56.

83 Andrew P. Roach and Alex Marshall, 'The dynamics of the drugs trade: a model for the study of the medieval trade in slaves?', in Gruszczyńsky, Jankowiak, and Shepard (eds), *Viking-Age Trade*, pp. 75–96.

84 Hardt, 'The importance of the slave trade', pp. 81–93.

85 Rio, *Slaving and the Funding of Elite Status*, pp. 39–57.

86 Rio, *Slaving and the Funding of Elite Status*, pp. 31–2.

87 Holm, 'The slave trade of Dublin', 320–1.

Epilogue

As we have seen, slave raiding appears to have declined through the second half of the eleventh century, albeit more sharply in some areas than in others. Slave trading can be seen to follow a similar trajectory (see Map 5), though outside England there is evidence for its continuance on a small scale into the second half of the twelfth century. Slaving was no longer a primary source of income or the basis of long-distance connections, and instead continued to support localised legal hierarchies. This epilogue examines the end of slave trading in the British Isles and the Czech lands and the reason for its disappearance, and ultimately proposes a model for early medieval slave trading suggested by these two case studies.

The twelfth century

Throughout the eleventh and twelfth centuries references to raiding and slave trading diminish and disappear from sources in which they had once been common. Amongst the English, raiding and slave taking appear only once or twice a decade in the *Anglo-Saxon Chronicle* after 1016, and after 1066 they disappear entirely.[1] As discussed in Chapter 4, this is almost certainly due to the new outcomes of warfare introduced with the Norman Conquest in 1066, in which combatants took captives exclusively for ransom. English narrative sources of the twelfth century that describe earlier slave trading make clear that it was considered an abhorrent and defunct practice in the author's own lifetime, meaning that slave trading did not long outlive the Council of Westminster's prohibition in 1102.[2] Hagiographers in Britain no longer counted the redemption of slaves among their subjects' accomplishments; Wulfstan of Worcester (d. 1095) and Margaret of Scotland (d. 1093) appear as the last saints concerned for the welfare of slaves.

Elsewhere, slave raiding seems to have continued into at least the first three or four decades of the twelfth century, though slave trading becomes far less detectable, suggesting reversion to a system that privileged ransoming and direct enslavement over sale. Raiding by the peoples of Scotland diminished and was usually undertaken by Galwegians and Highland *Scotti* rather than the Scots of Lothian, and accounts by English authors became increasingly stereotyped as time went on.[3] Nevertheless, a papal legate extracted a pledge from Galwegians in 1138 to return all captive girls and women whom they had taken in a previous campaign into England under David I.[4] Raiding and slave trading by Scandinavian inhabitants of the Western Isles, Orkney, and Shetland probably continued, but changes were likely to have been afoot with the ascension of David I to the Scots throne.[5] Although he seems to have had limited ability to prevent his armies from enslaving people, David himself had been raised to knighthood at the Anglo-Norman court, and his reign saw the subsequent introduction of Norman lordship to Scotland, all of which would have hastened the decline of slave-holding in the kingdom of the Scots.

In Wales and Ireland, raiding continued even as captive taking became less visible. In Ireland, this shift occurs around 1115, after which only a few annals indicate anything on a scale comparable to the tenth and eleventh centuries, though cattle rustling remained frequent.[6] Despite close connections between the English and Dublin churches and nobilities throughout the eleventh century, the importation of English slaves to Ireland only faced internal opposition in 1169, when the Council of Armagh believed the Norman invasion to be God's punishment for the importation of English slaves.[7] It may have been this Irish Sea slave trading by both the Irish and Scandinavians that prompted continued raiding by the Welsh, whom John of Worcester accused of selling innumerable people into slavery abroad during a rebellion against the Norman lord Richard FitzGilbert.[8] The Welsh may have been enslaving captives as late as the 1197 sacking of Aberystwyth, though the complete disappearance of slave trading from the source material by this point suggests it was not for the purpose of sale.[9]

Bohemian slave raiding continued in a similar manner, becoming rare in surviving sources after the first quarter of the century and ultimately disappearing altogether. Bohemians took captives on early twelfth-century campaigns into Poland, and the chronicler Gallus Anonymus claims that they encouraged the Holy Roman Emperor to invade Poland in 1109 because they were 'accustomed to living off raiding and plunder'.[10] The last mention of slave raiding appears in the chronicle of the Canon of Vyšehrad, who claimed that the Přemyslid duke Soběslav I carried off captives and plunder from Poland in 1132 and 1133.[11] Nevertheless, any contemporary slave trading could not have been substantial. As in Britain, concern for captives fails to appear after the first half of the eleventh century in hagiographical traditions of holy men other than Adalbert, and the last tangential reference to trade is in Vladislav's prohibition of Jewish ownership of Christians in 1124. Local transactions, largely invisible throughout the early Middle Ages, may have continued for a time, and slave populations could still theoretically be replenished via inherited status.[12] That said, saleability is a fundamental aspect of chattel slave status, and we must consider that, when slaving appears to have ceased, significant changes must have been under way.

Until the last known legal injunctions against slave trading were issued in the twelfth century, there is little to suggest that previous restrictive rulings were effective enough to be the major force behind the disappearance of slaving. The reissue and revision of laws and canons in England imply that few of these precipitated long-term change in and of themselves, and there were almost always limitations on the types of people and trade the laws sought to restrict. That injunctions against the sale of Christians to non-Christians do not appear any later than the first half of the eleventh century could have as much to do with the Christianisation of Scandinavia, and therefore the change of a pagan market into a Christian one, as they do the successful enforcement of these prohibitions. In Ireland, the Council of Armagh focused only on the enslavement of the English, and, in the Czech lands, Vladislav was concerned only with those Christians enslaved to Jews. The Council of Westminster is unique in its blanket prohibition and may stem from the moral context of England under the Norman lords, whose style of warfare was already separate from enslavement.[13]

There are several problems with assigning these measures causal roles in the end of slave trading, particularly long-distance slave trading, either via the power of the 'state' or the Church. Chapter 7 established that ending the slave trade was not in the economic interest of rulers, and most rulings inspired by Christian mores do not portray slavery or even slave trading as wholly immoral. Instead, these twelfth-century laws and canons may have been the last of their kind, because of broader social and economic changes that were already taking place. As discussed in Chapters 4 and 6, enslavement and slave trading were already in decline in the second half of the eleventh century. Raiding within England appears to have become greatly reduced during Cnut's reign, which in turn must have reduced the scale of enslavement. A gradual decline in the creation of saleable slaves must have accelerated when the shift to Norman warfare meant that war captives were no longer enslaved.[14] Any void in long-distance slave trading created by this sharp change may have been filled for a time by the purchase of slaves from Ireland or people sold directly from areas most devastated by Danish, Norwegian, and Norman armies, but this could not have been an extended practice. Other forms of unfreedom, particularly unfree tenancy, had become increasingly prevalent before 1066, and a dramatic reduction in slave supply may have accelerated this process.[15] The Council of Westminster's canon gives the appearance of an official clerical position regarding a declining activity, but this blanket ban was not wholly effective, since English slaves and captives were still being brought to Ireland as late as 1169. By the second half of the twelfth century, however, the flow of enslaved English into Ireland could not have been substantial, and Gerald of Wales strongly implies that willing involvement in slave trading by the English had ended by the late twelfth century, their ways having been corrected by Norman rule.[16]

For Ireland, external markets had also gradually dried up over the course of the eleventh and twelfth centuries. The cessation of dirham flows into Gotland in the late tenth century suggests that captives from Ireland could not have been connected to demand in central and western Asia, and the flurry of new settlement in the North Atlantic was complete by this time.[17] The potential export of Irish slaves to the Continent would also have slowed, as unfree tenancy became the favoured scheme for agricultural labour as early as the tenth century, and the Norman conquests of England and Wales probably heralded changing demand for slaves in those regions. Any demand still extant in Wales could be satisfied by raiding Norman estates. There may still have been demand for slaves in areas of Scotland, particularly those under Norse control, but overall export would have diminished considerably.

Bohemia likewise experienced social and economic changes that must have significantly, if indirectly, reduced the role of slave trading. Other forms of agrarian unfreedom in western Europe had gradually become prevalent over the course of the ninth through eleventh centuries, possibly as a result of increasing seigneurial powers, which would have diminished the demand for chattel slaves there.[18] A recent assessment of charters suggests that serfs – or, rather, unfree tenants who were not chattel slaves but not juridically serfs – were present on Czech estates as early as the eleventh century, and that by 1124 they were well established.[19] The internal demand for chattel slaves must have waned as a consequence of these changes when external demand from the neighbouring Frankish realm seemingly disappeared altogether. The collapse of the Umayyad Caliphate also would have been a significant blow to slave trading in Prague, as civil wars and increasingly weak rulers ultimately led to the deposition of the last caliph in 1031.[20] The Umayyads were the chief consumers of slaves, and, with less money and stability for importing slaves, servants, and concubines, the market for expensive *saqāliba* imported over vast distances may have withered, and we see a corresponding end to the steady export of these people into north Africa.[21]

In the British Isles and the Czech lands, twelfth-century rulings against slave trading seem to have been issued at a point when this practice, especially the export of slaves, was already seriously reduced, and the profitability for rulers and ecclesiastical institutions was a fraction of what it had been a century previously. What this situation indicates is that central authority – secular or ecclesiastical – played a secondary role in ending the slave trade. Most of the laws and canons assumed to mark the end of slave trading were just as selective as those issued during its peak, pointing to the primary importance of the social and economic changes of the eleventh and twelfth centuries, which reduced the general demand for chattel slave labour across Europe.

Towards a model of slaving

Slaving in the British Isles and the Czech lands bears sufficient similarities to establish a possible model of slave raiding and trading, if not for early medieval Europe as a whole then, at least, for the politically fragmented regions on the fringes of the former Roman Empire. The comparison of the two regions in this book has suggested that norms present in early medieval contexts, such as endemic warfare, tensions related to Christianisation, and the consolidation and centralisation of power, led to similar patterns of slaving in disparate, unconnected areas. The processes and participants were not identical, being ultimately defined by the particulars of individual societies and polities, but broad patterns nevertheless emerge in both small- and large-scale trading contexts.

Similarities

The peoples of the British Isles and the Czech lands practised slavery from the earliest emergence of our source material through to the twelfth century. As in much of Europe, enslaved people served predominantly in domestic roles at a household level and could be deployed on larger estates in England and the Czech lands in agricultural and pastoral roles. There is very little evidence of changes in the scale of slave labour or its importance to the societies that benefited from it, despite slavery's increasing visibility over a period of between four to eight centuries depending on the area. This is not the case for the eastern and western ends of the Mediterranean, where slavery existed on a far greater scale than in the rest of Europe and was deeply ingrained in household economies and in ideas about the display of wealth. The limited reproductive capabilities of enslaved populations in the Islamic world and restricted access to people residing within the House of Islam created a constant and voracious demand for enslaved Europeans. The lesser Byzantine demand for foreign slaves and the demand for labourers in settlement-era Iceland added to this milieu, creating a perfect storm of demand on the European periphery in the ninth and tenth centuries. The lands between the slaving zones and these areas of demand served primarily as transit zones, where middlemen moved enslaved people through territories that were well connected to demand centres. The extreme separation of zones of supply and zones of demand was an essential factor in the escalation of early medieval slave trading, which supplied deracinated and exoticised foreigners to caliphal armies and administration as well as to Byzantine workshops and elite households.

Within the slaving zones, only the enslavement of captives could respond elastically to the demand fostered by the interlinkage of these regions, but demand did make judicially or customarily enslaved people vulnerable to slaving networks. Endemic warfare in the slaving zones facilitated the enslavement of captives, all of which visibly escalated in response to the expansion of trade connectivity in northern and east central Europe in the second half of the ninth century and the tenth. It is probably not a coincidence that the British Isles and the Czech lands were both politically fragmented areas where new, highly mobile raiders had appeared on the scene. Captive taking was common to all raiders in Europe, but these were pagan outsiders with the ability to attack across wide geographical ranges, who disregarded political borders. Political fragmentation made it more difficult for people in the British Isles and east central Europe to coordinate strong responses, as was done against vikings in al-Andalus and to some degree in Francia. The development of new trade networks in turn linked slaving zones to areas of high demand via raiders' home territory, namely the maritime routes of the North and Irish Seas across Scandinavia to the rivers of eastern Europe, and Magyar connections to the Black Sea and the borders of Byzantium. This enabled raiders to simultaneously become high-volume slave traders.

This is not to say that substantial external demand introduced commercial slave trading to either region. As long as people were saleable, they could be caught up in trade networks that served to move luxury and mundane goods over long distances. English and Moravian slaves could be trafficked as far as the Mediterranean in the eighth and ninth centuries, respectively, by professional merchants operating as middlemen between suppliers and consumers, though in many of the documented cases the people being sold had not been captured by those seeking primarily to exploit the profitability of slave trading. Instead, ransoming practices and local trading meant that slave sales were often ad hoc, serving as a response to specific circumstances within a household. Long-distance slave trading was also a solution to significant political problems caused by the capture of notable individuals who could not be executed. New networks introduced by foreign raiders changed this slaving landscape dramatically, but evidence of ad hoc sales through the eleventh century demonstrates that not all long-distance slave trading needed to be part of large-scale operations.

Even as trade networks expanded, we have to remember that these routes served to move many different types of goods and that slave trading, although it clearly increased along with such connectivity, was only one part of these vast systems. Viking and Magyar raids were not initially prompted by the profitability of slaving, but, once trade had linked these peoples to demand in the Abbasid Caliphate and Byzantium, slaving became an important aspect of their martial activity. Increasing wealth derived from these networks encouraged native elites within the slaving zones to partake, leading to the diversification of these slaving systems. As routes and participants became less exclusive, long-distance demand could continue to be supplied even through periods of pacification between various groups, such as the English and the Danes in the second half of the ninth century or the Franks and the Magyars in the first half of the tenth. Shifting political landscapes in fragmented regions meant that raiding was always being undertaken by someone, and a multitude of routes and participants continued to move slaves across Europe.

Commercial slave trading did not move along linear, designated routes, though it probably operated in stages along primary and secondary corridors of trade. Market hubs allowed for local sales and shorter-distance commercial trade, which dispersed enslaved people within the slaving zones (from England to Ireland, for example) and accommodated long-distance traders who moved enslaved people through neighbouring transit zones. It is very likely that some people initially sold out of the slaving zones were purchased for households within the transit zones, and we cannot be sure of the proportion of people who were trafficked the full extent of the routes made possible by interconnected networks, such as from Ireland to Baghdad or from Prague to Egypt via al-Andalus. Ethnicity, gender, and age may have impacted the distances along which certain people were transported, with castrated Slavic boys in the tenth century probably making the longest journeys, beginning with their capture in eastern Europe, their transport westward across the European continent, and their export to north Africa and the Middle East via Iberia.

Despite the enormous changes in the scale of slave trading from the seventh through the eleventh centuries, there were two absolute constants: diversity of merchants and diversity of the enslaved. There is very little evidence to support the idea of slave trading monopolies by Jews or Vikings, or to demonstrate that the enslavement of Slavs was driven by restrictions on the sale of Christians to non-Christians. Anyone of any origin or religion could become a chattel slave or traffic people, and raiders and traders seem to have had few qualms about selling people with a shared language, culture, or religion to distant lands. Although rulers endeavoured to protect their own people from unjust enslavement and paid lip service to ecclesiastical disgust at the sale of Christians to non-Christians, they themselves ultimately benefited from the wide variety of people who bought and sold slaves within their realms through tax revenues. Their own participation in slaving attracted wealth and followers that allowed rulers to consolidate power while simultaneously weakening enemies, meaning that slaving functioned as a driver of centralising power in these fragmented areas.

This context, alongside continued selectivity of legislation, suggests that slaving did not end in the eleventh and twelfth centuries primarily because of moral outrage or the increasing ability of rulers to restrict enslavement and slave trading. The most important blow to these networks was, instead, a decline in demand for northern and Slavic slaves from the principal centres of consumption, predominantly in the Islamic world. Changes to political landscapes, such as the unification of England, Denmark, and Norway in 1016, and to mentalities of warfare that reduced the scope for enslavement were both important contributing factors in England, but a desire for the protection of co-religionists everywhere was not. Slaving in early medieval Europe remained diverse and flexible until its demise.

Regional differences

Even with these broad regional similarities between slaving in the British Isles and the Czech lands, there are some important differences that need to be highlighted. The first is chronology, indicating that the scaling up and subsequent diversification of raiding and slave trading did not happen within a particular timeframe. In the British Isles, Scandinavian conquest and settlement and subsequent political alliances between these peoples and native groups established a context in which these changes to slaving could occur more rapidly. Direct connection to Scandinavia, which was linked to Abbasid demand already in the first half of the ninth century and became a source of higher demand itself from around 870 to 940, also led to the development of large-scale slaving over the course of the second half of the ninth century. In the Czech lands, direct connections took longer to form, probably due both to the relatively abrupt termination of Great Moravian networks in the early tenth century and to Bohemia's initial role as a broker for Magyar and Ottonian slaving. It was not until the second half of the tenth century that Bohemia, where Prague was already known as a regional slave-trading hub, began to expand its own slaving interests, assisted by political decentralisation on the eastern Frankish marches and the formation and breakdown of alliances between the Přemyslid rulers of Bohemia, the Piast rulers of Poland, the Slavic confederations between the rivers Elbe and Oder, and the Ottonian kings and emperors in Francia.

Prague's position as a redistribution hub in trans-European trade networks is another key difference between the slaving zones studied here. For much of the tenth century Bohemians benefited financially from long-distance slave-trading networks, though they themselves had little direct participation in them. By hosting the market(s) that attracted traders, they ensured that a stream of captives could be brought in by other raiders – a situation facilitated by the severe disruption of Abbasid trade farther east, which led to a shift in the directional focus of Polish slave trading. Nowhere in the British Isles appears to have followed a similar pattern. Although Dublin ultimately came to be supplied principally with captives taken in Irish raids on other Irish kingdoms, large-scale slave trading initially developed there because the Scandinavian raiders and settled Hiberno-Norse sourced enslaved captives themselves. The evidence available makes it very difficult to ascertain whether Prague's development as a slave-trading hub was by chance or due to deliberate positioning by its rulers, but it seems highly likely that they would have encouraged such a profitable trade under circumstances that posed little political or military risk to themselves.

Drawing out the broad similarities in the development of slave trading in two unconnected regions offers the opportunity to place slaving firmly within the particular political, economic, and even social spheres in which it operated. By establishing regional differences, we can understand how individual contexts created divergent paths that could ultimately lead to similar outcomes. In less abstract terms, such a model illustrates the profound significance of trade connections in the early medieval world. Distinct practices of slavery in areas typically treated as peripheral to Europe could prompt changes in warfare, economic development, and even rulership in distant lands that were otherwise completely disparate. The similar trajectories of polities and trade networks typically portrayed in scholarship as entirely unrelated begs the question of how such trends of connectivity and control were replicated globally in other early medieval slave-trading contexts, such as sub-Saharan links to Islamic states in Asia and north Africa and during the development of geographically extensive centralised states in Central and South America. As made clear throughout this study, the supply, treatment, and disposal of human chattel prompted unique considerations regarding trade, and the model proposed here is unlikely to hold relevance for the exchange of other types of goods. Nevertheless, slave trading has been perpetrated for much of human history, and themes such as the importance of network connections, the roles of slaving and transit zones, and the diversity of participants echo slaving systems outside the medieval period, in which wealthy centralised states with high levels of economic organisation prompted the exploitation of politically fragmented areas far away.

For early medieval Europe more specifically, comparison between the British Isles in the Viking Age and the Czech lands in the tenth and eleventh centuries supports two important conclusions. First, there was a marked increase in slave-trading activity, which began as early as the late ninth century and peaked in the late tenth and early eleventh centuries, though the precise timings of peaks and other significant waves of activity varied due to the economic and political factors impacting each region and its networks. Second, even with more commercialised systems of larger-scale slave trading, connections between areas of slave supply and slave demand were almost certainly not linear in nature. They involved diverse raiders, traders, and victims moving gradually towards points of highest demand rather than direct highways transporting people and goods from one area to another and vice versa. Slave trading was nothing new to early medieval societies, but by the tenth century its scope and the goals of its active participants had undeniably changed. It had become a large-scale system that constituted, without a doubt, the highest volume of human trafficking seen in northern and eastern Europe since the fall of the Western Roman Empire.

Notes

1 Followers of William II Rufus captured and sold the Bishop of Durham's men in 1088, but Matthew Strickland believes that, given the context of 'forcible distraint', these were unfree tenants rather than freemen. Strickland, *War and Chivalry*, p. 316. *Symeonis Monachi Opera Omnia*, ed. Thomas Arnold, 2 vols (London: Longman & Co., 1885), i, p. 173.
2 Orderic Vitalis, *The Ecclesiastical History of Orderic Vitalis*, vol. 4: *Books VII and VIII*, ed. and trans. Marjorie Chibnall (Oxford: Oxford University Press, 1983), pp. 138–9. William of Malmesbury, *Vita Wulfstani*, pp. 102–3. Gerald of Wales, *Expugnatio Hibernica*, p. 70.
3 Strickland, *War and Chivalry*, pp. 294–304.
4 Richard of Hexam, *De gestis regis Stephani et de bello Standardii*, in J. Raine (ed.), *The Priory of Hexham, Its Chroniclers, Endowments and Annals*, 2 vols (Durham: Surtees Society 44, 1868), i, p. 99. John of Hexham, Historia Johannis, Prioris Haugustadensis ecclesiae, in Raine (ed.), *The Priory of Hexham*, i, pp. 116, 121.
5 Strickland, *War and Chivalry*, pp. 315, 324–8.
6 See p. 16, n. 26.
7 Patrick F. Wallace, 'The English presence in Viking Dublin', in Blackburn (ed.), *Anglo-Saxon Monetary History*, pp. 203–7.
8 *The Chronicle of John of Worcester*, vol. 3, ed. and trans. P. McGurk (Oxford: Oxford University Press, 1998), pp. 220–1. The *Gesta Stephani* records that the captives were young people of both sexes. *Gesta Stephani*, ed. and trans. K. R. Potter (Oxford: Oxford University Press, 1976), pp. 18–19.
9 *Brut y Tywysogyon: Red Book of Hergest Version*, ed. and trans. Thomas Jones (Cardiff: University of Wales Press, 1955), s. a. 1196, p. 179.

10 Gallus Anonymus, *Gesta Principium Polonorum*, pp. 161, 209, 229.
11 *Canonici Wissegradensis continuatio Cosmae*, ed. Josef Emler, in *Fontes Rerum Bohemicarum*, 8 vols (Prague: Nákladatelství Musea Království Českého, 1874), ii, p. 216.
12 For example, in the United States the importation of slaves was made illegal in 1807, but slavery itself did not end officially for another 56 years, with the issue of the Emancipation Proclamation in 1863.
13 Whitelock et al. (eds), *Councils & Synods I*, §28, ii, p. 678. Strickland, 'Slaughter, slavery or ransom', pp. 41–59. Alice Rio has argued that Norman lords may have been willing to let claims to free status go unchallenged on their new lands to prevent resistance to their lordship. Rio, *Slavery after Rome*, pp. 208–9.
14 Strickland, 'Slaughter, slavery or ransom', pp. 41–59.
15 Pelteret, *Slavery in Early Mediaeval England*, pp. 251–4.
16 Gerald of Wales, *Expugnatio Hibernica*, p. 70.
17 The rate of settlement in Greenland was always much lower than in Iceland. J. Arneborg, 'The Norse settlements in Greenland', in Fitzhugh and Ward (eds), *Vikings: The North Atlantic Saga*, p. 591. Hereditary slave status in Iceland would have reduced the need to import captives. Karras, *Slavery and Society*, pp. 50–3.
18 Wendy Davies, 'On servile status in the early Middle Ages', in M. L. Bush (ed.), *Serfdom and Slavery: Studies in Legal Bondage* (London: Longman, 1996), pp. 242–5. The use of enslaved women in Mediterranean Europe continued beyond the demise of agricultural slavery. Stuard, 'Ancillary evidence', 3–28.
19 Petráček, *Power and Exploitation*, pp. 104–6.
20 Collins, *Caliphs and Kings*, pp. 195–204.
21 Hugh Kennedy, *Muslim Spain and Portugal: A Political History of Al-Andalus* (Harlow: Longman, 1996), pp. 132–3, 140.

Bibliography

Primary sources

Ælfric's Colloquy, ed. G. N. Garmonsway, 2nd edn (London: Methuen, 1947).
Adalbert of Magdeburg, *Continuatio Regionis*, ed. F. Kurze, MGH SS rer. Germ. 50 (Hanover, 1890), pp. 154–79.
Adam of Bremen, *Gesta Hammaburgensis Ecclesiae Pontificum*, ed. Bernhard Schmeidler, MGH, SS. Rer. Germ. 2 (Hanover, 1917).
Adam of Bremen, *History of the Archbishops of Hamburg–Bremen*, trans. Francis J. Tschan (New York, NY: Columbia University Press, 1959).
Adomnán's Life of Columba, ed. and trans. Alan Orr Anderson and Marjorie Ogilvie Anderson (Oxford: Oxford University Press, 1991).
Agobard of Lyon to Louis the Pious, ed. E. Dümmler, MGH, Epist. 5 (Hanover, 1899), pp. 182–5.
Alcuin to Higbald, ed. E. Dümmler, MGH, Epist. 4 (Hanover, 1895), pp. 57–8.
Das altenglische Bussbuch, ed. Robert Spindler (Leipzig: Bernhard Tauchnitz, 1934).
Die altenglische Version des Halitgar'schen Bussbuches, ed. Josef Raith (Hamburg: H. Grand, 1933).
Altfrid, *Vita Liudgeri episcopi Mimigardefordensis*, ed. G. H. Pertz, MGH, SS rer. Merov. 2 (Hanover, 1879), pp. 403–19.
The Ancient Laws and Institutes of Ireland, ed. and trans. W. N. Hancock et al., 6 vols (Dublin: Stationery Office, 1865–1901).
Annala Rioghachta Eireann: Annals of the Kingdom of Ireland by the Four Masters, ed. and trans. J. O'Donovan (Dublin: Hodges and Smith, 1848).
Annales Cambriae AD 682–954: Texts A–C in Parallel, ed. and trans. David N. Dumville (Cambridge: Department of Anglo-Saxon, Norse, and Celtic, 2002).
Annales Corbeienses, ed. G. Pertz, MGH, SS 3 (Hanover, 1839), pp. 1–18.
Annales Fuldenses, ed. G. Pertz and F. Kurze, MGH, SS rer. Germ. 7 (Hanover, 1891).
Annales Hildesheimenses, ed. G. Waitz, MGH, SS rer. Germ. 8 (Hanover, 1878).

Annales Quedlinburgenses, ed. M. Giese, MGH, SS rer. Germ. 72 (Hanover, 2004).
Annales Regni Francorum, ed. F. Kurze, MGH, SS rer. Germ. 6 (Hanover, 1895).
The Annals of Inisfallen (MS. Rawlinson B. 503), ed. and trans. Seán Mac Airt (Dublin: Dublin Institute for Advanced Studies, 1944).
The Annals of Ulster, ed. and trans. Seán Mac Airt and Gearóid Mac Niocaill (Dublin: Dublin Institute of Advanced Studies, 1983).
Annals of Ulster, ed. and trans. W. M. Hennessy and B. MacCarthy (Dublin: Stationery Office, 1887).
The Anglo-Saxon Chronicle: A Collabourative Edition, ed. David Dumville and Simon Keynes, 17 vols (Cambridge and Woodbridge: Brewer, 1983–2007).
Bartoňková, Dagmar (ed. and trans.), *Magnae Moraviae Fontes Historici*, 5 vols (Brno: Masaryk University Press, 1967).
Bavarian Geographer, *Descriptio civitatum et regionum ad septentrionalem plagam Danubii*, in Erwin Herrmann (ed.), *Slawisch–germanische Beziehungen im südostdeutschen Raum von der Spätantike bis zum Ungarnsturm* (Munich: R. Lerche, 1965), pp. 212–21.
Bede's Ecclesiastical History of the English People, ed. and trans. Bertram Colgrave and R. A. B. Mynors (Oxford: Oxford University Press, 1969).
Bernold of Constans, *Chronicon*, ed. I. S. Robinson, MGH, SS rer. Germ. N.S. 14 (Hanover, 2003), pp. 383–540.
Bieler, Ludwig (ed. and trans.), *The Irish Penitentials* (Dublin: Dublin Institute of Advanced Studies, 1963).
Bieler, Ludwig (ed.), *Libri Epistolarum Sancti Patricii Episcopi* (Dublin: Royal Irish Academy, 1952; repr. 1993).
Binchy, D. A., 'The saga of Fergus Mac Léti', *Ériu*, 16 (1952), 33–48.
Birch, Walter de Gray (ed.), *Cartularium Saxonicum*, 3 vols (London: Whiting & Co., 1893).
Bitterauf, T. (ed.), *Die Traditionen des Hochstifts Freising*, vol. 1: *744–926* (Munich: Rieger'sche Universitätsbuchhandlung, 1905).
Brut y Tywysogion: Peniarth MS. 20 Version, ed. and trans. Thomas Jones (Cardiff: University of Wales Press, 1952).
Brut y Tywysogyon: Red Book of Hergest Version, ed. and trans. Thomas Jones (Cardiff: University of Wales Press, 1955).
Cáin Adamnáin: An Old-Irish Treatise on the Law of Adamnan, ed. and trans. Kuno Meyer (Oxford: Oxford University Press, 1905).
Canonici Wissegradensis continuatio Cosmae, ed. Josef Emler, in *Fontes Rerum Bohemicarum*, 8 vols (Prague: Nákladatelství Musea Království Českého, 1874), pp. 203–37.
The Chronicle of John of Worcester, vol. 3, ed. and trans. P. McGurk (Oxford: Oxford University Press, 1998).
Chronicum Scotorum, ed. and trans. William M. Hennessy (London: Longmans, 1866).
Codex Diplomaticus et Epistolaris Regni Bohemiae, ed. G. Friedrich, 3 vols (Prague: Czech Academy of Sciences, 1904).

Cormac Úa Cuilennáin, *Sanas Cormaic*, in Kuno Meyer (ed.), *Anecdota from Irish Manuscripts*, vol. 4 (Dublin: Hodges, Figgis & Co., 1912), pp. 1–128.

Cosmas of Prague, *The Chronicle of the Czechs*, ed. János M. Bak and Pavlína Rychterová, trans. Pavla Mutlová and Martyn Rady (Budapest: Central European University Press, 2020).

Cronica Regum Mannie and Insularum, ed. and trans. George Broderick, 2nd edn (Douglas: Manx National Heritage, 1995).

Dado of Rouen, *Vita Eligii ep. Noviomagensis*, ed. B. Krusch, MGH, SS rer. Merov. 4 (Hanover, 1902), pp. 635–761.

Davies, Wendy (ed.), *The Llandaff Charters* (Aberystwyth: National Library of Wales, 1979).

El 'Ḏikr al-Aqālīm' de Isḥāq ibn al-Ḥasan al-Zayyāt, ed. and trans. Fransisco Castelló (Barcelona: University of Barcelona, 1989).

Domesday Book, vol. 2: *Sussex*, ed. John Morris (Chichester: Phillimore, 1976).

The Earliest Life of Gregory the Great, ed. B. Colgrave (Lawrence, KS: University of Kansas Press, 1968).

Eirik the Red's Saga, trans. Keneva Kunz, in Gísli Sigurðsson (ed.), *The Vinland Sagas* (London: Penguin, 2008), pp. 23–50.

Epistola Theotmari episcopi, ed. Fritz Lošek MGH, *Studien und Texte* 15 (Hanover, 1997).

Evans, J. G. (ed.), *The Text of the Book of Llan Dâv* (Oxford: Oxford University Press, 1893).

Fowler, Roger, 'A late Old English handbook for the use of a confessor', *Anglia*, 83 (1965), 1–34.

Fragmentary Annals of Ireland, ed. and trans. Joan Newlon Radner (Dublin: Dublin Institute for Advanced Studies, 1978).

Freshfield, Edwin Hanson (ed. and trans.), *Roman Law in the Later Byzantine Empire* (Cambridge: Bowes & Bowes, 1938).

Gallus Anonymus, *Gesta Principium Polonorum*, ed. and trans. Paul W. Knoll and Frank Schaer (Budapest: Central European University Press, 2003).

Gayangos, Pascual de (trans.), *The History of the Mohammedan Dynasties in Spain*, 2 vols (London: Oriental Translation Fund, 1840–1843).

Gerald of Wales, *Expugnatio Hibernica*, ed. and trans. A. B. Scott and F. X. Martin (Dublin: Royal Irish Academy, 1978).

Gesta Stephani, ed. and trans. K. R. Potter (Oxford: Oxford University Press, 1976).

Gildas: The Ruin of Britain and Other Works, ed. and trans. Michael Winterbottom (London: Philimore & Co, 1978).

Golb, Norman, and Omeljan Pritsak (eds), *Khazarian Hebrew Documents of the Tenth Century* (Ithaca, NY: Cornell University Press, 1982).

Gúbretha Caratniad, in Rudolf Thurneysen (ed.), 'Aus dem irischen Recht III', *Zeitschrift für Celtische Philologie*, 15 (1925), 302–70.

Haddan, Arthur West, and William Stubbs (eds), *Councils and Ecclesiastical Documents Relating to Great Britain and Ireland*, 3 vols (Oxford, 1869–1878).

Haji, Hamid (ed. and trans.), *Founding the Fatimid State: The Rise of an Islamic Empire* (London: I.B. Tauris, 2006).
Herman of Reichenau (Contractus), *Chronicon*, ed. G. H. Pertz, MGH, SS 5 (Hanover, 1849), pp. 67–133.
The Hibernensis, ed. and trans. Roy Flechner (Washington, DC: Catholic University of America Press, 2019).
Howlett, D. R. (ed.), *The Book of Letters of Saint Patrick the Bishop* (Dublin: Four Courts Press, 1994).
Hudson, Benjamin T., 'The Scottish Chronicle', *The Scottish Historical Review*, 77:204 (1998), 129–61.
Inquisitio de thelonis Raffelstettensis, ed. A. Boretius and V. Kraus, MGH, Capit. 2 (Hanover, 1897), pp. 249–53.
Jurasinski, Stefan, and Lisi Oliver (eds and trans.), *The Laws of Alfred: The* Domboc *and the Making of Anglo-Saxon Law* (Cambridge: Cambridge University Press, 2021).
Kaiser, Daniel H. (ed. and trans.), *The Laws of Rus': Tenth to Fifteenth Centuries* (Salt Lake City, UT: Charles Schlacks, Jr., 1992).
Kennedy, A. G., 'Cnut's law code of 1018', *Anglo-Saxon England*, 11 (1982), 57–81.
Kupfer, Frantiszek, and Tadeusz Lewicki (eds and trans.), *Źródła Hebajskie do Dziejów Słowian I Niektórych Innych Ludów Środkowej I Wschodniej Europy* [*Hebrew Sources for the History of the Slavs and Some Other Peoples of Central and Eastern Europe*] (Warsaw: Polish Academy, 1956).
Landnámabók, trans. H. Pálsonn and P. Edwards (Winnipeg: University of Manitoba Press, 1972).
Lantbert, *Vita Herberti Archiep. Coloniensis*, ed. G. Pertz, MGH SS 4 (Hanover, 1841), pp. 739–53.
Lapidge, Michael (ed.), *The Cult of St Swithun* (Oxford: Oxford University Press, 2003).
The Law of Hywel Dda: Law Texts from Medieval Wales, ed. and trans. Dafydd Jenkins (Llandysul: Gomer Press, 1986).
The Laws of the Isaurian Era: The Ecloga *and Its Appendices*, trans. Mike Humphreys (Liverpool: Liverpool University Press, 2017).
Laxdæla Saga, trans. M. Magnusson (London: Penguin, 1969).
Lebor na Cert, ed. and trans. M. Dillon (Dublin: Irish Texts Society, 1962).
Legenda Christiani, ed. and trans. Jaroslav Ludvíkovský (Prague: Vyšehrad, 1978).
Lewicki, Tadeusz, 'Opis Pragi w arabskim słowniku geograficznym al-Himjarīego (XV wiek)' ['Description of Prague in the Arabic geographical dictionary of al-Himjarī (15th century)'], *Archeologia Polski* 16 (1971), 695–700.
Lewicki, Tadeusz (ed. and trans.), *Źródła arabskie do dziejów Słowiańszczyzny* [*Arabic Sources for the History of the Slavs*], vol. 1 (Wrocław: Wyd. Polskeij Academii Nauk, 1956).

Lewis, Bernard (ed. and trans.), *Islam from the Prophet Muhammad to the Capture of Constantinople*, 2 vols (Oxford: Oxford University Press, 1987).

Lex Baiwariorum, ed. E. de Schwind, MGH, Leges 3 (Hanover, 1926), pp. 261–335.

Le Liber Pontificalis, ed. L. Duchesne, 2 vols (Paris: E. Thorin, 1886).

Liebermann, Felix (ed.), *Die Gesetze der Angelsachsen*, 3 vols (Halle: Max Niemeyer, 1903–1916).

The Life of Bishop Wilfrid by Eddius Stephanus, ed. and trans. Bertram Colgrave (Cambridge: Cambridge University Press, 1985).

Life of Saint Adalbert Bishop of Prague and Martyr, ed. and trans. C. Gaşpar, in G. Klaniczay (ed.), *Saints of the Christianisation Age of Central Europe (Tenth–Eleventh Century)* (Budapest: Central European University Press, 2013), pp. 77–182.

The Life of Saint Basil the Younger, ed. and trans. Denis F. Sullivan, Alice-Mary Talbot, and Stamatina McGrath (Washington, DC: Dumbarton Oaks, 2014).

Liutprand of Cremona, *Antapodosis*, ed. J. Becker, MGH, SS rer. Germ. 41 (Hanover, 1915), pp. 1–158.

The Lives of the Eighth-Century Popes (Liber Pontificalis), trans. Raymond Davis, 2nd edn (Liverpool: Liverpool University Press, 2007).

Ludvíkovský, Jaroslav, 'Nově zjištěný rukopis legendy *Crescente fide* a jeho význam pro datování Kristiána' ['A newly discovered manuscript of the legend *Crescente fide* and its significance for dating Christian'], *Listy Filologické*, 81 (1958), 56–68.

Lunde, Paul and Caroline Stone (eds and trans.), *Ibn Fadlān and the Land of Darkness: Arab Travellers in the Far North* (London: Penguin, 2012).

MacLean, Simon, *History and Politics in Late Carolingian and Ottonian Europe: The* Chronicle *of Regino of Prüm and Adalbert of Magdeburg* (Manchester: Manchester University Press, 2009).

Marcus, J. R. (ed. and trans.), *The Jew in the Medieval World: A Sourcebook, 315–1791* (Cincinnati: Hebrew Union College Press, 1999).

Medieval Slavic Lives of Saints and Princes, ed. and trans. M. Kantor (Ann Arbor, MI: Michigan Slavic Publications, 1983).

The Metrical Dindsenchas, ed. and trans. Edward Gwynn, 5 vols (Dublin: Hodges, Figgis, 1903–1935).

Nicephorus, *The Life of St Andrew the* Fool, ed. and trans. Lennart Rydén, 2 vols (Uppsala: Uppsala University Press, 1995).

Novellae, ed. Rudolph Schoell, *Corpus Iuris Civilis*, vol. 3, 6th edn (Berlin: Wiedmann, 1956).

The Novels of Justinian: A Complete Annotated English Translation, ed. David J. D. Miller and Peter Sarris (Cambridge: Cambridge University Press, 2018).

The Old English Canons of Theodore, ed. R. D. Fulk and Stefan Jurasinski (Oxford: Oxford University Press, 2012).

The Old English History of the World: An Anglo-Saxon Rewriting of Orosius, ed. and trans. Malcolm Godden (Cambridge, MA: Harvard University Press, 2016).

Online Decreta Regni Mediaevalis Hungariae: The Laws of the Medieval Kingdom of Hungary (2019). All complete monographs 4. https://digitalcommons.usu.edu/lib_mono/4 (accessed 22 July 2023).

Orderic Vitalis, *The Ecclesiastical History of Orderic Vitalis*, vol. 4: *Books VII and VIII*, ed. and trans. Marjorie Chibnall (Oxford: Oxford University Press, 1983).

Owen, A. (ed. and trans.), *Ancient Laws and Institutes of Wales* (London: Public Records Commissioners, 1841).

Pactum Hlotharii I, ed. A. Boretius and V. Krause, MGH Capit. 2 (Hanover, 1897), pp. 130–5.

The Poetic Edda, vol. 2: *Mythological Poems*, ed. and trans. Ursula Dronke (Oxford: Oxford University Press, 1997).

Rabin, Andrew (ed. and trans.), *The Political Writings of Archbishop Wulfstan of York* (Manchester: Manchester University Press, 2015).

Raine, J. (ed.), *The Priory of Hexham, Its Chroniclers, Endowments and Annals*, 2 vols (Durham: Surtees Society 44, 1868).

Regino of Prüm, *Chronicon*, ed. F. Kurze, MGH SS rer. Germ. 50 (Hanover, 1890), pp. 1–153.

Rees, W. J. (ed.), *Lives of the Cambro British Saints* (London: Longman, 1853).

Reuter, Timothy (trans.), *The Annals of Fulda* (Manchester: Manchester University Press, 1992).

Rimbert, *Vita Anskarii*, ed. G. Waitz, MGH, SS rer. Germ. 55 (Hanover, 1884).

Robinson, I. S., *Eleventh-Century Germany: The Swabian Chronicles* (Manchester: Manchester University Press, 2008).

The Russian Primary Chronicle: Laurentian Text, trans. S. H. Cross and O. P. Sherbowitz-Wetzor (Cambridge, MA: Medieval Academy of America, 1953).

S. Gregorii Magni Opera: Registrum Epistularum Libri I–VII, ed. Dag Norberg (Turnhout: Brepols, 1982).

Stengel, Edmund E. (ed.), *Urkundenbuch des Klosters Fulda*, vol. 1 (Marburg: Elwert, 1913; repr. 1958).

Stokes, Whitely (ed. and trans.), *The Annals of Tigernach*, 2 vols (Felinfach: Llanerch, 1993).

Squatriti, Paolo (ed. and trans.), *The Complete Works of Liutprand of Cremona* (Washington, DC: Catholic University of America Press, 2007).

Symeonis Monachi Opera Omnia, ed. Thomas Arnold, 2 vols (London: Longman & Co., 1885).

Tair Colofn Cyfraith: Three Columns of Law in Medieval Wales, ed. and trans. T. M. Charles-Edwards and P. Russell (Bangor: Welsh Legal History Society, 2005).

Thietmari Merseburgensis episcopi chronicon, ed. R. Holtzmann, MGH, SS rer. Germ. N.S. 9 (Berlin, 1935).

Thorpe, Benjamin (ed.), *Diplomatarium Anglicum Ævi Saxonici* (London: Macmillan, 1865).
Thurneysen, Rudolf (ed. and trans.), *Irisches Recht* (Berlin: Verlag der Akademie der Wissenschaften, 1931).
Turgot, *Life of St Margaret Queen of Scotland*, trans. W. Forbes-Leith (Edinburgh: W. Paterson, 1884).
Die Urkunden Heinrichs IV, part 3, ed. Alfred Gawlik, MGH, Diplomata (Hanover, 1978).
Die Urkunden Konrads II, ed. H. Bresslau, MGH, Diplomata (Hanover, 1909).
Vašica, Josef, 'Církevněslovanský penitenciál českého puvodů' ['A Church Slavonic penitential of Bohemian provenance'], *Slavia*, 29 (1960), 31–48.
Vita Amandi Episcopi I, ed. B. Krusch and W. Levison, MGH, SS rer. Merov. 5 (Hanover, 1910), pp. 431–49.
Vita Filiberti Abbatis Gemeticensis et Heriensis, ed. B. Krusch and W. Levison, MGH, SS rer. Merov. 5 (Hanover, 1910), p. 568–606.
Vita Findani, ed. O. Holder-Egger, MGH, SS 55 (Hanover, 1887), pp. 502–6.
Vita Griffini Filii Conani, ed. and trans. Paul Russell (Cardiff: University of Wales Press, 2005).
Vita Prima Sanctae Brigitae, ed. Ioannus Bollandus and Godefridus Henschenius, *Acta Sanctorum* (repr. Paris: Éditions Culture et Civilisation, 1863), Februarii I, pp. 118–29.
Vita Sanctae Balthildis A, ed. B. Krusch, MGH, SS rer. Merov. 2 (Hanover, 1888), pp. 475–508.
Vita Sancti Ciarani Abbatis de Cluain mic Nois, in *Vitae Sanctorum Hiberniae*, ed. Charles Plummer, 2 vols (Oxford: Oxford University Press, 1910), i, pp. 200–16.
Wandalbert of Prüm, *Miracula Sancti Goaris*, ed. W. Wattenbach, MGH, SS 15.1 (Hanover, 1887), pp. 361–73.
Wasserschleben, F. W. H. (ed.), *Die Bussordnungen der abendländischen Kirche* (Halle: Ch. Graeger, 1851).
The War of the Gaedhil with the Gaill, ed. and trans. James Henthorn Todd (London: Longman, 1867).
Warner, David A., *Ottonian Germany: The* Chronicon *of Thietmar of Merseburg* (Manchester: Manchester University Press, 2001).
Warner of Rouen, *Moriuht*, ed. and trans. Christopher J. McDonough (Toronto: Pontifical Institute of Medieval Studies, 1995).
Whitelock, Dorothy (ed. and trans.), *Anglo-Saxon Wills* (Cambridge: Cambridge University Press, 1930).
Whitelock, Dorothy (ed.), *English Historical Documents*, vol. 1: *500–1042* (Oxford: Oxford University Press, 1955).
Whitelock, Dorothy, M. Brett, and C. N. L. Brooke (eds), *Councils and Synods with Other Documents Relating to the English Church*, vol. 1: *871–1204*, 2 parts (Oxford: Oxford University Press, 1981).
Widukind of Corvey, *Deeds of the Saxons*, trans. Bernard S. Bachrach and David S. Bachrach (Washington, DC: Catholic University of America Press, 2014).

Widukind of Corvey, *Res Gestae Saxonicae*, ed. H. E. Lohmann and Paul Hirsch, MGH, SS rer. Germ. 60 (Hanover, 1935).

The Will of Æthelgifu: A Tenth Century Anglo-Saxon Manuscript, ed. Dorothy Whitelock (Oxford: Roxburghe Club, 1968).

William of Malmesbury, *Gesta Regum Anglorum*, ed. R. A. B. Mynors, R. M. Thomson, and M. Winterbottom, 2 vols (Oxford: Oxford University Press, 1998).

William of Malmesbury: Saints' Lives: Lives of ss. Wulfstan, Dunstan, Patrick, Benignus and Indract, ed. and trans. R. M. Thompson and M. Winterbottom (Oxford: Oxford University Press, 2002).

Wulfstan of York, *Sermo Lupi ad Anglos*, ed. Dorothy Whitelock (Exeter: Exeter University Press, 1976).

Zakon Sudnyj Ljudem, ed. and trans. H. W. Dewey and A. M. Kleimola (Ann Arbor, MI: Michigan Slavic Publications, 1977).

Secondary sources

Abrams, Lesley, 'Diaspora identity in the Viking Age', *Early Medieval Europe*, 20:1 (2012), 17–38.

Alexandre-Bidon, D. and D. Lett, *Children in the Middle Ages: Fifth–Fifteenth Centuries* (Notre Dame, IN: University of Notre Dame Press, 1999).

Amitai, Reuven, 'The Mamlūk institution, or one thousand years of military slavery in the Islamic world', in Christopher Leslie Brown and Paul D. Morgan (eds), *Arming Slaves: From Classical Times to the Modern Age* (New Haven, CT: Yale University Press), pp. 40–78.

Androshchuk, Fedir, *Vikings in the East: Essays on Contacts along the Road to Byzantium* (Uppsala: Uppsala University, 2013).

Arneborg, J., 'The Norse settlements in Greenland', in W. W. Fitzhugh and E. Ward (eds), *Vikings: The North Atlantic Saga* (Washington, DC: Smithsonian Institution, 2000), pp. 304–17.

Ayalon, David, 'On the eunuchs in Islam', *Jerusalem Studies in Arabic and Islam*, 1 (1979), 67–124.

Ayalon, David, *Eunuchs, Caliphs and Sultans: A Study in Power Relationships* (Jerusalem: Magnes, 1999).

Bachrach, Bernard S., *Early Carolingian Warfare: Prelude to Empire* (Philadelphia, PA: University of Pennsylvania Press, 2001).

Bachrach, David S., *Warfare in Tenth-Century Germany* (Woodbridge: Boydell, 2012).

Bagge, Sverre, *Kings, Politics, and the Right Order of the World in German Historiography c.950–1150* (Leiden: Brill, 2002).

Bak, J., and P. Lukin, 'Consensus and assemblies in early medieval central and eastern Europe', in P. S. Barnwell and M. Mostert (eds), *Political Assemblies in the Earlier Middle Ages* (Turnhout: Brepols, 2003), pp. 95–113.

Balcárek, Petr, *Byzantium in the Czech Lands (4th–16th Centuries)* (Leiden: Brill, 2023).

Balcárková, A., et al., 'Archeologický výzkum raně středověkého sídliště Kostice Zadní hrúd v letech 2009–2011' ['Archaeological investigation at the early medieval settlement Kostice Zadní hrúd in 2009–2011'], *Archeologické rozhledy*, 65 (2013), 735–75.

Banaji, Jarius, 'Late antiquity to the early Middle Ages: what kind of transition?', *Historical Materialism*, 19:1 (2011), 109–44.

Barker, Hannah, *That Most Precious Merchandise: The Mediterranean Trade in Black Sea Slaves, 1260–1500* (Philadelphia, PA: University of Pennsylvania Press, 2019).

Bartlett, Robert, *The Making of Europe: Conquest, Colonisation and Cultural Change 950–1350* (Princeton, NJ: Princeton University Press, 1994).

Bažantová, Nina, 'Romanesque and early Gothic silk textiles from Czech sources', in Petr Charvát and Jiří Prosecký (eds), *Ibrahim ibn Ya'qub at-Turtushi: Christianity, Islam and Judaism Meet in East-Central Europe, c. 800–1300 AD* (Prague: Czech Academy of Sciences, 1996), pp. 93–102.

Benedictow, Ole Jørgen, 'The demography of the Viking Age and the High Middle Ages in the Nordic countries', *Scandinavian Journal of History*, 21:3 (1996), 151–82.

Berend, Nora, Przemysław Urbánczyk, and Przemysław Wiszewski, *Central Europe in the High Middle Ages: Bohemia, Hungary and Poland c. 900–c. 1300* (Cambridge: Cambridge University Press, 2013).

Betti, Maddalena, 'La *Descriptio civitatum et regionum ad septentrionalem plagam Danubii:* lo spazio oltre il "*limes*" nel IX secolo', *Mélanges de l'École française de Rome – Moyen Âge*, 125:1 (2013), https://doi.org/10.4000/mefrm.1078 (accessed 3 October 2023).

Betti, Maddalena, *The Making of Christian Moravia (858–882): Papal Power and Political Reality* (Leiden: Brill, 2014).

Biermann, Felix, and Marek Jankowiak (eds), *The Archaeology of Slavery in Early Medieval Northern Europe: The Invisible Commodity* (Cham: Springer, 2021).

Bláhová, M., 'Verschriftlichte Mündlichkeit in der Böhmischen Chronik des Domherrn Cosmas von Prag', in A. Adamska and M. Mostert (eds), *The Development of Literate Mentalities in East Central Europe* (Turnhout: Brepols, 2004), pp. 323–42.

Blair, John, *The Church in Anglo-Saxon Society* (Oxford: Oxford University Press, 2005).

Blair, John, *Building Anglo-Saxon England* (Princeton, NJ: Princeton University Press, 2018).

Blinkhorn, Paul, *The Ipswich Ware Project* (Dorchester: Medieval Pottery Research Group, 2012).

Bloch, Marc, 'Comment et pourquoi finit l'esclavage antique', *Annales. Économies, Sociétés, Civilisations*, 2:2 (1947), 30–44, 161–70.

Boháčová, Ivana, 'Prague, Budeč, and Boleslav: the reflection of state formation in early medieval archaeological sources', in Jiří Macháček and Šimon Ungerman (eds), *Frühgeschichtliche Zentralorte in Mitteleuropa* (Bonn: Habelt, 2011), pp. 371–95.

Bois, Guy, *The Transformation of the Year One Thousand: The Village of Lounard from Antiquity to Feudalism*, trans. Jean Birrell (Manchester: Manchester University Press, 1992).

Bolton, Timothy, *Cnut the Great* (New Haven, CT: Yale University Press, 2017).

Bonnassie, Pierre, *From Slavery to Feudalism in South-Western Europe*, trans. Jean Birrell (Cambridge: Cambridge University Press, 1991).

Bosworth, C. E., et al., 'al-Sakāliba', in P. Bearman et al. (eds), *The Encyclopaedia of Islam*, vol. 8, 2nd edn (Leiden: Brill, 1995), pp. 872–81.

Brady, Lindy, 'The "dark Welsh" as slaves and slave traders in Exeter Book riddles 52 and 72', *English Studies*, 95:3 (2014), 235–55.

Brink, Stefan, *Thraldom: A History of Slavery in the Viking Age* (Oxford: Oxford University Press, 2021).

Bromberg, Erik I., 'Wales and the mediaeval slave trade', *Speculum*, 17:2 (1942), 263–9.

Brugge, David M., 'The Spanish borderlands', in Jacob Ernest Cooke (ed.), *Encyclopedia of the North American Colonies*, 3 vols (New York, NY: Maxwell Macmillan, 1993), ii, pp. 91–101.

Buchanan, Courtney Helen, 'Scandinavians in Strathclyde: multiculturalism, material culture and manufactured identities in the Viking Age', in Anna Ritchie (ed.), *Historic Bute: Land and People* (Edinburgh: Scottish Society for Northern Studies), pp. 17–32.

Buko, Andrzej, '"Tribal" societies and the rise of early medieval trade', in Joachim Henning (ed.), *Post-Roman Towns, Trade and Settlement in Europe and Byzantium*, 2 vols (Berlin: De Gruyter, 2007), i, pp. 431–50.

Byrne, Mary E., 'On the punishment of sending adrift', *Ériu*, 11 (1932), 97–102.

Cameron, Catherine M., *Captives: How Stolen People Changed the World* (Lincoln, NE: University of Nebraska Press, 2016).

Campbell, James, 'The late Anglo-Saxon state: a maximum view', in James Campbell (ed.), *The Anglo-Saxon State* (London: Hambledon, 2000), pp. 1–30.

Caswell, Fuad Matthew, *The Slave Girls of Baghdad: The Qiyan in the Early Abbasid Era* (London: I.B. Tauris, 2011).

Charles-Edwards, T. M., 'The Welsh law of theft: Iorwerth versus the rest', in T. M. Charles-Edwards and P. Russell (eds and trans.), *Tair Colofn Cyfraith: Three Columns of Law in Medieval Wales* (Bangor: Welsh Legal History Society, 2005), pp. 109–30.

Charles-Edwards, T. M., *Wales and the Britons, 350–1064* (Oxford: Oxford University Press, 2014).

Charvát, Petr, 'Who are Ibrahim's "Turks"? (a discussion note)', in Petr Charvát and Jiří Prosecký (eds), *Ibrahim ibn Ya'qub*

at-Turtushi: Christianity, Islam and Judaism Meet in East-Central Europe, c. 800–1300 AD (Prague: Czech Academy of Sciences, 1996), pp. 72–3.
Charvát, Petr, *Boleslav II: Sjednotitel českého státu* [*Boleslav II: Unifier of the Czech State*] (Prague: Vyšehrad, 2004).
El Cheikh, Nadia Maria, 'Revisiting the Abbasid harems', *Journal of Middle East Women's Studies*, 1:3 (2005), 1–19.
El Cheikh, Nadia Maria, 'Servants at the gate: eunuchs at the court of Al-Muqtadir', *Journal of the Economic and Social History of the Orient*, 48:2 (2005), 234–52.
El Cheikh, Nadia Maria *Women, Islam and Abbasid Identity* (Cambridge, MA: Harvard University Press, 2015).
Christys, Ann, *Vikings in the South: Voyages to Iberia and the Mediterranean* (London: Bloomsbury, 2015).
Clarke, H. B., 'Domesday slavery (adjusted for slaves)', *Midland History*, 1:4 (1972), 37–46.
Collins, Roger, *Caliphs and Kings: Spain, 796–1031* (Chichester: Wiley, 2012).
Connolly, Seán, '*Vita Prima Sanctae Brigitae:* background and historical value', *Journal of the Royal Society of Antiquaries of Ireland*, 119 (1989), 5–49.
Constable, Olivia Remie, 'Spain and Mediterranean slavery: the medieval slave trade as an aspect of Muslim–Christian relations', in Scott L. Waugh and Peter D. Diehl (eds), *Christendom and Its Discontents: Exclusion, Persecution, and Rebellion, 1000–1500* (Cambridge: Cambridge University Press, 1996), pp. 264–82.
Constable, Olivia Remie, *Trade and Traders in Muslim Spain* (Cambridge: Cambridge University Press, 1996).
Crone, Patricia, *Slaves on Horses: The Evolution of the Islamic Polity* (Cambridge: Cambridge University Press, 1980).
Cubitt, Catherine, 'As the lawbook teaches: reeves, lawbooks and urban life in the anonymous Old English Legend of the Seven Sleepers', *English Historical Review*, 124 (2009), 1021–49.
Darby, H. C., *The Domesday Geography of Eastern England* (Cambridge: Cambridge University Press, 1952).
Darby, H. C., *Domesday England* (Cambridge: Cambridge University Press, 1977).
Davies, Wendy, *An Early Welsh Microcosm: Studies in the Llandaff Charters* (London: Royal Historical Society, 1978).
Davies, Wendy, 'On servile status in the early Middle Ages', in M. L. Bush (ed.), *Serfdom and Slavery: Studies in Legal Bondage* (London: Longman, 1996), pp. 225–46.
Davis, David Brion, *The Problem of Slavery in Western Culture* (Oxford: Oxford University Press, 1966).
Delvaux, Matthew C., Transregional slave networks of the Northern Arc, 700–900 CE (PhD thesis, Boston College, 2019).

Devroey, Jean-Pierre, 'Men and women in early medieval serfdom: the ninth-century north Frankish evidence', *Past & Present*, 166 (2000), 3–30.

Dockès, Pierre, *Medieval Slavery and Liberation*, trans. A. Goldhammer (Chicago, IL: Chicago University Press, 1982).

Edwards, Nancy, *The Archaeology of Early Medieval Ireland* (London: Routledge, 1990).

Efthymiadis, Stephanos, 'Hagiography from the "Dark Age" to the age of Symeon Metaphrastes (eighth–tenth centuries)', in Stephanos Efthymiadis (ed.), *The Ashgate Research Companion to Byzantine Hagiography*, 2 vols (Farnham: Ashgate, 2011), i, pp. 95–142.

Ellis, Caitlin, 'Perceptions of the slave trade in Britain and Ireland: "Viking" and "Celtic" stereotypes', *Quaestio Insularis*, 19 (2018), 126–56.

Eska, C. M., 'Women and slavery in the early Irish laws', *Studia Celtica Fennica*, 8 (2011), 29–39.

Etchingham, Colmán, *Viking Raids on Irish Church Settlements in the Ninth Century* (Maynooth: Department of Old and Middle Irish, 1996).

Etchingham, Colmán, 'Slavery or ransom? Why vikings took captives in Ireland and beyond', in Matthias Toplak, Hanne Østhus, and Rudolf Simek (eds), *Viking-Age Slavery* (Vienna: Fassbaender, 2021), pp. 117–46.

Faith, Rosamund, *The English Peasantry and the Growth of Lordship* (London: Leicester University Press, 1997).

Finley, Moses, *Ancient Slavery and Modern Ideology*, expanded edn, ed. Brent D. Shaw (Princeton, NJ: Marcus Wiener, 1998).

Flechner, Roy, and Janel M. Fontaine, 'The admission of former slaves into churches and monasteries: reaching behind the sources', *Early Medieval Europe*, 29:4 (2021), 586–611.

Fontaine, Janel M., 'Early medieval slave-trading in the archaeological record: comparative methodologies', *Early Medieval Europe*, 25:4 (2017), 469–73.

Fontaine, Janel M., 'Archbishop Wulfstan and the slave trade', in Matthias Toplak, Hanne Østhus, and Rudolf Simek (eds), *Viking-Age Slavery* (Vienna: Fassbaender, 2021), pp. 147–64.

Fontaine, Janel M. 'Slave resistance in early medieval England', *Anglo-Saxon England*, 49 (2022), 253–84.

Foote, Peter E., 'Þrælahald Á íslandi', *Saga*, 15 (1977), 41–74.

Fouracre, Paul, and Richard A. Gerberding, *Late Merovingian France: History and Hagiography 640–720* (Manchester: Manchester University Press, 1996).

Franklin, S., and J. Shepard, *The Emergence of Rus, 750–1200* (Routledge: London, 1996).

Fransson, Ulf, et al. (eds), *Cultural Interaction between East and West: Archaeology, Artefacts and Human Contacts in Northern Europe* (Stockholm: Stockholm University, 2007).

Franz, Kurt, 'Slavery in Islam: legal norms and social practice', in Reuven Amitai and Christoph Cluse (eds), *Slavery and the Slave Trade in the*

Eastern Mediterranean (c. 1000–1500) (Turnhout: Brepols, 2017), pp. 51–142.

Fraser, James E., *From Caledonia to Pictland: Scotland to 795* (Edinburgh: Edinburgh University Press, 2009).

Friedmann, Bernhard, *Untersuchungen zur Geschichte des abodritischen Fürstentums* (Berlin: Duncker & Humblot, 1986).

Fynn-Paul, Jeffrey, 'Empire, monotheism and slavery in the greater Mediterranean region from antiquity to the early modern era', *Past and Present*, 205 (2009), 3–40.

Fynn-Paul, Jeffrey, and Damian A. Pargas (eds), *Slaving Zones: Cultural Identities, Ideologies, and Institutions in the Evolution of Global Slavery* (Leiden: Brill, 2018).

Gaiser, Adam, 'Slaves and silver across the Strait of Gibraltar: politics and trade between Umayyad Iberia and Khājirite north Africa', *Medieval Encounters*, 19 (2013), 41–70.

Galuška, Luděk, 'O otrocích na Velké Moravě a okovech ze Starého Města' ['On slaves in Great Moravia and the surroundings of Staré Město'], in Jan Klápště, Eva Plešková, and Josef Žemlička (eds), *Dějiny ve věku nejistot: Sborník k příležitosti 70. narozenin Dušana Třeštíka* [*History in an Age of Uncertainty: A Collection on the Occasion of Dušan Třeštík's 70th Birthday*] (Prague: Nakladatelství Lidové noviny, 2003), pp. 75–86.

Galuška, Luděk, *Slované doteky předků: O životě na Moravě 6.–10. století* [*Slav Contacts with the Ancestors: On Life in Moravia 6th–10th Centuries*] (Brno: Moravské Zemské Muzeum, 2004).

Galuška, Luděk, et al., 'The glass of Great Moravia: vessel and window glass, and small objects', *Journal of Glass Studies*, 54 (2012), 65–7.

Gardeła, Leszek, *Bad Death in the Early Middle Ages: Atypical Burials from Poland in a Comparative Perspective* (Rzeszów: Wydowca, 2017).

Gil, Moshe, 'The Rādhānite merchants and the land of Rādhān', *Journal of the Economic and Social History of the Orient*, 17 (1974), 299–328.

Gillingham, John, 'Christian warriors and the enslavement of fellow Christians', in Martin Aurell and Catalina Girbea (eds), *Chevalerie et Christianisme aux XIIe et XIIIe siècles* (Rennes: Presses de universitaires de Rennes, 2011), pp. 237–56.

Gillingham, John, 'Women, children, and the profits of war', in Janet L. Nelson et al. (eds), *Gender and Historiography: Studies in the Earlier Middle Ages in Honour of Pauline Stafford* (London: Institute of Historical Research, 2012), pp. 61–74.

Godden, Malcolm, 'Apocalypse and invasion in late Anglo-Saxon England', in Malcolm Godden, Douglas Gray, and T. F. Hoad (eds), *From Anglo-Saxon to Early Middle English: Studies Presented to E. G. Stanley* (Oxford: Oxford University Press, 1994), pp. 130–62.

Golb, Norman, *The Caliph's Favourite: New Light on Manuscript Sources of Hasdai ibn Shaprut of Cordova* (Chicago, IL: Oriental Institute of the University of Chicago, 2011).

Goldberg, Eric J., *Struggle for Empire: Kingship and Conflict under Louis the German, 817–876* (Ithaca, NY: Cornell University Press, 2006).

Gordon, Matthew S., 'Preliminary remarks on slaves and slave labour in the Abbasid Empire', in Laura Culbertson (ed.), *Slaves and Households in the Near East* (Chicago, IL: University of Chicago Press, 2011), pp. 71–84.

Graus, František, *Dějiny venkovského lidu v Čechách v době Předhusitské* [*History of Rural People in Bohemia in the Pre-Hussite Age*], 2 vols (Prague: Státní nakladatelství politické literatury, 1953).

Grimmer, Martin, 'Britons in early Wessex: the evidence of the law code of Ine', in Nicholas Higham (ed.), *Britons in Anglo-Saxon England* (Woodbridge: Boydell & Brewer, 2007), pp. 102–14.

Gruszczynski, J., M. Jankowiak, and J. Shepard (eds), *Viking-Age Trade: Silver, Slaves and Gotland* (Abingdon: Routledge, 2021).

Gulløv, H. C., 'Natives and Norse in Greenland', in W. W. Fitzhugh and E. Ward (eds), *Vikings: The North Atlantic Saga* (Washington, DC: Smithsonian Institution, 2000), pp. 318–26.

Hadley, Dawn, et al., 'The winter camp of the Viking Great Army, AD 872–3, Torksey, Lincolnshire', *The Antiquaries Journal*, 96 (2016), 23–67.

Hall, Richard, 'A check-list of Viking-Age coin finds from Ireland', *Ulster Journal of Archaeology*, 36/37 (1973/74), 71–86.

Halsall, Guy 'Anthropology and the study of pre-conquest warfare and society: the ritual war in Anglo-Saxon England', in Sonia Chadwick Hawkes (ed.), *Weapons and Warfare in Anglo-Saxon England* (Oxford: Oxford University Press, 1989), pp. 155–77.

Halsall, Guy, *Warfare and Society in the Barbarian West, 450–900* (London: Routledge, 2003).

Hamerow, Helena, *Rural Settlements and Society in Anglo-Saxon England* (Oxford: Oxford University Press, 2012).

Hammer, Carl I., *A Large-Scale Slave Society of the Early Middle Ages: Slaves and Their Families in Early Medieval Bavaria* (Burlington, VT: Ashgate, 2002).

Hanuliak, Milan, 'Ungewöhnliche Bestattungen in Siedlungsgruben des 9. bis 12. Jh.', *Ethnographische-Archäologische Zeitschrift*, 36:1 (1995), 125–36.

Hardt, Matthias, 'The importance of the slave trade for the Slavic princes of the Early and High Middle Ages', in G. Bührer-Thierry, R. Le Jan, and V. Loré (eds), *Acquérir, prélever, contrôler les ressources en compétition (400–1100)* (Turnhout: Brepols, 2017), pp. 81–93.

Harper, Kyle, *Slavery in the Late Roman World, AD 275–425* (Cambridge: Cambridge University Press, 2011).

Harvey, P. D. A., '*Rectitudines Singularum Personarum* and *Gerefa*', *English Historical Review*, CVIII:426 (1993), 1–22.

Havelková, P., et al., 'Enthesopathies and activity patterns in the early medieval Great Moravian population: evidence of division of labour', *International Journal of Osteoarchaeology*, 21:4 (2011), 487–504.

Havelková, P., M. Hladík, and P. Velemínský, 'Entheseal changes: do they reflect socioeconomic status in the early medieval central European population? (Mikulčice – Klášteřisko, Great Moravian Empire, 9th–10th century)', *International Journal of Osteoarchaeology*, 23:2 (2013), 237–51.

Helgason, A., et al., 'mtDNA and the origin of the Icelanders: deciphering signals of recent population history', *American Journal of Human Genetics*, 66:3 (2000), 999–1016.

Helgason, A., et al., 'Estimating Scandinavian and Gaelic ancestry in the male settlers of Iceland', *American Journal of Human Genetics*, 67:3 (2001), 723–37.

Hemer, Katie A., 'To tread the paths, and traverse the moors: investigating slavery in early medieval western Britain', in Felix Biermann and Marek Jankowiak (eds), *The Archaeology of Slavery in Early Medieval Northern Europe: The Invisible Commodity* (Cham: Springer, 2021), pp. 43–52.

Henderson, Julian, 'The politics of production, glass provenance and social context on the early Islamic silk roads', *Journal of Islamic Archaeology*, 8:2 (2021), 203–37.

Hendy, Michael F., *Studies in Byzantine Monetary Economy c. 300–1450* (Cambridge: Cambridge University Press, 1985).

Henning, Joachim, 'Gefangenenfesseln im slawischen Siedlungsraum und der europäische Sklavenhandel im 6.–12. Jahrhundert', *Germania*, 70 (1992), 403–26.

Henning, Joachim, 'Slavery or freedom? The causes of early medieval Europe's economic advancement', *Early Medieval Europe*, 12:3 (2003), 269–77.

Henning, Joachim, 'Strong rulers, weak economy? Rome, the Carolingians, and the archaeology of slavery in the first millennium AD', in Jennifer R. Davis and Michael McCormick (eds), *The Long Morning of Medieval Europe* (Burlington, VT: Ashgate, 2008), pp. 33–53.

Henning, Joachim, and Matthias Ruttkay, 'Frühmittelalterliche Burgwälle an der mittleren Donau im ostmitteleuropäischen Kontext: ein deutsch–slowakisches Forschungsprojekt', in Jiří Machaček and Šimon Ungerman (eds), *Frühgeschichtliche Zentralorte in Mitteleuropa* (Bonn: Habelt, 2011), pp. 259–88.

Herold, Hajnalka, 'Fortified settlements of the 9th and 10th centuries AD in central Europe: structure, function and symbolism', *Medieval Archaeology*, 56 (2012), 60–84.

Hilsch, Peter, 'Die Juden in Böhmen und Mähren im Mittelalter und die Ersten Privilegien', in F. Seibt (ed.), *Die Juden in den böhmischen Ländern* (Munich: R. Oldenburg Verlag, 1983), pp. 13–26.

Hodges, Richard, *Dark Age Economics: The Origins of Towns and Trade, AD 600–1000* (London: Duckworth, 1982).

Hogendorn, Jan S., 'The location of the "manufacture" of eunuchs', in Miura Toru and John Edward Philips (eds), *Slave Elites in the Middle East and Africa* (London: Keagan Paul International, 2000), pp. 41–68.

Holm, Poul, 'The slave trade of Dublin, ninth to twelfth centuries', *Peritia*, 5 (1986), 317–45.

Holsoe, Svend E. 'Slavery and economic response among the Vai (Liberia and Sierra Leone)', in Suzanne Miers and Igor Kopytoff (eds), *Slavery in Africa: Historical and Anthropological Perspectives* (Madison, WI: University of Wisconsin Press, 1977), pp. 287–304.

Horne, Tom, *A Viking Market Kingdom in Ireland and Britain* (London: Routledge, 2021).

Howard-Johnston, James, 'The fur trade in the early Middle Ages', in J. Gruszczyńsky, M. Jankowiak, and J. Shepard (eds), *Viking-Age Trade: Silver, Slaves and Gotland* (Abingdon: Routledge, 2021), pp. 57–74.

Hudson, John, 'Kings and crime: ideology and practice in the tenth and twelfth centuries', in P. Chassaigne and J. Genet (eds), *Droit et société en France et en Grande Bretagne (XIIe–XXe siècles)* (Paris: Éditions de la Sorbonne, 2003), pp. 15–38.

Hudson, John, *The Oxford History of the Laws of England: 871–1216* (Oxford: Oxford University Press, 2012).

Huml, V., Z. Dragoun, and R. Novy, 'Der archäologische Beitrag zur Problematik der Entwicklung Prags in der Zeit vom 9. bis zur Mitte des 13. Jahrhunderts und die Erfassung der Ergebnisse der historisch-archäologischen Erforschung Prags', *Zeitschrift für Archäologie des Mittelalters*, 18/19 (1990), 33–69.

Hyams, Paul, 'Feud and the state in late Anglo-Saxon England', *Journal of British Studies*, 40:1 (2001), 1–43.

Hyams, Paul, 'Servitude in Anglo-Saxon England: searching for the Serfs', in Stefan Jurasinski and Andrew Rabin (eds), *Languages of the Law in Early Medieval England: Essays in Memory of Lisi Oliver* (Leuven: Peeters, 2019), pp. 127–53.

Ivanova, Mirela, 'Rethinking the *Life of Constantine-Cyril the Philosopher*', *Slavonic and East European Review*, 98:3 (2020), 434–63.

Iversen, Tore, *Trelldommen: Norsk slaveri i middelalderen* (Bergen: University of Bergen, 1994).

Jan, Libor, 'Zrod zemského soudu v Čechách' ['The birth of provincial courts in Bohemia'], in A. Barciak (ed.), *Kultura Prawna w Europie Środkowej* [*Legal Culture in Central Europe*] (Katowice: Instytut Górnośląski, 2006), pp. 227–39.

Jankowiak, Marek, 'Two systems of trade in the Western Slavic lands in the 10th century', in Mateusz Bogucki and Marian Rębkowski (eds), *Economies, Monetisation and Society in the West Slavic Lands, 800–1200 AD* (Szczecin: Polish Academy of Sciences, 2013), pp. 137–48.

Jankowiak, Marek, 'Dirham flows into northern and eastern Europe and the rhythms of the slave trade with the Islamic world', in J. Gruszczynski, M. Jankowiak, and J. Shepard (eds), *Viking-Age Trade: Silver, Slaves and Gotland* (Abingdon: Routledge, 2021), pp. 105–31.

Jankowiak, Marek, 'Tracing the Saqaliba: slave trade and the archaeology of the Slavic lands in the tenth century', in Felix Biermann and Marek Jankowiak (eds), *The Archaeology of Slavery in Early Medieval Northern Europe: The Invisible Commodity* (Cham: Springer, 2021), pp. 161–81.

Jenkins, Dafydd, 'Crime and tort and the Three Columns of Law', in T. M. Charles-Edwards and P. Russell (eds and trans.), *Tair Colofn Cyfraith: Three Columns of Law in Medieval Wales* (Bangor: Welsh Legal History Society, 2005), pp. 1–25.

Ježek, Martin, 'A Mass for the slaves: from early medieval Prague', in Jiří Macháček and Šimon Ungerman (eds), *Frühgeschichtliche Zentralorte in Mitteleuropa* (Bonn: Habelt, 2011), pp. 623–42.

Jiwal, Shainool 'From slaves to supporters: the role of Slavs in the Fatimid Mediterranean empire in the fourth/tenth century', *Medieval Studies*, 77 (2015), 103–25.

Jochens, Jenny, *Women in Old Norse Society* (Ithaca, NY: Cornell University Press, 1995).

De Jong, F. P. C., 'Rival schoolmasters in early eleventh-century Rouen with special reference to the poetry of Warner of Rouen (fl. 996–1027)', *Anglo-Norman Studies*, XXXIX (2016), 45–63.

Jurasinski, Stefan, *The Old English Penitentials and Anglo-Saxon Law* (Cambridge: Cambridge University Press, 2015).

Jurasinski, Stefan, 'The Old English penitentials and the law of slavery', in S. Jurasinski, L. Oliver, and A. Rabin (eds), *English Law before Magna Carta: Felix Liebermann and* Die Gesetze der Angelsachsen (Leiden: Brill, 2010), pp. 97–118.

Kalhous, David, *Anatomy of a Duchy: The Political and Ecclesiastical Structures of Early Přemyslid Bohemia* (Leiden: Brill, 2012).

Kalhous, David, Legenda Christiani *and Modern Historiography* (Leiden: Brill, 2015).

Kalhous, David, 'Problémy formování církevní správy v českých zemích v ránem středověku' ['Problems of the formation of church administration in the Czech lands in the early Middle Ages'], *Studia Mediaevalia Bohemica*, 7 (2015), 7–36.

Kalhous, David, 'Creating bonds, creating memories: monasteries Kladruby and Opatovice in twelfth century and their forgeries', *Studia Historica Brunensia*, 65:1 (2018), 37–50.

Kalhous, David, 'Graves, churches, culture and texts: the processes of Christianisation in the early Middle Ages and their social and cultural context', in Jiří Macháček and Martin Wihoda (eds), *The Fall of Great Moravia: Who Was Buried in Grave H153 at Pohansko near Břeclav?* (Leiden: Brill, 2019), pp. 110–29.

Kaplony, A., 'Routen, Anschlussrouten, Handelshorizonte im Brief von Hasdāy b. Šaprūt an den hazarischen König', in Petr Charvát and Jiří Prosecký (eds.), *Ibrahim ibn Ya'qub at-Turtushi: Christianity, Islam and*

Judaism Meet in East-Central Europe, c. 800–1300 AD (Prague: Czech Academy of Sciences, 1996), pp. 140–68.

Karras, Ruth Mazo, *Slavery and Society in Medieval Scandinavia* (New Haven, CT: Yale University Press, 1988).

Karras, Ruth Mazo, 'Concubinage and slavery in the Viking Age', *Scandinavian Studies*, 62 (1990), 141–62.

Karras, Ruth Mazo, 'Desire, descendants, and dominance: slavery, the exchange of women, and masculine power', in Allen Frantzen and Douglas Moffat (eds), *The Work of Work: Servitude, Slavery, and Labour in Medieval England* (Glasgow: Cruithne, 1994), pp. 16–29.

Katona, Csete, *Vikings of the Steppe: Scandinavians, Rus', and the Turkic World (c. 750–1050)* (London: Routledge, 2022).

Katuninec, Milan, 'The mission of the Thessaloniki brothers in Great Moravia: between Constantinople and Rome', *Hiperboreea*, 8:2 (2021), 159–83.

Kazhdan, Alexander P. 'The concepts of freedom (*eleutheria*) and slavery (*duleia*) in Byzantium', in George Makdisi et al. (eds), *La Notion de liberté au Moyen Âge: Islam, Byzance, Occident. Penn–Paris–Dumbarton Oaks Colloquia, IV, session des 12–15 octobre 1983* (Paris: Société d'Edition les Belles Lettres, 1985), pp. 215–26.

Keene, Derek, 'London from the post-Roman period to 1300', in D. M. Palliser (ed.), *The Cambridge Urban History of Britain*, vol. 1: *600–1540* (Cambridge: Cambridge University Press, 2000), pp. 187–216.

Keller, Rodolphe, 'Pillage et pouvoirs aux marges orientales de la Germanie ottonienne (919–1024)', in Laurent Feller and Ana Rodríguez (eds), *Objets sous contrainte: Circulation des richesses et valeur des choses au Moyen Âge* (Paris: Éditions de la Sorbonne, 2013), https://books.openedition.org/psorbonne/26844 (accessed 2 August 2023).

Kelly, Fergus, *A Guide to Early Irish Law* (Dublin: Dublin Institute for Advanced Studies, 1988).

Kelly, Fergus, *Early Irish Farming* (Dublin: Dublin Institute of Advanced Studies, 1998).

Kennedy, Hugh, *Muslim Spain and Portugal: A Political History of Al-Andalus* (Harlow: Longman, 1996).

Kennedy, Hugh, *The Prophet and the Age of the Caliphates: The Islamic Near East from the 6th to the 11th Century*, 3rd edn (London: Routledge, 2015).

Kenny, Michael, 'The geographical distribution of Irish Viking-Age coin hoards', *Proceedings of the Royal Irish Academy*, 87C (1987), 507–25.

Kershaw, Jane, 'Gold as a means of exchange in Scandinavian England', in Jane Kershaw and Gareth Williams (eds), *Silver, Butter, Cloth: Monetary and Social Economies in the Viking Age* (Oxford: Oxford University Press, 2018), pp. 227–50.

Kershaw, Jane, et al., 'The scale of dirham imports to the Baltic in the ninth century: new evidence from archaeometric analyses of early Viking-Age silver', *Fornvännen*, 116 (2021), 185–204.

Keynes, Simon, 'Royal government and the written word in late Anglo-Saxon England', in R. McKitterick (ed.), *The Uses of Literacy in Early Mediaeval Europe* (Cambridge: Cambridge University Press, 1990), pp. 226–57.
Keynes, Simon, 'Crime and punishment in the reign of King Æthelred the Unready', in Ian Wood and Niels Lund (eds), *People and Places in Northern Europe 500–1600: Essays in Honour of Peter Hayes Sawyer* (Woodbridge: Boydell, 1991), pp. 67–81.
Keynes, Simon, 'An abbot, an archbishop, and the viking raids of 1006–7 and 1009–12', *Anglo-Saxon England*, 36 (2007), 151–220.
Klein, Martin A., 'Servitude among the Wolof and Sereer of Senegambia', in Suzanne Miers and Igor Kopytoff (eds), *Slavery in Africa: Historical and Anthropological Perspectives* (Madison, WI: University of Wisconsin Press, 1977), pp. 335–66.
Korpela, Jukka, *Slaves from the North: Finns and Karelians in the Eastern European Slave Trade, 900–1600* (Leiden: Brill, 2019).
Kosto, Adam, *Hostages in the Middle Ages* (Oxford: Oxford University Press, 2012).
Kouřil, Pavel, 'The Magyars and their contribution to the collapse and fall of Great Moravia: allies, neighbours, enemies', in Jiří Macháček and Martin Wihoda (eds), *The Fall of Great Moravia: Who Was Buried in Grave H153 at Pohansko near Břeclav?* (Leiden: Brill, 2019), pp. 62–93.
Kristjánsson, J., 'Ireland and the Irish in Icelandic tradition', in H. B. Clarke et al. (eds), *Ireland and Scandinavia in the Early Viking Age* (Dublin: Four Courts Press, 1998), 259–76.
Krofta, Kamil, *Dějiny selského stavu* [*A History of Peasant Status*] (Prague: Rolnická tiskárna, 1949).
Kruse, S., and J. Tate, 'XRF analysis of Viking Age silver hoards in Scotland', in J. Graham-Campbell (ed.), *The Viking-Age Gold and Silver of Scotland, AD 850–1100* (Edinburgh: National Museums Scotland, 1995), pp. 73–9.
Kučera, Matúš, *Slovensko po páde Velkej Moravy: Štúdie o hospodárskom a sociálnom vývine v 9.-13. storočí* [*Slovakia after the Fall of Great Moravia: A Study of Economic and Social Developments in the 9th–13th Centuries*] (Bratislava: Veda, 1974).
Kučerovská, Taťána, 'Kelčský nález' ['A Kelč find'], *Folia Numismatika*, 8/9 (1993), 63–187.
Laiou, Angeliki E., and Cécile Morrisson, *The Byzantine Economy* (Cambridge: Cambridge University Press, 2007).
Lambert, Tom, 'Theft, homicide and crime in late Anglo-Saxon law', *Past and Present*, 214 (2012), 3–43.
Lambert, Tom, *Law and Order in Anglo-Saxon England* (Oxford: Oxford University Press, 2017).
Lavelle, Ryan, 'The use and abuse of hostages in later Anglo-Saxon England', *Early Medieval Europe*, 14:3 (2006), 269–96.

Lebecq, Stéphane, 'Use of the word 'Frisian' in the 6th–10th centuries written sources: some interpretations', in S. McGrail (ed.), *Maritime Celts, Frisians and Saxons* (London: Council for British Archaeology, 1990), pp. 85–90.

Lebecq, Stéphane, 'Long distance merchants and the forms of their ventures at the time of the Dorestad heyday', in H. Sarfatij et al. (eds), *In Discussion with the Past: Archaeological Studies Presented to W. A. van Es* (Zwolle: Amersfoort, 1999), pp. 233–7.

Lebecq, Stéphane, and Alban Gautier, 'Routeways between England and the Continent in the tenth century', in David Rollason, Conrad Leyser, and Hannah Williams (eds), *England and the Continent in the Tenth Century: Studies in Honour of Wilhelm Levison (1876–1947)* (Turnhout: Brepols, 2010), pp. 17–34.

Lemanski, S. Jay, 'Slave or free: the *æhtemann* in Anglo-Saxon rural society', *Haskins Society Journal*, 29 (2017), 53–80.

Lenski, Noel 'Slavery in the Byzantine Empire', in Craig Perry et al. (eds), *Cambridge World History of Slavery*, vol. 2: *AD 500–1420* (Cambridge: Cambridge University Press, 2021), pp. 453–81.

Lenski, Noel, and Catherine M. Cameron (eds), *What Is a Slave Society? The Practice of Slavery in Global Perspective* (Cambridge: Cambridge University Press, 2018).

LeVeen, E. Philip, 'The African slave supply response', *The African Studies Review*, 18:1 (1975), 9–28.

Lewis-Simpson, Shannon, 'Old age in Viking-Age Britain', in Shannon Lewis-Simpson (ed.), *Youth and Age in the Medieval North* (Leiden: Brill, 2008), pp. 243–64.

Lovejoy, Paul E., 'The impact of the Atlantic slave trade on Africa: a review of the literature', *Journal of African History*, 30:3 (1989), 365–94.

Lucas, A. T., *Cattle in Ancient Ireland* (Kilkenny: Boethius, 1989).

Macháček, Jiří, 'Early medieval centre in Pohansko near Břeclav/Lundeburg: *munitio*, *emporium*, or *palatium* of the rulers of Moravia?', in Joachim Henning (ed.), *Post-Roman Towns, Trade and Settlement in Europe and Byzantium*, 2 vols (Berlin: De Gruyter, 2007), i, pp. 476–98.

Macháček, Jiří, *The Rise of Medieval Towns and States in Central Europe* (Leiden: Brill, 2010).

Macháček, Jiří, 'Slave trade in Great Moravia: reality or fiction?', in Felix Biermann and Marek Jankowiak (eds), *The Archaeology of Slavery in Early Medieval Northern Europe: The Invisible Commodity* (Cham: Springer, 2021), pp. 113–26.

Macháček, Jiří and Jan Videman, 'Monetisation of early medieval Moravia in light of new archaeological discoveries in the Lower Dyje region (Czech Republic)', in Mateusz Bogucki and Marian Rębkowski (eds), *Economies, Monetisation and Society in the West Slavic Lands, 800–1200 AD* (Szczecin: Polish Academy of Sciences, 2013), pp. 177–99.

Macháček, Jiří, Petr Dresler, and Renáta Přichystalová, 'Das Ende Großmährens: Überlegungen zur relativen und absoluten Chronologie des ostmitteleuropäischen Frühmittelalters', *Praehistorische Zeitschrift*, 93:2 (2018), 307–48.

Machula, J., 'Foreign items and outside influences in the material culture of tenth-century Bohemia', *Annual of Medieval Studies at the CEU*, 8 (2002), 65–88.

Maddicott, J. R., 'London and Droitwich, c. 650–750: trade, industry and the rise of Mercia', *Anglo-Saxon England*, 34 (2005), 7–58.

Maitland, F. W., *Domesday Book and Beyond: Three Essays in the Early History of England* (Cambridge: Cambridge University Press, 1987).

Maldonado, Adrián, *Crucible of Nations: Scotland from Viking Age to Medieval Kingdom* (Edinburgh: National Museums Scotland, 2021).

Manzano Moreno, Eduardo, 'Circulation de biens et richesses entre al-Andalus et l'Occident européen aux viiie–xe siècles', in Laurent Feller and Ana Rodríguez (eds), *Objets sous contrainte: Circulation des richesses et valeur des choses au Moyen Âge* (Paris: Éditions de la Sorbonne, 2013), http://books.openedition.org/psorbonne/26817 (accessed 31 May 2023).

Martin, Janet, *Medieval Russia: 980–1584* (Cambridge: Cambridge University Press, 2007).

Mařík, Jan, 'Hinterlands of early medieval central places in Bohemia: archaeological and historical sources', in Jiří Machaček and Šimon Ungerman (eds), *Frühgeschichtliche Zentralorte in Mitteleuropa* (Bonn: Habelt, 2011), pp. 397–403.

McCormick, Michael, *Origins of the European Economy* (Cambridge: Cambridge University Press, 2001),

McCormick, Michael, 'New light on the "Dark Ages": how the slave trade fueled the Carolingian economy', *Past and Present*, 177 (2002), 17–54.

McGovern, Thomas H., and Orri Vésteinsson, 'The peopling of Iceland', *Norwegian Archaeological Review*, 45:2 (2012), 206–18.

Metcalf, David, 'The monetary history of England in the tenth century viewed in the perspective of the eleventh century', in M. A. S. Blackburn (ed.), *Anglo-Saxon Monetary History: Essays in Memory of Michael Dolley* (Leicester: Leicester University Press, 1986), pp. 133–57.

Meillassoux, Claude, *The Anthropology of Slavery: The Womb of Iron and Gold*, trans. A. Dasnois (Chicago, IL: Chicago University Press, 1991).

Meouak, Mohamed, *Saqaliba: Eunuques et esclaves à la conquête du pouvoir* (Helsinki: Academia Scientiaria Fennica, 2004).

Metcalf, M., and W. Op Den Velde, 'Series E reconsidered', in T. Abramson (ed.), *Studies in Early Medieval Coinage*, vol. 2: *New Perspectives* (Woodbridge: Boydell, 2011), pp. 104–10.

Middleton, Neil, 'Early medieval port customs, tolls and controls of foreign trade', *Early Medieval Europe*, 13 (2005), 313–58.

Militký, Jiří, 'Nový pohled na zlatou byzantskou minci z Libice nad Cidlinou' ['A new view on a gold Byzantine coin from Libice nad Cidlinou'], *Numismatický sborník*, 21 (2006), 125–36.

Miller, Joseph C., *The Problem of Slavery as History* (New Haven, CT: Yale University Press, 2012).

Mishin, Dmitri, 'The saqāliba slaves in the Aghlabid state', *Annual of Medieval Studies at CEU 1996/97* (1998), 236–44.
Molyneaux, George, 'The *Ordinance concerning the Dunsæte* and the Anglo-Welsh frontier in the late tenth and eleventh centuries', *Anglo-Saxon England*, 40 (2011), 249–72.
Molyneaux, George, *Formation of the English Kingdom in the 10th Century* (Oxford: Oxford University Press, 2015).
Moore, J. S., 'Domesday slavery', *Anglo-Norman Studies*, XI (1988), 191–220.
Morrison, C., 'Byzantine coins in early medieval Britain: a Byzantinist's assessment', in M. Allen, R. Naismith, and E. Screen (eds), *Early Medieval Monetary History* (Farnham: Ashgate, 2014), pp. 207–42.
Müller-Mertens, Eckhard, 'The Ottonians as kings and emperors', in Timothy Reuter (ed.), *The New Cambridge Medieval History*, vol. 3: *c. 900–1024* (Cambridge: Cambridge University Press, 1999), pp. 233–66.
Murray, Kevin, '*Lebor na Cert*: language and date', in Kevin Murray (ed.), *Lebor na Cert: Reassessments* (London: Irish Texts Society, 2013), pp. 77–102.
Myrdal, Janken, 'Milking and grinding, digging and herding: slaves and farmwork 1000–1300', in Bjørn Poulsen and Søren Michael Sindbæk (eds), *Settlement and Lordship in Viking and Early Medieval Scandinavia* (Turnhout: Brepols, 2011), pp. 293–307.
Naismith, Rory, 'Islamic coins from early medieval England', *The Numismatic Chronicle*, 165 (2005), 193–222.
Naismith, Rory, 'The land market and Anglo-Saxon society', *Historical Research*, 89:243 (2015), 19–41.
Naismith, Rory, 'The Ely Memoranda and the economy of the late Anglo-Saxon fenland', *Anglo-Saxon England*, 45 (2016), 333–77.
Naismith, Rory, *Medieval European Coinage with a Catalogue of Coins in the Fitzwilliam Museum, Cambridge*, vol. 8: *Britain and Ireland c. 400–1066* (Cambridge: Cambridge University Press, 2017).
Nazmi, Ahmad, *Commercial Relations between Arabs and Slavs (9th–11th Centuries)* (Warsaw: Wydawnictwo Akademickie Dialog, 1998).
Norseng, Per, 'Law codes as a source for Nordic history in the early Middle Ages', *Scandinavian Journal of History*, 16:3 (1991), 137–66.
Nový, Rostislav, *Přemyslovský stát 11. a 12. století* [*The Přemyslid State in the 11th and 12th Centuries*] (Prague: Charles University, 1972).
Ó Cróinín, Dáibhí, *Early Medieval Ireland, 400–1200*, 2nd edn (Abingdon: Routledge, 2017).
Oakley, Francis, *Kingship: The Politics of Enchantment* (Malden, MA: Blackwell, 2006).
Origo, Iris, 'The domestic enemy: the eastern slaves in Tuscany in the fourteenth and fifteenth centuries', *Speculum*, 30:3 (1955), 321–66.
Padel, Oliver, *Slavery in Saxon Cornwall: The Bodmin Manumissions* (Cambridge: Cambridge University Press, 2009).
Paolella, Christopher, *Human Trafficking in Medieval Europe* (Amsterdam: Amsterdam University Press, 2020).

Patterson, Orlando, *Slavery and Social Death* (Cambridge, MA: Harvard University Press, 1982).

Pelteret, David, 'Slave raiding and slave trading in early England', *Anglo-Saxon England*, 9 (1981), 99–114.

Pelteret, David, 'Slavery in the Danelaw', in Ross Samson (ed.), *Social Approaches to Viking Studies* (Glasgow: Cruithne, 1991), pp. 179–88.

Pelteret, David, *Slavery in Early Mediaeval England: From Alfred the Great until the Twelfth Century* (Woodbridge: Boydell, 1995).

Pelteret, David, 'The manumissions in the Durham *Liber Vitae*', in D. Rollason and L. Rollason (eds), *The Durham* Liber Vitae, 3 vols (London: British Library, 2007), i, pp. 66–72.

Pestell, Tim, 'The kingdom of East Anglia, Frisia and Continental connections, c. AD 600–900', in John Hines and Nelleke Ijessennagger-van der Pluijm (eds), *Frisians and Their North Sea Neighbours: From the Fifth Century to the Viking Age* (Woodbridge: Boydell, 2017), pp. 193–222.

Petráček, Tomáš, *Power and Exploitation in the Czech Lands in the 10th–12th Centuries* (Leiden: Brill, 2017).

Phillips, Jr., William D., *Slavery in Medieval and Early Modern Iberia* (Philadelphia, PA: University of Pennsylvania Press, 2014).

Pipes, Daniel, *Slave Soldiers and Islam: The Genesis of a Military System* (New Haven, CT: Yale University Press, 1981).

Plomp, Kimberly A., et al., 'The composition of the founding population of Iceland: a new perspective from 3D analyses of basicranial shape', *PLoS ONE*, 16:2 (2021), 1–16.

Poláček, Lumir, 'Ninth-century Mikulčice: the "market of the Moravians"? The archaeological evidence of trade in Great Moravia', in Joachim Henning (ed.), *Post-Roman Towns, Trade and Settlement in Europe and Byzantium*, 2 vols (Berlin: De Gruyter, 2007), i, pp. 499–524.

Popović, Alexandre, *The Revolt of African Slaves in Iraq in the 3rd/9th Century* (Princeton, NJ: Marcus Wiener, 1999).

Poulík, Josef, 'Svědectví výzkumů a pramenů archeologických o Velké Moravě' ['Evidence of research and archaeological sources on Great Moravia'], in Bohuslav Chropovský and Josef Poulík (eds), *Velká Morava a počátky Československé státnosti* (Prague: Academia, 1985), pp. 9–80.

Pratt, David, 'Written law and the communication of authority in tenth-century England', in David Rollason, Conrad Leyser, and Hannah Williams (eds), *England and the Continent in the Tenth Century: Studies in Honour of Wilhelm Levison (1876–1947)* (Turnhout: Brepols, 2010), pp. 331–50.

Prinzing, Günther 'On slaves and slavery', in Paul Stephenson (ed.), *The Byzantine World* (London: Routledge, 2012), pp. 92–102.

Profantová, Naďa, 'Byzantine coins from the 9th–10th century from the Czech Republic', in Marcin Wołoszyn (ed.), *Byzantine Coins in Central Europe between the 5th and 10th Century* (Cracow: Polish Academy of Arts and Sciences, 2009), pp. 581–98.

La Puente, Cristina de, 'Free fathers, slave mothers and their children: a contribution to the study of family structures in al-Andalus', *Imago Temporis: Medium Aevum*, 7 (2013), 27–44.

La Puente, Christina de, 'The ethnic origin of female slaves in al-Andalus', in Matthew S. Gordon and Kathryn A. Hain, *Concubines and Courtesans: Women and Slavery in Islamic History* (Oxford: Oxford University Press, 2017), pp. 124–42.

Purcell, Emer, 'The first generation in Ireland, 795–812: viking raids and viking bases?', in Howard B. Clarke and Ruth Johnson (eds), *The Vikings in Ireland and Beyond* (Dublin: Four Courts Press, 2015), pp. 41–54.

Purcell, Emer, and John Sheehan, 'Viking Dublin: enmities, alliances and the cold gleam of silver', in D. M. Hadley and Letty ten Harkel (eds), *Everyday Life in Viking-Age Towns: Social Approaches to Towns in England and Ireland, c. 800–1100* (Oxford: Oxbow, 2013), pp. 35–60.

Raffield, Ben, 'The slave markets of the Viking world: comparative perspectives on an "invisible archaeology"', *Slavery & Abolition*, 40:4 (2019), 682–705.

Raffield, Ben, Neil Price, and Mark Collard, 'Polygyny, concubinage, and the social lives of women in Viking-Age Scandinavia', *Viking and Medieval Scandinavia*, 13 (2017), 167–209.

Redknap, Mark, 'Viking-Age settlement in Wales and the evidence from Llanbedrgoch', in J. Hines et al. (eds), *Land, Sea and Home* (Leeds: Maney, 2004), pp. 139–75.

Reuter, Timothy, 'Plunder and tribute in the Carolingian Empire', *Transactions of the Royal Historical Society*, 35 (1985), 75–94.

Reuter, Timothy, *Germany in the Early Middle Ages 800–1056* (London: Longman, 1991).

Reynolds, Andrew, *Anglo-Saxon Deviant Burial Customs* (Oxford: Oxford University Press, 2009).

Reynolds, Dwight F., 'The *Qiyan* of al-Andalus', in Matthew S. Gordon and Kathryn A. Hain (eds), *Concubines and Courtesans: Women and Slavery in Islamic History* (Oxford: Oxford University Press, 2017), pp. 100–23.

Richardson, David, 'Shipboard revolts, African authority, and the Atlantic slave trade', *The William and Mary Quarterly*, 58:1 (2001), 69–92.

Rio, Alice, 'Self-sale and voluntary entry into unfreedom', *Journal of Social History*, 45:3 (2012), 661–85.

Rio, Alice, 'Penal enslavement in the early Middle Ages', in A. Lichtenstein and C. de Vito (eds), *Global Convict Labour* (Leiden: Brill, 2015), pp. 79–107.

Rio, Alice, *Slavery after Rome 500–1100* (Oxford: Oxford University Press, 2017).

Rio, Alice, *Slaving and the Funding of Elite Status in Early Medieval Europe (ca. 800–1000 AD)* (Berlin: EB Verlag, 2024).

Roach, Andrew P., 'The people-trafficking princes: slaves, silver and state formation in Poland', *Slavonica*, 25:2 (2020), 132–56.

Roach, Andrew P., and Alex Marshall, 'The dynamics of the drugs trade: a model for the study of the medieval trade in slaves?', in J. Gruszczyńsky, M. Jankowiak, and J. Shepard (eds), *Viking-Age Trade: Silver, Slaves and Gotland* (Abingdon: Routledge, 2021), pp. 75–96.

Roach, Levi, 'Law codes and legal norms in later Anglo-Saxon England', *Historical Research*, 86 (2013), 465–86.

Ross, Margaret Clunies, 'Concubinage in Anglo-Saxon England', *Past & Present*, 108 (1985), 3–34.

Rotman, Youval, *Byzantine Slavery and the Mediterranean World* (Cambridge, MA: Harvard University Press, 2009).

Samson, Ross, 'The end of early medieval slavery', in Allen Frantzen and Douglas Moffat (eds), *The Work of Work: Servitude, Slavery, and Labour in Medieval England* (Glasgow: Cruithne, 1994), pp. 95–124.

Sandnes, Jørn, *Ødetid og gjenreisning: Trøndsk busetnings historie ca. 1200–1660* (Oslo: Universitetsforlaget, 1971).

Sandnes, Jørn, 'Bondesamfunnet', in Ingrid Semmingsen et al. (eds), *Norges kulturhistorie*, vol. 1: *Vår fjerne fortid* (Oslo: H. Auschehoug, 1979), pp. 39–68.

Sandnes, Jørn, '"Tolv kyr, to hester og tre træler": litt om omfanget av træleholdet i Norge i vikingtid og tidlig kristen tid', *Historisk Tidsskrift*, 62 (1983), 79–82.

Sawyer, Peter H., 'Kings and merchants', in Peter H. Sawyer and Ian N. Wood (eds), *Early Medieval Kingship* (Leeds: University of Leeds, 1977), pp. 139–58.

Sawyer, Peter H., *Kings and Vikings* (London: Routledge, 1982).

Sayers, William, 'Management of the Celtic fact in *Landnámabók*', *Scandinavian Studies*, 66:2 (1994), 129–53.

Schaeken, Jos, *Voices on Birchbark: Everyday Communication in Medieval Russia* (Leiden: Brill, 2019).

Scheil, Andrew P., *In the Footsteps of Israel: Understanding Jews in Anglo-Saxon England* (Ann Arbor, MI: University of Michigan Press, 2004).

Schledermann, P., and K. M. McCullough, 'Inuit–Norse contact in the Smith Sound region', in James H. Barrett (ed.), *Contact, Continuity, and Collapse: The Norse Colonization of the North Atlantic* (Turnhout: Brepols, 2003), pp. 183–205.

Serfass, Adam, 'Slavery and Pope Gregory the Great', *Journal of Early Christian Studies*, 14:1 (2006), 77–103.

Sheehan, John, 'The *longphort* in Viking Age Ireland', *Acta Archaeologica*, 79:1 (2008), 282–95.

Shepard, Jonathan, 'Back in Old Rus and the USSR: archaeology, history and politics', *English Historical Review*, 131:549 (2016), 384–405.

Sigurðsson, Gísli, *The Gaelic Influence in Iceland* (Reykjavik: University of Iceland Press, 2000).

Sindbæk, Søren Michael, 'The small world of the Vikings: networks in early medieval communication and exchange', *Norwegian Archaeological Review*, 40:1 (2007), 59–74.

Sjöholm, Elsa, *Gesetze als Quellen mittelalterlicher Geschichte des Nordens* (Stockholm: Almqvist & Wiksell, 1977).

Sjöholm, Elsa, 'Sweden's medieval laws: European legal tradition – political change', *Scandinavian Journal of History*, 15:1/2 (1990), 65–87.

Skre, Dagfinn, 'The social context of settlement in Norway in the first millennium AD', *Norwegian Archaeological Review*, 34:1 (2001), 1–12.

Sláma, Jiří, 'Poznámky k problému historického významu některých raně středověkých hradišť ve středních Čechách' ['Comments on the historical problem of the significance of some early medieval hillforts in central Bohemia'], *Archeologické rozhledy*, 29 (1977), 60–79.

Sláma, Jiří, 'K některým ekonomickým a politickým projevům raně středověkého přemyslovského státu' ['Towards some economic and political discourses of the early medieval Přemyslid state'], *Archeologické rozhledy*, 37 (1985), 334–42.

Smith, Romney David, 'The business of human trafficking: slaves and money between western Italy and the House of Islam before the Crusades (*c.* 900–*c.* 1100)', *Journal of Medieval History*, 45:5 (2019), 523–52.

Smyth, Alfred P., 'The earliest Irish annals: their first contemporary entries, and the earliest centres of recording', *Proceedings of the Royal Irish Academy*, 72 C (1972), 1–48.

Smyth, Alfred P., *Scandinavian Kings in the British Isles 850–880* (Oxford: Oxford University Press, 1977).

Solymosi, László, 'Liberty and servitude in the age of Saint Stephen', in Attila Zsoldos (ed.), *Saint Stephen and His Country. A Newborn Kingdom in Central Europe: Hungary* (Budapest: Győző Cholnoky, 2001), pp. 69–79.

Sommar, Mary, *The Slaves of the Churches* (Oxford: Oxford University Press, 2020).

Sommer, Petr, 'České kláštery 10.–13. století ve světle archeologických vyzkumů' ['Czech monasteries in the 10th–13th centuries in light of the archaeological investigation'], *Archeologia Historica*, 3:1 (1978), 337–48.

Sommer, Petr, *Svatý Prokop: Z počátků českého státu a církve* [*Saint Procopius: From the Beginnings of the Czech State and Church*] (Prague: Vyšehrad, 2007).

Sommer, Petr, 'České křestanství doby knížete Václava' ['Czech Christianity at the time of Prince Wenceslas'], in Petr Kubín (ed.), *Svatý Václav na památku 1100: Výročí narození knížete Václava Svatého* [*St Wenceslas on the Memorial 1100: Anniversary of the Birth of the Prince St Wenceslas*] (Prague: Charles University, 2010), pp. 65–79.

Stacey, Robin Chapman, *The Road to Judgment: From Custom to Court in Medieval Ireland and Wales* (Philadelphia, PA: University of Pennsylvania Press, 1994).

Stenton, F. M., *Anglo-Saxon England*, 3rd edn (Oxford: Oxford University Press, 1971).

Strickland, Matthew, 'Slaughter, slavery or ransom: the impact of the Conquest on conduct in warfare', in Carole Hicks (ed.), *England in the Eleventh Century: Proceedings of the 1990 Harlaxton Symposium* (Stamford: Paul Watkins, 1992), pp. 41–59.

Strickland, Matthew, *War and Chivalry: The Conduct and Perception of War in England and Normandy, 1066–1217* (Cambridge: Cambridge University Press, 1996).

Strzelczyk, Jerzy, 'Bohemia and Poland: two examples of successful western Slavonic state-formation', in Timothy Reuter (ed.), *The New Cambridge Medieval History*, vol. 3: *c. 900–1024* (Cambridge: Cambridge University Press, 1999), pp. 514–35.

Stuard, Susan Mosher, 'Ancillary evidence for the decline of medieval slavery', *Past and Present*, 149 (1995), 3–28.

Suchodolski, Stanisław, 'Change of transcontinental contacts as indicated by coins in the Baltic zone around 1000', in Przemysław Urbańczyk (ed.), *Europe around the Year 1000* (Warsaw: Wydawnictwo DIG, 2001), pp. 85–100.

Sutherland, P. D., 'The Norse and native North Americans', in W. W. Fitzhugh and E. Ward (eds), *Vikings: The North Atlantic Saga* (Washington, DC: Smithsonian Institution, 2000), pp. 238–47.

Sutt, Cameron, *Slavery in Árpád-Era Hungary in a Comparative Context* (Leiden: Brill, 2015).

Sutt, Cameron, 'Sexual access to slave women: Árpádian Hungary as a case study', in Andrea-Bianka Znorovszky and Christopher Mielke (eds), *Same Bodies, Different Women: Witches, Whores, and Handicapped. 'Other' Women in the Middle Ages and the Early Modern Period* (Budapest: Trivent Publishing, 2019), pp. 152–68.

Swift, Catherine, 'Taxes, trade and trespass in *Lebor na Cert*', in Kevin Murray (ed.), *Lebor na Cert: Reassessments* (London: Irish Texts Society, 2013), pp. 34–61.

Štefan, Ivo, 'Slavery and slave trade in early medieval Bohemia: archaeology of slavery or slavery of archaeology?', in Felix Biermann and Marek Jankowiak (eds), *The Archaeology of Slavery in Early Medieval Northern Europe: The Invisible Commodity* (Cham: Springer, 2021), pp. 127–40.

Štefan, Ivo, Petra Stránská, and Hana Vondrová, 'The archaeology of early medieval violence: the mass grave at Budeč, Czech Republic', *Antiquity*, 90:351 (2016), 759–76.

Šusta, Josef, 'Otroctví a velkostatek v Čechách' ['Slavery and the estate in Bohemia'], *Český Časopis Historický*, 5:1 (1899), 69–92.

Taylor, Alice, '*Lex scripta* and the problem of enforcement: Anglo-Saxon, Welsh and Scottish law compared', in F. Pirie and J. Scheele (eds), *Legalism: Community and Justice* (Oxford: Oxford University Press, 2014), pp. 47–75.

Tits-Dieuaide, M.-J., 'Grands domaines, grandes et petites exploitations en Gaule mérovingienne', in Adriaan Verhulst (ed.), *Le Grand domaine aux époques mérovingienne et carolingienne: Actes du colloque international, Gand, 8–10 Septembre 1983* (Ghent: Belgisch Centrum voor Landelijke Geschiedenis, 1985), pp. 23–50.

Toch, Michael, 'Jews and commerce: modern fancies and medieval realities', in S. Cavaciocchi (ed.), *Il ruolo economico delle minoranze in Europa: Secc. XIII–XVIII* (Florence: Instituto Francesco Datini, Prato, 2000), pp. 43–58.

Toch, Michael, *The Economic History of European Jews* (Leiden: Brill, 2013).

Toch, Michael, 'Was there a Jewish slave trade (or commercial monopoly) in the early Middle Ages?', in S. Hanβ and J. Schiel (eds), *Mediterranean Slavery Revisited (500–1800)* (Zurich: Chronos, 2014), pp. 421–44.

Tomková, Kateřina, 'Bohemian coins in the tenth-to-twelfth-century silver hoards', in Petr Charvát and Jiří Prosecký (eds), *Ibrahim ibn Ya'qub at-Turtushi: Christianity, Islam and Judaism Meet in East-Central Europe, c. 800–1300 AD* (Prague: Czech Academy of Sciences, 1996), pp. 78–92.

Tougher, Shaun, *The Eunuch in Byzantine History and Society* (London: Routledge, 2008).

Treharne, Elaine, *Living through Conquest: The Politics of Early English, 1020–1220* (Oxford: Oxford University Press, 2012).

Třeštík, Dušán, 'Trh Moravanů – ústřední trh Staré Moravy' ['Market of the Moravians – the central market of Old Moravia'], *Československý časopis historický*, 21 (1973), 869–94.

Třeštík, Dušan, 'The baptism of the Czech princes in 845 and the Christianisation of the Slavs', *Historica*, 2 (1995), 7–59.

Třeštík, Dušán, '"Veliké město Slovanů jménem Praha": státy a otroci ve střední Evropě v 10. století' ['"The great city of the Slavs named Prague": states and slaves in Central Europe in the 10th century'], in Lumír Polanský, Jiří Sláma, and Dušán Třeštík (eds), *Přemyslovský Stát kolem Roku 1000: Na pamět knížete Boleslava II* (Prague: Nakladatelství Lidové noviny, 2000), pp. 49–70.

Třeštík, Dušán, '"Eine grosse Stadt der Slawen namens Prag": Staaten und Sklaven in Mitteleuropa im 10. Jahrhundert', in Petr Sommer (ed.), *Boleslav II. – der tschechische Staat um das Jahr 1000: internationales Symposium Praha 9.–10. Februar 1999* (Prague: Filosofia, 2001), pp. 93–138.

Tůma, Oldřich, 'Great Moravia's trade contacts and the mediating role of Venice', *Byzantinoslavica*, 46 (1985), 67–77.

Valante, Mary, 'Castrating monks: Vikings, slave trade, and the value of eunuchs', in Larissa Tracey (ed.), *Castration and Culture in the Middle Ages* (Woodbridge: Boydell, 2013), pp. 174–87.

Valante, Mary, 'Dublin's economic relations with the hinterland and periphery in the Viking age', in Séan Duffy (ed.), *Medieval Dublin I* (Dublin: Four Courts Press, 1999), pp. 69–83.

de la Vassière, Étienne, *Samarcande et Samarra: Élites d'Asie central dans l'empire Abbasside* (Paris: Association pour l'Avancement des Études Iraniennes, 2007).

Venco, Clément, 'Par-delà la frontière: marchands et commerce d'esclaves entre la Gaule carolingienne et al-Andalus (VIIIe–Xe siècles)', in Sébastien Gasc et al. (eds), *Las fronteras pirenaicas en la Edad Media (siglos VI–XV)* (Zaragoza: University of Zaragoza, 2018), pp. 1–28.

Verlinden, Charles, 'L'origine de *sclavus* = esclave', *Bulletin du Cange: Archivum Latinitatis Medii Aevi*, 17 (1943), 97–128.

Verlinden, Charles, *L'Esclavage dans l'Europe médiévale*, 2 vols (Bruges: De Tempel, 1955, 1977).

Verlinden, Charles, 'Slavery, slave trade', in J. Strayer (ed.), *Dictionary of the Middle Ages*, 13 vols (New York, NY: Charles Scribner's Sons, 1982–1989), xi, pp. 334–40.
Vésteinsson, Orri, 'Ethnicity and class in settlement-period Iceland', in John Sheehan and Donnchadh Ó Corráin (eds), *The Viking Age: Ireland and the West* (Dublin: Four Courts Press, 2010), pp. 494–510.
Vinogradoff, Paul, *The Growth of the Manor*, 3rd edn (London: G. Allen & Unwin, 1920).
Vytlačil, Zdeněk, et al., 'Residential mobility in Great Moravia: strontium isotope analysis of a population sample from the early medieval site of Mikulčice-Valy (ninth–tenth centuries)', *Archaeological and Anthropological Sciences*, 13:8 (2021), 1–15.
Wallace, Patrick F., 'The English presence in Viking Dublin', in M. A. S. Blackburn (ed.), *Anglo-Saxon Monetary History: Essays in Memory of Michael Dolley* (Leicester: Leicester University Press, 1986), pp. 201–21.
Whitelock, Dorothy, 'The so-called laws of Edward and Guthrum', *English Historical Review*, 56 (1941), 1–21.
Wickham, Chris, *Framing the Early Middle Ages* (Oxford: Oxford University Press, 2005).
Wolverton, Lisa, *Hastening toward Prague: Power and Society in the Medieval Czech Lands* (Philadelphia, PA: University of Pennsylvania Press, 2001).
Wormald, Patrick, '*Lex scripta* and *verbum regis*: legislation and Germanic kingship from Euric to Cnut', in Patrick Wormald (ed.), *Legal Culture in the Early Medieval West: Law as Text, Image and Experience* (London: Bloomsbury, 1999), pp. 1–43.
Wormald, Patrick, '"Inter cetera bona genti suae": law-making and peace-keeping in the earliest English kingdoms', in Patrick Wormald (ed.), *Legal Culture in the Early Medieval West: Law as Text, Image and Experience* (London: Bloomsbury, 1999), pp. 179–99.
Wormald, Patrick, 'Giving God and king their due: conflict and its regulation in the early English state', in Patrick Wormald (ed.), *Legal Culture in the Early Medieval West: Law as Text, Image and Experience* (London: Bloomsbury, 1999), pp. 333–57.
Wormald, Patrick, *The Making of English Law: King Alfred to the Twelfth Century* (London: Blackwell, 1999).
Wyatt, David, 'The significance of slavery: alternative approaches to Anglo-Saxon slavery', *Anglo-Norman Studies*, XXIII (2001), 327–47.
Wyatt, David, *Slaves and Warriors in Medieval Britain and Ireland, 800–1200* (Leiden: Brill, 2009).
Yorke, Barbara, *Kings and Kingdoms of Early Anglo-Saxon England* (London: Routledge, 1990).
Žemlička, Josef, 'Das "Reich" der bohmischen Boleslavs und die Krise an der Jahrtausendwende', *Archeologické Rozhledy*, 47 (1995), 267–78.
Žemlička, Josef, *Čechy v době knížecí (1034–1198)* [*Bohemia in the Age of Princes (1034–1198)*] (Prague: Nakladatelství lidové noviny, 1997).

Index

Note: 'n.' after a page reference indicates the number of a note on that page

Æthelberht's law code 21, 28, 208
Æthelgifu 21–2, 28, 33, 56
Æthelred II 'the Unready' 121, 191
law codes 78, 175, 214–15
Æthelstan 171, 211
Abbasid Caliphate 47–50, 62, 63, 83, 166, 170, 220, 237, 239
Adalbert of Prague, St 79, 123, 132, 179, 183, 204–5, 216, 218, 232
Adomnán of Iona, St 31, 109, 153
Africa 11, 47
Islamic 11, 47, 48, 50, 156, 165, 173, 234, 238, 240
pre-colonial slavery in 76, 91
sub-Saharan 47, 48
see also trans-Atlantic slave trade
age 47, 55, 75–6, 81, 82, 89–90, 94, 209, 237
see also children
Al-Andalus 48, 50, 83, 132, 156, 172, 173–4, 176, 182–7, 236, 237
see also Cordoba; Iberia
Alba 121, 222, 223
Alfred of Wessex 120, 169, 170, 211
Domboc 81, 86, 208, 212, 214
treaty with Guthrum 55, 226n.48
Amand, St 60, 151, 152
Ancilla 7–8, 21, 22–3, 36, 60–1, 64, 65
Anglo-Saxon Chronicle 88, 118, 120, 121, 129, 130, 173, 221, 230
annals 9, 82, 89, 106, 109, 111–23, 131, 133, 170, 173, 177, 231
armies 111, 118, 122, 127, 215, 233
captive taking by 113–14, 116, 119–34 *passim*, 170, 231
enslavement of 110
Viking Great 119, 167, 168
see also mamluks; military slaves

Baghdad 48, 50, 55, 155, 237
Balthild, St 60, 151–2
Baltic region 62, 56, 127, 156, 166, 168–9, 174, 176, 185–6, 215
Bavaria 61, 114, 116, 127, 156, 157, 179, 189
Bede 21, 78, 90, 109–10, 113, 146, 148–9, 150, 152
Bernold of Constans 88, 132, 190
Birka 55, 167, 168
Black Sea 6, 50, 83, 124, 169, 236

Bohemia 3, 4, 6, 11, 32
Přemyslid Duchy of 34, 37, 79–80, 123–8, 158, 178–92 *passim*, 216, 220
Boleslav I of Bohemia 126, 127, 185
Boleslav II of Bohemia 127, 179, 185, 186, 191, 216, 217, 218
Bolesław I Chrobry of Poland 127, 131, 175, 220
Břetislav I of Bohemia 35, 79–80, 132, 133, 190, 204–5
Břevnov monastery 179, 217
Brian Boru 88, 122, 221
Brigit, St 27, 28, 144, 145, 150
Bristol 145, 177, 203, 215, 218–19
burials of slaves 10, 33, 55, 172
Byzantium 12, 46, 51–4, 59, 63, 65, 83, 111, 124, 127, 156, 174, 181, 190–1, 216, 235–6, 237
see also Moravia, Byzantine mission to; silk

canon law 28, 29, 64, 108, 205, 232–3, 234
see also penitentials
Carpathian basin 64, 190, 191
Caspian Sea 6, 50, 166, 169, 174, 189
castration 47, 49, 83–4, 94, 156, 173, 183, 184, 186–7, 237
see also eunuchs; *Někotoraja Zapověd*
cattle 8, 27, 35, 120, 130–1, 132, 231
charters 6, 10, 30, 31, 35–7, 61, 64, 157, 179–80, 217–18, 234
chattel slavery 7, 8, 20, 23, 30, 34, 36, 60–2, 64–5, 76–84 *passim*, 202, 232, 234
children 23, 61, 76
of mixed-status relationships 25, 47, 56, 65, 144, 146
of slaves 47, 48, 52
sale of 76, 80–4, 95, 131, 145, 182, 201, 209
targets of raiding 23, 85, 91, 94, 107, 108, 120, 126, 127, 130, 170
chivalry 107, 128, 129
Christianisation 3–5, 10, 55, 87, 108, 149, 203, 215, 232, 235
chronicles 8, 9, 54, 106, 109, 111, 113, 124, 170
see also individual authors and titles
Clement of Ohrid, St 90, 115, 155
Cnut of England, Denmark, and Norway 121–2, 129, 175, 215, 233
law codes 78–9, 122, 145, 175, 212, 214–15
see also Danish conquest of England
coinage 50, 122, 149, 150, 154, 157, 169, 171, 172, 185–6, 189, 191, 220, 221
see also dirhams; silver
concubinage 25, 33, 47–8, 55, 56, 62–5, 182, 234
see also sexual access to slaves
Constantinople 51–2, 54, 155, 180, 182, 190–1, 192
Cordoba 50, 84, 123, 179, 184, 188
Cosmas of Prague 34–5, 79, 127, 132, 180, 183, 190, 204, 212
Council of Armagh 177, 231, 232
Council of Westminster 215, 230, 232, 233
Cracow 32, 185, 188, 218
Cumal 26–8, 91
Cyril (Constantine), St 32–4, 115
see also Moravia, Byzantine mission to

Dál Riada 31, 121
Danelaw 54, 55
Danes 175, 221, 237
see also armies, Viking Great

Danish conquest of England 37, 78, 121, 122, 129, 134, 175–6, 211
  see also Cnut of England, Denmark, and Norway
Danube river 91, 113, 117, 155–6, 179, 186, 188–90, 192
Denmark 54, 55, 56, 58, 129, 168, 175, 176, 215, 238
diaspora 54–8
dirhams 167–73, 184–5, 187, 189, 220, 233
  see also silver
Domesday Book 20, 22–4, 219
Dublin 29, 54, 58, 88, 92–4, 106, 119–22 *passim*, 130, 168, 171, 173, 221, 231, 239
dukes 32, 35–6, 115, 117, 123, 180–1, 204–5, 212–18 *passim*, 223
  see also rulers

East Anglia 149, 152
Ecloga 33, 53, 79, 92, 207
Edward the Elder 120, 221
  laws of 171, 207, 208, 214
Elbe river 113, 125, 126, 218, 239
Eligius, St 60, 151–2
elites 5, 9, 27, 63, 111, 122, 134, 150, 207, 215, 216, 237
emporia 148–9, 151, 157, 166, 174, 222
  see also wics
estates 21–4, 26, 28, 31, 34–5, 60–1, 64, 78, 150, 166, 176, 180–1, 234–5
eunuchs 11, 48–50, 52, 83, 91, 94, 173, 187, 191
execution 77–8, 92–3, 95, 107

farming 24, 30, 65
farms 31, 35, 57, 59, 166, 169, 174
feud 86, 110, 149, 210
Findan, St 54, 86, 94, 145–7, 167–8
Finley, Moses 19, 51
fortifications 113–14, 118, 120–6 *passim*, 134, 156–7, 198n.98
Francia 46, 60–2, 119, 155–6, 168–9, 181, 187, 192, 204, 213, 236, 239
  Carolingian 6, 60, 111–13, 117, 125, 128, 169, 187
  East 61, 111, 113–17, 125, 134, 186
  Merovingian 60, 149–53
Frisian merchants 110, 146, 148–9, 151, 153, 158, 219
fur 166, 168, 179, 228n.81

Gallus Anonymus 132, 232
gender *see* labour, gendered; women
Gerald of Wales 82, 177, 233
gifting slaves and captives 7, 19, 32, 121
Gillingham, John 91, 106–7
glass 114, 156, 168
Gotland 55, 168–70, 186, 233
Graus, František 32, 180–1
Great Army *see* armies, Viking Great
Greater Poland 32, 185, 189, 221
  see also Piasts
Gregory I, Pope 90, 151–2, 205
Gynaeceum 36, 60

hagiography 8–9, 52, 87, 151, 153, 180, 203
  see also individual saints
harem *see* concubinage
Henry II of Germany 127, 132
Henry III of Germany 93, 132
Henry IV of Germany 88, 132, 190
Hiberno-Norse 29, 58, 106, 122, 171, 215, 239
  see also Dublin
Hlothhere and Eadric's law code 86, 146, 208
Holm, Poul 106–7, 131, 221

Holy Roman Empire 128, 176, 186, 190, 232
hostages 93–4, 113
Hungary 3, 32, 46, 80, 127, 180–91 *passim*, 218
  slavery in 46, 59, 60, 64–5
  see also Magyars

Iberia 11, 47–8, 173, 182, 187, 190–1, 238
  see also al-Andalus
ibn Fadlān, Ahmad 55, 62–3
ibn Rusta 62, 124
ibn Ya'qūb, Ibrāhīm 83–4, 123, 179–89 *passim*, 218
Iceland 186
  settlement of 46, 58–9, 119, 121–2, 134, 169–70, 174
  slavery in 11, 55, 58–9, 81, 235
Imma 110, 146–8, 150, 152, 155, 219
Ine's law code 26, 77–8, 98n.33, 151, 207–8, 212, 214
Irish Sea 121, 152, 172, 174, 176, 177, 219, 231, 236
Islamic law 46–7

Jews
  communities 65, 183
  merchants 115, 154–5, 158, 173, 176, 181–7, 192, 238
  slave ownership 2, 34–6, 64–5, 123, 132–3, 179, 183, 204, 216, 218, 232
  slaves 180, 190–1
  see also non-Christians; Radhanites
Ježek, Martin 34, 123, 181
Jurasinski, Stefan 82, 203

Keller, Rudolphe 125–6
kidnapping 76, 84–7, 89, 95, 146, 208–9, 213
kin 76–84 *passim*, 105, 145–7, 177, 209, 214
kings 21, 27, 29, 89, 118, 120–2, 130–1, 205–23 *passim*, 239
  see also dukes; rulers
Kučera, Matúš 32, 153
Kyiv 63, 186, 188

law codes 9, 23, 30, 32, 55–6, 63–4, 86, 205–7, 210–11
  see also individual texts
labour
  agricultural 5–6, 11, 19, 21–4 *passim*, 27, 31, 34, 37, 49–52 *passim*, 56, 60, 88, 91, 120, 233, 235
  craft-working 6, 11, 22, 33, 51, 56
  domestic 5–6, 11, 19, 23–9 *passim*, 33–7 *passim*, 49, 51–2, 56, 65, 80, 88, 91, 150, 182, 235
  gendered 27–8, 63, 91, 237
  household 21–6 *passim*, 34–5, 47, 49–53 *passim*, 59–62, 65, 150–1, 180, 183, 235–6, 237
  see also women
Landnámabók 58, 168
Laxdæla Saga 54, 58, 93, 172
Lebor na Cert 29, 37
Legenda Christiani 123, 179
letters 10, 63, 108, 116–17, 151–2, 184
Liutprand of Cremona 173, 183–4
London 23, 25, 39, 110, 120, 146, 149–50, 161n.29, 170, 176, 219
Louis the German 93, 113

Macháček, Jiří 33, 154, 157, 189–90
McCormick, Michael 7, 112, 116, 148, 153, 155, 181
Magyars 32, 64, 107, 113, 117, 124–6, 128, 134, 154, 236–7, 239
  see also Hungary

Malcolm III of Scotland 31, 130
Mamluks 48, 83
see also military slaves
mancipium 7–8, 61–2
manumission 8, 21–2, 24, 35, 47, 56, 60–1, 64, 76, 80–1, 84, 144
documents 26, 81, 219
marcher lords 124, 126–7
Margaret of Scotland, St 31, 130, 231
markets 4, 10–12, 19, 32, 50, 55, 57–8, 60, 90, 126, 144, 146–50 *passim*, 156–7, 168, 170–6 *passim*, 187, 189, 192, 219, 237, 239
see also individual locations; *emporia*; *wics*
marriage 8, 61, 64, 79–80, 108–9, 158, 212
Marxist theory 5–6, 32, 64, 153, 180–1
masculinity 25, 88, 105
Mediterranean
economic region 1, 3, 7, 65, 107, 112, 132, 154–6, 187, 190, 235
Sea 6, 169, 186, 236
Melkorka 55, 58, 93, 172
merchants 4, 11, 51, 147–8, 159, 169, 172–3, 177, 179, 183–7, 189, 205, 236, 238
see also individual peoples
Mercians 110, 120, 146, 219
Methodius, St 32, 90, 114–15, 155
see also Moravia, Byzantine mission to
Middle East 11, 47–8, 50, 181, 238
Mieszko I of Poland 127, 175, 185, 204, 220
Mikulčice 33, 156, 157
military slaves 11, 47, 49–50, 53, 65, 91, 94, 182
see also mamluks
Miller, Joseph C. 87, 203
Mojmirids 113, 115, 117
monasteries 28, 35, 77, 94, 108, 118, 132, 173, 181–2, 218
foundation 35–7, 60, 217–18
reform 24–5
morality of slavery 2, 84, 144, 177, 201–3, 209, 213, 232–3, 238
Moravia 3–4, 6, 32, 113, 186, 189
Byzantine mission to 32–3, 90, 114–15, 155
Great 3, 32–4, 79–80, 90, 92, 111, 113–17, 123–4, 146–7, 153–8, 178, 183, 206–7, 222, 239
Piast principality 127, 190
Přemyslid principality 35, 36, 189, 218
see also individual rulers; Cyril (Constantine), St; Methodius, St
Muslims 2, 64–5, 133, 216
see also non-Christians

Naum, St 115, 155, 156
Někotoraja Zapověd 83, 182, 186, 191, 210, 216
network theory 15n.24, 169
non-Christians
enslavement of Christians by 133, 147
merchants 158, 178
raiding by 89
sale of Christians to 8–10, 83, 154, 181, 201, 203, 205, 213–14, 216, 232, 238
slaves 179, 192, 222
see also Jews; Muslims; pagans
Norman Conquest
of England 9, 23–4, 107, 128–9, 134, 206, 230, 234
of Ireland 26
of Wales 234
Normandy 129, 173, 176, 215
North Atlantic 11, 58–9, 120, 122, 160, 170, 174, 177, 233

northern arc 166, 171–2, 184, 186
North Sea 148–50, 168, 173
Northumbria 31, 78, 109–10, 120, 150, 152–3
Norway 54–5, 57–8, 93, 129, 168, 176, 238

Olaf of Dublin 119, 168, 221
Olomouc 35, 36, 190, 218
Orkney 54, 94, 145, 231
Ottonian dynasty 124, 126–8, 134, 154, 239

pagans 2, 33, 89, 123, 125, 167, 222, 232
  captive taking by 85–7, 89, 105, 236
  raiding by 111, 118, 167
  slave ownership by 31, 108, 156, 179
  as slaves 123, 125, 156, 181, 202
  threat to Christians by 9, 85–6, 108, 133, 179
  see also non-Christians
Patrick, St 85, 108, 152
Pelteret, David 21, 24, 148, 202–3, 219
penal enslavement 11, 25, 33, 53, 61, 76–82, 115, 145, 157, 201, 205–8, 212–15
Penitential of Theodore 81–2, 91, 108–9, 151, 209
penitentials 8–9, 25, 82–3, 108–9, 144–5, 170, 203–16 *passim*
  see also canon law; *Penitential of Theodore*
Petráček, Tomáš 34–5, 181
Piasts 6, 127, 132, 185, 189, 204, 220, 222, 239
Picts 3, 31, 110, 119, 121
pirates 3, 85, 108, 177
plunder 90, 105–6, 112–27 *passim*, 131, 134, 173, 222, 232
Pohansko 33, 138n.44, 138n.57
Poland 3, 6, 63, 115, 127, 132–3, 180, 182, 190–1, 204, 218, 220–1, 232, 239
  see also Greater Poland; Piasts
polygyny 56, 144
  see also sexual access to slaves
Prague 34–6, 59, 63, 83–4, 90, 123–5, 128, 132, 134, 144, 178–92, 204, 216–18, 234, 237, 239
Přemyslids 3, 32, 35, 117, 123, 127–8, 132, 178–91 *passim*, 205, 216, 218, 220, 222, 239
  consolidation of power 36, 115, 124, 181, 204
  see also individual dukes; Bohemia, Přemyslid duchy of
prices 35, 64, 75, 77–8, 80, 90, 92, 94, 165, 168, 218

Radhanites 155, 183
  see also Jews, merchants
Raffelstetten customs tariff 91, 155–6, 179, 188
ransom 8, 34, 53, 77–8, 84, 86, 90–5, 105–11 *passim*, 118–34 *passim*, 146, 150, 153, 155, 167, 201, 230–1, 236
rape 40n.34, 52, 79, 88, 132, 145
  see also sexual access to slaves
Rastislav of Moravia 32, 90, 93, 114–15
reeves 171, 213, 219
Rio, Alice 23, 61, 76, 187, 203, 221
Roach, Andrew 204, 220, 222
Roman Empire 1, 52–3, 235, 241
Roman law 51, 65, 205
Rome 90, 152, 155–6
rulers 48, 59, 183, 234, 240
  captive taking by 93, 111, 124
  law 32, 206–17
  oversight of trade 59, 148, 217–22, 239
  power consolidation 4–5, 121, 238

response to slaving 2, 5, 7, 12, 76, 89, 127, 130, 185, 201, 203–23, 233–4, 238
warfare 107, 110, 113–17 *passim*, 239
see also dukes; kings; taxation
Rus 46, 54–5, 59–65 *passim*, 169–92 *passim*

sagas 55–6, 58
see also Laxdæla Saga
Samanids *see* dirhams; silver
Saqāliba 49–50, 61, 182, 185, 187–8, 234
sclavus 1, 49, 61
Scots 3, 9, 31, 59, 120, 130, 177, 231
self-sale 61, 80–2, 84, 95, 209
Sermo Lupi ad Anglos 78, 145, 175, 211
see also Wulfstan II of York
servus 7–8, 21–4, 34, 36, 64–5
sexual access to slaves 25, 28, 33, 52, 56–7, 88, 91, 144–5, 147
see also women
shackles 10, 110, 179, 188–9
silk 51, 114, 156, 166, 168–9, 176, 188–9, 191
silver 10–11, 27, 33, 122, 149, 157, 165–72 *passim*, 180, 185, 188–9, 191, 220–1
see also coinage; dirhams
slaving zones 7, 11, 46, 59, 65, 107, 165, 202, 221, 235–40 *passim*
Slavs 54, 89, 125, 133–4, 169, 221, 239
chattel slaves 1, 48–50, 52, 94, 124, 132, 134, 157, 165, 179–90 *passim*, 237–8
as merchants 179, 185
unfree 61–2, 170
warfare 111–14, 116–17, 125–8, 132
see also individual regions; *saqāliba*
soldiers *see* mamluks; military slaves
Sussex 21, 85, 219
Svatopluk of Moravia 90, 114–17
Sweden 54–5, 58, 167
Swein Forkbeard *see* Danish conquest of England
Swithun, St 25, 86, 146, 171

taxation 9, 12, 31, 91, 171, 176, 201, 204–5, 217–20, 222, 238
tenants 8, 23, 31, 34, 36–7, 60–1, 65, 77, 233–4
see also labour, agricultural
theft 93, 145
enslavement for 77, 79, 207, 212
of people 86–7, 146, 208–9
see also kidnapping
Theodore of Canterbury *see Penitential of Theodore*
Þeow 21, 23, 38n.5, 55, 78
Thietmar of Merseburg 94, 127, 132
Þræl 21, 28, 55
Torksey 119, 167, 172
towns 11, 25, 29, 170–1, 190
see also individual places; urbanisation
trans-Atlantic slave trade 1, 57, 75–6
Třeštík, Dušan 123, 181, 183–4, 204, 218, 220
Truso 169
Turks 48, 49, 199n.116

Umayyad Caliphate 48, 50, 83, 132, 176, 184, 191, 234
urbanisation 29, 37, 58, 65, 157
see also individual places; towns

Venice 54, 59, 90, 115, 153, 155–6, 186–7
Verdun 59, 173, 183–4, 186–7
Verlinden, Charles 7, 61, 154, 181–2

Vladislav I of Bohemia 34, 36, 183, 216, 232
Volga 62, 169

Warner of Rouen 88, 173, 176
The War of the Gaedhil and the Gaill 27, 29, 88
Weahl 21, 26, 61
Wenceslas of Bohemia, St 90, 123–5, 179
Wessex 24, 26, 35, 55, 118, 120, 146, 150, 206–7
Wics 148, 150–1, 157, 219
  see also emporia
Wihtred's law code 78, 151, 214
Wilfrid, St 21, 85, 86, 152
William I of England 22, 129, 177, 215, 218
William of Malmesbury 175, 177, 215, 218
wills 10, 21–2, 24, 32–3, 53, 56, 78
Winchester *see* Swithun, St
women
  capture of 114, 117, 120, 122, 126–7, 130, 170, 231
  enslavement of 23, 77, 79–81, 90–3, 107
  roles of enslaved 21, 25–30 *passim*, 36, 48–9, 52, 56, 63
  sale of 54, 62–4, 90, 144–5, 151, 172, 175, 177
  slave owners 21–2, 33–4, 53, 88, 158, 176
  see also concubinage; *gynaeceum*; labour, gendered; sexual access to slaves
Woodstown 167, 172
Wulfstan II of York 78–80, 82, 122, 145, 174–5, 183, 202, 207, 211–17 *passim*, 221
Wulfstan of Worcester, St 145, 177, 218, 231
Wyatt, David 88, 203

York 25, 58, 149, 168, 171

Zakon Suydnji Ljudem 33–4, 79–80, 86, 92, 115, 144, 146, 157, 206–8, 216

EU authorised representative for GPSR:
Easy Access System Europe, Mustamäe tee 50,
10621 Tallinn, Estonia
gpsr.requests@easproject.com

www.ingramcontent.com/pod-product-compliance
Ingram Content Group UK Ltd.
Pitfield, Milton Keynes, MK11 3LW, UK
UKHW020210280426
5425IPUK00002BA/4

* 9 7 8 1 5 2 6 1 6 0 0 9 6 *